Political System
and Change

Written under the auspices of the Center of International Studies, Princeton University. A list of other Center publications appears at the back of this book.

A *WORLD POLITICS* READER

Political System and Change

EDITED BY
IKUO KABASHIMA and
LYNN T. WHITE III

PRINCETON UNIVERSITY PRESS

Published by
Princeton University Press,
41 William Street,
Princeton, New Jersey 08540
In the United Kingdom:
Princeton University Press,
Guildford, Surrey

First Princeton Paperback
printing, 1986
First Hardcover printing, 1986
LCC 85-43377
ISBN 0-691-07698-7
ISBN 0-691-02244-5 (pbk.)

Clothbound editions of
Princeton University Press books
are printed on acid-free paper,
and binding materials are chosen
for strength and durability.
Paperbacks, while
satisfactory for personal
collections, are not usually
suitable for library rebinding.

Printed in
the United States of America
by Princeton University Press,
Princeton, New Jersey

To Cyril E. Black

CONTENTS

The Contributors   ix

INTRODUCTION

LYNN T. WHITE III
and IKUO KABASHIMA   Systematic Definitions
for Development Politics   3

POLITICAL SYSTEM: DEFINITIONS AND FUNCTIONS

DAVID EASTON   An Approach to the Analysis of
Political Systems   23

GABRIEL A. ALMOND   A Developmental Approach to
Political Systems   41

J. ROLAND PENNOCK   Political Development, Political
Systems, and Political Goods   73

POLITICAL ORDER

SAMUEL P. HUNTINGTON   Political Development and Political
Decay   95

TED GURR   Psychological Factors in Civil
Violence   140

ROBERT D. PUTNAM   Toward Explaining Military
Intervention in Latin American
Politics   174

CHALLENGES AND CHANGES

CLAUDE AKE   Modernization and Political
Instability: A Theoretical Exploration   205

C. S. WHITAKER, JR.   A Dysrhythmic Process of Political
Change   221

HOWARD J. WIARDA   Toward a Framework for the Study
of Political Change in the Iberic-
Latin Tradition: The Corporative
Model   249

IKUO KABASHIMA   Supportive Participation with
Economic Growth: The Case of
Japan   279

AGENDA FOR FUTURE STUDY

HARRY ECKSTEIN   The Idea of Political Development:
From Dignity to Efficiency   311

TONY SMITH   Requiem or New Agenda for Third
World Studies?   347

THE CONTRIBUTORS

LYNN T. WHITE III is Associate Professor of Politics and International Affairs at the Woodrow Wilson School, Princeton University.

IKUO KABASHIMA is Associate Professor of Political Science at the Institute of Socio-Economic Planning, University of Tsukuba (Japan).

DAVID EASTON is Distinguished Professor of Political Science at the University of California, Irvine, and Andrew MacLeish Distinguished Service Professor Emeritus at the University of Chicago.

GABRIEL A. ALMOND is Professor of Political Science Emeritus at Stanford University.

J. ROLAND PENNOCK is Professor Emeritus of Political Science at Swarthmore College.

SAMUEL P. HUNTINGTON is Clarence Dillon Professor of International Affairs at Harvard University.

TED GURR is Professor of Political Science and Director of the Center for Comparative Politics at the University of Colorado, Boulder.

ROBERT D. PUTNAM is Chairman, Department of Government, Harvard University.

CLAUDE AKE is Woodrow Wilson Scholar and Professor of Political Economy at the University of Port Harcourt (Nigeria).

C. SYLVESTER WHITAKER, JR. is Professor of Political Science and Africana Studies, and Director of International Programs at Rutgers University.

HOWARD J. WIARDA is Professor of Political Science at the University of Massachusetts at Amherst.

HARRY ECKSTEIN is Distinguished Professor and Professor of Political Science at the University of California, Irvine.

TONY SMITH is Professor of Political Science at Tufts University.

Introduction

SYSTEMATIC DEFINITIONS FOR DEVELOPMENT POLITICS

By LYNN T. WHITE III and IKUO KABASHIMA

THINKING implies comparisons. To make these, stable categories are needed for understanding politics and the ways it changes in various countries. Clearly defined, *un*changing terms—better yet, a set or "system" of interrelated and mutually consistent definitions—are inevitable for such study. There is no way to do without them. But a natural tension arises in political science, since politics has the nasty habit of not standing still. "System" and "change" conflict with each other.

To compare politics across different places in space or eras in time, the usual means is to define changes by functional categories. The functions are processes that a system performs so that it can last over time in its environment. Even thinkers who do not want to call themselves "systems theorists" often find it hard to avoid this approach. The only obvious alternative is to forgo any hope of comparison.[1] Let us begin with a look at classic approaches to definitions for comprehending the chaos of politics.

OLD IDEAS AND NEW POLITICS

In the 19th and early 20th centuries, Western political scientists were mainly interested in European-style polities. They created a legalistic, institutional set of definitions, which allowed them to compare politics in just a few European and English-speaking countries. The old *tria politica* of executive, legislative, and judicial functions provided a system to meet most of their interests.

The Depression of the 1930s, however, encouraged social scientists to rethink their disciplines. Many felt a need to move beyond institutional

---

[1] Anthropologists are the only notable group of social scientists to have taken up this alternative—and when they choose this tack, they try to adopt the analytic categories of the people whose behavior they study. This option has little currency in political science, where the tradition of trying to compare nations has long been strong. For more, see Clifford Geertz, *The Interpretation of Cultures* (New York: Basic Books, 1973), esp. chaps. 1 and 15. It is not surprising that when anthropologists turn to the study of larger collectivities and of development, they also adopt system-like units of analysis and emphasize the ecologies of these units. For example, see Geertz, *Agricultural Involution: The Processes of Ecological Change in Indonesia* (Berkeley: University of California Press, 1971), and *Islam Observed: Religious Development in Morocco and Indonesia* (Chicago: University of Chicago Press, 1968). For an exploration of the extent to which the anthropological approach is applicable to politics, see the essay by Harry Eckstein in this Reader, and the paragraphs of this introduction that apply to it.

studies toward research about actual behavior. They rejected an emphasis on preempirical ideas about how people ought morally or legally to act.

The number of states rose after World War II and soared by the early 1960s. Political scientists consequently had to face yet bigger problems. They needed approaches that stood a chance of holding true not only in European-style politics, but throughout the world. They were in danger of biting off more than they could chew; but political science would obviously be inadequate if it were irrelevant to the new states in cultures that had received scant attention before. New sets of analytic categories (subtler systems) were the only hope of avoiding intellectual chaos.

The first task was to gather basic data about little-known countries. The "Human Relations Area Files" and other encyclopedic projects offered straightforward descriptions of the politics, religions, economies, cultures, and international links of many new states.[2] Inventory, rather than theory, was the most obvious need.

But studies of individual countries showed that modern change was worldwide: urbanization, higher literacy, increasing product per capita, and wider use of media. Even descriptive studies had a tendency to be implicitly comparative, if only because they had to use English words as well as research categories that often had Western roots. In 1953, the Social Science Research Council established a Committee on Comparative Politics to explore the possibilities of evolving systematic ideas about quick-changing polities.

"Functionalist" ideas in sociology—especially the ambitious, very abstract notions of Talcott Parsons—therefore came to influence political science. Parsons tried to offer definitions for all "functions" of any "social system."[3] His scheme was subtle enough to link many sizes of human collectivity, from the individual to the international system, and it took seriously the need to consider human values as well as external constraints.[4] Above all, Parsons specified the definitions that make a "system" in terms

[2] The "Human Relations Area Files" were kept at Yale University, and a major series of books about particular countries was published in this project.

[3] Parsons' most comprehensive book is *The Social System* (Glencoe, IL: Free Press, 1951), but it is written in such convoluted and abstract English that it is now seldom read—even by graduate students. His more accessible work is an intellectual history of the bases of his approach, *The Structure of Social Action* (New York: McGraw-Hill, 1937)—vol. I on Marshall, Pareto, and Durkheim; vol. II on Weber. See also Emile Durkheim, *The Division of Labor in Society* (New York: Macmillan, 1933); D. F. Aberle and others, "The Functional Prerequisites of a Society" (an article by Parsons' students), *Ethics* 60 (January 1950), 100-111; and an application to one functional sector: Talcott Parsons and Neil J. Smelser, *Economy and Society* (New York: Free Press, 1956).

[4] For an attempt to apply this scheme, see Lynn White, "Shanghai's Polity in Cultural Revolution," in John W. Lewis, *The City in Communist China* (Stanford: Stanford University Press, 1971), 363-64.

of "functions" that contribute to the system's maintenance over time in its surroundings.

Crosscultural studies of politics seemed to need definitions as cagey and comprehensive as these. Even at the risk of abstraction, a system of functional definitions was unavoidable for any student who took seriously the job of comparing nations. As Gabriel Almond put it,

> instead of the concept of "the state," limited as it is by legal and institutional meanings, we prefer "political system"; instead of "powers," which again is a legal concept in connotation, we are beginning to prefer "functions"; instead of "offices" (legal again), we prefer "roles". . . .[5]

The journal *World Politics*, published under the auspices of Princeton's Center of International Studies by Princeton University Press, has been a major forum for refining the "systems" or "functional" approach to political change. It has also been a major forum for challenges to this approach. The essays in the present Reader are culled from *World Politics*, and many of them are precursors or summaries of studies that have become landmarks in the field of comparative politics. Some of them do so more cogently than the related longer books which appeared later.[6]

ARE "SYSTEM" AND "OUTPUT FUNCTIONS" INEVITABLE NOTIONS IN POLITICAL ANALYSIS?

David Easton, in "An Approach to the Analysis of Political Systems," uses a biological analogy to show the different processes of politics, while

[5] Gabriel A. Almond and James S. Coleman, eds., *The Politics of the Developing Areas* (Princeton: Princeton University Press, 1960), 4. This work was the first major publication of the S.S.R.C.'s Committee on Comparative Politics.

[6] Many of these books were published by Princeton University Press, under the sponsorship of either the Committee on Comparative Politics or Princeton's Center of International Studies: Almond and Coleman, *ibid.*; Gabriel A. Almond and Sidney Verba, *The Civic Culture: Political Attitudes and Democracy in Five Nations* (1963); Lucian W. Pye, ed., *Communications and Political Development* (1963); Joseph LaPalombara, ed., *Bureaucracy and Political Development* (1963); Robert E. Ward and Dankwart A. Rustow, eds., *Political Modernization in Japan and Turkey* (1964); Cyril E. Black and Thomas P. Thornton, eds., *Communism and Revolution: The Strategic Uses of Political Violence* (1964); James S. Coleman, ed., *Education and Political Development* (1965); Lucian W. Pye and Sidney Verba, eds., *Political Culture and Political Development* (1965); Harold and Margaret Sprout, *The Ecological Perspective on Human Affairs* (1965); Joseph LaPalombara and Myron Weiner, eds., *Political Parties and Political Development* (1966); Ted Robert Gurr, *Why Men Rebel* (1969); Leonard Binder, James S. Coleman, Joseph LaPalombara, Lucian W. Pye, Sidney Verba, and Myron Weiner, eds., *Crises and Sequences in Political Development* (1971). Other books from the same Press and Center have dealt with particular countries: Karl von Vorys, *Political Development in Pakistan* (1965); Harry Eckstein, *Division and Cohesion in Democracy: A Study of Norway* (1966); Henry Bienen, *Tanzania: Party Transformation and Economic Development* (1967); C. Sylvester Whitaker, *The Politics of Tradition: Continuity and Change in Northern Nigeria, 1946-1966* (1970); Francine R. Frankel, *India's Green Revolution: Economic Gains and Political Costs* (1971); and Henry Bienen, *Kenya: The Politics of Participation and Control* (1974).

at the same time linking them to each other. He takes a page from Hobbes's *Leviathan* and speaks, in effect, of a "political body" adapting to its environment. This is Easton's "system." Its parts interact to move toward, or maintain, an "equilibrium" in which the system as a whole can subsist in its surroundings. Since Easton's main concern is with politics (more than with other social processes, which are more extensively treated by Parsons), he chooses system "boundaries" defined by the resources and decisions of government authorities.[7]

The bounds of the system Easton defines are like membrane tissues for exchanging political resources ("inputs" such as taxes and votes) and political decisions ("outputs"). The problem with this way of looking at things is identical with its virtue: Easton mainly gives definitions, not observations, of functional sectors of politics. He maps the routes by which political inputs and outputs are conveyed in any system. He implies that we can understand one kind of complexity (politics) because we have knowledge of another (bodies).[8] The virtue of Easton's scheme is that it can link the traits of these "bodies" with what they find around them, over time and in different places. And it can do that only because Easton does not alter the definitions with which he begins. His definitions are deductive and abstract, not dependent on facts—and their inertia is exactly what makes them good tools for comparison.

This kind of thinking may seem too abstract because its concepts are hard to set down in definite terms. But Easton provides a basic grammar for attempting comparative study, even if his model seems to lack substance. It is stronger for its logic than for tight links with public, common notions about politics. That may be an inevitable form—and problem— of any approach which hopes to relate many different kinds of social facts. Practical people (students, for example, maybe more than professors!) have a tendency to react against the abstract generality of a functional schema such as Easton's. The main defense of this kind of theory, however, is that it may be implicit in any conscientious effort to show the relations of social things to each other.[9] Easton's kind of ambitiousness and

[7] Among Easton's books on this subject are *A Framework for Political Analysis* (Englewood Cliffs, NJ: Prentice-Hall, 1965) and *A Systems Analysis of Political Life* (New York: Wiley, 1965).

[8] A problem in analogizing a political "body" with a biological one is that species (not individuals) are what evolve in nature. The first paragraph of Durkheim, *The Division of Labor* (fn. 3), points out that social thinkers, not biologists, first saw the importance of functional differentiation.

[9] The idea that categories in a proper science should be consistent was accepted in the 1950s and most of the 1960s—and is still an ideal upheld implicitly by many scholars. Thomas S. Kuhn, *The Structure of Scientific Revolutions* (Chicago: University of Chicago Press, 1962)

abstraction may be necessary if we want to use understandings and words developed in one political situation to help describe another.

Gabriel Almond, in "A Developmental Approach to Political Systems," points out that systems theories are often accused of being inherently static. A system may change to match changes in its ecological niche, but the analytic definitions on which it is based must remain stable. Almond is determined to refine systems theory—to make it less abstract and rigid—while retaining its virtue of allowing comparisons. He is more specific than Easton when describing the functions a political system must perform in order to flourish.[10] He tries to set forth a more detailed list of tasks that a political system must accomplish lest it lose power. Easton emphasizes processes, especially how a "political system" absorbs resources. Almond's main interest lies in the processes it must perform to survive, and thus he stresses "output" processes in particular. But this focus of Almond's—which is not clearly inherent in the original need for clear definitions that first gave rise to the idea of "system"—also makes the logic of systems theory more flexible: it permits incoherence between the parts of a system (as long as the system has sufficient coordination to maintain itself). Above all, Almond's categories allow for more concrete comparisons, especially among developing systems.

The ideas of comparativists in the late 1950s and early 1960s grew apace—but so did the variety of new states. Third-world leaders at first had great expectations that economic growth would lead, more or less naturally, to greater social equality, then maybe to democracy—in any case, to "modernization." The whole happy process would abet political stability. Even if social scientists were more pessimistic, they did not quickly incorporate such worries into the structure of their comparative studies.

The optimistic view that political development walks hand-in-hand with economic growth was in for some unexpected shocks. In the 1960s, charismatic leaders and militarists had come to unprecedented promi-

---

nonetheless showed how consistent paradigms in natural science are refined until "crises" of new evidence arise with which their frameworks cannot deal. By the 1970s, this idea came into conflict with functionalist systems approaches in social science. The works of Clifford Geertz and Albert Hirschman were crucial to this change of thinking. For references, see fns. 1 and 22, and Hirschman, *A Bias for Hope* (New Haven: Yale University Press, 1971), 1-38 and 342-60.

[10] Almond's essay in this Reader refines, and adds sophistication to, the ideas in his introduction to Almond and Coleman (fn. 5)—which was later expanded to Gabriel A. Almond and G. Bingham Powell, Jr., *Comparative Politics: A Developmental Approach* (Boston: Little, Brown, 1966).

nence in the third world: Sukarno in Indonesia, Nkrumah in Ghana, and many others. These political changes were not totally inconsistent with systems theory; still, political scientists, always looking for linkages, had seldom argued that militarism or dictatorship arises as a matter of natural course. Systems theorists had tended to assume that history would bring *more* political efficiency, not less, to third-world nations. Military coups and political turmoil seemed to argue otherwise.

Roland Pennock, in "Political Development, Political Systems, and Political Goods," stands back from systems theory. He notices that its original logic makes one "output"—the stability of the system itself— more important than any other. Pennock argues this is a problem: governments should provide more welfare, security, justice, and liberty for their subjects, not just more order. Governments satisfy needs, "not just needs of the state as such . . . but human needs whose fulfillment makes the polity valuable to man, and gives it its justification." Stability should, Pennock writes, be merely a way to achieve human ends that systems theory fails to value enough. The proper measure of development should be outcomes like liberty—justifiable by norms that are independent of systems.

Pennock is more frank than Easton or Almond in introducing liberal values to systems theory, and he takes a more substantive approach than system logic would require to the "outputs" of government: *not* just stability, but also the crime rate, the incidence of independent political parties, fair trials, freedom of the press, official efforts in welfare, education, transport, and many other functions that are "development" for ordinary people.

Is "Order" the Fundamental Function?

In "Political Development and Political Decay," Samuel Huntington responds differently to the obvious breakdown of politics of newly independent countries during the 1960s. His ideas are more "realist" and less normative than Pennock's. Huntington emphasizes a single "output" of government—order—and finds that function to be the crucial one for political development.[11] The structure of Huntington's approach makes him a systems theorist; but he differs from his predecessors in that he shows broad reasons for pessimism about the ease of political progress.

[11] The essay in this volume summarizes the main idea developed in Huntington, *Political Order in Changing Societies* (New Haven: Yale University Press, 1968).

He has no hopes that an emphasis on liberal norms will shape political development.

Socioeconomic modernization increases the political participation of citizens, but it does not ensure that their demands can be met. Political development, for Huntington, differs from modernization, mobilization, and participation: it is an expansion in the ability of governments to deal with the onslaught of problems brought on by change. Here is a systems theorist without a smile, seeing danger in modernity, especially when elites lack practice in the "art of associating together" and lack institutions that can channel the social chaos that accompanies modern growth.

Modernization (in the form of higher output, urbanization, literacy, and so forth) thus bears no necessary relation to political development. In fact, political systems may decay because of socioeconomic progress. Aristotle's Athens and Republican Rome were politically developed in many ways, though they were not modern. By the same token, a country can modernize economically without any improvement of its political procedures. As Huntington shows, many countries follow just this course: political turmoil grows along with GNP, literacy, education, communication, and even voting. Political decay is one of the normal, not aberrant, paths to modernity.

Charismatic or military leaders often arise in third-world states—and they weaken nonpersonal institutions that might solve political problems. Such leaders are good at mobilizing people to serve in campaigns for goals such as literacy or industrialization, but a cost of their style is the lack of long-run political progress.

Huntington poses a dilemma: new states can have modernization or they can have political development; but unless they change slowly, they cannot usually have both. There is "no easy choice" between these values.[12] Huntington does not flinch from making bold policy recommendations to reduce the dilemma. First, he suggests that modernization be slowed. If university graduates are likely to foment political dissent, Huntington proposes that fewer students be funded. If free communications will undermine the political order, he recommends that regimes muzzle the press. Second, he finds no alternative to stronger regimes. Political parties—or just one of them, if more will cause trouble—are Huntington's key to institutionalization. Free elections and competition among elites, Huntington says, are no substitutes for political organization.

[12] See Samuel P. Huntington and Joan M. Nelson, *No Easy Choice: Political Participation in Developing Countries* (Cambridge: Harvard University Press, 1976).

That is strong medicine for an ailment which other liberals and systems theorists had failed to diagnose. Huntington has provoked many (including Ake, Whitaker, Wiarda, and Kabashima in this volume) to argue that the inherent looseness of all systems, or cultural checks on instability, may prevent civil disorder from getting out of hand. But Huntington's contribution to scientific thinking about political change is nonetheless path-breaking. Huntington retains a systemic framework, while discarding normative assumptions about progress that had been implicit in earlier work. He thereby brings the theory of developing systems back to face the facts of political decay that were obvious in many countries by the mid-1960s. Huntington's essay is the culmination of a line of argument in the first part of this book—from Easton's abstract logic of input and output processes, to Almond's laying out of more specifically political functions, to Pennock's normative emphasis on output functions that are socially desirable, finally to Huntington's stress on one particular output (order) without which no state can long survive. Most of the later essays in this volume assess the limits of the systems theory that Huntington makes realistic. His article, right or wrong, is the central pivot of this book.

But Huntington does not fully delve into the question, why does civil disorder arise? He points to its frequent occurrence in times of socioeconomic progress, and to the political effects of that chaos. But to get to the basic reasons for this link, one needs human psychology—and that discipline, relying often on concepts whose relation to facts are hard to specify, is intellectually riskier.

Ted Gurr's "Psychological Factors in Civil Violence" steps into this breach.[13] Referring explicitly to works by psychologists, especially on the causes of aggression, Gurr outlines a set of variables that explain the frequency and amount of civil violence. "Relative deprivation" arises when people achieve less than they expect—and it determines when they rebel. It is an awareness, most important when collective, among citizens that government interference prevents them from attaining what they want. Gurr offers a series of propositions that relate selected variables to the likelihood and magnitude of civil violence. In an article published several years after Gurr's, Huntington praises the comprehensiveness of Gurr's thinking and says that ideas about relative deprivation "dominated scholarly work on political instability" in subsequent years.[14] Gurr supplies

[13] Also see Gurr, *Why Men Rebel* (fn. 6).
[14] Samuel P. Huntington and Jorge I. Dominguez, "Political Development," in Fred I. Greenstein and Nelson Polsby, eds., *Handbook of Political Science* (New York: Wiley, 1975), 8.

reasons, in the psychologies of many individuals, for the collective political decay against which Huntington warns.

In "Toward Explaining Military Intervention in Latin American Politics," Robert Putnam explores whether political decay (as evidenced by coups) correlates with mobilization. He examines all 20 Latin American countries over two separate periods of time, 1906-1915 and 1956-1965. Social mobilization relates strongly—and negatively—to military intervention in these cases.

Putnam's approach is valuable because it provides a behavioral check (not just another plausible argument in logic) on Huntington's ideas. At first, Putnam may seem to disprove the notion that social mobilization and military intervention are two aspects of a single process—political decay. A closer look at what Putnam does with his data, however, suggests a general dilemma that faces attempts to attach empirical referents to concepts deduced from sets of definitions (and any systems theory is a set of definitions): Putnam shows correlations without being able to show the direction of causes. He proves that, over long time periods in many countries, mobilization and coups do not go together. He cannot, using correlations, tell whether this result arises because armies intervene to stop mobilization or, on the contrary, because lower mobilization gives the soldiers opportunities to intervene. This essay exemplifies the best potentials of inductive, empirical analysis; it also shows the limits of that approach.[15]

Do Reforms, Irregularities, and Traditions Weaken a System?

The original purpose of systems theory was to provide clear, linked, functional definitions that allow comparisons across different polities in space and time. But Huntington goes far beyond this original purpose. First, functionalist logic does not require that instability must always weaken a system. That happens only if the chaos goes beyond the regime's ability to cope. Second, systems theory does not require that all traits of a polity mesh perfectly with each other; it only directs attention to their links, whether tight or not. Third, the basic idea behind functionalism implies nothing about cultural differences that deeply affect actual

---

[15] The statistical correlations approach in Putnam's article differs from the implicit simultaneous equations approach that Gurr uses to explore the implications of the same theory. Gurr shows restraint in avoiding algebra for his propositions (since the symbols would obscure the meanings for most readers), but the two forms of mathematical interest contrast with each other nicely.

politics; but we cannot expect to understand how states change without taking cultural factors seriously.

These three aspects of the original notion of "system" have been implicitly ignored by many functionalists eager to describe development—and they provide the basis of a host of critiques, of Huntington in particular. Ake takes his predecessors to task on the first of these grounds. Whitaker emphasizes the second. Both Wiarda and Kabashima show the importance of the third.

In "Modernization and Political Instability: A Theoretical Exploration," Claude Ake challenges Huntington directly: "Political change is compatible with political stability, as long as the change occurs in accordance with prevailing expectations about how such change may legitimately come about." The original functionalist idea does not require us to think of *all* disorder, *all* efforts for social change, as threatening the end of a system. Huntington seems to imply that the chaos of modernization necessarily weakens political systems. But basic functionalist theory—which he follows in most respects—has a different implication: chaos will weaken regimes only if it becomes so extensive that it crosses a *threshold* above which the system cannot manage. Below that threshold, as Ake indicates, disorder may force reforms that strengthen a regime.

The classical quality of Ake's critique of Huntington—the fact that it harks back to the beginnings of this theory—is the main source of its power. If the polity is like a body, it may develop new immunities from the experience of becoming sick; it may become stronger rather than decay or die. The disagreement between Ake and Huntington echoes an antinomy that has concerned many social scientists in this century (notably Max Weber). On the one hand, modern bureaucratic development seems to constrain possibilities in politics. On the other, such change shows the need for leadership and political will, so that people remain in control of their fates.[16]

Ake also seems to depend on Emile Durkheim's point that increasingly different modern functions in society may lead to greater (not less) solidarity if these functions complement each other. In that case, violence, conflict, civil disorder, short regimes, and the lack of strong political institutions may not be as problematic as Huntington says. Ake also takes Lucian Pye to task for overstating the dangers of psychological anomie in modern times; and he criticizes David Apter for emphasizing the disrup-

---

[16] Max Weber, in his various writings, presented this dilemma most clearly. For an interpretation with this emphasis, and for further sources, see H. Stuart Hughes, *Consciousness and Society* (New York: Knopf, 1958). For a brilliant treatment of the American case, see E. E. Schattschneider, *The Semisovereign People* (Hinsdale, IL: Dryden, 1960).

tive political effects of modern changes in social roles.[17] Modernization, Ake admits, can be disintegrative; but it is not necessarily so. It may replace the structures that it attacks with new ones that will be just as strong or stronger.[18] There is nothing inherent in systems theory that should make us treat only change as news and lack of change as normal. Growth is as natural as growth pains.

The broad sociological—not just governmental—origins of systems theory also support Ake's point that *coups d'état* and executive crises (in which Huntington finds much danger) do not necessarily indicate political instability. Political authority is a phenomenon in many sizes of social collectivity, right down to the family. Too much stress on the importance of state leaders—who are very important to Huntington—reflects an unnecessary elitism.

In short, Ake is a systems theorist too, even though he criticizes other functionalists. He chastises them, in effect, for neglecting the original logic of the ideas they are trying to correct. They have forgotten, he implies, that "dysfunction" makes no vital threat to a system until it passes a threshold.

Sylvester Whitaker, in "A Dysrhythmic Process of Political Change," raises a similarly classic critique of other functionalists. He studies an African context, the complex society in Northern Nigeria, with its mix of Hausa-Fulani, Tiv, British, and other cultures.[19] People living there can choose among these traditions for various purposes that they determine. In education, both Islamic and Western forms are available. In politics, the emirs claim legitimacy on the basis of posts inherited from the colonial system as well as on the basis of their traditional roles. In any functional sphere, the peoples of Northern Nigeria use new as well as old bases for action. Whitaker does not repeat Ake's concern for thresholds, but he points to *loose links* in any system. He shows that modernizations in different parts of a unit of analysis march out of sync with each other. Choosing a metaphor appropriate to the culture he studies, Whitaker speaks of rhythms—and of "dysrhythmic political change." He does not reject the idea of system completely; he only shows there is no need for lockstep in the actual evolution of its sectors. The definitions were never anything but categories in which data could be explored, among which

[17] See Pye, *Politics, Personality, and Nation Building* (New Haven: Yale University Press, 1963), and David Apter, *The Politics of Modernization* (Chicago: University of Chicago Press, 1965).

[18] Ake's argument, which suggests some positive political functions of modern stress, is highly consistent with that made by the more general sociologist Lewis Coser, *The Functions of Social Conflict* (Glencoe, IL: Free Press, 1956). Ake's own functionalism is obvious in this close relation to Coser.

[19] Whitaker's book, *The Politics of Tradition* (fn. 6), elaborates on the ideas in this essay.

relations could be posited. Of course, variables may cluster in development—but this is always an empirical matter, to be researched anywhere. The clustering was never inherent to the business of definition. Whitaker maintains that other functionalists, if they imply modernization is a seamless web, forget the analytic quality of the notions they were trying to refine.

Howard Wiarda and Ikuo Kabashima carry a third line of criticism to Latin America and a special part of Asia. Each of these writers emphasizes the influence of culture on politics—and the inability of systems theory to explain actual developments in specific countries unless the "boundary" between politics and culture receives enough attention.

Wiarda, in "Toward a Framework for the Study of Political Change in the Iberic-Latin Tradition: The Corporative Model," shows that the policies of the Alliance for Progress in the 1960s were based on functionalist systems theory premises. The originators of these policies assumed that many Latin American countries were moving quickly toward revolution (as Cuba had already done), so that only urgent measures to promote moderate, liberal politics could prevent violence. They also assumed that if Latin American economies would grow, political democracy might soon follow. The result—a foreign aid program—was designed to meet the need and avert the danger.

What that analysis overlooked was the importance of cultural traditions in "Iberic-Latin" politics. Corporate and elite ideals made nonsense of the functionalist predictions. Revolution came slowly, and liberal democracy expanded little. In many large and important Latin American countries, armies seized power. "Semi-modernizing" movements such as the *Estado Nôvo* in Brazil, *Peronismo* in Argentina, and the carefully named *Partido Revolucionario Institucional* in Mexico had long been important in Latin America—yet the analysts of the early 1960s did not heed their implications for later change. Wiarda, referring specifically to Iberian ideals of authority that are still important though gradually changing, shows how system analysis fails when it ignores cultural ecologies.

Kabashima, in "Supportive Participation with Economic Growth: The Case of Japan," responds to Huntington's notions that modern participation endangers political order, and that participation must be limited if developing countries are to grow politically. But Kabashima shows how participation by have-nots may strengthen a system—if cultural conditions are right. In Japan after World War II, both political and economic mobilization was widespread, and a *supportive* kind of participation allowed a strengthening of institutions along with an increase of mobilization.

The supportive or nonsupportive *quality* of participation—not the *amount* of participation—determines the result in political order or decay. If the people who are negatively affected by modern economic change (peasants, in most developing countries) have a culture that inclines them to mobilize to help the regime help themselves, increased participation can raise the government's resources. In Japan, farmers who benefited little from economic development nonetheless participated a great deal in politics. As a result, there was some redistribution of income from urban to rural areas through the official budget, which counteracted the usual tendency toward inequality in development. A regime's cultural environment may tend to encourage supportive participation, especially among rural people; when it does, the result is modernization with order.

Kabashima offers an answer to the old question about how to link political and economic change. Students of comparative politics have long associated democracy with economic equality, because the former is egalitarian in principle. Some research, however, suggests that the degree of democratization is not related to economic equality.[20] Kabashima suggests that democracy (measured in terms of high political participation by have-nots) results in greater economic equality.

None of the critiques of Huntington that are raised by Ake, Whitaker, Wiarda, and Kabashima completely rejects systems theory. But all of them suggest that research should take adequate account of the cultural environment of politics. Even Ake, for whom the emphasis on culture is less obvious than for the other three, implies a need for more awareness that unusual political exchanges can be widespread in a system without leading to its collapse. Logics to accept this kind of inconsistency in systems have been best developed by anthropologists.[21] These culturalist methods are usable alongside systems theory.

What Is the Future of the Idea of a Developing Political System?

In his 1982 study, "The Idea of Political Development," Harry Eckstein sees a change "from dignity to efficiency." This insight allows Eckstein to choose between culturalist and systems approaches: the first

[20] See Robert W. Jackman, *Politics and Social Equality: A Comparative Analysis* (New York: Wiley, 1975).
[21] See Edmund R. Leach, *The Political Systems of Highland Burma* (Boston: Beacon Press, 1954). For studies in a different vein, see the works by Clifford Geertz cited in fn. 1.

is for regimes that emphasize the sacred qualities of politics, the second for systems in which functions have been specialized. He makes a bold argument based on past data rather than on a claim that we should begin with his premises.

Eckstein outlines the main change that polities have actually undergone as they develop. He would have us take seriously both the notions "political system" and "monotonic development." Many people sense some uniform change in modern polities, but they have a hard time pinning down what grows. Eckstein shows that "the early explorers" of political systems and change "were getting at something worth getting at"—something unavoidable, if we are to have clear definitions and see some regularities in modern change.

Originally, in primitive societies where work was not specialized, ceremonies were crucial to the legitimacy of leadership. As Eckstein notes, "power served pomp, not pomp power." Rituals of order were the heart of political life. The dignity of government, not its functional use, was its basis. Eckstein is no symbolic anthropologist (he is a systems theorist), but he relies on Geertz's ethnography of a "theatre-state"[22] to show how politics started.

When kings and courts began to extract and arrange social resources, they claimed a monopoly on violence and taxes, not just on cosmic right. As groups with separate interests arose, the functions of labor were differentiated (in governing as in all other social activities). Functional systems theory is thus a natural way to look at the vectored, monotonic change from politics whose main concern was sacred, to politics whose center is functional efficiency. And it is a natural analysis for politics that is no longer traditional.

Eckstein thus establishes a link between the use of systems theory and the use of the culturalist approach. For the analysis of modernizing polities, he suggests, there is no alternative to looking at functional sectors and their boundaries. He takes many current writers on development to task because they tend to study random or varied changes without paying attention to the need for clear definitions and categories that do not change over time and place. Without such definitions, there is no way to do comparative work. The impulse to be comparative, Eckstein shows, is not just an arbitrary choice, not just an intellectual fad. It relates to the central, most obvious, substantive changes in past politics.

Eckstein's sweeping review of political history leaves us with two basic points that seem perennial and inevitable. First, the idea of political "sys-

[22] Clifford Geertz, *Negara: The Theatre-State in Nineteenth-Century Bali* (Princeton: Princeton University Press, 1980).

tem" is not *passé*. On the contrary, the need to have consistent definitions of functions is basic to the study of modernizing polities. The symbolist alternative has its place mainly in the study of "primitive" polities or sacred politics. Second, some notion of political "development" remains necessary, despite the great effects cultures have in varying the kinds of change in different countries.

Tony Smith's 1985 essay, "Requiem or New Agenda for Third World Studies?" relates development functionalism to its main political alternative, dependency theory, just as Eckstein relates it to its main methodological alternative, symbolic cultural analysis. The *dependencistas'* unit of analysis is different from that of the developmentalists: it is a "world system" rather than separate national units. True to their Marxist heritage, dependency theorists define their main variables as economic rather than political. This theory holds that underdevelopment is not merely a stage of pre-development in national systems; on the contrary, it is an aspect of specifically capitalist development in the world system. Both *dependencismo* and developmentalism accept that history is the record of increasing functional differentiation; but the results are new when this division of labor is mainly conceived internationally rather than within countries, and when the functions being divided are basically economic.

The *dependencistas* argue against a political bias they see in development functionalism. They point out that an emphasis on the value of stability—whether because of a methodological need for sure definitions or because of an empirical need for political order—can be seen as a weak excuse for repressive authoritarianism. Emphasis on the inevitability of development may rationalize timidity and quietude—despite obvious injustice and poverty, e.g., in many countries of Latin America. Functionalists should have no false hope that such problems will disappear without any struggle.

By showing that dependency theory is flexible, and by emphasizing that dependency creates real problems which developmental functionalism fails to address, Smith takes this approach seriously.[23] But he also notes a weakness of many *dependencistas*: their tendency to insist on grand logics that ignore too many exceptions. Systems theory has the same flaw when it, too, is carried beyond the basic need for coherent definitions and is converted into hasty political recommendations.

Smith ends with an explicitly eclectic position—not because eclecti-

---

[23] For a subtle treatise from a nondogmatic *dependencista* viewpoint, see Gary Gereffi, *The Pharmaceutical Industry and Dependency in the Third World* (Princeton: Princeton University Press, 1983).

cism is nice or polite, but because the critiques of development function-alism (or of dependency theory, for that matter) leave it strong. Systems theory sensitizes us to the twin needs to use stable definitions and to look for regularities in historical change. It broadens our horizons of under-standing and makes us aware of issues in the real world. What more could we ask of a theory? Smith's essay suggests that developmental sys-tems theory will be with us for a long time.

Conclusion: Clarity for Comparisons as the Sole Point of the Theory of Developing Systems

Systems theory and dependency theory are not opposites. Most *depen-dencistas* now explicitly try to make comparisons between developing countries while at the same time trying to analyze a larger system (the whole world). Both the systems and dependency frameworks ideally use constant definitions, even if the *dependencistas* sometimes attempt to nar-row their project and show the overall importance only of "economic" functions. Both modes of thought are easiest to criticize when they limit the job of historical explanation to one function: order or monopoly are typical choices. Both are most convincing when they are flexible enough to take account of the many factors (political, economic, and cultural) that influence change in actual situations.

The earlier essays in this volume were written in the 1960s, when sys-tems theory flourished. Yet the concerns they raise have not disappeared. The four studies criticizing and refining these now classic efforts toward better comparisons, as well as the two evaluations from the 1980s, to-gether show that the main problems which arise with the idea of "devel-oping system" occur only when it is misapplied.

There is nothing new about the problem addressed by development functionalism or systems theory: how to keep order in a society that changes. Even before Durkheim, this question stirred people who thought about political and social integration, and it is a practical concern of modern governments. The abstraction of systems theory gives it the ability to serve as a framework for dealing with this question of order and development. Many critiques of particular versions of systems theory face other questions: issues of freedom and welfare, issues of how people should react to injustice, questions how cultural factors affect the possi-bilities of order, concerns for units smaller than the state, or concerns that international links may be exploitative. These other approaches have re-fined development functionalism—and made it a rich tradition.

Yet to the extent they do more than refine it, they start from questions basically different from the one it addresses. And that one does not go away. When systems theory is construed in terms of its original logic, without excluding any factor that is actually found to bear on the link between order and change, it organizes a great variety of thinking about that perennial question. If its purpose were more substantive and less definitional, it would not be able to do this.

The impulse toward a coherent set of definitions for looking at different polities, in distinct times and places, remains the most important intellectual challenge of comparative politics. We can solve the problem of using constant definitions in changing situations—but only if we accept it *as* a problem. We should not try to get around the antinomy by giving up either of two needs: to look for links between different kinds of social functions, and to take relevant evidence seriously even when it does not fit predefined categories.

Political System:
Definitions and Functions

AN APPROACH TO THE ANALYSIS
OF POLITICAL SYSTEMS*

By DAVID EASTON

I. Some Attributes of Political Systems

IN an earlier work I have argued for the need to develop general, empirically oriented theory as the most economical way in the long run to understand political life. Here I propose to indicate a point of view that, at the least, might serve as a springboard for discussion of alternative approaches and, at most, as a small step in the direction of a general political theory. I wish to stress that what I have to say is a mere orientation to the problem of theory; outside of economics and perhaps psychology, it would be presumptuous to call very much in social science "theory," in the strict sense of the term.

Furthermore, I shall offer only a Gestalt of my point of view, so that it will be possible to evaluate, in the light of the whole, those parts that I do stress. In doing this, I know I run the definite risk that the meaning and implications of this point of view may be only superficially communicated; but it is a risk I shall have to undertake since I do not know how to avoid it sensibly.

The study of politics is concerned with understanding how authoritative decisions are made and executed for a society. We can try to understand political life by viewing each of its aspects piecemeal. We can examine the operation of such institutions as political parties, interest groups, government, and voting; we can study the nature and consequences of such political practices as manipulation, propaganda, and violence; we can seek to reveal the structure within which these practices occur. By combining the results we can obtain a rough picture of what happens in any self-contained political unit.

In combining these results, however, there is already implicit the notion that each part of the larger political canvas does not stand alone but is related to each other part; or, to put it positively, that the operation of no one part can be fully understood without reference to the way in which the whole itself operates. I have suggested in my book, *The Political System,*[1] that it is valuable to adopt this implicit assump-

---

* The point of view expressed in this article was later fully developed in *A Framework for Political Analysis* (Englewood Cliffs, NJ: Prentice-Hall, 1965; reprinted by University of Chicago Press, 1979) and *A Systems Analysis of Political Life* (New York: Wiley, 1965; reprinted by University of Chicago Press, 1979).

[1] New York, 1953.

tion as an articulate premise for research and to view political life as a system of interrelated activities. These activities derive their relatedness or systemic ties from the fact that they all more or less influence the way in which authoritative decisions are formulated and executed for a society.

Once we begin to speak of political life as a system of activity, certain consequences follow for the way in which we can undertake to analyze the working of a system. The very idea of a system suggests that we can separate political life from the rest of social activity, at least for analytical purposes, and examine it as though for the moment it were a self-contained entity surrounded by, but clearly distinguishable from, the environment or setting in which it operates. In much the same way, astronomers consider the solar system a complex of events isolated for certain purposes from the rest of the universe.

Furthermore, if we hold the system of political actions as a unit before our mind's eye, as it were, we can see that what keeps the system going are inputs of various kinds. These inputs are converted by the processes of the system into outputs and these, in turn, have consequences both for the system and for the environment in which the system exists. The formula here is very simple but, as I hope to show, also very illuminating: inputs—political system or processes—outputs. These relationships are shown diagrammatically in Figure 1. This

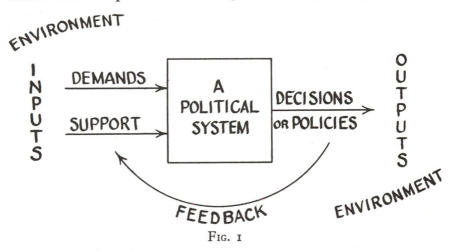

Fig. 1

diagram represents a very primitive "model"—to dignify it with a fashionable name—for approaching the study of political life.

Political systems have certain properties because they are systems.[2]

---

[2] My conceptions relating to system theory have been enriched through my participation in the Staff Theory Seminar of the Mental Health Research Institute at the Uni-

To present an over-all view of the whole approach, let me identify the major attributes, say a little about each, and then treat one of these properties at somewhat greater length, even though still inadequately.

(1) Properties of identification. To distinguish a political system from other social systems, we must be able to identify it by describing its fundamental units and establishing the boundaries that demarcate it from units outside the system.

(a) Units of a political system. The units are the elements of which we say a system is composed. In the case of a political system, they are political actions. Normally it is useful to look at these as they structure themselves in political roles and political groups.

(b) Boundaries. Some of the most significant questions with regard to the operation of political systems can be answered only if we bear in mind the obvious fact that a system does not exist in a vacuum. It is always immersed in a specific setting or environment. The way in which a system works will be in part a function of its response to the total social, biological, and physical environment.

The special problem with which we are confronted is how to distinguish systematically between a political system and its setting. Does it even make sense to say that a political system has a boundary dividing it from its setting? If so, how are we to identify the line of demarcation?

Without pausing to argue the matter, I would suggest that it is useful to conceive of a political system as having a boundary in the same sense as a physical system. The boundary of a political system is defined by all those actions more or less directly related to the making of binding decisions for a society; every social action that does not partake of this characteristic will be excluded from the system and thereby will automatically be viewed as an external variable in the environment.

(2) Inputs and outputs. Presumably, if we select political systems for special study, we do so because we believe that they have characteristically important consequences for society, namely, authoritative decisions. These consequences I shall call the outputs. If we judged that political systems did not have important outputs for society, we would probably not be interested in them.

Unless a system is approaching a state of entropy—and we can assume that this is not true of most political systems—it must have continuing inputs to keep it going. Without inputs the system can do no work; without outputs we cannot identify the work done by the

---

versity of Michigan. There has been such thorough mingling of ideas in this Seminar that rather than try to trace paternity, I shall simply indicate my obligation to the collective efforts of the Seminar.

system. The specific research tasks in this connection would be to identify the inputs and the forces that shape and change them, to trace the processes through which they are transformed into outputs, to describe the general conditions under which such processes can be maintained, and to establish the relationship between outputs and succeeding inputs of the system.

From this point of view, much light can be shed on the working of a political system if we take into account the fact that much of what happens within a system has its birth in the efforts of the members of the system to cope with the changing environment. We can appreciate this point if we consider a familiar biological system such as the human organism. It is subject to constant stress from its surroundings to which it must adapt in one way or another if it is not to be completely destroyed. In part, of course, the way in which the body works represents responses to needs that are generated by the very organization of its anatomy and functions; but in large part, in order to understand both the structure and the working of the body, we must also be very sensitive to the inputs from the environment.

In the same way, the behavior of every political system is to some degree imposed upon it by the kind of system it is, that is, by its own structure and internal needs. But its behavior also reflects the strains occasioned by the specific setting within which the system operates. It may be argued that most of the significant changes within a political system have their origin in shifts among the external variables. Since I shall be devoting the bulk of this article to examining some of the problems related to the exchange between political systems and their environments, I shall move on to a rapid description of other properties of political systems.

(3) Differentiation within a system. As we shall see in a moment, from the environment come both energy to activate a system and information with regard to which the system uses this energy. In this way a system is able to do work. It has some sort of output that is different from the input that enters from the environment. We can take it as a useful hypothesis that if a political system is to perform some work for anything but a limited interval of time, a minimal amount of differentiation in its structure must occur. In fact, empirically it is impossible to find a significant political system in which the same units all perform the same activities at the same time. The members of a system engage in at least some minimal division of labor that provides a structure within which action takes place.

(4) Integration of a system. This fact of differentiation opens up a

major area of inquiry with regard to political systems. Structural differentiation sets in motion forces that are potentially disintegrative in their results for the system. If two or more units are performing different kinds of activity at the same time, how are these activities to be brought into the minimal degree of articulation necessary if the members of the system are not to end up in utter disorganization with regard to the production of the outputs of interest to us? We can hypothesize that if a structured system is to maintain itself, it must provide mechanisms whereby its members are integrated or induced to cooperate in some minimal degree so that they can make authoritative decisions.

II. Inputs: Demands

Now that I have mentioned some major attributes of political systems that I suggest require special attention if we are to develop a generalized approach, I want to consider in greater detail the way in which an examination of inputs and outputs will shed some light on the working of these systems.

Among inputs of a political system there are two basic kinds: demands and support. These inputs give a political system its dynamic character. They furnish it both with the raw material or information that the system is called upon to process and with the energy to keep it going.

The reason why a political system emerges in a society at all—that is, why men engage in political activity—is that demands are being made by persons or groups in the society that cannot all be fully satisfied. In all societies one fact dominates political life: scarcity prevails with regard to most of the valued things. Some of the claims for these relatively scarce things never find their way into the political system but are satisfied through the private negotiations of or settlements by the persons involved. Demands for prestige may find satisfaction through the status relations of society; claims for wealth are met in part through the economic system; aspirations for power find expression in educational, fraternal, labor, and similar private organizations. Only where wants require some special organized effort on the part of society to settle them authoritatively may we say that they have become inputs of the political system.

Systematic research would require us to address ourselves to several key questions with regard to these demands.

(1) How do demands arise and assume their particular character in a society? In answer to this question, we can point out that demands have their birth in two sectors of experience: either in the environment

of a system or within the system itself. We shall call these the external and internal demands, respectively.

Let us look at the external demands first. I find it useful to see the environment not as an undifferentiated mass of events but rather as systems clearly distinguishable from one another and from the political system. In the environment we have such systems as the ecology, economy, culture, personality, social structure, and demography. Each of these constitutes a major set of variables in the setting that helps to shape the kind of demands entering a political system. For purposes of illustrating what I mean, I shall say a few words about culture.

The members of every society act within the framework of an ongoing culture that shapes their general goals, specific objectives, and the procedures that the members feel ought to be used. Every culture derives part of its unique quality from the fact that it emphasizes one or more special aspects of behavior and this strategic emphasis serves to differentiate it from other cultures with respect to the demands that it generates. As far as the mass of the people is concerned, some cultures, such as our own, are weighted heavily on the side of economic wants, success, privacy, leisure activity, and rational efficiency. Others, such as that of the Fox Indians, strive toward the maintenance of harmony, even if in the process the goals of efficiency and rationality may be sacrificed. Still others, such as the Kachins of highland Burma, stress the pursuit of power and prestige. The culture embodies the standards of value in a society and thereby marks out areas of potential conflict, if the valued things are in short supply relative to demand. The typical demands that will find their way into the political process will concern the matters in conflict that are labeled important by the culture. For this reason we cannot hope to understand the nature of the demands presenting themselves for political settlement unless we are ready to explore systematically and intensively their connection with the culture. And what I have said about culture applies, with suitable modifications, to other parts of the setting of a political system.

But not all demands originate or have their major locus in the environment. Important types stem from situations occurring within a political system itself. Typically, in every on-going system, demands may emerge for alterations in the political relationships of the members themselves, as the result of dissatisfaction stemming from these relationships. For example, in a political system based upon representation, in which equal representation is an important political norm, demands may arise for equalizing representation between urban and rural voting districts. Similarly, demands for changes in the process of recruitment of formal political leaders, for modifications of the way in which constitutions are amended, and the like may all be internally inspired demands.

I find it useful and necessary to distinguish these from external demands because they are, strictly speaking, not inputs of the system but something that we can call "withinputs," if we can tolerate a cumbersome neologism, and because their consequences for the character of a political system are more direct than in the case of external demands. Furthermore, if we were not aware of this difference in classes of demands, we might search in vain for an explanation of the emergence of a given set of internal demands if we turned only to the environment.

(2) How are demands transformed into issues? What determines whether a demand becomes a matter for serious political discussion or remains something to be resolved privately among the members of society? The occurrence of a demand, whether internal or external, does not thereby automatically convert it into a political *issue*. Many demands die at birth or linger on with the support of an insignificant fraction of the society and are never raised to the level of possible political decision. Others become issues, an issue being a demand that the members of a political system are prepared to deal with as a significant item for discussion through the recognized channels in the system.

The distinction between demands and issues raises a number of questions about which we need data if we are to understand the processes through which claims typically become transformed into issues. For example, we would need to know something about the relationship between a demand and the location of its initiators or supporters in the power structures of the society, the importance of secrecy as compared with publicity in presenting demands, the matter of timing of demands, the possession of political skills or know-how, access to channels of communication, the attitudes and states of mind of possible publics, and the images held by the initiators of demands with regard to the way in which things get done in the particular political system. Answers to matters such as these would possibly yield a conversion index reflecting the probability of a set of demands being converted into live political issues.

If we assume that political science is primarily concerned with the way in which authoritative decisions are made for a society, demands require special attention as a major type of input of political systems. I have suggested that demands influence the behavior of a system in a number of ways. They constitute a significant part of the material upon which the system operates. They are also one of the sources of change in political systems, since as the environment fluctuates it generates new types of demand-inputs for the system. Accordingly, without this attention to the origin and determinants of demands we would be at a loss to be able to treat rigorously not only the operation of a system at a moment of time but also its change over a specified interval. Both the statics and historical dynamics of a political system depend upon a detailed understanding of demands, particularly of the impact of the setting on them.

III. INPUTS: SUPPORT

Inputs of demands alone are not enough to keep a political system operating. They are only the raw material out of which finished products called decisions are manufactured. Energy in the form of actions or orientations promoting and resisting a political system, the demands arising in it, and the decisions issuing from it must also be put into the system to keep it running. This input I shall call support.[3] Without support, demands could not be satisfied or conflicts in goals composed. If demands are to be acted upon, the members of a system undertaking to pilot the demands through to their transformation into binding decisions and those who seek to influence the relevant processes in any way must be able to count on support from others in the system. Just how much support, from how many and which members of a political system, are separate and important questions that I shall touch on shortly.

What do we mean by support? We can say that A supports B either when A acts on behalf of or when he orients himself favorably toward B's goals, interests, and actions. Supportive behavior may thus be of two kinds. It may consist of actions promoting the goals, interests, and actions of another person. We may vote for a political candidate, or defend a decision by the highest court of the land. In these cases, support manifests itself through overt action.

On the other hand, supportive behavior may involve not external observable acts, but those internal forms of behavior we call orientations or states of mind. As I use the phrase, a supportive state of mind is a deep-seated set of attitudes or predispositions, or a readiness to act on behalf of some other person. It exists when we say that a man is loyal

---

[3] The concept support has been used by Talcott Parsons in an unpublished paper entitled "Reflections on the Two-Party System." I am pleased to note that in this article Professor Parsons also seems to be moving in the direction of input-output analysis of political problems, although the extent to which he uses other aspects of system theory is not clear to me.

to his party, attached to democracy, or infused with patriotism. What such phrases as these have in common is the fact that they refer to a state of feelings on the part of a person. No overt action is involved at this level of description, although the implication is that the individual will pursue a course of action consistent with his attitudes. Where the anticipated action does not flow from our perception of the state of mind, we assume that we have not penetrated deeply enough into the true feelings of the person but have merely skimmed off his surface attitudes.

Supportive states of mind are vital inputs for the operation and maintenance of a political system. For example, it is often said that the struggle in the international sphere concerns mastery over men's minds. To a certain extent this is true. If the members of a political system are deeply attached to a system or its ideals, the likelihood of their participating in either domestic or foreign politics in such a way as to undermine the system is reduced by a large factor. Presumably, even in the face of considerable provocation, ingrained supportive feelings of loyalty may be expected to prevail.

We shall need to identify the typical mechanisms through which supportive attitudes are inculcated and continuously reinforced within a political system. But our prior task is to specify and examine the political objects in relation to which support is extended.

(1) THE DOMAIN OF SUPPORT

Support is fed into the political system in relation to three objects: the community, the regime, and the government. There must be convergence of attitude and opinion as well as some willingness to act with regard to each of these objects. Let us examine each in turn.

(a) The political community. No political system can continue to operate unless its members are willing to support the existence of a group that seeks to settle differences or promote decisions through peaceful action in common. The point is so obvious—being dealt with usually under the heading of the growth of national unity—that it may well be overlooked; and yet it is a premise upon which the continuation of any political system depends. To refer to this phenomenon we can speak of the political community. At this level of support we are not concerned with whether a government exists or whether there is loyalty to a constitutional order. For the moment we only ask whether the members of the group that we are examining are sufficiently oriented toward each other to want to contribute their collective energies toward pacific settlement of their varying demands.

The American Civil War is a concrete illustration of the cessation of input of support for the political community. The war itself was definitive evidence that the members of the American political system could no longer contribute to the existence of a state of affairs in which peaceful solution of conflicting demands was the rule. Matters had come to the point where it was no longer a question of whether the South would support one or another alternative government, or whether it could envision its demands being satisfied through the normal constitutional procedures. The issue turned on whether there was sufficient mutual identification among the members of the system for them to be able to work together as a political community. Thus in any political system, to the extent that there is an in-group or we-group feeling and to the extent that the members of the system identify one another as part of this unit and exclude others according to some commonly accepted criteria, such as territoriality, kinship, or citizenship, we shall say that they are putting in support for the political community.

(b) The regime. Support for a second major part of a political system helps to supply the energy to keep the system running. This aspect of the system I shall call the regime. It consists of all those arrangements that regulate the way in which the demands put into the system are settled and the way in which decisions are put into effect. They are the so-called rules of the game, in the light of which actions by members of the system are legitimated and accepted by the bulk of the members as authoritative. Unless there is a minimum convergence of attitudes in support of these fundamental rules—the constitutional principles, as we call them in Western society—there would be insufficient harmony in the actions of the members of a system to meet the problems generated by their support of a political community. The fact of trying to settle demands in common means that there must be known principles governing the way in which resolutions of differences of claims are to take place.

(c) The government. If a political system is going to be able to handle the conflicting demands put into it, not only must the members of the system be prepared to support the settlement of these conflicts in common and possess some consensus with regard to the rules governing the mode of settlement; they must also be ready to support a government as it undertakes the concrete tasks involved in negotiating such settlements. When we come to the outputs of a system, we shall see the rewards that are available to a government for mobilizing support. At this point, I just wish to draw attention to this need on the part of a government for support if it is going to be able to make decisions with regard to demands. Of course, a government may elicit support in many ways: through persuasion, consent, or manipulation. It may also impose unsupported settlements of demands through threats of force. But it is a familiar axiom of political science that a government based upon force alone is not long for this world; it must buttress its position by inducing a favorable state of mind in its subjects through fair or foul means.

The fact that support directed to a political system can be broken down conceptually into three elements—support for the community, regime, and government—does not mean, of course, that in the concrete case support for each of these three objects is independent. In fact we might and normally do find all three kinds of support very closely intertwined, so that the presence of one is a function of the presence of one or both of the other types.

For example, withdrawal of support from the government of Louis XVI in effect also meant that members of the French monarchical system were challenging at least the regime; as it turned out in the ensuing revolution and civil war, there was even doubt whether the members of the system would continue to support a unified political community. In this case, what was initially opposition to the ruling sovereign—that is, to the government—quickly turned out to signify a lack of sufficient support for the regime and ultimately, to some extent, for the political community. But this is not always so and fortunately, from the point of view of social order, it is not typically the case. We are accustomed to calling for a change of government without thereby suggesting dissatisfaction with the regime or community. And at times, although this is less frequently true, the community shows sufficient intention to continue as a cooperating group to be able to accept a challenge to the regime. From 1832 to the 1880's England underwent a serious modification in its regime, introducing the basic elements of a system of popular democracy, without serious diminution of input of support at the community level. It is always a matter for empirical enquiry to discover the degree to which support at any one level is dependent upon support at the others.

This very brief discussion of support points up one major fact. If a system is to absorb a variety of demands and negotiate some sort of settlement among them, it is not enough for the members of the system to support only their own demands and the particular government that will undertake to promote these demands. For the demands to be processed into outputs it is equally essential that the members of the system stand ready to support the existence of a political community and some stable rules of common action that we call the regime.

(2) QUANTITY AND SCOPE OF SUPPORT

How much support needs to be put into a system and how many of its members need to contribute such support if the system is to be able to do the job of converting demands to decisions? No ready answer can be offered. The actual situation in each case would determine the amount and scope required. We can, however, visualize a number of situations that will be helpful in directing our attention to possible generalizations.

Under certain circumstances very few members need to support a system at any level. The members might be dull and apathetic, indifferent to the general operations of the system, its progress or decisions. In a loosely connected system such as India has had, this might well be the state of mind of by far the largest segment of the membership. Either in fact they have not been affected by national decisions or they have not perceived that they were so affected. They may have little sense of identification with the present regime and government and yet, with regard to the input of demands, the system may be able to act on the basis of the support offered by the known 3 per cent of the Western-oriented politicians and intellectuals who are politically active. In other words, we can have a small minority putting in quantitatively sufficient supportive energy to keep the system going. However, we can venture the hypothesis that where members of a system are putting in numerous demands, there is a strong probability that they will actively offer support or hostility at one of the three levels of the system, depending upon the degree to which these demands are being met through appropriate decisions.

Alternatively, we may find that all the members of a system are putting in support, but the amount may be so low as to place one or all aspects of the system in jeopardy. Modern France is perhaps a classic illustration. The input of support at the level of the political community is probably adequate for the maintenance of France as a national political unit. But for a variety of historical and contemporary reasons, there is considerable doubt as to whether the members of the French political system are putting in anything but a low order of support to the regime or any particular government. This low amount of support, even though spread over a relatively large segment of the population, leaves the French political system on somewhat less secure foundations than is the case with India. There support is less widespread but more active—that is, quantitatively greater—on the part of a minority. As this illustration indicates, the amount of support is not necessarily proportional to its scope.

It may seem from the above discussion as though the members of a political system either put in support or withhold it—that is, demonstrate hostility or apathy. In fact, members may and normally do simultaneously engage in supportive and hostile behavior. What we must be interested in is the net balance of support.

IV. MECHANISMS OF SUPPORT

To this point I have suggested that no political system can yield the important outputs we call authoritative decisions unless, in addition to demands, support finds its way into the system. I have discussed the possible object to which support may be directed, and some problems with regard to the domain, quantity, and scope of support. We are now ready to turn to the main question raised by our attention to support as a crucial input: how do systems typically manage to maintain a steady flow of support? Without it a system will not absorb sufficient energy from its members to be able to convert demands to decisions.

In theory, there might be an infinite variety of means through which members could be induced to support a system; in practice, certain well-established classes of mechanisms are used. Research in this area needs to be directed to exploring the precise way in which a particular system utilizes these mechanisms and to refining our understanding of the way in which they contribute to the making of authoritative policy.

A society generates support for a political system in two ways: through outputs that meet the demands of the members of society; and through the processes of politicization. Let us look at outputs first.

(1) OUTPUTS AS A MECHANISM OF SUPPORT

An output of a political system, it will be recalled, is a political decision or policy. One of the major ways of strengthening the ties of the members to their system is through providing decisions that tend to satisfy the day-to-day demands of these members. Fundamentally this is the truth that lies in the aphorism that one can fool some of the people some of the time but not all of them all of the time. Without some minimal satisfaction of demands, the ardor of all but the most fanatical patriot is sure to cool. The outputs, consisting of political decisions, constitute a body of specific inducements for the members of a system to support that system.

Inducements of this kind may be positive or negative. Where negative, they threaten the members of the system with various kinds of sanctions ranging from a small monetary fine to physical detention, ostracism, or loss of life, as in our own system with regard to the case of legally defined treason. In every system support stems in part from fear of sanctions or compulsion; in autocratic systems the proportion of coerced support is at a maximum. For want of space I shall confine myself to those cases where positive incentives loom largest.

Since the specific outputs of a system are policy decisions, it is upon the government that the final responsibility falls for matching or balancing outputs of decisions against input of demand. But it is clear that to obtain the support of the members of a system through positive incentives, a government need not meet all the demands of even its most influential and ardent supporters. Most governments, or groups such as political parties that seek to control governments, succeed in building up a reserve of support. This reserve will carry the government along even though it offends its followers, so long as over the extended short run these followers perceive the particular government as one that is in general favorable to their interests. One form that this reserve support takes in Western society is that of party loyalty, since the party is the typical instrument in a mass industrialized society for mobilizing and maintaining support for a government. However, continuous lack of specific rewards through policy decisions ultimately leads to the danger that even the deepest party loyalty may be shaken.

For example, labor has continued to support the Democratic Party even though much of the legislation promoted by members of that party has not served to meet labor's demands. In some measure, large sections of labor may continue to vote and campaign vigorously on behalf of the Democratic Party because they have no realistic alternative other than to support this party; but in addition the Democrats have built up in recent years, especially during the Roosevelt era, a considerable body of good will. It would take repeated neglect of labor's demands on the part of the Democratic Party to undermine the strong urban working-class support directed toward it and the government that the party dominates from time to time.

Thus a system need not meet *all the demands* of its members so long as it has stored up a reserve of support over the years. Nor need it satisfy even *some of the demands* of all its members. Just whose demands a system must seek to meet, how much of their demands, at what time, and under what conditions are questions for special research. We can say in advance that at least the demands of the most influential members require satisfaction. But this tells us little unless we know how to discover the influentials in a political system and how new sets of members rise to positions of influence.[4]

The critical significance of the decisions of governments for the support of the other two aspects of a system—namely, the political community and the regime—is clear from what I have said above. Not all withdrawal of support from a government has consequences for the success or failure of a regime or community. But persistent inability of a government to produce satisfactory outputs for the members of a system may well lead to demands for changing of the regime or for dissolution of the political community. It is for this reason that the input-output balance is a vital mechanism in the life of a political system.

(2) POLITICIZATION AS A MECHANISM OF SUPPORT

It would be wrong to consider that the level of support available to a system is a function exclusively of the outputs in the form of either sanctions or rewards. If we did so conclude, we could scarcely account for the maintenance of numerous political systems in which satisfaction of demands has been manifestly low, in which public coercion is limited, and yet which have endured for epochs. Alternately, it might be difficult to explain how political systems could endure and yet manage to flout or thwart urgent demands, failing thereby to render sufficient *quid pro quo* for the input of support. The fact is that whatever reserve of support has been accumulated through past decisions is increased and reinforced by a complicated method for steadily manufacturing support through what I shall call the process of politicization. It is an awkward term, but nevertheless an appropriately descriptive one.

As each person grows up in a society, through a network of rewards and punishments the other members of society communicate to and instill in him the various institutionalized goals and norms of that society. This is well known in social research as the process of socialization. Through its operation a person learns to play his various social roles. Part of these goals and norms relate to what the society considers desirable in political life. The ways in which these political patterns are learned by the members of society constitute what I call the process of politicization. Through it a person learns to play his political roles, which include the absorption of the proper political attitudes.

Let us examine a little more closely something of what happens during the process of politicization. As members of a society mature, they must absorb the various orientations toward political matters that one

[4] See C. W. Mills, *The Power Elite*, New York, 1956.

is expected to have in that society. If the expectations of the members of society with regard to the way each should behave in specific political situations diverged beyond a certain range, it would be impossible to get common action with regard to the making of binding decisions. It is essential for the viability of an orderly political system that the members of the system have some common basic expectations with regard to the standards that are to be used in making political evaluations, to the way people will feel about various political matters, and to the way members of the system will perceive and interpret political phenomena.

The mechanism through which this learning takes place is of considerable significance in understanding how a political system generates and accumulates a strong reserve of support. Although we cannot pursue the details, we can mention a few of the relevant dimensions. In the first place, of course, the learning or politicization process does not stop at any particular period for the individual; it starts with the child and, in the light of our knowledge of learning, may have its deepest impact through the teen age. The study of the political experiences of and the influences operating on the child and the adolescent emerges as an important and neglected area of research.[5]

In the second place, the actual process of politicization at its most general level brings into operation a complex network of rewards and punishments. For adopting the correct political attitudes and performing the right political acts, for conforming to the generally accepted interpretations of political goals, and for undertaking the institutionalized obligations of a member of the given system, we are variously rewarded or punished. For conforming we are made to feel worthy, wanted, and respected and often obtain material advantages such as wealth, influence, improved opportunities. For deviating beyond the permissible range, we are made to feel unworthy, rejected, dishonored, and often suffer material losses.

This does not mean that the pattern of rewards and punishments is by any means always effective; if it were, we would never have changed from the Stone Age. A measure of non-conformity may at certain stages in the life history of a political system itself become a respected norm.

[5] I am happy to say that, since I wrote this statement, the neglect has begun to be remedied. My colleagues at the University of Chicago, Robert Hess of the Committee of Human Development and Peter Rossi of the Department of Sociology, and I have undertaken a questionnaire-interview study of the development of the political attitudes, opinions, and images held by children and adolescents. This research is an attempt to develop some useful generalizations about major aspects of the processes of politicization in the American political system and to formulate a design that, for comparative purposes, could be applied in other political systems as well.

Even where this is not the case, the most seductive rewards and the severest punishments will never succeed in preventing some of the members of a system from pursuing what they consider to be their inextinguishable interests and from seeking, with varying degrees of success, to change the goals and norms of the system. This is one of the important sources of political change closely associated with changes in the inputs of demands that are due to a changing environment. But we cannot pursue this crucial matter of the nature of political change, as it would lead us off in a new direction.

In the third place, the means used for communicating the goals and norms to others tend to be repetitive in all societies. The various political myths, doctrines, and philosophies transmit to each generation a particular interpretation of the goals and norms. The decisive links in this chain of transmission are parents, siblings, peers, teachers, organizations, and social leaders, as well as physical symbols such as flags or totems, ceremonies, and rituals freighted with political meaning.

These processes through which attachments to a political system become built into the maturing member of a society I have lumped together under the rubric of politicization. They illustrate the way in which members of a system learn what is expected of them in political life and how they ought to do what is expected of them. In this way they acquire knowledge about their political roles and a desire to perform them. In stable systems the support that accrues through these means adds to the reservoir of support being accumulated on a day-to-day basis through the outputs of decisions.[6] The support obtained through politicization tends to be relatively—although, as we have seen, not wholly—independent of the vagaries of day-to-day outputs.

When the basic political attachments become deeply rooted or institutionalized, we say that the system has become accepted as legitimate. Politicization therefore effectively sums up the way in which legitimacy is created and transmitted in a political system. And it is an empirical observation that in those instances where political systems have survived the longest, support has been nourished by an ingrained belief in the legitimacy of the relevant governments and regimes.

What I am suggesting here is that support resting on a sense of the legitimacy of a government and regime provides a necessary reserve if the system is to weather those frequent storms when the more obvious outputs of the system seem to impose greater hardships than rewards. Answers to questions concerning the formation, maintenance, transmis-

---

[6] In primitive systems, politicization, not outputs of decisions, is normally the chief mechanism.

sion, and change of standards of legitimacy will contribute generously to an understanding of the way in which support is sufficiently institutionalized so that a system may regularly and without excessive expenditure of effort transform inputs of demand into outputs of decisions.

That there is a need for general theory in the study of political life is apparent. The only question is how best to proceed. There is no one royal road that can be said to be either the correct one or the best. It is only a matter of what appears at the given level of available knowledge to be the most useful. At this stage it appears that system theory, with its sensitivity to the input-output exchange between a system and its setting offers a fruitful approach. It is an economical way of organizing presently disconnected political data and promises interesting dividends.

A DEVELOPMENTAL APPROACH
TO POLITICAL SYSTEMS

By GABRIEL A. ALMOND

D URING the past decade two tendencies have come to dominate
the field of comparative politics. One of these is the concern for
theoretical explication and methodological rigor, and the second is the
emphasis on field studies of the "emerging," "new," and "non-Western" nations. The theoretical tendency has largely taken the form of
applications of "systems" theory to the study of politics, and the chief
criticism of this approach has been that it is a static theory, not suitable for the analysis and explanation of political change.

The great output of empirical studies of contemporary politics in
the new and emerging nations and the relative decline in the volume
of European political studies have similarly been criticized. Here the
argument is that the relative neglect of Western political studies, and
particularly of their historical dimension, handicaps us in our efforts
to work out the developmental theories and approaches which we
need for our research on the new and emerging nations.

Both of these criticisms have great cogency. Systems theory does
have a static, "equilibrium" bias; and the stress on the politics of the
new and emerging nations gives us an inadequate sampling of man's
experience with social and political change. The only answer to this
criticism is that this seems to be the way sciences develop—not by
orderly, systematic progression, but in a dialectical process involving
overemphases and neglects. If we are to come to grips more effectively
with political change, we shall have to redress this imbalance, adapt
systems theory in a developmental direction, and utilize historical
knowledge of Western political development (but not only Western
history) in elaborating theories of political systems and political change.

This article represents a move in this direction, an effort on the part
of one political systems theorist to define what political development
consists of and to take into account the variables which affect it.[1]

---

[1] Whatever merit this contribution to the theory of political change may have is
due to a long series of polemics which began with my paper, "Comparative Political
Systems" (*Journal of Politics*, xvii [August 1956], 391-409), and became somewhat
more lively after the appearance of my introductory essay in Almond and Coleman,
eds., *The Politics of the Developing Areas* (Princeton 1960). An early and partial
version of some of the ideas contained here appeared in Almond, "Political Systems
and Political Change," *American Behavioral Scientist*, vi (June 1963), 3-10. The
polemics were in part with myself, in part with graduate students in seminars, in part

I. System and Function

The term "system" has become increasingly common in the titles of texts and monographs in the field of comparative politics. Older texts tended to use such terms as "governments" or "foreign powers." Something more is involved here than mere style in nomenclature. The use of the concept of system reflects the penetration into political theory of the anthropological and sociological theory of functionalism. The chief social theorists whose names are associated with functionalism are the anthropologists Malinowski and Radcliffe-Brown and the sociologists Parsons, Merton, and Marion Levy.[2] Though they differ substantially in their concepts of system and function, what these men have been saying is that our capacity for explanation and prediction in the social sciences is enhanced when we think of social structures and institutions as performing *functions* in *systems*.

The point being made here is both simple and important. A circulatory system in an organism makes little sense by itself. When we view it as serving a purpose or set of purposes for the functioning of the organism as a whole, we can begin to comprehend its significance. Similarly, political parties or administrative agencies mean little by themselves. Their significance becomes clear when we see them as interacting with other institutions to produce public policies and enforcements of public policies in the domestic or international environments.

Functional-system theory as formulated by such writers as Talcott Parsons and Marion Levy implies three conditions: functional requisites, interdependence, and equilibrium. A particular system, whether it be an organism, a machine, or a family, has to behave in particular ways, perform a set of tasks, in order to "be" the particular organism, machine, or family. Levy calls these requirements "functional requisites," and lists nine activities as essential to the existence of any society.

---

with reviewers, and in most substantial part with my friends and colleagues of the Committee on Comparative Politics. These ideas were partly formulated during two summer workshops which the Committee held, one in 1962 and the second in 1963. Sidney Verba spent several weeks during both of these summers discussing "input-output" and "capabilities" theory with me. I am deeply in his debt for these formulations.

[2] Bronislaw Malinowski, *Magic, Science, and Religion* (Anchor Books: Garden City, N.Y., 1954); A. R. Radcliffe-Brown, *Structure and Function in Primitive Society* (Glencoe 1957); Talcott Parsons, *Essays in Sociological Theory Pure and Applied* (Glencoe 1949); Parsons, *The Social System* (Glencoe 1951); Talcott Parsons and Edward Shils, eds., *Toward a General Theory of Action* (Cambridge, Mass., 1951); R. K. Merton, *Social Theory and Social Structure* (Glencoe 1957); Marion Levy, Jr., *The Structure of Society* (Princeton 1952).

To illustrate, Levy includes among these requisites adaptation to the natural environment, differentiation of and recruitment to social roles, the maintenance of a common body of knowledge and beliefs, the socialization of the young, and the control of disruptive behavior.[3] Parsons speaks of four "imperatives of any system of action," including adaptation, goal gratification, integration, and latent pattern maintenance and tension management.[4] These and other writers also make the point that, for a system to continue in operation, these functions must be performed in certain ways. When a function is performed in such a way as to maintain the equilibrium of the system, the performance of the function by the agency or structure is referred to as "functional" (or *eufunctional*, in Marion Levy's formulation). When the performance upsets the equilibrium, then it is referred to as "dysfunctional." We shall come back to this concept of functionality-dysfunctionality at a later point.

We need to elaborate a little on the other two assumptions of systems theory—*interdependence* and *equilibrium*. By the interdependence of the parts of a system, we mean that when the properties of one component in a system change, all the others, and the system as a whole, are affected. Thus if the rings of an automobile erode, we speak of the car as "burning oil"; the functioning of other systems deteriorates; and the power of the car declines. Or, in the growth of organisms there are points, for example, when some change in the endocrine system affects the overall pattern of growth, the functioning of all the parts, and the general behavior of the organism. In political systems, the emergence of mass parties or mass media of communication changes the performance of all the other structures of the political system, and affects the general capabilities of the system in its domestic and foreign environments. In other words, when one variable in a system changes in magnitude or in quality, the others are subjected to strains and are transformed, and the system changes its pattern of performance; or the dysfunctional component is disciplined by regulatory mechanisms, and the equilibrium of the system is reestablished. Parsons and Shils argue that social systems tend toward equilibrium;[5] i.e., families, economies, churches, polities tend to preserve their character through time, or to change slowly. Hence the analytical scheme which they propose for generalized use in the social sciences is this concept of system, implying the interdependent interaction of struc-

---

[3] Levy, *Structure of Society*, 149ff.
[4] Talcott Parsons, *Economy and Society* (Glencoe 1956), 16ff.
[5] Parsons and Shils, eds., *Toward a General Theory of Action*, 107ff.

tures performing functions in such a way as to maintain the social system in equilibrium.

Even in this starkly simple form, the generic system model has value for the study of politics. The concept of function pushes us into realism and away from normative or ideological definitions. To answer functional questions we have to observe what a particular social system actually is and does. The concepts of functionality and dysfunctionality sensitize us to the factors making for social stability and social change, and enable us to perceive them in an orderly and thorough way. The concept of interdependence forces us to examine the performance of any structure or institution systemically; i.e., in all of its ramifications and interdependences. We can no longer be contented with describing a single institution or looking at bilateral interactions. Our research must assume interdependence and interaction among all components.

II. Critique of Functional Theory

The introduction of functionalism into the social sciences has stirred up a good deal of controversy and polemic.[6] Among the critics of functional theory, the logician Hempel has raised questions about the scientific status of functionalism, arguing that its exponents fail to provide operational criteria of function and dysfunction, and of the kind of interaction among variables which maintain a system in equilibrium. Gouldner's principal criticism is that the concept of system and function has come from biology and mechanics, and that there has been a tendency to attribute the properties of organismic and mechanical systems to social systems. He points out that interdependence and equilibrium may be of a radically different character in social systems. The autonomy of the components of social systems—i.e., the extent to which they may vary without significantly affecting other variables and the system as a whole—may be far greater than in mechanical and organismic systems.

Gouldner also argues that there is a static tendency in systems theory, a tendency to stress the functionality of institutions and the equilibrium of social systems. The distinction as formulated in anthropological and sociological theory tends to be dichotomous; i.e., structures perform either functionally or dysfunctionally. He argues that they should be viewed as continua, since without specification and measurement it is

[6] See *inter alia* Carl G. Hempel, "The Logic of Functional Analysis," and Alvin W. Gouldner, "Reciprocity and Autonomy in Functional Theory," in Llewellyn Gross, ed., *Symposium in Sociological Theory* (New York 1959), 241ff.

impossible to say what kind and degree of performance by given structures and institutions produce what kind of social equilibrium. Here Gouldner and Hempel would agree that what we need is a model of interaction of components in which the relations among variables and their consequences for system performance are left open to empirical investigation.

A further valuable criticism is Gouldner's argument that there is a tendency to treat each component in a social system as having a value equal to each of the others. Actually the significance and autonomy of the various parts of social systems may be quite unequal. Thus one may argue that the bureaucracy in differentiated political systems is in some sense the central structure of these systems, and that all other structures are significant by virtue of the way in which they affect the performance of the bureaucracy. Here again we need system models more appropriate for social and political phenomena.

Finally Gouldner argues that such a social system theorist as Parsons does not give sufficient stress to the special character of the interaction of social systems with their environments. He may attribute too great an impermeability to the boundaries of social systems. Thus political systems are quite porous, so to speak. The exchanges and movements which take place between political systems and their societies or their international environments, particularly in the modern world, are quite massive. It is impossible to account for either equilibrium or change in political systems without observing the volume and kind of their interactions with their social and international environments.

The main burden of these criticisms is that social system theory is still too much under the influence of biological and mechanical analogies, and that it fails to specify operational indices for such concepts as functionality, interdependence, and equilibrium. The criticisms have merit, but they should not obscure the importance of the original insights of the social system theorists. What we are engaged in here is simply an elaboration and adaptation of their work.

Before we drop the generic system concept and turn to the special characteristics of political systems, we need to deal with one or two other terms. Intrinsic to the concept of system is the notion of boundary and of exchanges or actions across boundaries. A system starts somewhere and stops somewhere. In dealing with an organism or a machine, it is relatively easy to locate the boundary and specify the interactions between it and its environment. The gas goes into the tank; the motor converts it into revolutions of the crankshaft and the driving wheels; and the car moves on the highway. In dealing with social systems, of which political systems are a class, the problem of boundary is not that easy. We may speak of what separates a social system from its environment as a boundary, but what we mean by this is not at all clear. Social systems are not made up of individuals but of roles; i.e., a family consists of the roles of mother and father, husband and wife, sibling and sibling, and the like. The family is only one set of interacting roles for a group of individuals who also may have extra-familial roles, and hence be involved in other social systems. In the same sense, a political system consists of the roles of nationals, subjects, voters, interacting—as the case may be—with legislators, bureaucrats, judges, and the like. The same individuals who perform roles in the political system perform roles in other social systems, such as the economy, religious community, family, and voluntary associations. As individuals expose themselves to political communication, vote, demonstrate, they shift from non-political to political roles. One might say that on election day as citizens leave their farms, plants, and offices to go to the polling places, they are crossing the boundary from the economy to the polity. It is crossing the boundary in both an objective and a subjective sense. In the objective sense, a man leaves his assembly line, where he is performing a role in a manufacturing process, to enter the polling booth, where he is performing a role in a political process. In a psychological sense, some shift of norms, values, expectations, and cognitions takes place as well.

The concept of boundary as we apply it to social and political systems is, of course, an analogy. What we really mean by this analogy can be specified only if we examine empirically the actual exchanges which take place between one system and another. Thus, when we speak of the interaction of personalities and the political system, we are thinking of the impulses, attitudes, and values entering into the performance of political roles by the individuals who make up the political system. At some point in this interactive process, properties which we associate with personality, such as hostility and rigidity, get converted into attitudes toward or choices of particular foreign or defense policies or candidates for public office. In other words, there are boundaries here between general affective and value tendencies, and political attitudes and choices.

There is a boundary between the polity and the economy. For example, an inflation may reduce the real income of certain groups in the population. When these changes in the economic situations of particular groups get converted into demands for public policy or changes in political personnel, there is an interaction between the economy and the polity. What really happens in the empirical sense is that certain psychic states resulting from changes in the economic capabilities of groups are converted into demands on the political system, demands on trade union or other pressure group leaders that they lobby for particular actions by the legislative or executive agencies, and the like. Somewhere along the line here a boundary is passed from one system to another, from the economic system to the political system.

That we are using an analogy when we speak of the boundaries of political systems, and a misleadingly simple analogy at that, becomes clear when we consider the variety of phenomena we include under it. We use it in a simple physical sense, as when we speak of the boundaries of nations or of subnational political jurisdictions. We use it in a behavioral sense, as when we refer to the interactions of voters and candidates, governmental officials and citizens, as these are separated from the interactions of these same individuals in their roles as workers and employers, parishioners and clergy. We use it in a psychological sense, as when we refer to attitudes toward politics, politicians, public officials, and public policies, as these are differentiated from the other contents of the psyches of the members of a polity. Whenever we use the term we need to be clear just which one, or which combination, of these phenomena we have in mind.

Another way of thinking about the interaction of political systems with their environments is to divide the process into three phases, as is usually done in systems theory—input, conversion, output. The inputs and outputs which involve the political system with other social systems are transactions between the system and its environment; the conversion processes are internal to the political system. When we talk about the sources of inputs and how they enter the political system, and how outputs leave the political system and affect other social systems, we shall in effect be talking about the boundaries of the political system.

III. THREE TYPES OF FUNCTIONS

One further thought before we leave this generic concept of system and turn to political systems, properly speaking. We have talked about the functions of systems and how they give the system its identity. Actually, we need to think of systems as functioning at different *levels*. One level of functioning involves the unit as a whole in its environment. An animal moves, while plants do not. Some machines process data; others produce power. An economy produces and distributes physical goods and services. Families produce children and socialize them into adult roles and disciplines. Religious systems regulate the relations of their members with authorities and norms to which supernatural qualities are attributed. What we focus on at this level is the behavior of the system as a unit in its relations with other social systems and the environment.

The second kind of functioning is internal to the system. Here we refer to "conversion processes," such as the digestion of food, the elimination of waste, the circulation of the blood, the transmission of impulses through the nervous system. The conversion processes or functions are the ways particular systems transform inputs into outputs. Obviously the two levels of behavior are related. In order for an animal to be able to move, hunt, dig, and the like, energy must be created in the organism and the use of the energy controlled and directed. The level and kind of performance of the system in its environment are tied up with a particular kind of structural-functional performance inside the system.

In talking about politics, we shall speak of the performance of the political system in its environment as the political system's "capabilities." What happens inside the political system we shall refer to as "conversion functions." To illustrate, we shall speak here of the "responsive capability" of political systems, meaning by the term the openness of the political system to demands coming from various groups in the society, or from the international political system. This capacity to respond is associated with the performance inside the political system of such functions as communication, interest articulation, aggregation, and rule-making.

Finally, we shall speak of "system-maintenance and adaptation functions." For an automobile to perform efficiently on the road, parts must be lubricated, repaired, replaced. New parts may perform stiffly; they must be "broken in." In a political system the incumbents of the various roles (diplomats, military officers, tax officials, and the like) must be recruited to these roles and learn how to perform them. New roles are created and new personnel "broken in." These functions (in machines, maintenance and replacement of parts; in politics, *recruitment* and *socialization*) do not directly enter into the conversion processes of the system; they affect the internal efficiency and operations of the system, and hence condition its performance.

When we compare classes of political systems with each other, or individual political systems with each other, we need to make these comparisons in terms of *capabilities, conversion functions,* and *system-maintenance and adaptation functions,* and the interrelations among these three kinds of functions. And when we talk about political development, it will also be in terms of the interrelations of these three kinds of political functions. A change in capability will be associated with changes in the performance of the conversion functions, and these changes in turn will be related to changes in political socialization and recruitment.

While the individual categories that we use may, on empirical test, turn out to be inappropriate, this threefold classification of functions is important for political analysis, and we believe it will hold up under testing and examination.[7] The theory of the political system will consist of the discovery of the relations among these different levels of functioning—capabilities, conversion functions, and system-maintenance and adaptation functions—and of the interrelations of the functions at each level. The theory of political change deals with those transactions between the political system and its environment that affect changes in general system performance, or capabilities that in turn are associated with changes in the performance of the system-adaptation functions and the conversion functions.

IV. THE POLITICAL SYSTEM: INPUTS AND OUTPUTS

This discussion of the concept of system has been useful, but we shall be open to the criticism of being carried away by an analogy if we fail to bring these analytical tools into the world of politics. What is the political system? What gives it its special identity? Much has been written on this subject, and it is difficult to get agreement among political theorists on the precise language of their definitions. Common to most of these definitions is the association of the political system with the use of legitimate physical coercion in societies. Easton speaks of *authoritative allocation of values,* Lasswell and Kaplan of *severe deprivations,* Dahl of *power, rule, and authority.*[8] Common to all of

---

[7] This approach to functional requisites analysis is related to earlier work but differs in its explicit differentiation of these three classes of function. For other applications of functional theory to the study of political systems, see in particular David Apter, *The Gold Coast in Transition* (Princeton 1955), 325ff.; Apter, "A Comparative Method for the Study of Politics," *American Journal of Sociology,* LXIV (November 1958), 221-37; and Apter's contribution to Harry Eckstein and David Apter, eds., *Comparative Politics* (New York 1963), 723ff.; also William C. Mitchell, *The American Polity* (New York 1962), 7ff.

[8] David Easton, *The Political System* (New York 1953), 130ff.; Harold Lasswell and Abraham Kaplan, *Power and Society* (New Haven 1950), 176; Robert Dahl, *Modern Political Analysis* (Englewood Cliffs, N.J., 1963), 5ff.

these definitions is their association of politics with legitimate heavy sanctions.[9] We have suggested elsewhere that "Legitimate force is the thread that runs through the inputs and outputs of the political system, giving it its special quality and salience and its coherence as a system. The inputs into the political system are all in some way related to claims for the employment of legitimate physical compulsion, whether these are demands for war or for recreational facilities. The outputs of the political system are also all in some way related to legitimate physical compulsion, however remote the relationship may be. Thus public recreational facilities are usually supported by taxation, and any violation of the regulations governing their use is a legal offense. . . ."[10] When we speak of the political system, we include all of the interactions—inputs as well as outputs—which affect the use or threat of use of physical coercion. "We mean to include not just the structures based on law, like parliaments, executives, bureaucracies, and courts, or just the associational or formally organized units, like parties, interest groups, and media of communication, but *all of the structures in their political aspects*, including undifferentiated structures like kinship and lineage, status and caste groups, as well as anomic phenomena like riots, street demonstrations, and the like."[11]

This is not the same thing as saying that the political system is solely concerned with force, violence, or compulsion, but only that its relation to coercion is its distinctive quality. Political elites may be concerned with peace, social welfare, individual freedom and self-realization, but their concern with these values as politicians is somehow related to compulsory actions such as taxation, law-making and law enforcement, foreign and defense policy. The political system is not the only system that makes rules and enforces them, but its rules and enforcements go "all the way" in compelling obedience or performance.

David Easton, who was the first political scientist to write about politics in explicit "system" terms, distinguishes two classes of inputs into the political system—*demands* and *supports*.[12] Demand inputs may be subclassified in a variety of ways. We suggest that they may be classified under four headings: (1) demands for goods and services, such as wage and hour laws, educational opportunities, recreational

[9] See Max Weber, "Politics as a Vocation," in Hans Gerth and C. Wright Mills, eds., *From Max Weber* (New York 1946), 78.

[10] Almond and Coleman, eds., *Politics of the Developing Areas*, 7.

[11] *Ibid.*, 8.

[12] "An Approach to the Analysis of Political Systems," *World Politics*, ix (April 1957), 383-400.

facilities, roads and transportation; (2) demands for the regulation of behavior, such as provision of public safety, control over markets and labor relations, rules pertaining to marriage and the family; (3) demands for participation in the political system, for the right to vote, hold office, petition governmental bodies and officials, organize political associations, and the like; and (4) symbolic inputs, such as demands for the display of the majesty and power of the political system in periods of threat or on ceremonial occasions, or demands for the affirmation of norms, or the communication of policy intent from political elites.

Support inputs may be classified under four headings: (1) material supports, such as the payment of taxes or other levies, and the provision of services, such as labor contributions or military service; (2) obedience to laws and regulations; (3) participation, such as voting, joining organizations, and communicating about politics; and (4) manifestation of deference to public authority, symbols, and ceremonials.

On the output side, we may speak of four classes of transactions initiated by the political system that tend to match up with the supports we have listed above and may or may not be responsive to demands, depending on the kind of political system that is involved. These are: (1) extractions, which may take the form of tribute, booty, taxes, or personal services; (2) regulations of behavior, which may take a variety of forms and affect some subset of the whole gamut of human behavior and relations; (3) allocations or distributions of goods and services, opportunities, honors, statuses, and the like; and (4) symbolic outputs, including affirmations of values, displays of political symbols, statements of policies and intents.

When we speak of a stable political system, what we usually have in mind is a particular pattern of flow into and out of the political system, a particular kind of input-output flow. In the political system, properly speaking, the inputs of demands and supports are *converted* into extractive, regulative, distributive, and symbolic outputs. The demands can be handled by the political system; the strains which they impose are bearable without any basic change in structure or culture. The outputs are responsive to the demands in expected or legitimate ways; and the supports are responsive to the outputs again in expected or legitimate ways. When these conditions obtain, the political system may be said to be in a state of equilibrium both internally (in the performance of conversion functions by political structures) and in its relations with its environments.

One last point should be made about the flow of inputs and outputs.

This is the question of the source of the inputs. We do not wish to leave the impression that inputs necessarily come only from the society of which the political system is a part, and that the political system must be viewed only in "conversion" terms. It is typical of political systems that inputs are generated internally by political elites—kings, presidents, ministers, legislators, and judges. Similarly, inputs may come from the international system in the form of demands and supports from foreign political systems. The flow of inputs and outputs includes transactions between the political system and the components of its domestic and foreign environments, and inputs may come from any one of these three sources—the domestic society, the political elites, and the international environment.

Something should be said about the relations between demands and supports. Generally speaking, demands stemming from inside or outside of the political system affect the policies or goals of the system, whether they be responsive, distributive, regulative, or the like, while supports of goods and services, obedience, deference, and the like provide the resources available to the political system which enable it to extract, regulate, and distribute—in other words, to carry out these goals.

V. The Conversion Functions

This brings us to the events which occur in the political system, properly speaking, or to what we have called the conversion functions. In every political system there is a set of political structures which initiates or processes inputs, and converts them into outputs. The demands entering the political system are articulated, aggregated, or combined; converted into policies, rules, regulations; applied, enforced, adjudicated. These kinds of conversion events occur in all political systems; they are incidental to any political process, no matter how simple or undifferentiated it may be. But the kinds of structures, institutions, or roles which perform these functions, and the way they perform them, vary from the intermittent political structure of a primitive band hardly distinguishable from the family, religious, and economic system, to the highly differentiated political systems of modern societies, with their complex interactions between domestic social and international systems, and the internal interaction of electorates, interest groups, political parties, media of communication, parliaments, bureaucracies, and courts. This conceptual language in regard to the political system enables us to discriminate effectively among these systems, to talk intelligently about their performance and prospects.

This list of political conversion functions is not derived from generic system theory, or from concepts in use in sociological theory. Whatever virtue this classification of functions has results from the fact that it is derived from the observation of political systems. In other words, we are not forcing our data into categories that fit system concepts formulated in other disciplines, but developing concepts which can help us codify and classify political events.

The problem of developing categories to compare the conversion processes in different kinds of political systems is not unlike the problem of comparative anatomy and physiology. Surely the anatomical structure of a unicellular organism differs radically from that of a vertebrate, but something like the functions which in the vertebrate are performed by a specialized nervous system, a gastro-intestinal tract, a circulatory system, are performed in the amoeba by intermittent adaptations of its single cell. Hence we may say that the amoeba performs the same physiological functions as does the vertebrate. In addition we use the functional concepts which we derive from the study of more advanced biological forms to compare them with the less differentiated forms. Indeed, it is only by using the categories of physiological functioning derived from the analysis of differentiated organisms that we can compare them with the more simple ones.

In the same sense, if we look at complex political systems, we can observe specialized structures performing distinctive tasks. We observe electorates, media of communication, pressure groups, parties, parliaments, bureaucracies, and courts. By observing these structures and their interactions, we can explicate what distinctive jobs are being done in the process of converting political inputs into outputs. And we can use these functional categories to compare complex political systems with one another, and these with the less differentiated ones.

We suggest a sixfold classification of political conversion functions: (1) the articulation of interests or demands, (2) the aggregation or combination of interests into policy proposals, (3) the conversion of policy proposals into authoritative rules, (4) the application of general rules to particular cases, (5) the adjudication of rules in individual cases, and (6) the transmission of information about these events within the political system from structure to structure and between the political system and its social and international environments.

VI. The Capabilities of Political Systems

More than four decades ago when Max Weber delivered his lecture on "Politics as a Calling," he discouraged us from thinking of politics in terms of performance. He told us: ". . . The state cannot be defined in terms of its ends. There is scarcely any task that some political association has not taken in hand, and there is no task that has always been exclusive and peculiar to political associations. . . . Ultimately, we can define the modern state only in terms of the specific means peculiar to it . . . namely, the use of physical force."[13] Contemporary empirical political theory tends to follow Weber in its stress on power and process, the "who" and the "how" of politics. It emphasizes two questions: (1) Who makes decisions? (2) How are decisions made?[14] The performance of political systems tends to be inferred from structure and process or evaluated according to moral and ideological norms. When we introduce the concept of capabilities, their development and transformation, we explicitly add two more questions to the "who?" and the "how?" The first of these is what impact does the political system have, what does it do, in its domestic and international environments? And the second question is, what impact does the society and the international environment have on the political system?

Parsons comes closer to meeting the needs of the contemporary political theorist when he speaks of the function of the polity as that of the ". . . mobilization of societal resources and their commitment for the attainment of collective goals, for the formation and implementation of 'public policy.' "[15] Francis Sutton similarly emphasizes the importance of the functions of political systems in their social and international environments, stressing integration for the internal environment and representation for the international.[16] The development of the concept of the capabilities of political systems represents a pursuit of these leads, but we have had to go farther in specifying types of relationships between the political system and its environments, for "goal attainment," "integration," and "representation" must be broken down into their components, and these elements treated as continua, if we are to be able to code the performance of political systems in the environment in a discriminating way.

The concept of capabilities, then, is a way of characterizing the performance of the political system and of changes in performance, and of comparing political systems according to their performance. Our particular classification of capabilities is a coding scheme, derived

---

[13] Gerth and Mills, eds., *From Max Weber*, 77.

[14] See, for example, Harold D. Lasswell, *Politics: Who Gets What, When and How* (Glencoe 1959); Dahl, *Modern Political Analysis*.

[15] Talcott Parsons, *Structure and Process in Modern Societies* (Glencoe 1960), 181.

[16] "Social Theory and Comparative Politics," in Eckstein and Apter, eds., *Comparative Politics*, 77.

from a kind of informal pre-testing operation. We have to try it out to determine whether it helps us discriminate among political systems, or handle political development in a meaningful way.

We suggest five categories of capability derived from our classification of inputs and outputs proposed at an earlier point. These are: (1) extractive, (2) regulative, (3) distributive, (4) symbolic, and (5) responsive. These five categories of capability may be viewed as functional requisites; that is, any political system—simple or complex—must in some measure extract resources from, regulate behavior in, distribute values in, respond to demands from, and communicate with other systems in its environments. There are surely other ways of categorizing the functional requisites of political systems at the system-environment level;[17] but this particular classification is presented as a useful starting point. It is the product of an informal coding of historical and contemporary political systems. A rigorous test of their usefulness can be made only by formal and explicit employment of these categories in coding historical and contemporary data.

But to say that these are functional requisites of any political system is only the beginning, since we are not interested in defining the minimal political system. We are concerned with characterizing real political systems both historical and contemporary, comparing them with one another at the system-environment level, dividing them into meaningful classes, and discovering their developmental properties.

For these purposes, we need to treat capabilities as performance magnitudes, either actual performance or potential performance. We stress that capability refers to performance and has to be separated from the institutions and agencies involved in the performance. To relate the institutions and structures to performance is one of the central problems of political analysis, and we ought not to confuse rates of performance with the means or instruments of performance.

Perhaps capabilities may be best thought of as ranges of particular kinds of performance. An examination of a particular political system may show variation in its rate of resource extraction over time. In war situations, the rate may be high; in normal periods, the rate may be substantially lower. But the problem of ascertaining the range of capability is more complex than examining rates of performance in normal and crisis situations. We may need to specify the extractive *potential* of a political system. What rate of extraction is this system capable of and under what conditions? This is only partly inferable

---

[17] See, for example, David Apter, "A Comparative Method for the Study of Politics," in *ibid.*, 82ff.

from past record of performance. To get at this aspect of the range of capability we need to look at the support aspects of capabilities.

It is also necessary to distinguish between capabilities and elite policies and goals. Elite policies and goals may and usually do involve more than one capability. For example, a policy of economic development will require increases in resource extraction, and regulation, perhaps holding the line on distribution, and coping with demand inputs by increasing the symbolic capability. From this point of view capabilities may be viewed as ends intermediate to the policy goals of the elites. Since policies are made up of different doses of the different classes of outputs, capabilities analysis is essential to rigorous comparative policy analysis. It may enable us to distinguish sharply and operationally among different kinds of economic development, welfare, and other kinds of public policies.

It may also be in order to point to the implications of capabilities analysis for normative political theory. The inclusion of the performance or capabilities aspect of political systems may help bridge the gap which has been developing between the scientific and normative study of political systems. Questions regarding the "proper ends" of the state need to be grounded on empirical evidence of the different ways different kinds of political systems interact with individuals and groups in their domestic societies, and with political and social systems in the international environment. Empirical studies of the *performance* of political systems, of the *what* of politics (in addition to the *who* and *how*), should enable us to grapple operationally with what we mean when we speak of good and evil, just and unjust, political systems.

We may turn now to definitions of the five categories of capability. By the *extractive* capability, we mean measures of the range of performance of the political system in drawing material and human resources from the domestic and international environment. We separate this capability out because there have been political systems like the Mongol Empire, the warlords in China, guerrilla chieftains in Mexico, which have had little more than an extractive capability. Thus it makes sense to treat it separately, since it is to be found in all political systems, and is the distinguishing mark of a particular class of political systems. The extractive capability may be estimated quantitatively as a proportion of the national product; and its variations may be estimated quantitatively over time.

The *regulative* capability refers to the flow of control over behavior and of individual and group relations stemming from the political system. It is even more difficult to express it in quantitative terms than is the extractive capability, though aspects of it are measurable, and in a general way its magnitude, its pattern, and changes in its magnitude and pattern can be estimated. Here we have to concern ourselves with the objects of regulation, the frequency and intensity of regulation, and the limits of tolerance of regulation. While formulating indices to measure changes in this capability is a complex problem, the utility of this concept as an approach to political classification and development is evident. With these two capability concepts we can distinguish between primarily extractive political systems such as those referred to above, and extractive-regulative ones such as the historic bureaucratic political systems described by Eisenstadt in his recent book.[18] Furthermore, we can chart the developmental process from the one to the other, as regulative outputs cease being primarily unintended consequences of or instrumental to extraction and acquire goals of their own, such as some conception of social justice, order, economic advantage, or religious conformity.

The *distributive* capability refers to the allocation of goods, services, honors, statuses, and opportunities of various kinds from the political system to individuals and groups in the society. It is the flow of activity of the political system as dispenser of values or as redistributor of values among individuals and groups. Some aspects of this capability are more readily measurable than others. The structure of taxation may be viewed in its distributive aspects. The magnitude of welfare and educational programs can be expressed quantitatively, as proportions, and in terms of the social strata affected. Thus, while the general impact of public policy on social stratification is difficult to express quantitatively, there are aspects of it which are measurable, and the total pattern may be characterized for comparative and developmental purposes.

What we have said about political capabilities suggests a logic of capability analysis. An extractive capability implies some regulation and distribution, though these consequences may be unintended. A regulative capability implies an extractive capability, if only to gain the resources essential to regulation; and it is difficult to conceive of a regulative capability which would not in some way affect the distribution of values and opportunities. They are not only logically related. They suggest an order of development. Thus political systems which are primarily extractive in character would appear to be the simplest ones of all. They do not require the degree of role differentiation and specialized orientations that extractive-regulative systems or extractive-

---

[18] S. N. Eisenstadt, *The Political Systems of Empires* (Glencoe 1963).

regulative-distributive ones do. Regulative systems cannot develop without extractive capabilities; thus the development of the one implies the development of the other. Increasing the extractive capability implies an increase in the regulative capability, as when, for example, political systems move from intermittent collection of tribute or raids to some form of regularized taxation. Similarly, a distributive system implies an extractive capability, and obviously can reach a higher distributive level if it is associated with a regulative capability as well.

At an earlier point we spoke of *symbolic* inputs, referring to demands for symbolic behavior on the part of political elites—displays of the majesty and power of the state in periods of threat or on ceremonial occasions, affirmations of norms, or communication of policy intent from political elites. We referred to symbolic supports, meaning such behavior as showing respect for, pride in, or enthusiasm for political elites, physical symbols of the state such as flags and monuments, and political ceremonials. And we spoke of symbolic outputs, including affirmations of values by elites, displays of physical symbols, displays of incumbents of sacred or honored offices, or statements of policies and intents. Thus we need to deal with the *symbolic capability* of political systems and treat its relations to the other forms of capability. Surely we do not mean by symbolic capability simply the quantitative flow of symbolic events into and out of the political system. If capability is a profile of rates of performance—e.g., rates of extraction, regulation, and distribution—then symbolic capability is a rate of *effective symbol flow*, from the political system into the society and the international environment. The displays of flags, troops, and ships, the conduct of ceremonies on the occasion of anniversaries, or on the birth, marriage, coronation, and death of princes, kings, presidents, and the like, the construction of monuments, visits by royalty or high officials, are symbolic outputs either in response to demands or independently initiated by elites. The effectiveness of symbolic outputs of this kind are difficult to measure, but political elites (and journalists and scholars) often attempt to do so by counting crowds and audiences, recording the decibels and duration of applause, examining reports on the demeanor of audiences, or conducting surveys of attitudes. Similarly, affirmations of values by elites may be effective or ineffective. They may create or mobilize reserves of support, as did Churchill's speeches during World War II. Statements of policies may facilitate other kinds of system capability, increasing the rate of acquiescence in extraction, obedience to regulation, acceptance of distribution, and reducing the input of demands.

Symbolic output is not the same thing as symbolic capability. The output of symbols may cease to be edifying, menacing, stirring, credible, or even observed, listened to, or read. Royalty or high officials may be spat upon, pelted with rotten vegetables, statues thrown down from high places, pamphlets cast aside, television and radio sets turned off. Or, as in the case of new nations, the symbolism may have little if any resonance. Symbolic messages may be transmitted but not received. The symbols of local authority may be the only ones granted legitimacy, while the central symbolic output may have little, if any, meaning or effect.

While extractive, regulative, distributive, and symbolic capabilities are ways of describing the pattern of *outputs* of the political system into the internal and external environments, the *responsive* capability is a relationship between *inputs*, coming from the society or the international political system, and *outputs*. The responsive capability is an estimate of the degree to which outgoing activity is the consequence of demands arising in the environments of the political system. Again, the usefulness of this concept is suggested by the fact that it implies operational measures, i.e., a given quantity of responses to demands over the total of the demands. We are not minimizing the difficulties in translating this concept of responsiveness into specific measurable relationships. Obviously, in reality we shall have to settle for approximations, for measurement of aspects of the relationship between inputs and outputs.

The reader must forgive the crudeness of this provisional formulation of the concept of political capability. It is the logical next step from treating the political system in terms of interaction with its foreign and domestic environments, in input-conversion-output terms. The capabilities of a political system are a particular patterning of input and output, particular performance profiles of political systems. We are more interested in demonstrating the importance of this level of analysis than in making claims for the effectiveness of this particular schema, more concerned with focusing and directing theoretical speculation and research than in presenting what would be a prematurely formalized theory. The truth of the matter is that we shall only arrive at a good capabilities theory through historical and contemporary studies in which we test out these and other coding schemes.

Tentatively we suggest that we may use the same capabilities scheme for the international interaction of political systems. Just as a political system may have an extractive capability in regard to its own society, so also may it have an extractive capability in regard to the international environment. Thus it may draw spoils, booty of war, and tribute from the international environment, or it may conduct or protect trade and investment, receive subsidies or loans. In the same sense a political system may have an international regulative capability, as in the conquest and the assimilation of other territories and peoples, or in limiting the freedom of other political systems in their political, religious, or military arrangements, or through participation in international organizations which affect the conduct of nations. An international distributive capability may be expressed in tariff arrangements, the granting of subsidies, subventions, loans, and technical aid. The international symbolic capability is a set of measures of the impact of symbol output on political systems in the international environment. Revolutionary symbol output may have great impact on the performance and development of other political systems, and increase the impact of other capabilities in the international environment. Symbol output into the international environment in the form of appeals to common culture and tradition may similarly affect the performance and development of other political systems, and initiate feedbacks which benefit the initiating political system. Statements by political elites of foreign policies and intents may have important effects on the other capabilities of the initiating political system, as well as on the capabilities of other political systems. An international responsive or accommodative capability may be expressed as a relation between its extractive, regulative, and distributive capabilities, and demands from the international environment.

Again this concept of capabilities enables us to handle the relations between internal and international capabilities more systematically than has been the case in the past, just as it enables us to handle the relations among capabilities. Thus a political system which has developed only an internal extractive capability is unlikely to develop other forms of capability in the international environment. Only when a political system develops the institutions and orientations necessary for societal regulation is it likely to pursue regulative goals in the international environment. Similarly, a political system which has not developed an internal distributive capability is unlikely to pursue distributive goals in the international environment. Finally, a political system which has a high internal responsive capability will manifest a different kind of international responsiveness than a system in which internal responsiveness is less well developed. What we suggest here is that there are relations between domestic and international capabilities. But beyond this we can only say that the interrelation among domestic and international capabilities is a matter for deductive and empirical method used together, rather than for simple reliance on logical inference.

Thus the aims of research on political systems must be: (1) to discover and compare capabilities profiles summarizing the flows of inputs and outputs between these political systems and their domestic and international environments; (2) to discover and compare the structures and processes which convert these inputs into outputs; and (3) to discover and compare the recruitment and socialization processes which maintain these systems in equilibrium or enable them to adapt to environmental or self-initiated changes.

We have also to speak of the capabilities of other social systems. Just as the political system has a particular level and range of performance which we can summarize in terms of a capabilities profile, so also do other social systems in the society of which the political system is a part, and the international political system of which it is a member, have capabilities. Such social systems as the economy, the religious community, or family, kinship, and tribal structures also extract resources from the environment, regulate behavior, distribute values, display and transmit symbols, and respond to demands. Similarly, political systems in the international environment have capabilities, and the international political system may have some extractive, regulative, distributive, symbolic, and responsive capability. The flow of inputs into political systems, the kinds of problems they confront, and the pressure on them to develop capabilities will vary with the performance patterns or the capabilities of these other social systems. The distributive capability of an economy will affect the rate and intensity of demands for distribution, regulation, and the like entering into the political system. The need for developing the regulative capability of a political system will vary with the regulative capability of other social systems, including the international political system. When we think of the factors affecting the capabilities of a particular political system, we must see this problem in the context of interacting social systems, of which the political system is only one.

VII. The Support Aspects of Capability

Thus far we have stressed the performance aspect of capability, the rates which may be computed from the volume of particular kinds of output over time. We have already suggested that the range of capability can only partly be inferred from these performance rates, since political systems may operate at "less than capacity," or they may be drawing on reserves which in time will be exhausted. To get at this aspect of capability we need to deal with the question of supports. If we undertook the task of estimating the extractive capability of a political system, we would look for measures of the quantity or value of the money receipts, goods, and services drawn from the society in proportion to the total product of the society. But there are two aspects of political extraction which such a measure of the extractive capability would leave out. The first of these is the relation between the quantities "levied" by the political system, and the quantities delivered. How much tax evasion is there? How much evasion of military service, desertion? Is a day's work given for a day's pay? Do troops stand under fire? We speak of French and Italian *incivisme*, meaning by that a tendency toward nonperformance, evasion, unresponsiveness, desertion. In other words, we need some way of estimating social performance in response to the outputs of the political system. Does the population pay its taxes, obey the laws, accept the reallocation of values, opportunities, and wealth stemming from the political system, respond to symbolic displays and appeals?

Related to this support performance is the idea of "support potential." The tax receipts of a political system, the proportion of taxes paid to taxes levied, will not tell us what the tax potential of a political system is. In the same sense, measures of the output of obedience to regulations will not tell us what the obedience potential of a political system is.

The support aspect of capability has to be measured, therefore, in terms of the resources delivered in relation to the resources levied, the obedience accorded in proportion to the obedience required, the allocations accepted in relation to the allocations imposed, the responsiveness of the population to symbolic outputs in relation to that which is expected. And in addition to these support performance measures, we need to know what rate of extraction, regulation, distribution, and symbol receptivity a society might accept, under varying conditions, from its political system without fundamental structural change in the relations between the political system and the society.

This may appear to be a needless conceptual complication, but we are constantly making judgments of this kind about political systems, estimating loyalty, morale, and commitment in relation to the performance and stability of political systems. What we are suggesting is that the support aspect of capability may be measured in two ways, by estimates of support performance—in other words, of behavior—and by probing the political culture in order to ascertain what the support possibilities are, the depth of the loyalty, the intensity of the commitment, the availability of support for various purposes, and the like. These constitute a kind of political system "reserve," and we need to know something about this reserve in comparing political systems, or in speculating about developmental prospects.

One further point must be made about the support aspect of capability, and particularly about its system reserve aspect. It is a general reserve up to a point. It may be drawn upon in the form of support for the extractive, regulative, distributive, or symbolic outputs of the political system. Political loyalty and commitment, for example, may be drawn upon for support of a higher rate of taxation, a greater extent of regulation, a greater degree of social distribution, a more aggressive international capability. But there may be, and usually are, rigidities in the exchangeability of support for one kind of activity as against another. There may be greater potential support available for extractive measures than for distributive ones, or greater potential support for distributive measures than for regulative ones. And these potential supports will vary in different strata of the population, and under different circumstances. The system reserve component of capability is an aspect of political culture, the "support propensities" which are distributed among the various strata of the population, and the various roles of the political system. We have to estimate the content of this reserve, its magnitude, and its mobility, if we are going to be able to explain and predict political performance.

VIII. Dysfunctional Inputs

What we have presented so far is more than a classification of variables and less than a theory of political systems. It is more than a taxonomy, since it suggests interrelations among capabilities, and between capabilities, the structure and culture of the political system, and the performance of the system maintenance and adaptation functions. These relations, derived at least in part deductively, may be formulated as hypotheses for empirical testing against historical data. It is less than a theory, since prior to systematic study it is an open question whether these particular categories of capability and of conversion and maintenance functions will help us to discriminate the variables we need to know about in order to construct a good theory.

They may be viewed as a proposed first step toward constructing a theory of the political system and of the development of political systems. For example, our analysis of capabilities is suggestive of a theory of political growth, obviously not in any simple or unilinear sense. It is clear from the logic of capabilities analysis that there can be no extractive capability without some regulative capability, no regulative capability without a particular kind and level of extractive capability, no distributive capability without both a regulative and extractive capability, and that these output capabilities will be greatly affected by the development of a responsive capability. In addition, support of political system performance will be affected by the magnitude, content, and interrelations of the other capabilities, and in particular by symbol capability, and in turn will affect them. Finally, the particular pattern of domestic capabilities will significantly limit and affect, and be limited and affected by, the pattern of international capability.

In addition, capabilities theory enables us to relate the performance of the political system in its domestic and international environments to its internal characteristics. We mean that any level or pattern of system-environment performance rests on a set of structural and cultural conditions. An extractive capability, no matter how simple it may be, rests on some structural specialization and role orientations. A regulative capability requires some military, policing, and bureaucratic structure, and "command-obedience" expectations and orientations. A distributive capability requires further specialization of structure (a welfare bureaucracy, an educational system) and the development of distributive, welfare, and egalitarian orientations within the political system. A symbolic capability rests on some political liturgy and iconography, revered and respected offices and officeholders, and the development of attitudes of reverence and respect for these political rites and ceremonials, political roles, political persons. A responsive capability rests on the development of a specialized infrastructure and a political culture of participation, and the adaptation of the rest of the political system to their emergence. Finally, changes in the level and pattern of system performance require system adaptation in the form of role differentiation, changing recruitment patterns, and new forms and contents of political socialization.

What we have presented is less than a theory in still another sense. An analysis of the capabilities of a political system will enable us to characterize the kind of development a political system has attained, but it does not tell us what factors affect political change or development, what produces change in capabilities.

Changes in capability are the consequence of the interaction of *certain kinds* of inputs with the political system. Consider, for a moment, a political system in equilibrium. There are flows of demands and supports from various groupings in the society; flows of demands and supports from the international political system; and inputs from the political elites (within the political system itself). There are flows of output—extractions, regulations, allocations, communications—from the political system into the society and the international political system. Within the political system the demand and support inputs are converted into extractions, regulations, allocations, communications. When all these flows have a particular range of content and level of magnitude, such that the existing structure and culture of the political system can cope with them, we may speak of the political system as being in equilibrium. But suppose there is a change in the content or magnitude of any one or combination of these input flows.

Suppose there is a depression and the unemployed in a political system demand jobs and food from the government, or a war breaks out and a neighboring power threatens its territory. Or suppose a new dynasty in a political system wants to engage in large-scale construction of temples, palaces, and tombs. Or suppose a political elite embarks on a radical departure in taxation; or requires religious conformity of its entire population and suppresses other religions; or embarks on a large-scale program of welfare. Any one of these input flows may be innovative, dysfunctional—i.e., they may require significant changes in the magnitude and kind of performance of the political system. These dysfunctional input flows are what "cause" changes in the capabilities of political systems, in the conversion patterns and structures of the political system, and in the performance of the socialization and recruitment functions. What we need to know is how these dysfunctional flows affect political development, what kinds of dysfunctional flows affect what kinds of capability patterns.

To cope with this question operationally we need to lay out the dimensions in which the flow of inputs may vary. We suggest that they may vary (1) quantitatively, (2) in their substance or content, (3) in their intensity, (4) in their source, and (5) in the *number of kinds* of dysfunctional inputs affecting the political system at a given point in time. We also need to keep in mind, in considering the significance of these flows for political development, the reactions of elites to dysfunctional inputs from the domestic and international environments, and the capabilities of systems other than the one we are examining—other social systems in the same society and the international political system—as they affect or are affected by the processes of the political system. We will take these questions up separately.

First, the quantitative dimension. Dysfunctional inputs may be incremental. Thus demands for participation may begin in the middle classes, spread among the urban working classes, and then to the rural workers. In other countries, demands for participation may be for universal suffrage all at once. For lack of better terms, we may speak of this quantitative variable as a continuum with one extreme labeled "incremental" and the other "high magnitude." The quantity of dysfunctional inputs are of importance for political development because this will affect the scale of the cultural and structural adaptations which the political system is called upon to make. An incremental increase in demands for participation may require only a small adjustment in attitude and a limited set of structural adaptations; while a high magnitude increase may require a fundamental cultural reorientation and the establishment of a complex political infrastructure.

Second, dysfunctional inputs pertain to particular subject matter areas, such as the regulation of land-tenure, or of market relations, enfranchisement or eligibility for public office, religious practices, and family relations. The substance or content of the innovative flow will also significantly affect the pattern of political development, for a political system may be able, for example, to tolerate welfare innovations more readily than regulatory or participatory ones. In other words, the dysfunctionality of a particular kind of input will vary with the existing culture and structure of the political system.

Third, dysfunctional inputs may vary in their intensity. Demands by new strata of the population for the right to vote may take the form of orderly petitions or of violent demonstrations. Low-intensity demands will confront the political system with a different problem of adaptation than high-intensity demands. Low-intensity demands may produce no system adaptation, while high-intensity demands may result either in a change in the responsive capability of the political system in the form of enfranchisement of a new stratum of the population, or a change in the regulative capability in the form of a substantial increase in police forces and repressive action.

Fourth, dysfunctional inputs may vary according to their source. It will make a great deal of difference for the adaptation of the political system if the innovative flow comes from the international political system, from the political elite, or from the domestic society. And in the case of the last it will make a great deal of difference as to which stratum or subsystem of the domestic society is the source of the flow of demands. A political system which has been exposed to large-scale wars over a long period of time will develop a very different capability profile, and political structure and culture, than one which has been relatively protected from threats to its security. Innovation stemming from the political elites may be more immediately translated into changes in political capability than innovations stemming from either the domestic society or the international political system. And dysfunctional demands from the upper classes may involve less of a structural and cultural change in the political system than those emanating from less advantaged strata of the population.

Fifth, it will make a great deal of difference whether the political system is simultaneously confronted by demands for more than one kind of innovation. For example, a political system may be confronted by the threat of war at the same time that it is confronted by a rise in demands for political participation or welfare. It may have to choose among dysfunctional demands, responding to some and suppressing others. The political culture and structure of political systems will be fundamentally affected by such "simultaneous" or cumulative revolutions, just as those which have had the advantage of being able to meet crises one by one will show the marks of such historical experience.

We may also view political development from the vantage point of dysfunctional outputs. Whatever the source of the innovative outputs may be—the domestic society, the political system, the international political system—they may initiate a process of social change which affects inputs into the political system, or which produces capabilities in other social systems that affect the flow of demands and supports into the political system. But the relation of dysfunctional outputs to political development are indirect, through "input feedbacks." Thus the development of a welfare capability may produce changes in social structure and attitudes which will increase the support inputs of some elements of the society and the demand inputs of others. A shift from an aggressive to an accommodative foreign policy may increase the resources available for the development of a welfare capability, and result in innovative welfare inputs by the political elites.

In talking about dysfunctional inputs, we have stressed changes in the quantity, content, intensity, and incidence of different kinds of *demands*. But dysfunctionality can result from fluctuations in the flow of *supports* as well—losses of morale, failures of recruitment campaigns, declines in tax yields, widespread disobedience to regulations. Needless to say, fluctuations in support will be affected by the kinds of demands made by political elites on the society, as well as by the responsiveness of elites to demands stemming from the society.

The extent to which the political system is loaded by dysfunctional flows will vary with the capabilities of other social systems in the domestic society and international system. An economy may develop new capabilities—new systems of production and distribution—and as a consequence the loading of the political system with distributive demands may be significantly reduced, thereby affecting political development. Or a religious system may develop regulative capabilities that reduce the flow of innovative demands on the political system. Or the international political system may develop a regulative or distributive capability that reduces the pressure on the political system. A case in point would be the international military or technical assistance units of the United Nations that reduce the pressure for the development of extractive and regulative capabilities in some of the new nations. Thus the existence of, or the development of, capabilities in other social systems may affect the rate of flow of dysfunctional inputs, keeping the flow at the incremental and low-intensity level, and perhaps help avoid some of the disruptive consequences of multi-issue dysfunctional pressures.

We must never lose sight of innovation and change outside the political system in trying to account for a particular pattern of political development. But one variable which we must treat in greater detail is the reaction pattern of political elites, the behavior of important role incumbents in the political system as they are exposed to dysfunctional demands or supports. Perhaps the term "reaction" is incorrect, for it may lead us to overlook the originative and creative activities of political elites. Political elites both originate innovative flows and respond to innovative flows which originate elsewhere. When political elites are themselves the source of innovation, when they develop new goals and new capabilities in the pursuit of these goals, then we must examine these changes in capability and follow through the consequences of such developments for the society and the international system, and from these environments back into the political system again.

When political elites are "reacting" to dysfunctional inputs, then we must examine the relation between these reactions and the loading of the political system. The reaction pattern of political elites will often determine whether a flow of innovative demands changes from a low magnitude to a high magnitude, from a low intensity to a high intensity, from a simple to a multi-issue flow, from a single source to many sources. This interaction between dysfunctional pressures and elite reaction is on the same level of importance as is the response patterns of other social systems from the point of view of the development of political system capabilities.

A political elite confronted by dysfunctional flows of demands and supports has available to it three possible modes of reaction or some combination of these reactions. It may react adaptively. For example, if there is a demand for the suffrage among strata in the population, it may yield to these demands and accept the changes in culture, structure, and performance that this requires. An adaptive reaction is an acquiescence to demands in terms of those demands. Thus demands for innovation in welfare programs are met by such innovation, although even such adaptive behavior usually will require some creativity on the part of the elites. The content of a welfare program has to be specifically elaborated, staff recruited and trained, and modes of enforcement devised, tested, perfected.

A second possible mode of elite reaction may be described as rejective. The rejection of demands may take the form of elite indifference ("Let them eat cake"), explicit refusal to accept demands for innovation, or repression of the demands. The mode of rejection will, of course, affect the development of capabilities. Indifference may result in an accumulation of demands, in increases in their number, intensity, and the groups involved in the demands. The rise in pressure for innovation may reach the point where the elite must react either adaptively or repressively. Either reaction will affect the capabilities, culture, and structure of the political system but in different ways. For example, adaptation may result in the swelling of the welfare capability; repression may result in a swelling of the regulative capability.

The third mode of elite response is substitutive. Demands for "bread" may be met with an increased output of "circuses." Demands for the suffrage may be met by a tender of symbolic affirmations of national glory, an aggressive foreign policy, or by welfare measures. The history of elite reactions to dysfunctional demands—particularly for welfare and political participation—is full of examples of substitutive responses of this and other kinds. The ways in which substitutive elite behavior affects the development of the political system are rather complex. The substitutive reaction may "absorb" the dysfunctional demands, as in the case of Germany in the period after the establishment of the Second Reich, when the middle classes tended to "forget" their liberal impulses in their satisfaction with national unity and glory. Or the substitutive reaction may postpone the rendezvous with the innovative demands. Or it may do some of both. In addition, the substitutive reaction may in itself involve a change in capability—e.g., an expansion of international capability with all that this might entail in the development of bureaucracy, in the relative power of military and civil elites, and in political culture.

IX. System Adaptation, Recruitment, and Socialization

New roles and new attitudes are the essence of system change. New capabilities or levels of capability, new political institutions and processes, call for new elites, changes in elite training and indoctrination, and changes in expectation, commitment, values, and beliefs among the various strata of the population. The socialization and recruitment processes of a political system have a special relation to political change. We need to consider the different ways in which these system adaptation functions can become involved in the process of political change.

One common way in which recruitment and socialization patterns affect political development is through changes occurring in other social systems. Consider, for example, the process of industrialization. The spread of industrial technology and associated phenomena such as urbanization and the spread of mass communication tend to mobilize (in Karl Deutsch's terms) new strata of the population, recruit them into new economic and social roles and attitudes. These changes in activity and attitude may spill over into political orientations and stimulate new demands for participation and welfare. New elites (middle- or working-class demagogues and organizers) may be recruited and constitute the source of demands for structural change in the political system. Adults recruited into the industrial economy will be resocialized; children raised in urban-industrial families will be socialized differently from children in rural-agricultural families. This illustrates a sequence in which industrialization affects general socialization, role differentiation, and recruitment, which affects political socialization and recruitment, which in turn builds up innovative pressure on the political system.

Changes in the religious system may have similar consequences. The Protestant Reformation and the rise of individual sects, such as Methodism, changed the content and form of socialization and recruitment in England. New religious elites—clerical and lay—were recruited and came to constitute a stratum from which political elites were drawn. In the case of Methodism, the early British trade union and labor leaders were in many cases recruited from the Methodist subculture; just as the "radical" middle-class elites of the first part of the nineteenth century were recruited in part from the earlier nonconformist sects.

A second way in which recruitment and socialization may affect political change is through actions originating with the political elites themselves. Thus a political elite may directly manipulate the socialization and recruitment processes. This is dramatically illustrated in the policies of totalitarian countries, where the whole social infrastructure of family, community, church, and school is infiltrated, and where the party sets up an organizational system to indoctrinate and recruit among the younger generations. Resocialization of adults through party and party-controlled organizations and control of the mass media is also a totalitarian tactic. While this pattern is more deliberately manipulative in totalitarian countries, it is common in many others. The introduction of civic training in the schools is a common practice in democratic countries; and in clerico-authoritarian countries the church and its schools are self-consciously used as a device for political socialization.

A third pattern is one in which elite reaction to innovative pressures may affect socialization and recruitment in an indirect way. An adaptive reaction by political elites to demands for participation and welfare will not only produce immediate changes in political culture, structure, and capabilities. It may also have the longer-run consequences of affecting family and community socialization processes, producing young adults committed to the political system, providing it with support in the form of goods, services, and loyalty. Passive or alienated adults may be resocialized by adaptive and responsive behavior among the political elites, changing from alienated to allegiant orientations. Rejective reactions among political elites may have the contrary effect, transforming allegiant to alienative orientations and affecting the flow of support into, and the support potential of, the political system.

The consequences for political socialization and recruitment of aggressive foreign policies and frequent warfare should also be stressed. If successful, an aggressive foreign policy may increase support and introduce a nationalist-militarist content into family, community, and school socialization. If unsuccessful or excessively costly, it may produce a withdrawal of support and alienative tendencies in a population. French and German political history is instructive in these connections. The radicalization and alienative tendencies of French political culture during the life of the Third and Fourth Republics have often been attributed in part to the humiliating defeats and costly victories of the Franco-Prussian War and World Wars I and II. The rapid growth of the French Communist Party has been attributed in part to the strong pacifist currents set in motion by the enormous casualties of World War I. The fall of the Fourth Republic was triggered off by army officers who had experienced military defeat and the collapse of the French colonial empire.

The failure of efforts to democratize Germany has been attributed to the bureaucratization and militarization of Prussian and German society in the course of their aggressive expansion in recent centuries. The German educational system and family life were shaped in this military-authoritarian society and tended to produce obedient subjects lacking in "civil courage." The National Socialist elites recruited heavily among the "irregulars" of World War I, the men who could not adjust to peaceful routines after years of battlefield life.

The sequence here involves a particular pattern of foreign policy which produces a feedback of socialization and recruitment consequences, which in turn affects the flow of demands and supports into the political system. In our efforts to relate political development to dysfunctional interaction among political systems and their social and international environments, we need particularly to illuminate the recruitment and socialization processes as they reflect social change and stimulate political change, as they are the direct instruments of political change, or as they become the instruments of political change through a particular pattern of public policy.

What we have been suggesting here is that the performance of a political system (e.g., its "immobilism" or "mobilism"), its conversion characteristics (e.g., the congruence or incongruence of its structures, the cohesion or fragmentation of its culture), the operations of its recruitment and socialization processes, are explainable in terms of a particular history of interaction between the political system and its social and international environments.

We are not simply making the obvious point that we can learn much about political development from the study of history. What we are proposing is an approach to political development in terms of systematic comparative history. This has to be done with a common coding scheme, a set of categories, and hypotheses about their interrelations. The adaptation of political systems theory proposed here may serve as a starting point. We need to meet both prongs of the critique of recent tendencies in comparative politics at the same time—by formulating a conception of the political system which is developmental, and by testing and elaborating this conception against the richness of knowledge of man's historical experience with politics.

POLITICAL DEVELOPMENT, POLITICAL SYSTEMS, AND POLITICAL GOODS

By J. ROLAND PENNOCK*

POLITICAL theorists from Plato to the present have concerned themselves not only with the nature of the polity as we know it, but with how it came to be, what purposes it serves, and by what stages it has developed. The last item, however, has more often than not been slighted. This lack now forces itself on our attention for an obvious reason: Never before have so many "new states" come into being in so short a span of time and never before have students of politics been provided with so many living examples of states at all stages of development, many of them conspicuously failing to perform vital functions, frequently to the extent that disorder and violent change prevail.

The modern approach to this exciting new specimen collection for political scientists makes major use of the concepts of "political development" and "political systems." Each concept presents its difficulties. In the case of political development, it is partly a matter of securing agreement upon definition and partly a matter of avoiding certain implications that easily attach to the term. In the case of "political systems," various writers have felt that the close linkage between systems theory and equilibrium analysis tends to color this approach with a static cast of thought.[1] My aim is to contribute to this discussion by introducing a third term, "political goods," and relating it to the other two. Before discussing this new element, it is essential to the subsequent argument to give a brief sketch of the schema to which it is to be added.

I. POLITICAL DEVELOPMENT AND THE POLITICAL SYSTEM

By an act of deliberate oversimplification, economists frequently reduce economic development to a single variable: per capita income. No comparable course is open to the student of political development,

* I gratefully acknowledge helpful comments and criticisms, at various stages, from John W. Chapman, Charles E. Gilbert, David G. Smith, and Bryce Wood.

[1] Two recent discussions by leaders in the theoretical elaboration of, respectively, "political development" and "political systems" have dealt with these problems. See Gabriel A. Almond, "A Developmental Approach to Political Systems," *World Politics*, xvii (January 1965), 183-214; and David Easton, *A Systems Analysis of Political Life* (New York 1965), esp. chap. 2.

for this phenomenon is not unilinear; it has many facets and dimensions, and none of them is easily measured.[2] At the very least, one must deal with the political culture, with informal political institutions, with governmental and constitutional arrangements, and with the operation of the whole, including the mutual relations of the various elements.

In "systems" terminology, one speaks of the political environment, the inputs (demands and supports), the conversion processes, communications (including feedback), and, to a limited degree, of outputs. Institutionalization and structural differentiation, while they find place in systems theory, tend to be assigned a minor importance.[3]

The political culture comprises a complex of attitudes, sentiments, myths, ideologies, and goals relating to government, to politics, to political roles, and to the entirety (the political system and the society of which it is an aspect). It includes the sense of individual identity and self-respect, and the concepts of rights and duties that characterize the people generally. The state of information and opinion on public matters is also a significant part of it. An inventory of a political culture will note not only the nature, content, and extent or intensity of each of these items but also the way in which they are distributed among the masses and various elites. In short, the political culture

[2] "Political development," "political modernization," and other locutions used to describe the same phenomena all have their drawbacks. It should be made clear that the biological connotations of inevitability, uniform stages, and unvarying patterns are excluded from the term "development" when it is applied to the political realm. Political development may be interrupted and its institutional manifestations may revert in part to earlier patterns, sometimes to the accompaniment of further development on another front—perhaps economic. One thinks of "Tudor despotism" following "Lancastrian constitutionalism." (One might think also of the child who had started to talk but who, on learning to walk, apparently loses the speech capability for several months.) Development may be arrested for long periods, as in Spain and Portugal; it may also be very uneven, with bureaucracy developing at one period at the expense of popular participation—or vice versa; and, of course, it may reverse its direction. See S. N. Eisenstadt, *The Political Systems of Empires* (Glencoe 1963), 342-53. Even the organic analogy, which should certainly not be pressed too far, is by no means incompatible with the notion of political deterioration, decay, and, for that matter, illness, and death. These terms supply the means for coping, terminologically, with phenomena that would otherwise call for such strange concepts as "undevelopment," or "backward development."

[3] David Easton, in his *A Framework for Political Analysis* (Englewood Cliffs 1965), states that "from the point of view of the analysis being developed, structure is definitely secondary, so much so that only incidentally and for secondary purposes need discussion of structures be introduced" (p. 49). Neither "institution" nor "institutionalization" appears in the index of this volume or in that of his *Systems Analysis of Political Life*, nor are they discussed at any length in these volumes. The closest he comes to such a discussion is in the elaboration of the concept of "authorities," while protesting that he is not lapsing into "arid legal formalism" (*A Systems Analysis*, 214).

itself has many dimensions. One might venture to summarize a large part of what constitutes development of these dimensions by saying that a polity becomes more developed as its political culture achieves a sense of national identity without being reduced to monolithic simplicity and also as it incorporates the prevailing world culture, including as elements of the latter the secularization of politics, achievement orientation, and rationality.

The second dimension (or category of dimensions) of political development comprises the elements of the political system itself, its institutions and organized structures. The informal political and semipolitical institutions that provide the means (if any) for popular participation in politics, ranging from mildest influence to final decision-making, come under this heading. They include elections, political parties, and semipolitical organizations such as labor unions, cooperatives, religious organizations, businessmen's and producers' organizations, youth organizations, and other voluntary organizations exerting political influence. Development in this area is measured by the extent of these provisions for political activity, by the degree to which political activities are differentiated from other forms of social activity, by the extent and depth of popular participation, and by the invention or adoption of methods, such as party competition, for making participation effective. One student has attempted to reduce the notion of political development to popular participation, by speaking of it as "changes in the direction of greater distribution and reciprocity of power."[4]

The informal political institutions would have little point were it not for the formal organs of government, ranging all the way from electoral systems through representative assemblies and electorally accountable political leadership, and including the organs of administration and adjudication. Development here begins with the simple matter of differentiation between structures that are distinctly political and those that are not. Division of labor among governmental organs for such special purposes as tax gathering, adjudication, determination of general policies, and so on, with the boundaries or jurisdictions sharply maintained, constitutes a further stage of political development. So, too, does the creation of devices for limiting arbitrariness and for the protection of rights, for enforcing accountability, and

[4] Frederick W. Frey, "Political Development, Power, and Communications in Turkey," in Lucian W. Pye, *Communications and Political Development* (Princeton 1963), 301. He adds to these ingredients the overall level of power, and notes, in a passage suggestive of the difficulties of this subject, that an increase in the distribution of power may have an adverse effect on its overall level (pp. 303, 324).

for the distribution of power, geographically or otherwise. All elements of the Weberian legal-rational model, such as a bureaucracy characterized by hierarchy, rationality, discipline, professionalization, achievement orientation, and so on, find place here. Bureaucracy, as Talcott Parsons has pointed out, is a powerful adaptive factor for any political system, enabling it to conduct military operations more successfully, to control its natural resources more effectively, to foster productive enterprise, to raise more money through taxation, and to maintain order and control deviant behavior among large and heterogeneous populations.[5] Much the same is true of a universalized legal order.

Whether political and governmental structures are formal or informal, incorporated in the legal structure or not, it is of greatest importance that they should be institutionalized; and the process of institutionalization is as surely part of development as are specialization of function and differentiation of structure. It is when certain forms and procedures become the accepted ways of doing things that they become effective instruments of stability and of legitimation.[6]

Part or all of a particular category of development may remain static or may even deteriorate while others are progressing. By means of a dictatorship, for example, a polity may be attaining greater national integration, not to mention order, stability, and satisfaction of needs, while the institutions (and perhaps even the organizational forms) for popular participation are neglected or suppressed. As was remarked above, one dimension of political development may, under certain circumstances, be elongated while another is truncated. One may find oneself comparing two polities, one of which is highly developed in a given respect (say, popular participation) and stunted in another (say, the rule of law), while the situation in the other polity is quite the reverse. In some such cases it may not be possible to make a sensible judgment that one is politically more developed than the other.[7]

[5] "Evolutionary Universals in Society," *American Sociological Review*, XXIX (June 1964), 339-57, at 349.

[6] This point is ably argued by Samuel P. Huntington in "Political Development and Political Decay," *World Politics*, XVII (April 1965), 386-430.

[7] This statement is entirely compatible with the opinion that development in both respects would be more functional, more favorable to the survival of the polity, and for this reason preferable. Parsons, for example, argues that the existence of a definitive link between popular participation and ultimate control of decision-making is so great an aid in building and maintaining support for the political-legal system as a whole and for its outputs (binding rules and decisions) that, for large-scale societies, the "democratic association" is an "evolutionary universal" ("Evolutionary Universals," 340-41, 353-55). Anticipating an objection, he declares, "I realize that to take this position I must maintain that communist totalitarian organization will

Other dimensions of political development involve the operation of the political system as a whole and the relations among its parts. Generally speaking, it is here that systems analysis has made its greatest contribution, especially through Parsons' elucidation of the functions of a system, such as "pattern maintenance" (including "tension management"), adaptation, and integration.[8]

The concept of legitimacy belongs here. The capacity of a political system to convert power into authority, to secure the popular acceptance of its acts as legitimate and to channel order-threatening struggles for power through the political machine, subjecting them to constitutional restraints, is a measure of its development. A key example, indeed a rather special and particularly important case of the legitimacy factor, is the ability of the system to provide for peaceful and orderly transfers of power.

David Easton identifies "persistence" as perhaps the central feature of a political system—the persistence, that is, not of any particular institutions or forms (thus differentiating the term from "pattern maintenance") but of "some kind of system for making and executing binding decisions."[9] He is not discussing political development as such, but presumably he would judge the development of a political system primarily in terms of its proven capacity to persist. This capacity would involve the ability to satisfy demands, to handle stressful situations, and to maintain support.

Other discussions vary the emphasis slightly by stressing the capacity of the polity to mobilize social forces and to direct the course and rate of social and economic change.[10] But enough has been said to provide the setting for a discussion of "political goods" as an additional dimension of political development, or at least as a category

---

probably not fully match 'democracy' in political and integrative capacity in the long run. I do indeed predict that it will prove to be unstable and will either make adjustments in the general direction of elective democracy and a plural party system or 'regress' into generally less advanced and politically less effective forms of organization, failing to advance as rapidly or as far as might otherwise be expected" (p. 356). Incidentally, this statement from the leading systems theorist needs to be taken into account by those who argue that systems theory tends to be static.

[8] See, for instance, Parsons, "Some Highlights of the General Theory of Action," in Roland Young, *Approaches to the Study of Politics* (Evanston 1958), 282-301, esp. 292-95.

[9] *A Framework*, 78; also 88, and chap. 6 generally.

[10] Pye, 18. Karl W. Deutsch declares that political development should mean the ability to absorb more and more information from the environment, the ability to respond to and change the environment more effectively, in accordance with needs, and an increase in the range and diversity of the goals that the organization can follow (*The Nerves of Government: Models of Political Communication and Control* [New York 1963], 139-40).

that needs to be duly taken into account in comparing polities and evaluating their development.

II. Goals, Outputs, Outcomes, and Political Goods

The discussion to this point has been largely confined to environmental and "internal" factors, i.e., to the political culture and to the organization and functioning of the political system rather than to its outputs. Such references as have been made to outputs deal principally with those that operate directly on the system itself, or on the political culture, as by building support for the system ("pattern maintenance"), regulating its own processes ("adaptation"), or maintaining its unity ("integration"). To be sure, it is also recognized that political systems develop their own autonomous political goals and that the attainment of these collective goals is one of their major functions, providing an important measure of their development.[11] But a question arises: Is one goal as good as another or are states to be judged partly by the goals they select? Here we enter the realm of political goods.[12]

Note that we are no longer discussing only "outputs," in the sense of binding policies and decisions; rather, we are considering "outcomes." We are talking about the consequences of outputs—consequences for the people, for the society as a whole, or for some subset other than the polity, as, for instance, the economy or the family. We are indeed still dealing with the attainment of political goals, but the focus of attention is upon those goals that satisfy "needs"—not just needs of the state as such, matters that will enable it to persist, but human needs whose fulfillment makes the polity valuable to man, and gives it its justification. I shall call these goals "political goods."

The degree to which a political system achieves these political goods may be considered yet another dimension of political development. The

[11] See Parsons, *Structure and Process in Modern Societies* (Glencoe 1960), 181-82; Parsons, " 'Voting' and the Equilibrium of the American Political System," in Eugene Burdick and Arthur J. Brodbeck, eds., *American Voting Behavior* (Glencoe 1959), 83ff.; and Karl von Vorys, "Toward a Concept of Political Development," *Annals of the American Academy of Political and Social Science*, Vol. 358 (March 1965), 14-19, at 19.

[12] The political-development literature is not devoid of references to this aspect of the subject, but for the most part they are brief and almost incidental. Pye, for instance, in the process of listing many of the items discussed in the preceding pages, lists, without elaboration, "a clear recognition of the rights and duties of citizens," and a care for "the public interest" (p. 18). In discussing the problems with which new states in particular are confronted, Almond mentions, along with two problems of the kind discussed above ("national integration" and "political participation"), two substantive problems: "international accommodation" and "welfare distribution" ("Political Systems and Political Change," *American Behavioral Scientist*, vi [June 1963], 3-10, 7).

important point, however, is that, when we seek to compare a political system either with another political system or with its own past, its output of political goods should constitute one important element in our evaluation.[13]

What is a "political good"? The particular goals pursued by political systems vary greatly from time to time and from place to place. Even the broad purposes they serve may vary somewhat in accordance with the polity's stage of development and its total situation. The maintenance of order and the provision of security for the group as a whole and for its individual members, however, appears to be almost a universal objective of political organization and activity, and it is certainly one of the principal values it supplies. And if indeed a polity does help create order and security it would be hard to deny that, to that extent, it was generating a political good.[14]

Other things being equal, then, I would contend that a political system that provides more security is more "developed" than one that provides less. Certain further comments are in order. In the first place, it is important to point out some of the items covered by that all-important "other things being equal." The extent to which a polity may be able to provide security, especially against attack from without, is only partly subject to its own control. To a certain degree Switzerland's record for security against foreign attack is doubtless attributable to her own policies and their implementation. To an even greater extent, however, it may be the accidents of geography that account for its good record in this regard. Surely one would not wish to give a polity low marks because of matters beyond its control. In fact the whole issue of security against attack from without, in the modern world at least, is so vexed that, save in clear and extreme cases, one would hesitate to give great weight to it in evaluating a state or judging its degree of development. At the same time one recognizes, with Almond, that "international accommodation" is one of the polity's

---

[13] Not all political goods result strictly from "outputs" of the political system. Some derive directly from the political process, as by-products, so to speak. For instance, political participation is part of the political process; it may help build up political support for the system in the future; it may provide guidance as to demand and need; and at the same time it may contribute directly to the welfare of the individuals concerned by giving them expressive outlets and contributing to their individual development. In these last-mentioned ways, it creates a political good, whether or not the polity had selected this good as one of its goals.

[14] I say "to that extent" because it might be that in a particular situation order is incompatible with other political goods and therefore, while it is good in itself, it should be temporarily sacrificed to make possible the creation of other goods. In such a discussion as this, the all-important qualifier "other things being equal" must be taken as understood even when it is not expressed.

important functions. "International order," to be sure, would be highly relevant for evaluating the development of the incipient world political system or of such a relatively undeveloped political system as that of NATO or the Organization of American States.

To go beyond security to a consideration of military power as an aspect of political development seems hardly proper. We would not say that the United States is more politically developed than, say, Canada, because it could undoubtedly defeat Canada in war. It is of course more powerful, but its greater power derives from its greater natural and human resources rather than from anything peculiar to the political systems of the two countries. Of course political development may have an effect on military potential. Doubtless superior political development has something to do with the fact that Israel is more than a match for the United Arab Republic, even though the population of the latter is over ten times as great. Obviously other factors, not in themselves political, help account for the difference. Current usage is right, I believe, in not including military might as itself an aspect or measure of political development, while still recognizing that political development will be one factor in determining the military potential of a country.

When it comes to the matter of internal security, however, the situation is quite different. The security a man enjoys in walking the streets at night, the assurance he has of the safety of his house and property, these are matters that are or should be within the state's control. Save under the most unusual circumstances—chaos created by some natural catastrophe, for example—it would appear to be altogether proper to rank a state higher, on developmental or other scales of evaluation, in proportion as its record for providing this kind of security is good.

From security, a relatively precise concept, we may move to "welfare," one of the most vague. I include here both material welfare and the more intangible elements of psychic or spiritual welfare. In the final analysis everything that contributes to happiness or contentment should probably find a home here if it is not included under one of the more specific headings.

The extent to which welfare is to be attributed to the political system is of course a matter for study in each case. For the most part, the poverty of the Eskimos can hardly be attributed to their political organization, or lack of it. Nor can the polity of Kuwait take credit for the high per capita income of its people. How far the state *assumes* responsibility for matters having to do with many aspects of welfare varies greatly with circumstances. Yet that variance itself often re-flects the degree of political development, although it is also a function of the way other social structures are operating. If the family is taking adequate care of its own needy members, the state may well abstain from action in this field. But when economic security or other human needs—education, for example—are not being taken care of to the extent that the resources of the society would justify, then whether and how effectively the political organization steps in is a measure of the society's political development. Generally speaking, the promotion of economic growth, whether indirectly by supplying the necessary infrastructure, by providing conditions that encourage the immigration of foreign capital and expertise, or more directly by governmental "planning" and enterprise, is today accepted as a proper function of government; and the effective energies spent on it constitute a measure of the society's political development.

Welfare includes much more than physical welfare. Such matters as growth in individual dignity and self-respect and the development of individual capacities (as long as they are not used to the detriment of others) come under this heading. The polity may make a contribution in this area by providing for widespread political participation. Robert Ward includes among the specifications of the modern polity "widespread popular interest and involvement in the political system, though not necessarily in the decision-making aspects thereof."[15] He is making a descriptive statement. I would simply add that, where participation in decision-making contributes to the achievement of consensus, legitimacy, or the achievement of political goals, it counts as a sign of political development; and moreover that, where it contributes to individual capacity and self-respect, it is also a measure of political development, in the absence of offsetting negative effects.

A third political good is justice. Again we are dealing with a concept that covers a large area. Some parts of the area are ill-defined and in dispute, but even without these sections we have a sizable parcel that has been well surveyed, and title to which, as within the political province, is well established. To settle disputes that threaten to lead to violence or to divide the polity and thus expose it to attack or civil war is clearly one of the first functions undertaken by the political system. Equally it is a mark of political development when the number and kinds of disputes among its members over which the judicial machinery of the polity successfully takes jurisdiction grows

[15] "Political Modernization and Political Culture in Japan," *World Politics,* xv (January 1963), 569-96, 571.

and approaches a monopoly. Likewise, we recognize that a political system is developing as it acquires standards, machinery, and modes of procedure that facilitate judgments based on full and accurate information, that treat like cases alike, and that protect society with a minimum of degradation and a maximum of rehabilitation for its deviant members.[16]

"Justice according to law," "the rule of law," and related concepts (e.g., "due process") do not of course exhaust the content of "justice." Nor do they exhaust the area in which we can find substantial agreement. Take equality of opportunity. As applied to the bureaucracy, and marked by appointment to office on a merit rather than an ascriptive basis, this principle is generally recognized as a test of political development. I would suggest that a polity that secures the application of this principle throughout the society, and not just in administrative and political circles, has achieved a significant political good. (Of course many people in this country and others would take issue with the universal application of the principle of equality of opportunity; but generally, I believe, it would be on the grounds that under the circumstances in question it would result in so much harm as to warrant the injustice done by limiting its application.)

How much further can one go in elaborating principles of justice to which general agreement could be secured? To answer that ques-

---

[16] It will be noted that I have here reverted to discussion of the processes and organization of government, but the point is that their value is to be judged by their outputs—or more specifically, by the out*comes* of these outputs.

It might be objected that modern totalitarian dictatorships may not subscribe to the standards of justice according to law outlined above. Are we then to call them less "developed" than modern constitutional regimes? I would suggest three replies to such an argument, any one of which would seem to me adequate. In the first place, we might avoid the issue by saying that whether or not you call these regimes "developed," to the extent that their standards of the administration of justice do not meet the principles outlined above—to that extent, all else apart—they are less productive of "political goods" than are polities that do conform to these principles. Secondly, I would be quite happy to say that to this extent they are in fact less developed, less fitted to fulfill the needs of men and society. Finally, I would doubt that in fact totalitarian regimes have questioned the principles set forth above. Where practices differ it is generally, I suggest, for one of two reasons. It may be claimed that values are in conflict and that "justice" in the legalistic sense has to be sacrificed to some more basic value, perhaps the security of the political system itself. Thus for instance when individuals are punished for the alleged crimes of others it is generally on the theory that the threat of such punishment is, under existing circumstances, a necessary mechanism of social control (cf. the Supreme Court's justification for our wartime treatment of the Japanese Americans). Alternatively, the problem may be one of disagreement as to what are "like" cases. If it is believed, for instance, that a Jew is a human being of an inferior type and that his behavior subverts sound Aryan standards, then even one who accepts the formal standards of justice belonging to the "Western" tradition must come to a differing conclusion because of his factual judgment of what a Jew is or does.

tion would take me far beyond the bounds of this article. A few hypothetical questions, however, may suggest that what has been said thus far by no means reaches the outer limits of the area of agreement. Is it unjust to punish willful injury to others, where no justification based on standards accepted by the society is offered? Is it unjust to compel an individual to live up to a contract that met the prevailing legal conditions for a contract when it was made? Is it unjust to require an individual to restore the acknowledged property of another person which has somehow come into his possession?

Finally, I would add, as a fourth political good, "liberty." One's first reaction might be that liberty is a peculiarly "Western," parochial value. But this is not the case. Meanings vary, and so does the relative importance attributed to liberty. Even so, as in the case of justice, the area of pure relativity is less extensive than might at first appear. Why is security so generally sought after? Is it because people wish to avoid uncertainty, suffering, and violent death? But this kind of security, as has often been pointed out, they could enjoy in a prison cell or, in a measure, as slaves. It can hardly be doubted that some freedom to move about and to make choices in areas of one's interests is a desideratum for virtually all sane human beings. And most certainly the demands and needs that lead to the formation and development of a political system include this element. Put in these terms, the point hardly seems to call for further justification. Clearly a major purpose of "law and order" is to make it possible for people to enjoy a predictable environment and to be free and feel free to exercise their own choices. For Communists, liberty is one of the highest goals. What we would consider serious abridgments of liberty in Communist countries they justify as necessary to the realization of the ultimate free society, or as restrictions on one kind of liberty (e.g., freedom of speech) for the protection of another ("economic" liberty), or for the preservation of a regime dedicated to the creation of the cooperative commonwealth. Even fascist regimes, while being extremely parsimonious with this particular kind of political good, give at least tacit recognition to its value by the justification they advance for their treatment of it. Liberty, they argue, must be restricted because it is destructive of political unity, or, as we might say, of the political culture. For the political system to allow it in great measure would be to lead, they believe, to the serious injury, perhaps the dissolution, of the body politic itself. The difference here between the fascist and the democratic view is not so much a matter of what is of ultimate value as it is a question of what is possible and what are the likely consequences

of a given policy. Typically, fascist regimes have risen where the bourgeois liberty of free speech has been charged, not always without
reason, with leading to stultifying deadlock destructive of all other
political goods.

III. FURTHER OBSERVATIONS

While the very general values discussed above as "political goods"
are, I believe, either expressly or tacitly recognized as goods with substantial universality, in many particular situations they are relativistic.
Those things necessary for the persistence of the political system, which
is essential to all else, must take priority. In a given case this necessity
may call for the abrogation or abridgment of interests and values
otherwise judged fundamental. Moreover, human interests are subject
to certain natural orderings. Just as life is essential to the enjoyment
of all human values, so the necessities of life must first be satisfied;
the hungry man will set small store by liberty or many elements of
welfare. A political system that fails to provide basic security or to
provide—or enable the economy to provide—minimum subsistence
cannot then be judged highly developed no matter how much liberty
it succeeds in guaranteeing.

Moreover, the production of political goods cannot serve as the sole
test for the development of the polity in the same way that the production of economic goods serves economists as a measure of economic
development. In the most simple society at least some of the goods we
have termed "political" may be enjoyed with little or no aid from the
political system, or at least from any distinct entity identifiable as a
political system. But this is only a limiting case. In large and complicated societies political goods are not forthcoming in satisfactory degree
without a considerable development of political culture, institutions,
and organization.

Political systems are subject to deterioration as well as to development. They may decline, and they may even be destroyed by internal
as well as external forces. Eisenstadt has described this process at length,
documented it for many cases, and explained something of its dynamics.[17] For instance, he points out that after a bureaucracy along
Weberian lines has become highly developed, its foundations may be
undermined by conflict between ruling groups and other major social
strata, with the consequence that the political system is gradually transformed in the direction of less differentiation and flexibility. It is sig-

[17] *Political Systems of Empires.*

nificant to note his finding that "one crucial aspect of such a break-down . . . was the tendency of the bureaucracy itself to displace its service goals to the rulers and the major strata—emphasizing goals of self-aggrandizement, and thus seriously impairing its own efficiency."[18] In other words the political system retrogresses whether judged by aspects of its structure, such as differentiation, or by its outputs and their effect on the welfare or other "good" of the society as a whole or of important parts of it.

IV. MEASUREMENT OF POLITICAL GOODS

I have spoken of the output of political goods as a basis for evaluation and even as a "dimension" of political development. Against this suggested mode of analysis it may be urged that the concepts dealt with are too vague, that they do not submit themselves to measurement. How much security, or welfare, or justice, or liberty is "produced" by a particular polity? How can one tell? To place these questions in proper perspective, one must see how they might apply to the generally recognized dimensions of political development, as discussed at the beginning of this article. What is the "support potential" of a particular polity?[19] Gross comparisons are possible; careful measurement would seem to be beyond our present reach. What is the degree of "legitimacy" enjoyed by a particular political system, or how much consensus characterizes its political culture? Is consensus complemented by enough but not too much cleavage? If political participation is an aspect of political development, does it follow that the greater the degree of participation the greater the development? Or is it a question of proportion? And if the latter, how is it measured? How does one measure secularization or capacity for social mobilization? I am by no means suggesting that these concepts are so vague as to be useless; but I am suggesting that the problems involved in measuring or weighing them are of an order of magnitude similar to that of problems entailed by the consideration of political goods.

Take the case of security. Here, as with the concept of a healthy political culture, one must break it up into smaller bits. One may examine the record of homicides, assaults, thefts, property damage, and the casualties resulting from civil strife. These items can be counted (and in developed polities they are). An overall view of such statistics gives at least an indication of the degree to which the political

---

[18] Ibid., 363. Cf. Aristotle on perverted forms of government (Politics, 1279a).
[19] This concept is developed in Almond, "A Developmental Approach," 204-5.

system in question is developed in one of its aspects, an indication suitable at least for purposes of comparing the system with other polities of similar size and complexity.

Welfare of course is a large and amorphous collection of specifics. Many of them, individually, submit rather readily to measurement: transportation and communication facilities, sanitation, education, poverty, housing. Sometimes one finds single indicators, such as life expectancy or caloric intake, that give considerable feel for the quality of a large area of a country's welfare map. This kind of test, however, must then be supplemented by study aimed at discovering how far the political system is responsible for the welfare of the society in question. What about such an indeterminate but vital characteristic as human dignity? No one would claim that he could measure it directly; but none of us would have any difficulty in naming measurable items—the existence and extent of slavery, for example—that would constitute important guides to the estate of human dignity in a particular society. The establishment of effective procedures to prevent the conviction and punishment of innocent persons would be another indicator. So would discrimination on the basis of race or color. Do people stand up for their rights, or submit to arbitrary or callous governmental action without resistance?[20]

In the case of justice, too, one could rely on survey techniques (Do people trust the integrity and impartiality of the courts? Are the courts better or worse than they were ten years ago?) and also on the more easily ascertainable facts of judicial procedure (Are the elements of a "fair trial" or their functional equivalents observed? What proportion of reported crimes go unpunished?). To what extent are vocational and other valued opportunities open to all on achievement-oriented rather than ascriptive qualifications? What is the extent of social and occupational mobility and what is the nature of the obstacles to it?

As to liberty, again one need only let his imagination roam. Is movement within the country or across national boundaries restricted, and if so, how much? Is preventive detention relied upon? What about freedom of expression? Are news media relatively free and independent? (Content analysis provides a useful tool for answering this question.) What about freedom of association, in political parties and otherwise? Does freedom of religious belief and exercise prevail? Are

---

[20] Some of the ways in which survey research techniques could be used to explore this kind of question are suggested by Almond and Sidney Verba's *The Civic Culture* (Princeton 1963).

arbitrary arrests, punishments, and expropriations common, and do people live in fear of such infringements on their rights? These are matters that can be ascertained with some degree of precision in most societies. Where they cannot, that fact is itself a significant indication of the scope of liberty.

V. Comparison of Polities in Terms of Political Goods

Although one may be able to measure important elements of security, welfare, and the like, the question remains of how one can compare different political goods, or different aspects of the broad categories of political good that have been discussed above. How much is it worth, in material terms, to enhance the dignity of citizens? Is a particular state buying security at too high a price in terms of butter or freedom? As in the case of measurement, it is doubtful whether questions of this kind are more difficult when applied to political goods than they are in the case of other dimensions of political development; but however that may be, they are worth considering in themselves.

Questions of the kind just posed have to do largely with how society *distributes* its outputs among various political goods rather than with the amount of political goods it produces. We might describe the difficulty as the lack of a market. A man, in certain societies, can trade a cow for a hut or a wife and can thereby (together with many similar transactions) establish their relative economic values. But he cannot similarly exchange some of his protection against violence for more honest courts, or some of his equality of opportunity for more security against poverty in his old age.

Difficult though this problem of commensurability is, it can, I believe, be tackled and minimized in a variety of ways. First, one can apply the principle of the Pareto optimum. One can say of two otherwise similar polities that the one with less violence is higher on the scale of political development. This "other-things-being-equal" approach has severe limitations, especially in a field in which there are so many "other things"; but it is not to be completely ignored. Probably, it has its greatest usefulness in comparing the same polity at two different times. Thus one can say of a state that, in the absence of retrogression in other respects, an increase in equality of opportunity for certain groups, the removal of censorship, or the expansion of free schools, with an attendant rise in the educational level of the populace, are evidences of political development.

A second point tends to make the Paretian method more useful than it might otherwise appear, and also in itself diminishes the extent of the problem. The political goods we have been discussing may sometimes conflict, but more frequently they do not. Political goods tend to be realized together and even to be mutually self-supporting. An improvement in the quality of justice administered by the courts is likely to improve personal security. Greater educational opportunities have positive repercussions on both liberty and welfare. Within limits, the same can be said of increased political participation (itself an aspect of welfare as well as a means to further political development). More broadly, an increase in security helps all the other political values or objectives—much as an improvement in the political culture helps the processes by which political inputs are converted into outputs—and an increase in justice, welfare, or even liberty more frequently than not contributes, directly or indirectly, to security.

It is no accident that many of the factors we have been discussing tend to develop together, in the same direction if not at the same pace, for many of them are aspects of the general Weberian rationality-legality pattern. Thus the elimination of special privilege and of discrimination throughout society is based upon the same principle of rationality as is the bureaucratic rule of appointments and promotions according to merit. The principle underlying the formal rationality of the rule of law is easily and not unnaturally extended to such "substantive" matters (in Weber's terminology) as assuring equal access to the courts and to legal counsel regardless of economic circumstance. True, the bureaucracy may move in a Weberian direction even while, on the political side, a charismatic leader may behave arbitrarily, resisting the pressure toward both rationalistic standards and public accountability. But even modern dictatorships and modern democracies are likely to show more developments in common with each other than either has in common with a traditional, ascriptive society.[21]

Much of the difficulty that appears when one thinks abstractly about such questions as the relative values of liberty and equality disappears

---

[21] It may be suggested that political development is characterized by a movement toward, or an increase in, each of the following elements, regardless of whether the polity is democratically or autocratically governed: dynamism; achievement orientation; differentiation of function; such elements of rationality as a bureaucracy organized on rational principles or, more generally, the breakdown of ascriptive bases for selection, access, and opportunities, in favor of rational criteria (perhaps qualified by a "political" component); secularization of politics; development of instrumentalities for political communication and for articulating and aggregating interests; popular political participation (not necessarily in decision-making); the capacity for social mobilization; and the acceptance of broad responsibility for welfare.

when one not only breaks these abstractions down into more concrete entities but also when one poses the problem of whether, *in a
particular situation*, if one has to choose, it is better to increase the one
or the other. In other words, an incremental approach often avoids
problems that otherwise seem insoluble.[22] *If* it is clear, for instance,
that in a given situation a second political party can be permitted only
at the price of such governmental instability as will discourage the
entrance of much needed foreign capital, *and if* it seems reasonable to
suppose that denial of a second party now will probably not foreclose
the opportunity a few years hence, then most people would be likely
to agree that freedom of association should be to this extent limited.
The difficulties about this choice reside in the "if" clauses. But these
are matters of calculating probable consequences, not of weighing one
value against another.

Finally, it was perhaps an exaggeration to say that politics (at least
in democratic regimes) has no substitute for the economic market as
a means of commensurating goods and establishing a common unit of
value. We have, after all, the political marketplace of elections and related elements of the democratic process itself. The democratic political process gives effect to political demands. Its outputs tend to maximize the satisfaction of political wants, with varying degrees of
accuracy.

This last point has brought us back to "process," specifically to
democratic processes, in our search for tests and measures of political
development. But we must note that process is only *one* index. The
political market—like the economic market—is subject to serious shortcomings. In the first place, it is not strictly comparable to the economic
market. For instance, it may fail to reflect intensity either of demand
or of need. It has, in fact, a certain all-or-nothing quality about it.
Minorities and minority rights are *guaranteed* no protection by the
electoral process, although they may achieve it.[23]

Also in politics, unlike economics, people do not bid (vote) directly
for their objectives, but for men or policies that they believe or hope
(perhaps mistakenly) will lead to the realization of those objectives.
In short, one cannot assume that what they get is an exact indication
of what they want. (Whether they get what they deserve, as is some-

[22] See David Braybrooke and Charles E. Lindblom, *A Strategy of Decision: Policy
Evaluation as a Social Process* (New York 1963).

[23] Such guarantees of course may be written into the constitution and protected by
judicial review or other devices, but this is not market action. Guarantees of this
nature do not reflect current pressures, but earlier decisions made by the constituent
power.

times argued, is another question.) Furthermore, people may be so divided as to means—as to how they believe liberty or justice or prosperity may best be obtained—that their political activities become completely self-defeating, nugatory, or worse. Also, especially in the short run, they may not know their own good. Their desires may not reflect their real needs. Finally, in most of the emerging nations, anything that could at all fairly be called a political market hardly exists. It certainly malfunctions too seriously to be used as an important test for political development. It is only where democratic institutions are working well that the test of the political marketplace provides an important measure for how well the ends of the state are being attained. And even here one need only consider the extent of political apathy and the lack of adequate information and communication in even the most advanced democracies to realize that at best the market test is subject to severe limitations.

VI. In Conclusion

"Political development" cannot be reduced to a simple formula. Not all facets of a developed polity mutually reinforce each other; some qualify each other. For instance, responsiveness to the wishes of the majority may run contrary to respect for individual rights; and by the same token the latter may limit the former. The quality of the political culture is a basic measure; but it is not all-sufficient and it is itself a composite of many characteristics. A formula like "free circulation of inputs and outputs through the institutional framework" is suggestive, and yet is so vague as to be of relatively little use for measurement or for comparison. A developed polity should not only respond to demands; it should respond to them effectively. Moreover, it should *encourage* them by identifying needs and specifying how they can be met.

Frey's suggestive phrase "the increase in the distribution and reciprocity of power" is both interesting and valuable. It covers a lot of important ground; but it is also rather vague and difficult to pin down in application. Moreover, Frey himself qualifies and complicates it by adding the element of the total amount of power. Surely this is important. But would one wish to say that the development of political power *without limit* was a sign of political development, even if the power were widely distributed?

Parsons' "collective goal attainment" also has its attractiveness—and its shortcomings. The phrase "collective goal" may conceal potential conflicts. A collectivity, too, may desire something that is bad for it as judged by outsiders or by the collectivity at a later date. Has American treatment of Negroes, to say nothing of Nazi treatment of Jews, been "collective goal attainment"? If so, does it signify "political development"? In other words, this formula tells us nothing about such things as rights, or security against arbitrary arrest, torture, or other forms of tyranny. Sometimes, too, people do not desire what they need. It is a proper and important function of the polity, and a mark of its development, to make its members conscious of their needs—for instance, for better education or for better sanitary conditions or for birth control.

Although no one formula or test has proved acceptable, it is tempting to think that a polity's record in producing political goods deserves a certain priority. *A priori*, the test of anything in terms of what it produces seems to make sense. Furthermore achievement as the test of development has the intuitive advantage of being an "unlimited value goal," as contrasted with an "optimum value goal." That is to say, such matters as stability or political participation are not necessarily the kind of goods of which the more the better, *ad infinitum*. After a certain point, additional increments may become actually disvalued.[24] Security, justice, liberty, and welfare, on the other hand, may be affirmed to have unlimited value, each in itself. (Of course, if more of one involves a decrease in one of the others, that is another matter.) To put it differently, these political goods are what the polity is *for*, in the sense that they give it whatever value and justification it has. On the other hand, what we have called the environmental and procedural elements are the causes, the conditions, indeed the necessary conditions, of these goods. Unlike the political culture and the structural and procedural elements, the political goods are not *parts* of the polity, although they are attributes of it; they are, in large measure, its fruits.

Primarily, however, the question is not whether outputs should be stressed more than inputs or processes; or, to speak more accurately, whether achievements are more important than the political culture or the structural elaboration and smooth operation of the political machine. They must all be taken into account. In politics, the distinctions between means and ends and between procedure and substance are never final. These elements are forever reacting upon each other and merging into one another. Analysis must not be allowed to ob-

---

[24] This discussion borrows heavily from Frederick W. Frey, in Pye, 300-301.

scure organic relations. Yet for scientific purposes the distinctions are important. It is common today to compare or rank states by the degree of party competition,[25] or their adoption and use of the major devices of representative government,[26] or their social mobilization.[27] It is my suggestion that, to see a more nearly complete picture and to make more highly discriminating judgments, anyone who is concerned with political development in any way involving measurement or comparison should take full account of some of the measurable elements of the political goods of security, justice, liberty, and welfare.

[25] See for example the valuable tables in Almond and James S. Coleman, eds., *The Politics of the Developing Areas* (Princeton 1960), Appendix.

[26] As worked out in detail by Phillips Cutright, "National Political Development: Measurement and Analysis," *American Sociological Review*, xxviii (April 1963), 253-64.

[27] See Deutsch, "Social Mobilization and Political Development," *American Political Science Review*, lv (September 1961), 493-514.

Political Order

POLITICAL DEVELOPMENT
AND POLITICAL DECAY

By SAMUEL P. HUNTINGTON*

AMONG the laws that rule human societies," de Tocqueville said, "there is one which seems to be more precise and clear than all others. If men are to remain civilized or to become so, the art of associating together must grow and improve in the same ratio in which the equality of conditions is increased."[1] In much of the world today, equality of political participation is growing much more rapidly than is the "art of associating together." The rates of mobilization and participation are high; the rates of organization and institutionalization are low. De Tocqueville's precondition for civilized society is in danger, if it is not already undermined. In these societies, the conflict between mobilization and institutionalization is the crux of politics. Yet in the fast-growing literature on the politics of the developing areas, political institutionalization usually receives scant treatment. Writers on political development emphasize the processes of modernization and the closely related phenomena of social mobilization and increasing political participation. A balanced view of the politics of contemporary Asia, Africa, and Latin America requires more attention to the "art of associating together" and the growth of political institutions. For this purpose, it is useful to distinguish political development from modernization and to identify political development with the institutionalization of political organizations and procedures. Rapid increases in mobilization and participation, the principal political aspects of modernization, undermine political institutions. Rapid modernization, in brief, produces not political development, but political decay.

I. POLITICAL DEVELOPMENT AS MODERNIZATION

Definitions of political development are legion. Most, however, share two closely related characteristics. First, political development is identified as one aspect of, or as intimately connected with, the broader processes of modernization in society as a whole. Moderniza-

* I am grateful to the Center for International Affairs, Harvard University, for the support which made this article possible and to Edward C. Banfield, Mather Eliot, Milton J. Esman, H. Field Haviland, Jr., and John D. Montgomery, for their helpful written comments on an earlier draft.

[1] *Democracy in America* (Phillips Bradley edn., New York 1955), ii, 118.

tion affects all segments of society; its political aspects constitute political development. Indeed, many authors seem to prefer the phrase "political modernization" as more descriptive of their primary concern. Second, if political development is linked with modernization, it is necessarily a broad and complex process. Hence most authors argue that political development must be measured by many criteria. The "multi-function character of politics," Lucian Pye has said, ". . . means that no single scale can be used for measuring the degree of political development."[2] It thus differs from economic development, on the character of which there seems to be more general agreement and which is measurable through fairly precise indices such as per capita national income. Definitions of political development hence tend to itemize a number of criteria. Ward and Rustow list eight characteristics of the modern polity; Emerson has five. Pye identifies four major aspects of political development plus half a dozen additional "factors." Eisenstadt finds four characteristics of political modernization.[3]

The definitions are many and multiple; but, with a few exceptions, the characteristics which they identify with political development are all aspects of the processes of modernization. Four sets of categories recur continuously in the definitions. One set, focusing on the Parsonian pattern variables, can perhaps best be summed up as *rationalization*. This involves movement from particularism to universalism, from diffuseness to specificity, from ascription to achievement, and from affectivity to affective neutrality. In terms of political development, functional differentiation and achievement criteria are particularly emphasized.[4] A second set of characteristics identified with development involves nationalism and *national integration*. Almost all writers recognize the problem of the "crisis of national identity" and the necessity of establishing a firmly delimited ethnic basis for the political community.[5] A developed polity, it is usually assumed, must,

---

[2] Lucian W. Pye, ed., *Communications and Political Development* (Princeton 1963), 16.

[3] Robert E. Ward and Dankwart A. Rustow, eds., *Political Modernization in Japan and Turkey* (Princeton 1964), 6-7; Rupert Emerson, *Political Modernization: The Single-Party System* (Denver 1963), 7-8; Pye, ed., *Communications and Political Development*, 17-18; S. N. Eisenstadt, "Bureaucracy and Political Development," in Joseph LaPalombara, ed., *Bureaucracy and Political Development* (Princeton 1963), 99.

[4] James S. Coleman, in Gabriel A. Almond and Coleman, eds., *The Politics of the Developing Areas* (Princeton 1960), 532; Fred W. Riggs, "Bureaucracy and Political Development: A Paradoxical View," in LaPalombara, ed., *Bureaucracy and Political Development*, 122; Eisenstadt, in *ibid.*, 99; Ward and Rustow, eds., *Political Modernization*, 7.

[5] See, e.g., Gabriel A. Almond, "Political Systems and Political Change," *American*

with rare exception, be a nation-state. "Nation-building" is a key aspect of political development. A third approach focuses on *democratization*: pluralism, competitiveness, equalization of power, and similar qualities. "Competitiveness," says Coleman, "is an essential aspect of political modernity. . . ." Hence, "the Anglo-American polities most closely approximate the model of a modern political system. . . ."[6] Frey argues that "the most common notion of political development in intellectual American circles is that of movement towards democracy." He finds this a congenial notion and offers his own definition of political development as "changes in the direction of greater distribution and reciprocity of power. . . ."[7]

Rationalization, integration, and democratization thus commonly appear in definitions of political development. The characteristic of political development or political modernization which is most frequently emphasized, however, is *mobilization*, or *participation*. Modernization, Karl Deutsch has emphasized, involves social mobilization, and "this complex of processes of social change is significantly correlated with major changes in politics." Increases in literacy, urbanization, exposure to mass media, industrialization, and per capita income expand "the politically relevant strata of the population," multiply the demands for government services, and thus stimulate an increase in governmental capabilities, a broadening of the elite, increased political participation, and shifts in attention from the local level to the national level.[8] Modernization means mass mobilization; mass mobilization means increased political participation; and increased participation is the key element of political development. Participation distinguishes modern politics from traditional politics. "Traditional society," says Lerner, "is non-participant—it deploys people by kinship into communities isolated from each other and from a center. . . ." Modern society, in contrast, is "participant society."[9] The "new world political culture," say Almond and Verba, "will be a political culture of participation. If there is a political revolution going on throughout the world, it is what might be called the participation explosion. In all the new nations of the world the belief that the ordinary man is polit-

Behavioral Scientist, vi (June 1963), 3-10; Ward and Rustow, eds., *Political Modernization*, 7.

[6] Coleman, in Almond and Coleman, eds., *Politics of Developing Areas*, 533.

[7] Frederick W. Frey, "Political Development, Power, and Communications in Turkey," in Pye, ed., *Communications and Political Development*, 301.

[8] Karl W. Deutsch, "Social Mobilization and Political Development," *American Political Science Review*, lv (September 1961), 493ff.

[9] Daniel Lerner, *The Passing of Traditional Society* (Glencoe 1958), 48-50.

ically relevant—that he ought to be an involved participant in the political system—is widespread. Large groups of people who have been
outside politics are demanding entrance into the political system."[10]
Political development, Rustow argues, may be defined as "(1) an increasing national political unity plus (2) a broadening base of political
participation. . . ." Similarly, Riggs declares that political development
"refers to the process of politicization: increasing participation or involvement of the citizen in state activities, in power calculations, and
consequences."[11]

All definitions are arbitrary. These definitions of political development as some combination or permutation of participation, rationalization, democratization, and nation-building are just as legitimate as
any other definition. While all definitions may be equally arbitrary
and equally legitimate, they do vary greatly, however, in their relevance
to particular problems and their usefulness for particular ends. Presumably one major purpose of concepts of political development is to
facilitate understanding of the political processes in contemporary
Asian, African, and Latin American societies. To be analytically useful, a concept must be precise and relevant. It must also have sufficient
generality of application to permit comparative analysis of differing
situations. Many approaches to political development suffer from one
or more of the following difficulties.

First, the identification of political development with modernization or with factors usually associated with modernization drastically
limits the applicability of the concept in both time and space. It is
defined in parochial and immediate terms, its relevance limited to
modern nation-states or the emergence of modern nation-states. It
becomes impossible to speak of a politically developed tribal authority,
city-state, feudal monarchy, or bureaucratic empire. Development is
identified with one type of political system, rather than as a quality
which might characterize any type of political system. All systems
which are not modern are underdeveloped, including presumably fifth-
century Athens, the third-century B.C. Roman republic, the second-
century A.D. Roman empire, the Han and T'ang empires in China,
or even eighteenth-century America. None of these political systems
was modern. Is it also useful to consider them underdeveloped? Would
it not be more appropriate to consider development or underdevelopment as a characteristic which might be found in any type of political

[10] Gabriel A. Almond and Sidney Verba, *The Civic Culture* (Princeton 1963), 4.
[11] Dankwart A. Rustow, "The Vanishing Dream of Stability," *AID Digest* (August
1962), 13; Riggs, in LaPalombara, ed., *Bureaucracy and Political Development*, 139.

system? City-states could be developed or underdeveloped; so also could be bureaucratic empires or modern nation-states. This approach would cast additional light on contemporary modernizing societies by furnishing a second set of categories (in addition to the traditional-modern set) for comparing the processes of change in those societies with the processes of change in other types of societies. Such an approach, of course, would also liberate the concept of development from the even more limited identification of it with the Western, constitutional, democratic nation-state.

The second problem with many definitions of political development is the obverse but also the corollary of the first. On the one hand, development is limited to the characteristics of the modern nation-state. On the other, it is also broadened to include almost all politically relevant aspects of the modernization process. It acquires comprehensiveness at the cost of precision. There is a natural tendency to assume that political development is all of a piece, that one "good thing" is compatible with another. In addition, studies of modernization have shown a very high degree of correlation among such indices as literacy, urbanization, media participation, and political participation.[12] Hence, it is easy to assume that a similar correlation exists among the various elements identified as contributing to political development. In fact, however, the four, eight, or twelve criteria of development may or may not have any systematic relation to each other. They may indeed be negatively correlated. There is no particular reason, for instance, why more participation and more structural differentiation should go together; in fact, there is some a priori reason to assume that more of one might mean less of the other. If this be the case, two contradictory tendencies (A, —B; —A, B) could both be labeled "political development." The broader the definition of development, moreover, the more inevitable development becomes. The all-encompassing definitions make development seem easy by making it seem inescapable. Development becomes an omnipresent first cause, which explains everything but distinguishes nothing. Almost anything that happens in the "developing" countries—coups, ethnic struggles, revolutionary wars—becomes part of the process of development, however contradictory or retrogressive this may appear on the surface. Political development thus loses its analytical content and acquires simply a geographic one. At the extreme, it becomes synonymous with the political history of Asia, Africa, and Latin America.[13]

[12] Lerner, Passing of Traditional Society, chap. 2.
[13] For the reductio ad absurdum, see Majid Khadduri, Modern Libya: A Study in

Thirdly, many definitions of political development fail to distinguish clearly the empirical relevance of the components going into the definition. Concepts of "developed" and "undeveloped" as ideal types or states of being are confused with concepts of "development" as a process which are, in turn, identified with the politics of the areas commonly called "developing." The line between actuality and aspiration is fogged. Things which are in fact occurring in the "developing" areas become hopelessly intertwined with things which the theorist thinks should occur there. Here again the tendency has been to assume that what is true for the broader processes of social modernization is also true for political changes. Modernization, in some degree, is a fact in Asia, Africa, Latin America: urbanization is rapid; literacy is slowly increasing; industrialization is being pushed; per capita gross national product is inching upward; mass media circulation is expanding; political participation is broadening. All these are facts. In contrast, progress toward many of the other goals identified with political development—democracy, stability, structural differentiation, achievement patterns, national integration—often is dubious at best. Yet the tendency is to think that because modernization is taking place, political development also must be taking place. As a result, many of the sympathetic Western writings about the underdeveloped areas today have the same air of hopeful unreality which characterized much of the sympathetic Western writing about the Soviet Union in the 1920's and 1930's. They are suffused with what can only be described as "Webbism": that is, the tendency to ascribe to a political system qualities which are assumed to be its ultimate goals rather than qualities which actually characterize its processes and functions.[14]

In actuality, only some of the tendencies frequently encompassed in the concept "political development" appear to be characteristic of the "developing" areas. Instead of a trend toward competitiveness and

---

Political Development (Baltimore 1963), and J. Clagett Taylor, *The Political Development of Tanganyika* (Stanford 1963). In the titles and content of both, "political development" has no analytical meaning. It is simply a synonym (euphemism?) for "political history." Both books are good history, but they are not social science.

[14] See, e.g., Milton J. Esman, "The Politics of Development Administration," to be published in John D. Montgomery and William Siffin, eds., *Politics, Administration and Change: Approaches to Development* (New York 1965). Esman bases his analysis on the assumption that the political leaders of modernizing societies are motivated by the goals of nation-building and social-economic progress and not by desire for personal power, wealth, status, or the territorial expansion of their countries. This assumption has about the same degree of truth and usefulness in explaining politics in the contemporary "developing" areas as the assumption that Stalin's policies were devoted to building communism has to the explanation of Soviet politics in the 1930's.

democracy, there has been an "erosion of democracy" and a tendency to autocratic military regimes and one-party regimes. Instead of stability, there have been repeated coups and revolts. Instead of a unifying nationalism and nation-building, there have been repeated ethnic conflicts and civil wars. Instead of institutional rationalization and differentiation, there has frequently been a decay of the administrative organizations inherited from the colonial era and a weakening and disruption of the political organizations developed during the struggle for independence.[15] Only the concept of political development as mobilization and participation appears to be generally applicable to the "developing" world. Rationalization, competitiveness, and nation-building, in contrast, seem to have only a dim relation to reality.

This gap between theory and reality suggests a fourth difficulty in many concepts of political development. They are usually one-way concepts. Little or no provision is made for their reversibility. If political development is thought to involve the mobilization of people into politics, account should also be taken of the possibility that political de-development can take place and people can be demobilized out of politics. Structural differentiation may occur, but so also may structural homogenization. National disintegration is a phenomenon as much as national integration. A concept of political development should be reversible. It should define both political development and the circumstances under which political decay is encouraged.

The failure to think of political development as a reversible process apparently stems from two sources. Insofar as development is identified with modernization, many aspects of modernization do appear to be practically irreversible. Urbanization is not likely to give way to ruralization. Increases in literacy are not normally followed by sharp declines. Capital once invested in factories or power plants stays invested. Even increases in per capita gross national product are, more often than not, permanent, except for minor dips or destruction caused by war or natural catastrophe. With varying slopes, with hesitancy in some sectors but with strength and steady progress in others, virtually all the indices of modernization progress steadily upward on the charts. But political changes have no such irreversibility.

In other instances, one feels that an underlying commitment to the theory of progress is so overwhelming as to exclude political decay as

---

[15] On the "erosion of democracy" and political instability, see Rupert Emerson, *From Empire to Nation* (Cambridge, Mass., 1960), chap. 15; and Michael Brecher, *The New States of Asia* (London 1963), chap. 2.

a possible concept. Political decay, like thermonuclear war, becomes unthinkable. Almond, for instance, measures not just political development but *political change* by "the acquisition by a political system of some new capability."[16] The specific capabilities he has in mind are those for national integration, international accommodation, political participation, and welfare distribution. Before the Renaissance, Almond argues, political systems "acquired and lost capabilities . . . in anything but a unilinear, evolutionary way." Modernization, however, reduces "the independence of man's political experiments." Change is "far from unilinear," but it is toward "the emergence of world culture." Surely, however, modern and modernizing states can change by losing capabilities as well as by gaining them. In addition, a gain in any one capability usually involves costs in others. A theory of political development needs to be mated to a theory of political decay. Indeed, as was suggested above, theories of instability, corruption, authoritarianism, domestic violence, institutional decline, and political disintegration may tell us a lot more about the "developing" areas than their more hopefully defined opposites.

II. Political Development as Institutionalization

There is thus much to be gained (as well as something to be lost) by conceiving of political development as a process independent of, although obviously affected by, the process of modernization. In view of the crucial importance of the relationship between mobilization and participation, on the one hand, and the growth of political organizations, on the other, it is useful for many purposes to define political development as the institutionalization of political organizations and procedures. This concept liberates development from modernization. It can be applied to the analysis of political systems of any sort, not just modern ones. It can be defined in reasonably precise ways which are at least theoretically capable of measurement. As a concept, it does not suggest that movement is likely to be in only one direction: institutions, we know, decay and dissolve as well as grow and mature. Most significantly, it focuses attention on the reciprocal interaction between the on-going social processes of modernization, on the one hand, and the strength, stability, or weakness of political structures, traditional, transitional, or modern, on the other.[17]

---

[16] Almond, *American Behavioral Scientist*, VI, 6.

[17] The concept of institutionalization has, of course, been used by other writers concerned with political development—most notably, S. N. Eisenstadt. His definition, however, differs significantly from my approach here. See, in particular, his "Initial

The strength of political organizations and procedures varies with their *scope of support* and their *level of institutionalization.* Scope refers simply to the extent to which the political organizations and procedures encompass activity in the society. If only a small upper-class group belongs to political organizations and behaves in terms of a set of procedures, the scope is limited. If, on the other hand, a large segment of the population is politically organized and follows the political procedures, the scope is broad. Institutions are stable, valued, recurring patterns of behavior. Organizations and procedures vary in their degree of institutionalization. Harvard University and the newly opened suburban high school are both organizations, but Harvard is much more of an institution than is the high school. The seniority system in Congress and President Johnson's select press conferences are both procedures, but seniority is much more institutionalized than are Mr. Johnson's methods of dealing with the press. Institutionalization is the process by which organizations and procedures acquire value and stability. The level of institutionalization of any political system can be defined by the adaptability, complexity, autonomy, and coherence of its organizations and procedures. So also, the level of institutionalization of any particular organization or procedure can be measured by its adaptability, complexity, autonomy, and coherence. If these criteria can be identified and measured, political systems can be compared in terms of their levels of institutionalization. Furthermore, it will be possible to measure increases and decreases in the institutionalization of particular organizations and procedures within a political system.

ADAPTABILITY-RIGIDITY

The more adaptable an organization or procedure is, the more highly institutionalized it is; the less adaptable and more rigid it is, the lower its level of institutionalization. Adaptability is an acquired organizational characteristic. It is, in a rough sense, a function of environmental challenge and age. The more challenges which have arisen in its environment and the greater its age, the more adaptable it is. Rigidity is more characteristic of young organizations than of old ones. Old organizations and procedures, however, are not necessarily adaptable if they have existed in a static environment. In addition, if over a period of time an organization has developed a set of responses

Institutional Patterns of Political Modernisation," *Civilisations,* xii (No. 4, 1962), 461-72, and xiii (No. 1, 1963), 15-26; "Institutionalization and Change," *American Sociological Review,* xxix (April 1964), 235-47; "Social Change, Differentiation and Evolution," *ibid.,* xxix (June 1964), 375-86.

for dealing effectively with one type of problem, and if it is then confronted with an entirely different type of problem requiring a different response, the organization may well be a victim of its past successes and be unable to adjust to the new challenge. In general, however, the first hurdle is the biggest one. Success in adapting to one environmental challenge paves the way for successful adaptation to subsequent environmental challenges. If, for instance, the probability of successful adjustment to the first challenge is 50 per cent, the probability of successful adjustment to the second challenge might be 75 per cent, to the third challenge $87\frac{1}{2}$ per cent, to the fourth $93\frac{3}{4}$ per cent, and so on. Some changes in environment, moreover, such as changes in personnel, are inevitable for all organizations. Other changes in environment may be produced by the organization itself; if, for instance, it successfully completes the task which it was originally created to accomplish. So long as it is recognized that environments can differ in the challenges which they pose to organizations, the adaptability of an organization can in a rough sense be measured by its age. Its age, in turn, can be measured in three ways.

One is simply chronological: the longer an organization or procedure has been in existence, the higher the level of institutionalization. The older an organization is, the more likely it is to continue to exist through any specified future time period. The probability that an organization which is one hundred years old will survive one additional year, it might be hypothesized, is perhaps one hundred times greater than the probability that an organization one year old will survive one additional year. Political institutions are thus not created overnight. Political development, in this sense, is slow, particularly when compared with the seemingly much more rapid pace of economic development. In some instances, particular types of experience may substitute for time: fierce conflict or other serious challenges may transform organizations into institutions much more rapidly than normal circumstances. But such intensive experiences are rare, and even with such experiences time is still required. "A major party," Ashoka Mehta has observed, in commenting on why communism is helpless in India, "cannot be created in a day. In China a great party was forged by the revolution. Other major parties can be or are born of revolutions in other countries. But it is simply impossible, through normal channels, to forge a great party, to reach and galvanize millions of men in half a million villages."[18]

[18] Ashoka Mehta, in Raymond Aron, ed., *World Technology and Human Destiny* (Ann Arbor 1963), 133.

A second measure of adaptability is generational age. So long as an organization still has its first set of leaders, so long as a procedure is still performed by those who first performed it, its adaptability is still in doubt. The more often the organization has surmounted the problem of peaceful succession and replaced one set of leaders with another, the more highly institutionalized it is. In considerable measure, of course, generational age is a function of chronological age. But political parties and governments may continue for decades under the leadership of one generation. The founders of organizations—whether parties, governments, or business corporations—are often young. Hence the gap between chronological age and generational age is apt to be greater in the early history of an organization than later in its career. This gap produces tensions between the first leaders of the organization and the next generation immediately behind them, which can look forward to a lifetime in the shadow of the first generation. In the middle of the 1960's the Chinese Communist Party was forty-five years old, but in large part it was still led by its first generation of leaders. An organization may also change leadership without changing generations of leadership. One generation differs from another in terms of its formative experiences. Simple replacement of one set of leaders by another, i.e., surmounting a succession crisis, counts for something in terms of institutional adaptability, but it is not as significant as a shift in leadership generations, i.e., the replacement of one set of leaders by another set with significantly different organizational experiences. The shift from Lenin to Stalin was an intra-generation succession; the shift from Stalin to Khrushchev was an inter-generation succession.

Thirdly, organizational adaptability can be measured in functional terms. An organization's functions, of course, can be defined in an almost infinite number of ways. (This is a major appeal and a major limitation of the functional approach to organizations.) Usually an organization is created to perform one particular function. When that function is no longer needed, the organization faces a major crisis. It either finds a new function or reconciles itself to a lingering death. An organization which has adapted itself to changes in its environment and has survived one or more changes in its principal functions is more highly institutionalized than one which has not. Not functional specificity but functional adaptability is the true measure of a highly developed organization. Institutionalization makes the organization more than simply an instrument to achieve certain purposes.[19]

[19] See the very useful discussion in Philip Selznick's small classic, *Leadership in Administration* (New York 1957), 5ff.

Instead its leaders and members come to value it for its own sake, and it develops a life of its own quite apart from the specific functions it may perform at any given time. The organization triumphs over its function.

Organizations and individuals thus differ significantly in their cumulative capacity to adapt to changes. Individuals usually grow up through childhood and adolescence without deep commitments to highly specific functions. The process of commitment begins in late adolescence. As the individual becomes more and more committed to the performance of certain functions, he finds it increasingly difficult to change those functions and to unlearn the responses which he has acquired to meet environmental changes. His personality has been formed; he has become "set in his ways." Organizations, on the other hand, are usually created to perform very specific functions. When the organization confronts a changing environment, it must, if it is to survive, weaken its commitment to its original functions. As the organization matures, it becomes "unset" in its ways.

In practice, organizations vary greatly in their functional adaptability. The YMCA, for instance, was founded in the mid-nineteenth century as an evangelical organization to convert the single young men who, during the early years of industrialization, were migrating in great numbers to the cities. With the decline in need for this function, the Y successfully adjusted to the performance of many other "general service" functions broadly related to the legitimizing goal of "character development." Concurrently, it broadened its membership base to include first non-evangelical Protestants, then Catholics, then Jews, then old men as well as young, and then women as well as men![20] As a result, the organization has prospered although its original functions disappeared with the dark satanic mills. Other organizations, such as the WCTU and the Townsend Movement, have had greater difficulty in adjusting to a changing environment. The WCTU "is an organization in retreat. Contrary to the expectations of theories of institutionalization, the movement has not acted to preserve organizational values at the expense of past doctrine."[21] The Townsend Movement has been torn between those who wish to remain loyal to the original function

[20] See Mayer N. Zald and Patricia Denton, "From Evangelism to General Service: The Transformation of the YMCA," *Administrative Science Quarterly*, VIII (September 1963), 214ff.

[21] Joseph R. Gusfield, "Social Structure and Moral Reform: A Study of the Woman's Christian Temperance Union," *American Journal of Sociology*, LXI (November 1955), 232; and Gusfield, "The Problem of Generations in an Organizational Structure," *Social Forces*, XXXV (May 1957), 323ff.

and those who put organizational imperatives first. If the latter are successful, "the dominating orientation of leaders and members shifts *from the implementation of the values the organization is taken to represent* (by leaders, members, and public alike), *to maintaining the organizational structure as such*, even at the loss of the organization's central mission."[22] The conquest of polio posed a similar acute crisis for the National Foundation for Infantile Paralysis. The original goals of the organization were highly specific. Should the organization dissolve when these goals were achieved? The dominant opinion of the volunteers was that the organization should continue. "We can fight polio," said one town chairman, "if we can organize people. If we can organize people like this we can fight anything." Another felt that: "Wouldn't it be a wonderful story to get polio licked, and then go on to something else and get that licked and then go on to something else? It would be a challenge, a career."[23]

The problems of functional adaptability are not much different for political organizations. A political party gains in functional age when it shifts its function from the representation of one constituency to the representation of another; it also gains in functional age when it shifts from opposition to government. A party which is unable to change constituencies or to acquire power is less of an institution than one which is able to make these changes. A nationalist party whose function has been the promotion of independence from colonial rule faces a major crisis when it achieves its goal and has to adapt itself to the somewhat different function of governing a country. It may find this functional transition so difficult that it will, even after independence, continue to devote a large portion of its efforts to fighting colonialism. A party which acts this way is less of an institution than one, like the Congress Party, which after achieving independence drops its anti-colonialism and quite rapidly adapts itself to the tasks of governing. Industrialization has been a major function of the Communist Party of the Soviet Union. A major test of the institutionalization of the Communist Party will be its success in developing new functions now that the major industrializing effort is behind it. A governmental organ which can successfully adapt itself to changed functions, such as the British Crown in the eighteenth and nineteenth

[22] Sheldon L. Messinger, "Organizational Transformation: A Case Study of a Declining Social Movement," *American Sociological Review*, xx (February 1955), 10; italics in original.

[23] David L. Sills, *The Volunteers* (Glencoe 1957), p. 266. Chap. 9 of this book is an excellent discussion of organizational goal replacement with reference to the YMCA, WCTU, Townsend Movement, Red Cross, and other case studies.

centuries, is more of an institution than one which cannot, such as the French monarchy in the same period.

COMPLEXITY-SIMPLICITY

The more complicated an organization is, the more highly institutionalized it is. Complexity may involve both multiplication of organizational subunits, hierarchically and functionally, and differentiation of separate types of organizational subunits. The greater the number and variety of subunits, the greater the ability of the organization to secure and maintain the loyalties of its members. In addition, an organization which has many purposes is better able to adjust itself to the loss of any one purpose than an organization which has only one purpose. The diversified corporation is obviously less vulnerable than that which produces one product for one market. The differentiation of subunits within an organization may or may not be along functional lines. If it is functional in character, the subunits themselves are less highly institutionalized than the whole of which they are a part. Changes in the functions of the whole, however, are fairly easily reflected by changes in the power and roles of its subunits. If the subunits are multifunctional, they have greater institutional strength, but they may also, for that very reason, contribute less flexibility to the organization as a whole. Hence, a political system with parties of "social integration," in Neumann's terms, has less institutional flexibility than one with parties of "individual representation."[24]

Relatively primitive and simple traditional political systems are usually overwhelmed and destroyed in the modernization process. More complex traditional systems are more likely to adapt to these new demands. Japan, for instance, was able to adjust its traditional political institutions to the modern world because of their relative complexity. For two and a half centuries before 1868, the emperor had reigned and the Tokugawa shogun had ruled. The stability of the political order, however, did not depend solely on the stability of the shogunate. When the authority of the shogunate decayed, another traditional institution, the emperor, was available to become the instrument of the modernizing samurai. The collapse of the shogun involved not the overthrow of the political order but the "restoration" of the emperor.

The simplest political system is that which depends on one individual. It is also, of course, the least stable. Tyrannies, Aristotle pointed

[24] Sigmund Neumann, "Toward a Comparative Study of Political Parties," in Neumann, ed., *Modern Political Parties* (Chicago 1956), 403-5.

out, are virtually all "quite short-lived."[25] A political system with several different political institutions, on the other hand, is much more likely to adapt. The needs of one age may be met by one set of institutions; the needs of the next by a different set. The system possesses within itself the means of its own renewal and adaptation. In the American system, for instance, President, Senate, House of Representatives, Supreme Court, and state governments have played different roles at different times in history. As new problems arise, the initiative in dealing with them may be taken first by one institution, then by another. In contrast, the French system of the Third and Fourth Republics centered authority in the National Assembly and the national bureaucracy. If, as was frequently the case, the Assembly was too divided to act and the bureaucracy lacked the authority to act, the system was unable to adapt to environmental changes and to deal with new policy problems. When in the 1950's the Assembly was unable to handle the dissolution of the French Empire, there was no other institution, such as an independent executive, to step into the breach. As a result, an extraconstitutional force, the military, intervened in politics, and in due course a new institution, the de Gaulle Presidency, was created which was able to handle the problem. "A state without the means of some change," Burke observed of an earlier French crisis, "is without the means of its conservation."[26]

The classical political theorists, preoccupied as they were with the problem of stability, arrived at similar conclusions. The simple forms of government were most likely to degenerate; the "mixed state" was more likely to be stable. Both Plato and Aristotle suggested that the most practical state was the "polity" combining the institutions of democracy and oligarchy. A "constitutional system based absolutely, and at all points," Aristotle argued, "on either the oligarchical or the democratic conception of equality is a poor sort of thing. The facts are evidence enough: constitutions of this sort never endure." A "constitution is better when it is composed of more numerous elements."[27] Such a constitution is more likely to head off sedition and revolution. Polybius and Cicero elaborated this idea more explicitly. Each of the "good" simple forms of government—kingship, aristocracy, and democracy—is likely to degenerate into its perverted counterpart—tyranny, oligarchy, and mobocracy. Instability and degeneration can be avoided only by combining elements from all the good forms into a mixed

[25] *Politics* (Ernest Barker trans., London 1946), 254.
[26] *Reflections on the Revolution in France* (Gateway edn., Chicago 1955), 37.
[27] *Politics*, 60, 206.

state. Complexity produces stability. "The simple governments," Burke echoed two thousand years later, "are fundamentally defective, to say no worse of them."[28]

AUTONOMY-SUBORDINATION

A third measure of institutionalization is the extent to which political organizations and procedures exist independently of other social groupings and methods of behavior. How well is the political sphere differentiated from other spheres? In a highly developed political system, political organizations have an integrity which they lack in less developed systems. In some measure, they are insulated from the impact of non-political groups and procedures. In less developed political systems, they are highly vulnerable to outside influences.

At its most concrete level, autonomy involves the relations between social forces, on the one hand, and political organizations, on the other. Social forces include the groupings of men for social and economic activities: families, clans, work groups, churches, ethnic and linguistic groupings. Political institutionalization, in the sense of autonomy, means the development of political organizations and procedures which are not simply expressions of the interests of particular social groups. A political organization which is the instrument of a social group—family, clan, class—lacks autonomy and institutionalization. If the state, in the traditional Marxist claim, is really the "executive committee of the bourgeoisie," then it is not much of an institution. A judiciary is independent to the extent that it adheres to distinctly judicial norms and to the extent that its perspectives and behavior are independent of those of other political institutions and social groupings. As with the judiciary, the autonomy of political institutions is measured by the extent to which they have their own interests and values distinguishable from those of other social forces. As with the judiciary, the autonomy of political institutions is likely to be the result of competition among social forces. A political party, for instance, which expresses the interests of only one group in society—whether labor, business, or farmers—is less autonomous than one which articulates and aggregates the interests of several social groups. The latter type of party has a clearly defined existence apart from particular social forces. So also with legislatures, executives, and bureaucracies. Political procedures, like political organizations, also have varying degrees of autonomy. A highly developed political system has procedures to minimize, if not to eliminate, the role of vio-

[28] *Reflections on the Revolution in France*, 92.

lence in the system and to restrict to explicitly defined channels the influence of wealth in the system. To the extent that political officials can be toppled by a few soldiers or influenced by a few dollars, the organizations and procedures lack autonomy. Political organizations and procedures which lack autonomy are, in common parlance, said to be corrupt.

Political organizations and procedures which are vulnerable to non-political influences from within the society are also usually vulnerable to influences from outside the society. They are easily penetrated by agents, groups, and ideas from other political systems. Thus, a *coup d'état* in one political system may easily "trigger" a *coup d'état* by similar groups in other less-developed political systems.[29] In some instances, apparently, a regime can be overthrown by smuggling into the country a few agents and a handful of weapons. In other instances, a regime may be overthrown by the exchange of a few words and a few thousand dollars between a foreign ambassador and some disaffected colonels. The Soviet and American governments presumably spend substantial sums attempting to bribe high officials of less well-insulated political systems which they would not think of wasting in attempting to influence high officials in each other's political system.

In every society affected by social change, new groups arise to participate in politics. Where the political system lacks autonomy, these groups gain entry into politics without becoming identified with the established political organizations or acquiescing in the established political procedures. The political organizations and procedures are unable to stand up against the impact of a new social force. Conversely, in a developed political system, the autonomy of the system is protected by mechanisms which restrict and moderate the impact of new groups. These mechanisms either slow down the entry of new groups into politics or, through a process of political socialization, impel changes in the attitudes and behavior of the most politically active members of the new group. In a highly institutionalized political system, the most important positions of leadership can normally be achieved only by those who have served an apprenticeship in less important positions. The complexity of a political system contributes to its autonomy by providing a variety of organizations and positions in which individuals are prepared for the highest offices. In a sense, the top positions of leadership are the inner core of the political system; the less powerful positions, the peripheral organizations, and the semi-

---

[29] See Samuel P. Huntington, "Patterns of Violence in World Politics," in Huntington, ed., *Changing Patterns of Military Politics* (New York 1962), 44-47.

political organizations are the filters through which individuals desiring access to the core must pass. Thus the political system assimilates new social forces and new personnel without sacrificing its institutional integrity. In a political system which lacks such defenses, new men, new viewpoints, new social groups may replace each other at the core of the system with bewildering rapidity.

COHERENCE-DISUNITY

The more unified and coherent an organization is, the more highly institutionalized it is; the greater the disunity of the organization, the less its institutionalization. Some measure of consensus, of course, is a prerequisite for any social group. An effective organization requires, at a minimum, substantial consensus on the functional boundaries of the group and on the procedures for resolving disputes on issues which come up within those boundaries. The consensus must extend to those active in the system. Non-participants or those only sporadically and marginally participant in the system do not have to share the consensus and usually, in fact, do not share it to the same extent as the participants.[30] In theory, an organization can be autonomous without being coherent and coherent without being autonomous. In actuality, however, the two are often closely linked together. Autonomy becomes a means to coherence, enabling the organization to develop an esprit and style which become distinctive marks of its behavior. Autonomy also prevents the intrusion of disruptive external forces, although, of course, it does not protect against disruption from internal sources. Rapid or substantial expansions in the membership of an organization or in the participants in a system tend to weaken coherence. The Ottoman Ruling Institution, for instance, retained its vitality and coherence as long as admission was restricted and recruits were "put through an elaborate education, with selection and specialization at every stage." The Institution perished when "everybody pressed in to share its privileges. . . . Numbers were increased; discipline and efficiency declined."[31]

Unity, esprit, morale, and discipline are needed in governments as well as in regiments. Numbers, weapons, and strategy all count in war, but major deficiencies in any one of those may still be counterbalanced by superior coherence and discipline. So also in politics. The problems

[30] See, e.g., Herbert McCloskey, "Consensus and Ideology in American Politics," *American Political Science Review*, XVIII (June 1964), 361ff.; Samuel Stouffer, *Communism, Conformity, and Civil Liberties* (New York 1955), *passim.*

[31] Arnold J. Toynbee, *A Study of History* (Abridgement of Vols. I-VI by D. C. Somervell, New York 1947), 176-77.

of creating coherent political organizations are more difficult but not fundamentally different from those involved in the creation of coherent military organizations. "The sustaining sentiment of a military force," David Rapoport has argued, "has much in common with that which cements any group of men engaged in politics—the willingness of most individuals to bridle private or personal impulses for the sake of general social objectives. Comrades must trust each other's ability to resist the innumerable temptations that threaten the group's solidarity; otherwise, in trying social situations the desire to fend for oneself becomes overwhelming."[32] The capacities for coordination and discipline are crucial to both war and politics, and historically societies which have been skilled at organizing the one have also been adept at organizing the other. "The relationship of efficient social organization in the arts of peace and in the arts of group conflict," one anthropologist has observed, "is almost absolute, whether one is speaking of civilization or subcivilization. Successful war depends upon team work and consensus, both of which require command and discipline. Command and discipline, furthermore, can eventually be no more than symbols of something deeper and more real than they themselves."[33] Societies, such as Sparta, Rome, and Britain, which have been admired by their contemporaries for the authority and justice of their laws have also been admired for the coherence and discipline of their armies. Discipline and development go hand in hand.

One major advantage of studying development in terms of mobilization and participation is that they are measurable. Statistics are readily available for urbanization, literacy, mass media exposure, and voting. Hence, comparisons are easily made between countries and between different stages of the same country. What about institutionalization? Are the criteria of adaptability, complexity, autonomy, and coherence also measurable? Quite obviously the difficulties are greater. The UN has not conveniently collected in its *Statistical Yearbook* data on the political institutionalization of its members. Nonetheless, no reason exists why with a little imagination and effort sufficient information could not be collected to make meaningful comparisons of the levels of political institutionalization of different countries or of the same country at different times. Adaptability can be measured by chronological age, leadership successions, generational changes, and functional changes. Complexity can be measured by the number

[32] David C. Rapoport, "A Comparative Theory of Military and Political Types," in Huntington, ed., *Changing Patterns of Military Politics*, 79.
[33] Harry Holbert Turney-High, *Primitive War* (Columbia, S.C., 1949), 235-36.

and diversity of organizational subunits and by the number and diversity of functions performed by the organizations. Autonomy is perhaps the most difficult of the criteria to pin down: it can, however, be measured by the distinctiveness of the norms and values of the organization compared with those of other groups, by the personnel controls (in terms of cooptation, penetration, and purging) existing between the organization and other groups, and by the degree to which the organization controls its own material resources. Coherence may be measured by the ratio of contested successions to total successions, by the cumulation or non-cumulation of cleavages among leaders and members, by the incidence of overt alienation and dissent within the organization, and, conceivably, by opinion surveys of the loyalties and preferences of organization members.

Experience tells us that levels of institutionalization differ. Measuring that difference may be difficult, but it is not impossible. Only by measuring institutionalization will we be able to buttress or disprove hypotheses about the relation between social, economic, and demographic changes, on the one hand, and variations in political structure, on the other.

III. Mobilization vs. Institutionalization: Public Interests, Degeneration, and the Corrupt Polity

MOBILIZATION AND INSTITUTIONALIZATION

Social mobilization and political participation are rapidly increasing in Asia, Africa, and Latin America. These processes, in turn, are directly responsible for the deterioration of political institutions in these areas. As Kornhauser has conclusively demonstrated for the Western world, rapid industrialization and urbanization create discontinuities which give rise to mass society. "The *rapid* influx of large numbers of people into *newly* developing urban areas invites mass movements."[34] In areas and industries with very rapid industrial growth, the creation and institutionalization of unions lag, and mass movements are likely among the workers. As unions are organized, they are highly vulnerable to outside influences in their early stages. "The rapid influx of large numbers of people into a new organization (as well as a new area) provides opportunities for mass-oriented elites to penetrate the organization. This is particularly true during the formative periods of organizations, for at such times external constraints must carry the burden of social control until the

---

[34] William Kornhauser, *The Politics of Mass Society* (Glencoe 1959), 145.

new participants have come to internalize the values of the organization."[35]

So also in politics. Rapid economic growth breeds political instability.[36] Political mobilization, moreover, does not necessarily require the building of factories or even movement to the cities. It may result simply from increases in communications, which can stimulate major increases in aspirations that may be only partially, if at all, satisfied. The result is a "revolution of rising frustrations."[37] Increases in literacy and education may bring more political instability. By Asian standards, Burma, Ceylon, and the Republic of Korea are all highly literate, but no one of them is a model of political stability. Nor does literacy necessarily stimulate democracy: with roughly 75 per cent literacy, Cuba was the fifth most literate country in Latin America (ranking behind Argentina, Uruguay, Chile, and Costa Rica), but the first to go Communist; so also Kerala, with one of the highest literacy rates in India, was the first Indian state to elect a Communist government.[38] Literacy, as Daniel Lerner has suggested, "may be dysfunctional—indeed a serious impediment—to modernization in the societies now seeking (all too rapidly) to transform their institutions."[39]

Increased communication may thus generate demands for more "modernity" than can be delivered. It may also stimulate a reaction against modernity and activate traditional forces. Since the political arena is normally dominated by the more modern groups, it can bring into the arena new, anti-modern groups and break whatever consensus exists among the leading political participants. It may also mobilize minority ethnic groups who had been indifferent to politics but who now acquire a self-consciousness and divide the political system along ethnic lines. Nationalism, it has often been assumed, makes for national integration. But in actuality, nationalism and other forms of ethnic consciousness often stimulate political disintegration, tearing apart the body politic.

Sharp increases in voting and other forms of political participation can also have deleterious effects on political institutions. In Latin

[35] *Ibid.*, 146.

[36] See Mancur Olson, Jr., "Rapid Growth as a Destabilizing Force," *Journal of Economic History*, XXVII (December 1963), 529-52; and Bert F. Hoselitz and Myron Weiner, "Economic Development and Political Stability in India," *Dissent*, VIII (Spring 1961), 172-79.

[37] See Daniel Lerner, "Toward a Communication Theory of Modernization," in Pye, ed., *Communications and Political Development*, 330ff.

[38] Cf. Deutsch, *American Political Science Review*, LV, 496.

[39] Daniel Lerner, "The Transformation of Institutions" (mimeo.), 19.

America since the 1930's, increases in voting and increases in political instability have gone hand in hand. "Age requirements were lowered, property and literacy requirements were reduced or discarded, and the unscrubbed, unschooled millions on the farms were enfranchised in the name of democracy. They were swept into the political life of the republics so rapidly that existing parties could not absorb many of them, and they learned little about working within the existing political system."[40] The personal identity crises of the elites, caught between traditional and modern cultures, may create additional problems: "In transitional countries the political process often has to bear to an inordinate degree the stresses and strains of people responding to personal needs and seeking solutions to intensely personal problems."[41] Rapid social and economic change calls into question existing values and behavior patterns. It thus often breeds personal corruption. In some circumstances this corruption may play a positive role in the modernizing process, enabling dynamic new groups to get things done which would have been blocked by the existing value system and social structure. At the same time, however, corruption undermines the autonomy and coherence of political institutions. It is hardly accidental that in the 1870's and 1880's a high rate of American economic development coincided with a low point in American governmental integrity.[42]

Institutional decay has become a common phenomenon of the modernizing countries. *Coups d'état* and military interventions in politics are one index of low levels of political institutionalization: they occur where political institutions lack autonomy and coherence. According to one calculation, eleven of twelve modernizing states outside Latin America which were independent before World War II experienced *coups d'état* or attempted coups after World War II. Of twenty states which became independent between World War II and 1959, fourteen had coups or coup attempts by 1963. Of twenty-four states which became independent between 1960 and 1963, seven experienced coups or attempted coups before the end of 1963.[43] Instability in Latin America was less frequent early in the twentieth century than it was in the middle of the century. In the decade from 1917 to 1927, military men occupied the presidencies of the twenty

[40] John J. Johnson, *The Military and Society in Latin America* (Stanford 1964), 98-99.
[41] Lucian W. Pye, *Politics, Personality and Nation Building* (New Haven 1962), 4-5.
[42] See, in general, Ronald E. Wraith and Edgar Simpkins, *Corruption in Developing Countries* (London 1963).
[43] These figures are calculated from the data in the Appendix of Fred R. von der Mehden, *Politics of the Developing Nations* (Englewood Cliffs, N.J., 1964).

Latin American republics 28.7 per cent of the time; in the decade from 1947 to 1957, military men were presidents 45.5 per cent of the time.[44] In the 1930's and 1940's in countries like Argentina and Colombia, military intervention in politics occurred for the first time in this century. Seventeen of the twenty Latin American states experienced coups or coup attempts between 1945 and 1964, only Chile, Mexico, and Uruguay having clean records of political stability.

In many states the decline of party organizations is reflected in the rise of charismatic leaders who personalize power and weaken institutions which might limit that power. The increasing despotism of Nkrumah, for instance, was accompanied by a marked decline in the institutional strength of the Convention People's Party. In Turkey, Pakistan, and Burma, the Republican People's Party, Muslim League, and AFPFL deteriorated and military intervention eventually ensued. In party organizations and bureaucracies, marked increases in corruption often accompanied significant declines in the effectiveness of governmental services. Particularistic groups—tribal, ethnic, religious— frequently reasserted themselves and further undermined the authority and coherence of political institutions. The legitimacy of postcolonial regimes among their own people was often less than that of the colonial regimes of the Europeans. Economists have argued that the gap between the level of economic well-being of the underdeveloped countries and that of highly developed countries is widening as the absolute increases and even percentage increases of the latter exceed those of the former. Something comparable and perhaps even more marked is occurring in the political field. The level of political institutionalization of the advanced countries has, with a few exceptions such as France, remained relatively stable. The level of political institutionalization of most other countries has declined. As a result, the political gap between them has broadened. In terms of institutional strength, many if not most of the new states reached their peak of political development at the moment of independence.

The differences which may exist in mobilization and institutionalization suggest four ideal-types of politics (see Table 1). Modern, developed, civic polities (the United States, the Soviet Union) have high levels of both mobilization and institutionalization. Primitive polities (such as Banfield's backward society) have low levels of both. Contained polities are highly institutionalized but have low levels of

---

[44] Computed from figures in R. W. Fitzgibbon, "Armies and Politics in Latin America," paper, 7th Round Table, International Political Science Association, Opatija, Yugoslavia, September 1959, 8-9.

TABLE I. TYPES OF POLITICAL SYSTEMS

SOCIAL MOBILIZATION	POLITICAL INSTITUTIONALIZATION	
	High	*Low*
High	Civic	Corrupt
Low	Contained	Primitive

mobilization and participation. The dominant political institutions of contained polities may be either traditional (e.g., monarchies) or modern (e.g., political parties). If they are the former, such polities may well confront great difficulties in adjusting to rising levels of social mobilization. The traditional institutions may wither or collapse, and the result would be a corrupt polity with a high rate of participation but a low level of institutionalization. In the corrupt society, politics is, in Macaulay's phrase, "all sail and no anchor."[45] This type of polity characterizes much, if not most, of the modernizing world. Many of the more advanced Latin American countries, for instance, have achieved comparatively high indices of literacy, per capita national income, and urbanization. But their politics remains notably underdeveloped. Distrust and hatred have produced a continuing low level of political institutionalization. "There is no good faith in America, either among men or among nations," Bolivar once lamented. "Treaties are paper, constitutions books, elections battles, liberty anarchy, and life a torment. The only thing one can do in America is emigrate."[46] Over a century later, the same complaint was heard: "We are not, or do not represent a respectable nation . . . not because we are poor, but because we are disorganized," argued an Ecuadorian newspaper. "With a politics of ambush and of permanent mistrust, one for the other, we . . . cannot properly organize a republic . . . and without organization we cannot merit or attain respect from other nations."[47] So long as a country like Argentina retains a politics of coup and countercoup and a feeble state surrounded by massive social forces, it cannot be considered politically developed, no matter how urbane and prosperous and educated are its citizens.

In reverse fashion, a country may be politically highly developed, with modern political institutions, while still very backward in terms of modernization. India, for instance, is typically held to be the epit-

[45] Thomas B. Macaulay, letter to Henry S. Randall, Courtlandt Village, New York, May 23, 1857, printed in "What Did Macaulay Say About America?" *Bulletin of the New York Public Library*, XXIX (July 1925), 477-79.

[46] Simon Bolivar, quoted in K. H. Silvert, ed., *Expectant Peoples: Nationalism and Development* (New York 1963), 347.

[47] *El Dia*, Quito, November 27, 1943, quoted in Bryce Wood, *The Making of the Good Neighbor Policy* (New York 1961), 318.

ome of the underdeveloped society. Judged by the usual criteria of modernization, it was at the bottom of the ladder during the 1950's: per capita GNP of $72, 80 per cent illiterate, over 80 per cent of the population in rural areas, 70 per cent of the work force in agriculture, a dozen major languages, deep caste and religious differences. Yet in terms of political institutionalization, India was far from backward. Indeed, it ranked high not only in comparison with other modernizing countries in Asia, Africa, and Latin America, but also in comparison with many much more modern European countries. A well-developed political system has strong and distinct institutions to perform both the "input" and the "output" functions of politics. India entered independence with not only two organizations, but two highly developed—adaptable, complex, autonomous, and coherent—institutions ready to assume primary responsibility for these functions. The Congress Party, founded in 1885, was one of the oldest and best-organized political parties in the world; the Indian Civil Service, dating from the early nineteenth century, has been appropriately hailed as "one of the greatest administrative systems of all time."[48] The stable, effective, and democratic government of India during the first fifteen years of independence rested far more on this institutional inheritance than it did on the charisma of Nehru. In addition, the relatively slow pace of modernization and social mobilization in India did not create demands and strains which the Party and the bureaucracy were unable to handle. So long as these two organizations maintain their institutional strength, it is ridiculous to think of India as politically underdeveloped, no matter how low her per capita income or how high her illiteracy rate.

Almost no other country which became independent after World War II was institutionally as well prepared as India for self-government. In countries like Pakistan and the Sudan, institutional evolution was unbalanced; the civil and military bureaucracies were more highly developed than the political parties, and the military had strong incentives to move into the institutional vacuum on the input side of the political system and to attempt to perform interest aggregation functions. This pattern, of course, has also been common in Latin America. In countries like Guatemala, El Salvador, Peru, and Argentina, John J. Johnson has pointed out, the military is "the country's best organized institution and is thus in a better position to give objective expression to the national will" than are parties or

[48] Ralph Braibanti, "Public Bureaucracy and Judiciary in Pakistan," in LaPalombara, ed., *Bureaucracy and Political Development*, 373.

interest groups.[49] In a very different category is a country like North Vietnam, which fought its way into independence with a highly disciplined political organization but which was distinctly weak on the administrative side. The Latin American parallel here would be Mexico, where, as Johnson puts it, "not the armed forces but the PRI is the best organized institution, and the party rather than the armed forces has been the unifying force at the national level." In yet a fourth category are those unfortunate states, such as the Congo, which were born with neither political nor administrative institutions. Many of these new states deficient at independence in one or both types of institutions have also been confronted by high rates of social mobilization and rapidly increasing demands on the political system (see Table 2).

TABLE 2. INSTITUTIONAL DEVELOPMENT AT MOMENT OF INDEPENDENCE

INPUT INSTITUTIONS	OUTPUT INSTITUTIONS	
	High	*Low*
High	India	North Vietnam
Low	Sudan	Congo

POLITICAL INSTITUTIONS AND PUBLIC INTERESTS

A society with weak political institutions lacks the ability to curb the excesses of personal and parochial desires. Politics is a Hobbesian world of unrelenting competition among social forces—between man and man, family and family, clan and clan, region and region, class and class—a competition unmediated by more comprehensive political organizations. The "amoral familism" of Banfield's village has its counterparts in amoral clanism, amoral groupism, and amoral classism. Without strong political institutions, society lacks the means of defining and realizing its common interests. The capacity to create political institutions is the capacity to create public interests.

Traditionally the public interest has been approached in three ways.[50] It has been identified either with abstract, substantive ideal values and norms such as natural law, justice, or right reason; or with the specific interest of a particular individual ("L'état, c'est moi"), group, class (Marxism), or majority; or with the result of a competitive process among individuals (classic liberalism) or groups (Bentleyism).

[49] Johnson, *Military and Society*, 143.
[50] See, in general, Glendon Schubert, *The Public Interest* (Glencoe 1960); Carl J. Friedrich, ed., *Nomos V: The Public Interest* (New York 1962); Douglas Price, "Theories of the Public Interest," in Lynton K. Caldwell, ed., *Politics and Public Affairs* (Bloomington, Ind., 1962), 141-60.

The problem in all these approaches is to arrive at a definition which is concrete rather than nebulous and general rather than particular. Unfortunately, in most cases what is concrete lacks generality and what is general lacks concreteness. One partial way out of the problem is to define the public interest in terms of the concrete interests of the governing institutions. A society with highly institutionalized governing organizations and procedures is, in this sense, more able to articulate and achieve its public interests. "Organized (institutionalized) political communities," as Friedrich argues, "are *better adapted* to reaching decisions and developing policies than unorganized communities."[51] The public interest, in this sense, is not something which exists *a priori* in natural law or the will of the people. Nor is it simply whatever results from the political process. Rather it is whatever strengthens governmental institutions. The public interest is the interest of public institutions. It is something which is created and brought into existence by the institutionalization of government organizations. In a complex political system, many governmental organizations and procedures represent many different aspects of the public interest. The public interest of a complex society is a complex matter.

We are accustomed to think of our primary governing institutions as having representative functions—that is, as expressing the interests of some other set of groups (their constituency). Hence, we tend to forget that governmental institutions have interests of their own. These interests not only exist; they are also reasonably concrete. The questions, "What is the interest of the Presidency? What is the interest of the Senate? What is the interest of the House of Representatives? What are the interests of the Supreme Court?" are difficult but not completely impossible to answer. The answers would furnish a fairly close approximation of the "public interest" of the United States. Similarly, the public interest of Great Britain might be approximated by the specific institutional interests of the Crown, Cabinet, and Parliament. In the Soviet Union, the answer would involve the specific institutional interests of the Presidium, Secretariat, and Central Committee of the Communist Party.

Institutional interests differ from the interests of individuals who are in the institutions. Keynes's percipient remark that "In the long run, we are all dead" applies to individuals, not institutions. Individual interests are necessarily short-run interests. Institutional interests, how-

[51] Carl J. Friedrich, *Man and His Government* (New York 1963), 150; italics in original.

ever, exist through time: the proponent of the institution has to look to its welfare through an indefinite future. This consideration often means a limiting of immediate goals. The "true policy," Aristotle remarked, "for democracy and oligarchy alike, is not one which ensures the greatest possible amount of either, but one which will ensure the longest possible life for both."[52] The official who attempts to maximize power or other values in the short run often weakens his institution in the long run. Supreme Court justices may, in terms of their immediate individual desires, wish to declare an act of Congress unconstitutional. In deciding whether it is in the public interest to do so, however, presumably one question they should ask themselves is whether it is in the long-term institutional interest of the Supreme Court for them to do so. Judicial statesmen are those who, like John Marshall in *Marbury vs. Madison*, maximize the institutional power of the Court in such a way that it is impossible for either the President or Congress to challenge it. In contrast, the Supreme Court justices of the 1930's came very close to expanding their immediate influence at the expense of the long-term interests of the Court as an institution.

The phrase "What's good for General Motors is good for the country" contains at least a partial truth. "What's good for the Presidency is good for the country," however, contains more truth. Ask any reasonably informed group of Americans to identify the five best Presidents and the five worst Presidents. Then ask them to identify the five strongest Presidents and the five weakest Presidents. If the identification of strength with goodness and weakness with badness is not 100 per cent, it will almost certainly not be less than 80 per cent. Those Presidents—Jefferson, Lincoln, the Roosevelts, Wilson—who expanded the powers of their office are hailed as the beneficent promoters of the public welfare and national interest. Those Presidents, such as Buchanan, Grant, Harding, who failed to defend the power of their institution against other groups are also thought to have done less good for the country. Institutional interest coincides with public interest. The power of the Presidency is identified with the good of the polity.

The public interest of the Soviet Union is approximated by the institutional interests of the top organs of the Communist Party: "What's good for the Presidium is good for the Soviet Union." Viewed in these terms, Stalinism can be defined as a situation in which the personal interests of the ruler take precedence over the institution-

[52] *Politics*, 267.

alized interests of the Party. Beginning in the late 1930's Stalin consistently weakened the Party. No Party Congress was held between 1939 and 1952. During and after World War II the Central Committee seldom met. The Party secretariat and Party hierarchy were weakened by the creation of competing organs. Conceivably this process could have resulted in the displacement of one set of governing institutions by another, and some American experts and some Soviet leaders did think that governmental organizations rather than Party organizations would become the ruling institutions in Soviet society. Such, however, was neither the intent nor the effect of Stalin's action. He increased his personal power, not the governmental power. When he died, his personal power died with him. The struggle to fill the resulting vacuum was won by Khrushchev, who identified his interests with the interests of the Party organization, rather than by Malenkov, who identified himself with the governmental bureaucracy. Khrushchev's consolidation of power marked the reemergence and revitalization of the principal organs of the Party. While they acted in very different ways and from different motives, Stalin weakened the Party just as Grant weakened the Presidency. Just as a strong Presidency is in the American public interest, so also a strong Party is in the Soviet public interest.

In terms of the theory of natural law, governmental actions are legitimate to the extent that they are in accord with the "public philosophy."[53] According to democratic theory, they derive their legitimacy from the extent to which they embody the will of the people. According to the procedural concept, they are legitimate if they represent the outcome of a process of conflict and compromise in which all interested groups have participated. In another sense, however, the legitimacy of governmental actions can be sought in the extent to which they reflect the interests of governmental institutions. In contrast to the theory of representative government, under this concept governmental institutions derive their legitimacy and authority not from the extent to which they represent the interests of the people or of any other group, but from the extent to which they have distinct interests of their own apart from all other groups. Politicians frequently remark that things "look different" after they obtain office than they did when they were competing for office. This difference is a measure of the institutional demands of office. It is precisely this

[53] See Walter Lippmann, *The Public Philosophy* (Boston 1955), esp. 42, for his definition of the public interest as "what men would choose if they saw clearly, thought rationally, acted disinterestedly and benevolently."

difference in perspective which legitimizes the demands which the officeholder makes on his fellow citizens. The interests of the President, for instance, may coincide partially and temporarily first with those of one group and then with those of another. But the interest of the Presidency, as Neustadt has emphasized,[54] coincides with that of no one else. The President's power derives not from his representation of class, group, regional, or popular interests, but rather from the fact that he represents none of these. The Presidential perspective is unique to the Presidency. Precisely for this reason, it is both a lonely office and a powerful one. Its authority is rooted in its loneliness.

The existence of political institutions (such as the Presidency or Presidium) capable of giving substance to public interests distinguishes politically developed societies from undeveloped ones. The "ultimate test of development," as Lucian Pye has said, "is the capacity of a people to establish and maintain large, complex, but flexible organizational forms."[55] The level of organization in much of the world, however, is low. "Except in Europe and America," Banfield notes, "the concerting of behavior in political associations and corporate organizations is a rare and recent thing."[56] The ability to create public organizations and political institutions is in short supply in the world today. It is this ability which, above all else, the Communists offer modernizing countries.

DEGENERATION AND THE CORRUPT POLITY

Most modernizing countries are buying rapid social modernization at the price of political degeneration. This process of decay in political institutions, however, has been neglected or overlooked in much of the literature on modernization. As a result, models and concepts which are hopefully entitled "developing" or "modernizing" are often only partially relevant to the countries to which they are applied. More relevant in many cases would be models of corrupt or degenerating societies, highlighting the decay of political organization and the increasing dominance of disruptive social forces. Who, however, has advanced such a theory of political decay or a model of a corrupt political order which might be useful in analyzing the political processes of the countries that are usually called "developing"? Perhaps the most relevant ideas are the most ancient ones. The evolution of

[54] See Richard E. Neustadt, *Presidential Power* (New York 1960), *passim*, but esp. 33-37, 150-51.

[55] Pye, *Politics, Personality and Nation Building*, 51.

[56] Edward C. Banfield, *The Moral Basis of a Backward Society* (Glencoe, Ill., 1958), 7-9, 15ff.

many contemporary new states, once the colonial guardians have departed, has not deviated extensively from the Platonic model. Independence is followed by military coups as the "auxiliaries" take over.[57] Corruption by the oligarchy inflames the envy of rising groups. Conflict between oligarchy and masses erupts into civil strife. Demagogues and street mobs pave the way for the despot. Plato's description of the means by which the despot appeals to the people, isolates and eliminates his enemies, and builds up his personal strength is a far less misleading guide to what has taken place in Ghana and other new states than many things written yesterday.[58]

Plato is one of the few theorists, ancient or contemporary, with a highly explicit theory of political degeneration.[59] The concept of a "corrupt society," however, is a more familiar one in political theory. Typically it refers to a society which lacks law, authority, cohesion, discipline, and consensus, where private interests dominate public ones, where there is an absence of civic obligation and civic duty, where, in short, political institutions are weak and social forces strong. Plato's degenerate states are dominated by various forms of appetite: by force, wealth, numbers, and charisma. "Those constitutions," says Aristotle, "which consider only the personal interest of the rulers are all wrong constitutions, or perversions of the right forms."[60] So also, Machiavelli's concept of the corrupt state, in the words of one commentator, "includes all sorts of license and violence, great inequalities of wealth and power, the destruction of peace and justice, the growth of disorderly ambition, disunion, lawlessness, dishonesty, and contempt for religion."[61] Modern equivalents of the classical corrupt society are Kornhauser's theory of the mass society (where, in the absence of institutions, elites are accessible to masses and masses are available for

---

[57] For comments on the short time lag between independence and the first coup, see Dankwart A. Rustow, "The Military in Middle Eastern Society and Politics," in Sydney N. Fisher, ed., *The Military in the Middle East: Problems in Society and Government* (Columbus, Ohio, 1963), 10.

[58] See, in general, *The Republic*, Book VIII, and especially the description of the despotic regime (Cornford trans., New York 1945), 291-93.

[59] Perhaps the closest contemporary model comes not from a social scientist but from a novelist: William Golding. The schoolboys (newly independent elites) of *The Lord of the Flies* initially attempt to imitate the behavior patterns of adults (former Western rulers). Discipline and consensus, however, disintegrate. A demagogic military leader and his followers gain or coerce the support of a majority. The symbol of authority (the conch) is broken. The voices of responsibility (Ralph) and reason (Piggy) are deserted and harassed, and reason is destroyed. In the end, the naval officer (British Marine Commandos) arrives just in time to save Ralph (Nyerere) from the "hunters" (mutinous troops).

[60] *Politics*, 112.

[61] George H. Sabine, *A History of Political Thought* (rev. edn., New York 1950), 343.

mobilization by the elite) and Rapoport's concept of the praetorian state where "private ambitions are rarely restrained by a sense of public authority; [and] the role of power (i.e., wealth and force) is maximized."[62] Typical of the corrupt, praetorian, or mass societies is the violent oscillation between extreme democracy and tyranny. "Where the pre-established political authority is highly autocratic," says Kornhauser, "rapid and violent displacement of that authority by a democratic regime is highly favorable to the emergence of extremist mass movements that tend to transform the new democracy in anti-democratic directions."[63] Aristotle and Plato saw despotism emerging out of the extremes of mob rule. Rapoport finds in Gibbon an apt summary of the constitutional rhythms of the praetorian state, which "floats between the extremes of absolute monarchy and wild democracy."[64] Such instability is the hallmark of a society where mobilization has outrun institutionalization.

IV. Strategies of Institutional Development

If decay of political institutions is a widespread phenomenon in the "developing" countries and if a major cause of this decay is the high rate of social mobilization, it behooves us, as social scientists, to call a spade a spade and to incorporate these tendencies into any general model of political change which we employ to understand the politics of these areas. If effective political institutions are necessary for stable and eventually democratic government and if they are also a precondition of sustained economic growth, it behooves us, as policy analysts, to suggest strategies of institutional development. In doing this, we should recognize two general considerations affecting probabilities of success in institution-building.

First, the psychological and cultural characteristics of peoples differ markedly and with them their abilities at developing political institutions. Where age-old patterns of thought and behavior have to be changed, quite obviously the creation of political institutions is a far more difficult task than otherwise. "The Tokugawa Japanese could not, as did the Chinese, put family above government," one expert

---

[62] Kornhauser, *Politics of Mass Society, passim*; David C. Rapoport, "Praetorianism: Government Without Consensus" (Ph.D. dissertation, University of California, Berkeley 1959); and Rapoport in Huntington, ed., *Changing Patterns of Military Politics*, 72, where the quotation occurs.

[63] Kornhauser, *Politics of Mass Society*, 125.

[64] Edward Gibbon, *The Decline and Fall of the Roman Empire* (New York 1899), I, 235, quoted by Rapoport in Huntington, ed., *Changing Patterns of Military Politics*, 98.

has observed. "The samurai was expected to be loyal to his official superior first, his family second. In mores generally the primacy of the organization over the person was constantly reiterated."[65] This difference in Japanese and Chinese attitudes toward authority undoubtedly accounts in part for their differences in modernization and development. The Japanese peacefully and smoothly created new political institutions and amalgamated them with old ones. The weakness of traditional Chinese political institutions, on the other hand, led to forty years of revolution and civil war before modern political institutions could be developed and extended throughout Chinese society.

Second, the potentialities for institution-building differ markedly from society to society, but in all societies political organizations can be built. Institutions result from the slow interaction of conscious effort and existing culture. Organizations, however, are the product of conscious, purposeful effort. The forms of this effort may vary from a Meiji Restoration to a Communist Revolution. But in each case a distinct group of identifiable people set about adapting old organizations or building new ones. "Nation-building" has recently become a popular subject, and doubts have been raised about whether nations can be "built."[66] These doubts have a fairly solid basis. Nations are one type of social force, and historically they have emerged over long periods of time. Organization-building, however, differs from nation-building. Political organizations require time for development, but they do not require as much time as national communities. Indeed, most of those who speak of nation-building in such places as tropical Africa see organization-building as the first step in this process. Political parties have to be welded out of tribal groups; the parties create governments; and the governments may, eventually, bring into existence nations. Many of the doubts which people have about the possibilities of nation-building do not apply to organization-building.

Given our hypotheses about the relation of social mobilization to institutionalization, there are two obvious methods of furthering institutional development. First, anything which slows social mobilization presumably creates conditions more favorable to the preservation and strengthening of institutions. Secondly, strategies can be developed and applied directly to the problem of institution-building.

[65] John Whitney Hall, "The Nature of Traditional Society: Japan," in Ward and Rustow, eds., *Political Modernization in Japan and Turkey*, 19.

[66] See Karl W. Deutsch and William J. Foltz, eds., *Nation-Building* (New York 1963), *passim*, but especially the contributions of Joseph R. Strayer and Carl J. Friedrich.

SLOWING MOBILIZATION

Social mobilization can be moderated in many ways. Three methods are: to increase the complexity of social structure; to limit or reduce communications in society; and to minimize competition among segments of the political elite.[67]

In general, the more highly stratified a society is and the more complicated its social structure, the more gradual is the process of political mobilization. The divisions between class and class, occupation and occupation, rural and urban, constitute a series of breakwaters which divide the society and permit the political mobilization of one group at a time. On the other hand, a highly homogeneous society, or a society which has only a single horizontal line of division between an oligarchy that has everything and a peasantry that has nothing, or a society which is divided not horizontally but vertically into ethnic and communal groups, has more difficulty moderating the process of mobilization. Thus, mobilization should be slower in India than in the new African states where horizontal divisions are weak and tribal divisions strong, or in those Latin American countries where the middle strata are weak and a small oligarchy confronts a peasant mass. A society with many horizontal divisions gains through the slower entry of social groups into politics. It may, however, also lose something in that political organizations, when they do develop, may form along class and stratum lines and thus lack the autonomy of more broadly based political organizations. Political parties in countries like Chile and Sweden have been largely the spokesmen for distinct classes; caste associations seem destined to play a significant role in Indian politics. The disruptive effects of political organizations identified with social strata may be reduced if other political institutions exist which appeal to loyalties across class or caste lines. In Sweden, loyalty to the monarchy and the Riksdag mitigates the effects of class-based parties, and in India the caste associations must, in general, seek their goals within the much more extensive framework of the Congress Party. In most societies, the social structure must be largely accepted as given. Where it is subject to governmental manipulation and influence, mobilization

[67] These are not, of course, the only ways of slowing mobilization. Myron Weiner, for instance, has suggested that one practical method is "localization": channeling political interests and activity away from the great issues of national politics to the more immediate and concrete problems of the village and community. This is certainly one motive behind both community development programs and "basic democracies."

will be slowed by government policies which enhance the complexity of social stratification.

The communications network of a society is undoubtedly much more subject to governmental influence. Rapid gains in some of the most desired areas of modernization—such as mass media exposure, literacy, and education—may have to be purchased at the price of severe losses in political stability. This is not to argue that political institutionalization as a value should take precedence over all others: if this were the case, modernization would never be good. It is simply to argue that governments must balance the values won through rapid increases in communications against the values jeopardized by losses in political stability. Thus, governmental policies may be wisely directed to reducing the number of university graduates, particularly those with skills which are not in demand in the society. Students and unemployed university graduates have been a concern common to the nationalistic military regime in South Korea, the socialist military regime in Burma, and the traditional military regime in Thailand. The efforts by General Ne Win in Burma to cut back the number of university graduates may well be imitated by other governments facing similar challenges. Much has been made of the problems caused by the extension of the suffrage to large numbers of illiterates. But limited political participation by illiterates may well, as in India, be less dangerous to political institutions than participation by literates. The latter typically have higher aspirations and make more demands on government. Political participation by illiterates, moreover, is more likely to remain limited, whereas participation by literates is much more likely to snowball with potentially disastrous effects on political stability. A governing elite may also affect the intensity of communications and the rate of political mobilization by its policies on economic development. Large, isolated factories, as Kornhauser has shown, are more likely to give rise to extremist movements than smaller plants more closely integrated into the surrounding community.[68] Self-interest in political survival may lead governing elites to decrease the priority of rapid economic change.

The uncontrolled mobilization of people into politics is also slowed by minimizing the competition among political elites. Hence mobilization is likely to have less disturbing effects on political institutions in one-party systems than in two-party or multiparty systems. In many new states and modernizing countries, a vast gap exists between the modernized elite and the tradition-oriented mass. If the elite di-

[68] Kornhauser, *Politics of Mass Society*, 150-58.

vides against itself, its factions appeal to the masses for support. This produces rapid mobilization of the masses into politics at the same time that it destroys whatever consensus previously existed among the politically active on the need for modernization. Mobilization frequently means the mobilization of tradition; modern politics become the vehicle of traditional purposes. In Burma during the first part of this century, the "general pattern was one in which the modernizers first fell out among themselves whenever they were confronted with demanding choices of policy, and then tended to seek support from among the more traditional elements, which in time gained the ascendency."[69] In Turkey a rough balance between the mobilization of people into politics and the development of political institutions existed so long as the Republican People's Party retained a political monopoly. The conscious decision to permit an opposition party, however, broadened the scope of political competition beyond the urban, Westernized elite. The Democratic Party mobilized the peasants into politics, strengthened the forces of traditionalism, and broke the previous consensus. This led the party leaders to attempt to maintain themselves in power through semilegal means and to induce the army to join them in suppressing the Republican opposition. The army, however, was committed to modernization and seized power in a *coup d'état*, dissolving the Democratic Party and executing many of its top leaders. In due course, the military withdrew from direct conduct of the government, and democratic elections led to a multiparty system in which no party has a clear majority. Thus from a relatively stable one-party system, Turkey passed through a brief two-party era to military rule and a multiparty system: the familiar syndrome of states where mobilization has outrun institutionalization. In the process, not only were political institutions weakened, but the traditional-minded were brought into politics in such a way as to create obstacles to the achievement of many modernizing goals.

CREATING INSTITUTIONS

"Dans la naissance des sociétés ce sont les chefs des républiques qui font l'institution; et c'est ensuite l'institution qui forme les chefs des républiques," said Montesquieu.[70] But in the contemporary world, political leaders prefer modernization to institution-building, and no matter who leads modernization, the process itself generates con-

---

[69] Pye, *Politics, Personality and Nation Building*, 114.

[70] Charles de Secondat, Baron Montesquieu, *Considérations sur les causes de la grandeur des romains et de leur décadence*, in *Oeuvres*, I (Paris 1828), 119-20.

flicting demands and inducements which obstruct the growth of political institutions. Where modernization is undertaken by traditional
leaders working through traditional political institutions, the efforts
of the traditional leaders to reform can unleash and stimulate social
forces which threaten the traditional political institutions. Traditional leaders can modernize and reform their realms, but, where substantial social elements oppose reform, they have yet to demonstrate
they can put through reforms without undermining the institutions
through which they are working. The problem is: how can the traditional political institutions be adapted to accommodate the social
forces unleashed by modernization? Historically, except for Japan,
traditional political institutions have been adapted to the modern
world only where a high degree of political centralization was not
required for modernization and where traditional (i.e., feudal) representative institutions retained their vitality (as in Great Britain and
Sweden). If modernization requires the centralization of power in a
"reform monarch" or "revolutionary emperor," it means the weakening or destruction of whatever traditional representative institutions
may exist and thus complicates still further the assimilation of those
social forces created by modernization. The concentration of power
also makes the traditional regime (like the eighteenth-century French
monarchy) more vulnerable to forcible overthrow. *The vulnerability
of a traditional regime to revolution varies directly with the capability
of the regime for modernization.* For traditional rulers, the imperatives of modernization conflict with the imperatives of institution-
building.

If the traditional political institutions are weak, or if they have
been displaced and suppressed during periods of colonial rule, adaptation is impossible. In societies which have undergone colonial rule,
incubation can serve as a substitute for adaptation. Unfortunately, the
opportunity for incubation was missed in most colonial societies, with
a few prominent exceptions such as India and the Philippines. Incubation requires a colonial administration which is willing to permit
and *to contend with* a nationalist movement for many years, thus
furnishing the time, the struggle, and the slowly increasing responsibility which are the ingredients of institution-building. In general,
however, colonial powers tend to postpone incubation for as long as
possible and then, when they see independence as inevitable, to bring
it about as quickly as possible. Consequently, most of the states which
became independent in the 1950's and 1960's had little opportunity to
incubate political institutions while still under colonial tutelage.

Where traditional political institutions are weak, or collapse, or are overthrown, authority frequently comes to rest with charismatic leaders who attempt to bridge the gap between tradition and modernity by a highly personal appeal. To the extent that these leaders are able to concentrate power in themselves, it might be supposed that they would be in a position to push institutional development and to perform the role of "Great Legislator" or "Founding Father." The reform of corrupt states or the creation of new ones, Machiavelli argued, must be the work of one man alone. A conflict exists, however, between the interests of the individual and the interests of institutionalization. Institutionalization of power means the limitation of power which might otherwise be wielded personally and arbitrarily. The would-be institution-builder needs personal power to create institutions but he cannot create institutions without relinquishing personal power. Resolving this dilemma is not easy. It can be done only by leaders who combine rare political skill and rare devotion to purpose. It was done by Mustafa Kemal who, for almost two decades, managed to maintain his own personal power, to push through major modernizing reforms, and to create a political institution to carry on the government after his death. Atatürk has been a conscious model for many contemporary modernizing leaders, but few, if any, seem likely to duplicate his achievement.

The military junta or military dictatorship is another type of regime common in modernizing countries. It too confronts a distinct set of problems in the conflict between its own impulses to modernization and the needs of institution-building. The military officers who seize power in a modernizing country frequently do so in reaction to the "chaos," "stalemate," "corruption," and "reactionary" character of the civilian regimes which preceded them. The officers are usually passionately devoted to measures of social reform, particularly those which benefit the peasantry (whose interests have frequently been overlooked by the anterior civilian regime). A rationalistic approach to societal problems often makes the officers modernizers par excellence. At the same time, however, they are frequently indifferent or hostile to the needs of political institution-building. The military typically assert that they have taken over the government only temporarily until conditions can be "cleaned up" and authority restored to a purified civilian regime. The officers thus confront an organizational dilemma. They can eliminate or exclude from politics individual civilian politicians, but they are ill-prepared to make fundamental changes in political processes and institutions. If they turn back power to the civilians, the same conditions to which they originally objected tend to reappear (Burma). If they attempt to restore civilian government and to continue in power as a civilian political group (Turkey, South Korea), they open themselves to these same corrupting influences and may pave the way for a second military takeover by a younger generation of colonels who purge the civilianized generals, just as the generals had earlier purged the civilians. Finally, if the military leaders retain power indefinitely, they need to create authoritative political organizations which legitimize and institutionalize their power. Concern with their own personal authority and unfamiliarity with the needs of political institution-building create problems in the fulfillment of this task. It is still too early to say for certain what sort of authoritative political institutions, if any, will be produced by regimes led by military officers such as Nasser and Ayub Khan.

THE PRIMACY OF PARTY

Charismatic leaders and military chiefs have thus had little success in building modern political institutions. The reason lies in the nature of modern politics. In the absence of traditional political institutions, the only modern organization which can become a source of authority and which can be effectively institutionalized is the political party. *The importance of the political party in providing legitimacy and stability in a modernizing political system varies inversely with the institutional inheritance of the system from traditional society.* Traditional systems do not have political parties. Unlike bureaucracy, the party is a distinctly modern form of political organization. Where traditional political institutions (such as monarchies and feudal parliaments) are carried over into the modern era, parties play secondary, supplementary roles in the political system. The other institutions are the primary source of continuity and legitimacy. Parties typically originate within the legislatures and then gradually extend themselves into society. They adapt themselves to the existing framework of the political system and typically reflect in their own operations the organizational and procedural principles embodied in that system. They broaden participation in the traditional institutions, thus adapting those institutions to the requirements of the modern polity. They help make the traditional institutions legitimate in terms of popular sovereignty, but they are not themselves a source of legitimacy. Their own legitimacy derives from the contributions they make to the political system.

Where traditional political institutions collapse or are weak or non-existent, the role of the party is entirely different from what it is in those polities with institutional continuity. In such situations, strong party organization is the only long-run alternative to the instability of a corrupt or praetorian or mass society. The party is not just a supplementary organization; it is instead the source of legitimacy and authority. In the absence of traditional sources of legitimacy, legitimacy is sought in ideology, charisma, popular sovereignty. To be lasting, each of these principles of legitimacy must be embodied in a party. Instead of the party reflecting the state, the state becomes the creation of the party and the instrument of the party. The actions of government are legitimate to the extent that they reflect the will of the party. The party is the source of legitimacy because it is the institutional embodiment of national sovereignty, the popular will, or the dictatorship of the proletariat.

Where traditional political institutions are weak or non-existent, the prerequisite of stability is at least one highly institutionalized political party. States with one such party are markedly more stable than states which lack such a party. States with no parties or many weak parties are the least stable. Where traditional political institutions are smashed by revolution, post-revolutionary order depends on the emergence of one strong party: witness the otherwise very different histories of the Chinese, Mexican, Russian, and Turkish revolutions. Where new states emerge from colonialism with one strong party, the problem is to maintain the strength of that party. In many African countries the nationalist party was the single important modern organization to exist before independence. The party "was generally well organized. The conditions of the political struggle and the dedication of the top elite to the party as the prime instrument of political change led the elite to give the major portion of their energies and resources to building a solid, responsive organization capable of disciplined action in response to directives from the top and able to ferret out and exploit feelings of dissatisfaction among the masses for political ends."[71] After independence, however, the dominant political party is often weakened by the many competing demands on organizational resources. A marked dispersion of resources means a decline in the overall level of political institutionalization. "Talents that once were available for the crucial work of party organization," one observer has warned, "may now be preoccupied with running a ministry or government bureau. . . . Unless new sources of loyal organizational

[71] William J. Foltz, "Building the Newest Nations: Short-Run Strategies and Long-Run Problems," in Deutsch and Foltz, eds., *Nation-Building*, 121.

and administrative talents can be found immediately, the party's organization—and, therefore, the major link between the regime and the masses—is likely to be weakened."[72]

The need for concentration applies not only to the allocation of resources among types of organizations but also to the scope of organization. In many modernizing countries, the political leaders attempt too much too fast; they try to build mass organizations when they should concentrate on elite organizations. Organizations do not have to be large to be effective and to play a crucial role in the political process: the Bolshevik Party in 1917 is one example; the Indian Civil Service (which numbered only 1,157 men at independence) is another. Overextension of one's resources in organization-building is as dangerous as overextension of one's troops in a military campaign. (The strategic hamlet program in South Vietnam is an example of both.) Concentration is a key principle of politics as well as strategy. The pressures for broad organizational support, however, seem to push towards the all-inclusive organization. In his efforts to create a political structure to bolster his military regime in Egypt, for instance, Nasser first created the Liberation Rally in 1953, which soon came to have from 5 to 6 million members. The organization was simply too big to be effective and to achieve its purpose. After the adoption of a new constitution in 1956, the Liberation Rally was replaced by the National Union, which was designed to be the school of the nation and also to be universal in membership (except for reactionaries). Again the organization was too broad to be effective. Hence in 1962, after the break with Syria, a new organization, the Arab Socialist Union, was organized with the advice of organizational and ideological experts from Yugoslavia. It was designed to be a more exclusive, more tightly organized body, its membership limited to 10 per cent of the population. Inevitably, however, it also mushroomed in size, and after two years it had 5 million members. In a fourth effort, early in 1964 President Nasser reportedly formed still another group limited to only 4,000 members and called the "Government Party," which would form the core of the Arab Socialist Union. The new organization was to be designed by Nasser "to enforce a peaceful transfer of power and a continuation of his policies if anything happens to him."[73] Whether this organization, unlike its predecessors, becomes an institution remains to be seen. Its likelihood of success depends upon its limitation in size.

[72] Ibid., 123-24.
[73] Washington Post, February 9, 1964, p. A-17.

American social scientists have devoted much attention to the competitiveness of political systems, devising various ways of measuring that competitiveness and classifying systems according to their degree of competitiveness.[74] The more parties which exist within a system, presumably the more competitive it is. Yet the proliferation of parties usually means the dispersion of organization and leadership talents and the existence of a large number of weak parties. If sufficient resources are available to support more than one well-organized party, this is all to the good. But most modernizing countries will be well off if they can create just one strong party organization. *In modernizing systems, party institutionalization usually varies inversely with party competitiveness.* Modernizing states with multiparty systems are much more unstable and prone to military intervention than modernizing states with one party, with one dominant party, or with two parties. The most unstable systems and those most prone to military

TABLE 3. DISTRIBUTION OF COUPS AND COUP ATTEMPTS
IN MODERNIZING COUNTRIES SINCE INDEPENDENCE

Type of Political System	Number of Countries	Countries with Coups Number	Countries with Coups Per cent
Communist	3	0	0
One-party	18	2	11
One-party dominant	12	3	25
Two-party	11	5	45
Multiparty	22	15	68
No effective parties	17	14	83

SOURCE: Figures are somewhat revised and adapted from the similar table in Fred R. von der Mehden, *Politics of the Developing Nations* (Englewood Cliffs, N.J., 1964), 65.

intervention are the multiparty systems and the no-party systems. The weak institutionalization of parties in the multiparty system makes that system extremely fragile. The step from many parties to no parties and from no parties to many parties is an easy one. In their institutional weakness, the no-party system and the multiparty system closely resemble each other.

[74] See James S. Coleman, in Almond and Coleman, eds., *Politics of the Developing Areas*, Conclusion; Phillips Cutright, "National Political Development: Its Measurement and Social Correlates," in Nelson W. Polsby, Robert A. Dentler, and Paul A. Smith, eds., *Politics and Social Life* (Boston 1963), 569-82; von der Mehden, *Politics of the Developing Nations*, 54-64.

POLITICAL DEVELOPMENT AND AMERICAN POLICY

The Bolshevik concept of the political party is directly relevant to modernizing countries. It provides a conscious and explicit answer to the problem of mobilization vs. institutionalization. The Communists actively attempt to expand political participation. At the same time they are the most energetic and intense contemporary students of de Tocqueville's "art of associating together." Their specialty is organization, their goal the mobilization of the masses into their organizations. For them mobilization and organization go hand in hand. "There are only two kinds of political tasks," a leading Chinese Communist theorist has said: "one is the task of propaganda and education, the other is the task of organization."[75] The party is initially a highly select group of those who have achieved the proper degree of revolutionary consciousness. It expands gradually as it is able to win the support and participation of others. Peripheral organizations and front groups provide an organizational ladder for the gradual mobilization and indoctrination of those who in due course become full-fledged party members. If the political struggle takes the form of revolutionary war, mobilization occurs on a gradual territorial basis as village after village shifts in status from hostile control to contested area to guerrilla area to base area. The theory is selective mobilization; the political involvement of masses who have not reached the proper level of revolutionary consciousness can only benefit reaction. The "opportunist" Menshevik, Lenin warned, "strives to proceed from the bottom upward, and, therefore, wherever possible and as far as possible, upholds autonomism and 'democracy'. . . ." The Bolshevik, on the other hand, "strives to proceed from the top downward, and upholds an extension of the rights and powers of the center in relation to the parts."[76]

Communist doctrine thus recognizes the need to balance mobilization and organization and stresses the party as the key to political stability. The American approach, on the other hand, tends to ignore the requirements of political organization and to deprecate the importance of party. American attitudes are rooted in the secondary, instrumental role of party in the American constitutional system. In addition, American distaste for politics leads to an emphasis on the

---

[75] Ai Ssu-chi, quoted in Frederick T. C. Yu, "Communications and Politics in Communist China," in Pye, ed., *Communications and Political Development*, 261-62.

[76] V. I. Lenin, *One Step Forward, Two Steps Back* (*The Crisis in Our Party*), in *Collected Works* (Fineberg and Jochel trans., London 1961), 396-97.

output aspects of the political system. The stress, as Lucian Pye has pointed out, has been on the efficient administrator rather than the wily politician.[77] Aid missions advise governments on administrative organization and economic planning, but seldom do they advise political leaders on how to create a strong party. To meet the problems of interest aggregation, Americans have resorted to a variety of alternatives to political organization. Some Americans have urged that the military, as the strongest organization in many modernizing countries, should assume a major role in the responsibilities of government.[78] At times American policy has relied on individual political leaders, such as Magsaysay, Diem, or Ayub Khan. Alternatively, the American government has stressed adherence to particular structural forms, such as free elections.

All of these approaches are doomed to failure. Neither military juntas nor charismatic personalities nor free elections can be a long-term substitute for effective political organization. Charismatic leaders are reluctant to substitute party control for personal control. Military officers are usually even more explicitly anti-party. They contrast the venal party politics of the civilians with the honest devotion to the nation of the military. Military coups and military juntas may spur modernization, but they cannot produce a stable political order. Instead of relying on the military, American policy should be directed to the creation within modernizing countries of at least one strong non-Communist political party. If such a party already exists and is in a dominant position, support of that party should be the keystone of policy. Where political life is fragmented and many small parties exist, American backing should go to the strongest of the parties whose goals are compatible with ours. If it is a choice between a party and a personality, choose the party: better the Baath than Nasser. Where no parties exist and the government (whether traditional, military, or charismatic) is reasonably cooperative with the United States, American military, economic, and technical assistance should be conditioned upon the government's making efforts to develop a strong supporting party organization.

Several years ago Guy Pauker warned that "What is most urgently

[77] Pye, *Politics, Personality and Nation Building*, 297-301; and Pye, "The Policy Implications of Social Change in Non-Western Societies" (M.I.T. Center for International Studies, Cambridge 1957, mimeo.), 69-80.

[78] Guy J. Pauker, "Southeast Asia as a Problem Area in the Next Decade," *World Politics*, xi (April 1959), 325-45; Lucian W. Pye, "Armies in the Process of Political Modernization," in John J. Johnson, ed., *The Role of the Military in Underdeveloped Countries* (Princeton 1962), 69-90.

needed in Southeast Asia today is organizational strength."[79] Organizational strength is also the most urgent need in southern Asia, the Middle East, Africa, and Latin America. Unless that need is met with American support, the alternatives in those areas remain a corrupt political system or a Communist one.

[79] Pauker, *World Politics*, xi, 343.

PSYCHOLOGICAL FACTORS IN
CIVIL VIOLENCE

By TED GURR*

UNTIL recently many political scientists tended to regard violent civil conflict as a disfigurement of the body politic, neither a significant nor a proper topic for their empirical inquiries. The attitude was in part our legacy from Thomas Hobbes's contention that violence is the negation of political order, a subject fit less for study than for admonition. Moreover, neither the legalistic nor the institutional approaches that dominated traditional political science could provide much insight into group action that was regarded by definition as illegal and the antithesis of institutionalized political life. The strong empirical bent in American political science led to ethnocentric inquiry into such recurring and salient features of American political life as voting and legislative behavior. The American Revolution and Civil War appeared as unique events, grist for exhaustive historical inquiry but unlikely subjects for systematic comparative study or empirical theory. Representative of the consequences of these attitudes is a recent judgment that political violence "by its very nature [is] beyond any simple or reasonable laws of causation."[1]

This article proposes, first, that civil violence *is* a significant topic of political inquiry and, second, not only that it is capable of explanation, but that we know enough about the sources of human violence to specify in general, theoretical terms some of the social patterns that dispose men to collective violence.

The proposition that civil violence is important as a genus is widely but not yet universally accepted, even by scholars concerned with some of its forms, revolution in particular.[2] This is the case, one suspects, be-

* This article is a revision of a paper read to the panel on "The Psychology of Political Unrest," at the Annual Meeting of the American Psychological Association, New York, September 2-6, 1966. Harry Eckstein's careful and helpful evaluation of draft versions of this paper is gratefully acknowledged. Others who have provided useful, though not always satisfiable, criticism of the theoretical model include Leonard Berkowitz, Alfred de Grazia, Mohammed Guessous, Marion J. Levy, Jr., John T. McAlister, Jr., Mancur L. Olson, Jr., Joel Prager, Bryant Wedge, and Oran R. Young. Theoretical work was supported by an award from a National Science Foundation institutional grant to New York University and by the Center for Research on Social Systems (formerly SORO) of American University.

[1] Arnold Forster, "Violence on the Fanatical Left and Right," *Annals of the American Academy of Political and Social Science*, cccLxiv (March 1966), 142.
[2] For example, Lawrence Stone, "Theories of Revolution," *World Politics*, xviii

cause revolutions have traditionally been regarded as the most significant form of civil strife, because the universe of such events has been defined by reference to their consequences rather than their common
characteristics or preconditions, and because the older theoretical generalizations have emphasized primarily the processes of such events and
categorization of their concomitants at a low level of generality.[3] But the
evidence both of recent history and of systematic attempts at specifying the incidence of civil strife suggests that revolutions are but one of
an extraordinarily numerous variety of interrelated forms of strife;[4] that
some of these forms, among them coups d'état, guerrilla war, and massive rioting, can alter political processes and social institutions as drastically as any of the classic revolutions; and that the forms themselves
are mutable, or rather, that by reifying our arbitrary distinctions among
forms of strife we have overlooked some fundamental similarities.[5]
Examination of those special conditions and processes that lead from
turmoil to revolution provides a partial understanding of revolution
per se, but for a sufficient explanation we require a more general
theory, one capable of accounting for the common elements of that
much larger class of events called civil strife.

(January 1966), 159-76, advances the curious argument that collective violence generally
cannot be the object of useful theorizing because it is at the same time both pervasive
and somehow peripheral.

[3] The emphasis on processes is evident in the major theoretical analyses of the
"classic" revolutions, including Lyford P. Edwards, *The Natural History of Revolutions*
(Chicago 1927); Crane Brinton, *The Anatomy of Revolution* (New York 1938); George
S. Pettee, *The Process of Revolution* (New York 1938); Louis R. Gottschalk, "Causes of
Revolution," *American Journal of Sociology*, L (July 1944), 1-9; and Rex D. Hopper,
"The Revolutionary Process: A Frame of Reference for the Study of Revolutionary
Movements," *Social Forces*, XXVIII (March 1950), 270-79.

[4] A great many counts of the incidence of civil strife events have recently been reported. Harry Eckstein reports 1,632 "internal wars" in the period 1946-1959 in "On
the Etiology of Internal Wars," *History and Theory*, IV, No. 2 (1965), 133-63. Rummel
and Tanter counted more than 300 "domestic conflict events" per year during the years
1955-1960, including an annual average of 13 guerrilla wars and 21 attempted overthrows
of government; see Raymond Tanter, "Dimensions of Conflict Behavior Within Nations,
1955-60: Turmoil and Internal War," *Peace Research Society Papers*, III (1965), 159-84.
Most important to the argument that civil strife is a single universe of events are results
of Rudolph Rummel's factor analysis of 236 socioeconomic and political variables, including nine domestic conflict measures, for a large number of nations. Eight of the
conflict measures—e.g., number of riots, of revolutions, of purges, of deaths from group
violence—are strongly related to a single factor but not significantly related to any
others, empirical evidence that they comprise a distinct and interrelated set of
events. See *Dimensionality of Nations Project: Orthogonally Rotated Factor Tables for
236 Variables*, Department of Political Science, Yale University (New Haven, July 1964),
mimeographed.

[5] The "French Revolution" was a series of events that would now be characterized
as urban demonstrations and riots, peasant uprisings, and a coup d'état. It is called a
revolution in retrospect and by virtue of the Duc de Liancourt's classic remark to
Louis XVI. The American Revolution began with a series of increasingly violent urban
riots and small-scale terrorism that grew into a protracted guerrilla war.

The resort to illicit violence is the defining property that distinguishes these collective events from others. We can regard this as just a definitional point,[6] but it has a crucial theoretical consequence: to direct attention to psychological theories about the sources of human aggression.

Some types of psychological theories about the sources of aggressive behavior can be eliminated at the outset. There is little value in pseudo-psychological speculation about revolutionaries as deviants, fools, or the maladjusted. Psychodynamic explanations of the "revolutionary personality" may be useful for microanalysis of particular events but scarcely for general theory. Aggression-prone victims of maladaptive socialization processes are found in every society, and among the actors in most outbreaks of civil violence, but they are much more likely to be mobilized by strife than to be wholly responsible for its occurrence. Nor can a general theory of civil strife rest on culturally specific theories of modal personality traits, though it might well take account of the effects of these traits. Some cultures and subcultures produce significantly more aggression-prone than cooperative personalities, but an explanation of this order says little of the societal conditions that elicit aggression from the aggression-prone, and nothing at all of the capacity for civil violence of even the most apparently quiescent populations.

The only generally relevant psychological theories are those that deal with the sources and characteristics of aggression in all men, regardless of culture. Such psychological theories do not directly constitute a theory of civil strife. They do offer alternative motivational bases for such a theory and provide means for identifying and specifying the operation of some crucial explanatory variables. As is demonstrated in the following section, one or another of these theories is implicit in most theoretical approaches to civil strife that have no explicit motivational base, although only one of them appears highly plausible in the light of empirical evidence.

PSYCHOLOGICAL THEORIES OF AGGRESSION

There are three distinct psychological assumptions about the generic sources of human aggression: that aggression is solely instinctual, that

---

[6] The universe of concern, civil violence, is formally defined as *all collective, non-governmental attacks on persons or property, resulting in intentional damage to them, that occur within the boundaries of an autonomous or colonial political unit.* The terms "civil strife," "violent civil conflict," and "civil violence" are used synonymously in this article. The universe subsumes more narrowly defined sets of events such as "internal war," which Harry Eckstein defines as "any resort to violence within a political order to change its constitution, rulers, or policies" (in "On the Etiology of Internal Wars," 133), and "revolution," typically defined in terms of violently accomplished fundamental change in social institutions.

it is solely learned, or that it is an innate response activated by frustration.[7] The instinct theories of aggression, represented, among others, by Freud's attribution of the impulse to destructiveness to a death instinct and by Lorenz's view of aggression as a survival-enhancing instinct, assume that most or all men have within them an autonomous source of aggressive impulses, a drive to aggress that, in Lorenz's words, exhibits "irresistible outbreaks which recur with rhythmical regularity."[8] Although there is no definitive support for this assumption, and much evidence to the contrary, its advocates, including Freud and Lorenz, have often applied it to the explanation of collective as well as individual aggression.[9] The assumption is evident in Hobbes's characterization of man in the state of nature and is perhaps implicit in Nieburg's recent concern for "the people's capability for outraged, uncontrolled, bitter, and bloody violence,"[10] but plays no significant role in contemporary theories of civil strife.

Just the opposite assumption, that aggressive behavior is solely or primarily learned, characterizes the work of some child and social psychologists, whose evidence indicates that some aggressive behaviors are learned and used strategically in the service of particular goals—aggression by children and adolescents to secure attention, by adults to express dominance strivings, by groups in competition for scarce values, by military personnel in the service of national policy.[11] The assumption that violence is a learned response, rationalistically chosen and dispassionately employed, is common to a number of recent theoretical approaches to civil strife. Johnson repeatedly, though not consistently, speaks of civil violence as "purposive," as "forms of behavior *intended* to disorient the behavior of others, thereby bringing about the demise

[7] Bryant Wedge argues (in a personal communication) that much human aggression, including some civil strife, may arise from a threat-fear-aggression sequence. Leonard Berkowitz, however, proposes that this mechanism can be subsumed by frustration-aggression theory, the inferred sequence being threat (anticipated frustration)-fear-anger-aggression, in *Aggression: A Social Psychological Analysis* (New York 1962), chap. 2. It may be conceptually useful to distinguish the two mechanisms; it nonetheless appears likely that most variables affecting the outcome of the frustration-aggression sequence also are operative in the postulated threat-aggression sequence.

[8] Konrad Lorenz, *On Aggression* (New York 1966), xii.

[9] Sigmund Freud, *Civilization and Its Discontents*, trans. Joan Riviere (London 1930); Lorenz, chaps. 13, 14. Freud's instinctual interpretation of aggression is advanced in his later works; his early view was that aggression is a response to frustration of pleasure-seeking behavior. For a review and critique of other instinct theories of aggression, see Berkowitz, chap. 1.

[10] H. L. Nieburg, "The Threat of Violence and Social Change," *American Political Science Review*, LVI (December 1962), 870.

[11] A characteristic study is Albert Bandura and Richard H. Walters, *Social Learning and Personality Development* (New York 1963). For a commentary on instrumental aggression, see Berkowitz, esp. 30-32, 182-83, 201-2.

of a hated social system."[12] Parsons attempts to fit civil violence into the framework of social interaction theory, treating the resort to force as a way of acting chosen by the actor(s) for purposes of deterrence, punishment, or symbolic demonstration of their capacity to act.[13] Schelling is representative of the conflict theorists: he explicitly assumes rational behavior and interdependence of the adversaries' decisions in all types of conflict.[14] Stone criticizes any emphasis on violence as a distinguishing or definitional property of civil strife on grounds that it is only a particular means, designed to serve political ends.[15]

The third psychological assumption about aggression is that it occurs primarily as a response to frustration. A "frustration" is an interference with goal-directed behavior; "aggression" is behavior designed to injure, physically or otherwise, those toward whom it is directed. The disposition to respond aggressively when frustrated is considered part of man's biological makeup; there is an innate tendency to attack the frustrating agent. Learning can and does modify the tendency: what is perceived to be frustrating, modes of aggressive response, inhibition through fear of retaliation, and appropriate targets are all modified or defined in the learning process, typically but not solely during socialization.

Frustration-aggression theory is more systematically developed, and has substantially more empirical support, than theories that assume either that all men have a free-flowing source of destructive energy or that all aggression is imitative and instrumental. Moreover, the kinds of evidence cited in support of theories of the latter type appear to be subsumable by frustration-aggression theory, whereas the converse is not the case.

One crucial element that frustration-aggression theory contributes to the study of civil violence concerns the drive properties of anger. In the recent reformulation of the theory by Berkowitz, the perception of frustration is said to arouse anger, which functions as a drive. Aggressive responses tend not to occur unless evoked by some external cue, but their occurrence is an inherently satisfying response to that anger.[16] Similar-

[12] Chalmers Johnson, *Revolutionary Change* (Boston 1966), 12, 13, italics added.
[13] Talcott Parsons, "Some Reflections on the Place of Force in Social Process," in Harry Eckstein, ed., *Internal War: Problems and Approaches* (New York 1964), 34-35.
[14] Thomas C. Schelling, *The Strategy of Conflict* (Cambridge, Mass., 1960), 4.
[15] P. 161.
[16] The most influential and systematic statement of the theory is John Dollard and others, *Frustration and Aggression* (New Haven 1939). Two important recent syntheses of the evidence are Berkowitz, *Aggression*, and Aubrey J. Yates, *Frustration and Conflict* (New York 1962). Also see Leonard Berkowitz, "The Concept of Aggressive Drive: Some Additional Considerations," in Berkowitz, ed., *Advances in Experimental Psychology*, Vol. II (New York 1965), 307-22.

ly, Maier has amassed extensive evidence that the innate frustration-induced behaviors (including regression, fixation, and resignation, as well as aggression) are for the actor ends in themselves, unrelated to further goals and qualitatively different from goal-directed behavior.[17]

To argue that aggression is innately satisfying is not incompatible with the presence of learned or purposive components in acts of individual or collective aggression. Cues that determine the timing, forms, and objects of aggression are learned, just as habits of responding aggressively to moderate as well as severe frustration can be learned. The sense of frustration may result from quite rational analysis of the social universe. Leaders can put their followers' anger to rational or rationalized uses. If anger is sufficiently powerful and persistent it may function as an autonomous drive, leading to highly rational and effective efforts by both leaders and the led to satisfy anger aggressively. The crucial point is that rationalization and organization of illicit violence are typically subsequent to, and contingent upon, the existence of frustration-induced anger. Collective violence may be a calculated strategy of dispassionate elite aspirants, and expectations of gains to be achieved through violence may be present among many of its participants. Nonetheless the implication of frustration-aggression theory is that civil violence almost always has a strong "appetitive," emotional base and that the magnitude of its effects on the social system is substantially dependent on how widespread and intense anger is among those it mobilizes.

If anger implies the presence of frustration, there is compelling evidence that frustration is all but universally characteristic of participants in civil strife: discontent, anger, rage, hate, and their synonyms are repeatedly mentioned in studies of strife. Moreover, the frustration assumption is implicit or explicit in many theoretical analyses of the subject. Smelser's concept of "strain" as one of the major determinants of collective behavior, particularly hostile outbursts and value-oriented movements (revolutions), can be readily reformulated in terms of perceived frustration.[18] So can Willer and Zollschan's notion of "exigency" as a precursor of revolution.[19] Ridker characterizes the consequence of

[17] Norman R. F. Maier, *Frustration: The Study of Behavior Without a Goal* (New York 1949), 92-115, 159-61. Maier postulates a frustration threshold that may open the way to any of four classes of "goal-less" behavior of which aggression is only one. His findings have not been related adequately to the body of research on the frustration-aggression relationship. One can suggest, however, that the nonaggressive responses—fixation, regression, and apparent resignation—can be treated as more or less innate responses in a response hierarchy which are resorted to in the absence of aggression-evoking cues.

[18] Neil J. Smelser, *Theory of Collective Behavior* (New York 1963).

[19] David Willer and George K. Zollschan, "Prolegomenon to a Theory of Revolu-

failure to attain economic expectations as "discontent," analogous in source and consequence to anger.[20] In Davies' theory of revolution, the reversal of a trend of socioeconomic development is said to create frustration, which instigates revolution.[21] Galtung's theory of both intranational and international aggression recognizes that "the external conditions leading to aggression ... probably have to pass through the minds of men and precipitate as perceptions with a high emotive content before they are acted out as aggression."[22]

In none of these approaches to theory, however, has frustration-aggression theory been systematically exploited nor have its variables been taken into account.[23] The primary object of this article is to demonstrate that many of the variables and relationships identified in social psychological research on the frustration-aggression relationship appear to underlie the phenomenology of civil violence. Juxtaposition of these two diverse types of material provides a basis for an interrelated set of propositions that is intended to constitute the framework of a general theory of the conditions that determine the likelihood and magnitude of civil violence. These propositions are of two types, whose proposed relationships are diagrammed in Figure 1: (1) propositions about the operation of *instigating variables*, which determine the magnitude of anger, and (2) propositions about *mediating variables*, which determine the likelihood and magnitude of overt violence as a response to anger.[24]

This approach does not deny the relevance of aspects of the social structure, which many conflict theorists have held to be crucial. The supposition is that theory about civil violence is most fruitfully based on systematic knowledge about those properties of men that determine how they react to certain characteristics of their societies.

---

tions," in George K. Zollschan and Walter Hirsch, eds., *Explorations in Social Change* (Boston 1964), 125-51.

[20] Ronald G. Ridker, "Discontent and Economic Growth," *Economic Development and Cultural Change*, xi (October 1962), 1-15.

[21] James C. Davies, "Toward a Theory of Revolution," *American Sociological Review*, xxvii (February 1962), 5-19.

[22] Johan Galtung, "A Structural Theory of Aggression," *Journal of Peace Research*, ii, No. 2 (1964), 95.

[23] Ivo K. and Rosalind L. Feierabend, in "Aggressive Behaviors Within Polities, 1948-1962: A Cross-National Study," *Journal of Conflict Resolution*, x (September 1966), 249-71, have formally equated political instability with aggressive behavior and have derived and tested several hypotheses about stability from frustration-aggression theory. They have attempted no general theoretical synthesis, however.

[24] The term "instigating" is adapted from the behavioristic terminology of Dollard and others. Instigating variables determine the strength of instigation, i.e., stimulus or motivation, to a particular kind of behavior. Mediating variables refer to intervening conditions, internal or external to the actors, which modify the expression of that behavior.

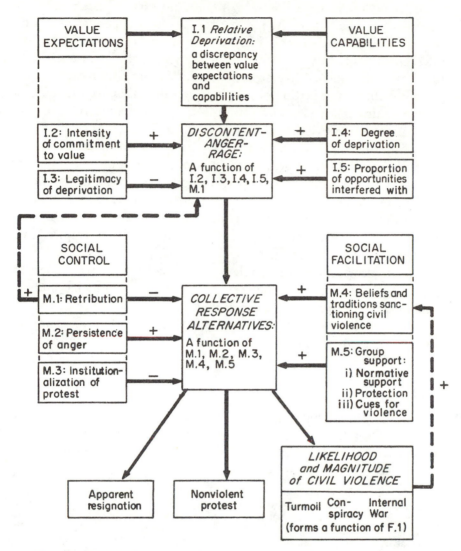

a. The direction(s) of proposed effects on magnitude of civil violence are indicated by + and −.

FIGURE 1. VARIABLES DETERMINING THE LIKELIHOOD AND MAGNITUDE
OF CIVIL VIOLENCE

RELATIVE DEPRIVATION: VARIABLES
DETERMINING THE MAGNITUDE OF ANGER

My basic premise is that the necessary precondition for violent civil conflict is relative deprivation, defined as actors' perception of discrepancy between their *value expectations* and their environment's apparent *value capabilities*.[25] Value expectations are the goods and conditions of life to which people believe they are justifiably entitled. The referents of value capabilities are to be found largely in the social and physical environment: they are the conditions that determine people's perceived chances of getting or keeping the values they legitimately expect to attain. In a comparable treatment, Aberle defines relative deprivation as "a negative discrepancy between legitimate expectation and actuality," viewing expectations as standards, not mere prophecies or hopes.[26] For purposes of general theoretical specification I assume that perceived discrepancies between expectations and capabilities with respect to any collectively sought value—economic, psychosocial, political —constitute relative deprivation. The extent to which some values may be more salient than others is a subject of theoretical and empirical inquiry not evaluated here.

Relative deprivation can be related to the concept of frustration by extending Yates's distinction between the frustrating situation and the frustrated organism.[27] A frustrating situation is one in which an actor is, by objective standards, thwarted by some social or physical barrier in attempts to attain or continue enjoyment of a value. The actor can be said to be frustrated, however, only when he is aware of interference or thwarting. The awareness of interference is equivalent to the concept of relative deprivation as defined above.

A further distinction is necessary between two general classes of deprivation: those that are personal and those that are group or category experiences.[28] For given groups, and for some classes of societies, it is

[25] The phrase "relative deprivation" was first used systematically in Samuel A. Stouffer and others, *The American Soldier: Adjustment During Army Life*, Vol. I (Princeton 1949), to denote the violation of expectations. J. Stacy Adams reviews the concept's history and some relevant evidence and suggests that feelings of injustice intervene between the condition of relative deprivation and responses to it, in "Inequity in Social Exchange," in Berkowitz, ed., *Advances in Experimental Psychology*, 267-300. The "injustice" aspect is implicit in my definition and use of relative deprivation as *perceived* discrepancy between what people think they will get and what they believe they are entitled to. The Stouffer concept has been related to levels of social satisfaction and to anomie, but has not, so far as I know, been associated with the discontent-anger-rage continuum in the frustration-aggression relationship.

[26] David F. Aberle, "A Note on Relative Deprivation Theory," in Sylvia L. Thrupp, ed., *Millennial Dreams in Action: Essays in Comparative Study* (The Hague 1962), 209-14. Bert Hoselitz and Ann Willner similarly distinguish between expectations, regarded by the individual as "what is rightfully owed to him," and aspirations, which represent "that which he would like to have but has not necessarily had or considered his due," in "Economic Development, Political Strategies, and American Aid," in Morton A. Kaplan, ed., *The Revolution in World Politics* (New York 1962), 363.

[27] Pp. 175-78.

[28] Aberle, 210.

possible to identify events and patterns of conditions that are likely to be widely seen as unjust deprivation. Such events may occur abruptly—for example, the suppression of a political party or a drastic inflation—or slowly, like the decline of a group's status relative to other social classes. Such conditions can be called collective frustrations[29] to distinguish them from such unexpected personal frustrations as failure to obtain an expected promotion or the infidelity of a spouse, which may be relatively common but randomly incident in most populations.

Whether empirical research ought to focus on conditions defined as collectively frustrating or directly on perceived deprivation is an operational question whose answer depends on the researcher's interest and resources, not upon the following theoretical formulation. Survey techniques permit more or less direct assessment of the extent and severity of relative deprivation.[30] To the extent that the researcher is prepared to make assumptions about measurable conditions that are collectively frustrating in diverse nations, cross-national aggregate data can be used in correlational studies.[31]

The basic relationship can be summarized in a proposition analogous to and assuming the same basic mechanism as the fundamental theorem of frustration-aggression theory:[32]

Proposition I.1: The occurrence of civil violence presupposes the likelihood of relative deprivation among substantial numbers of individuals in a society; concomitantly, the more severe is relative deprivation, the greater are the likelihood and intensity of civil violence.

This proposition may be truistic, although theories were noted above which attempt to account for civil strife without reference to discontent. Moreover, relative deprivation in some degree can be found in any society. The usefulness of the basic proposition is best determined by reference to the set of propositions that qualify it. These propositions specify the conditions that determine the severity and in some cases the

[29] The Feierabends use the comparable term "systemic frustration" to describe the balance between "social want satisfaction" and "social want formation."

[30] Hadley Cantril's work offers examples, especially *The Pattern of Human Concerns* (New Brunswick 1965).

[31] This approach is exemplified by the Feierabends' work and by Bruce M. Russett, "Inequality and Instability: The Relation of Land Tenure to Politics," *World Politics*, xvi (April 1964), 442-54.

[32] The basic postulate of Dollard and others is that "the occurrence of aggressive behavior always presupposes the existence of frustration and, contrariwise, that the existence of frustration always leads to some form of aggression" (p. 1). It is evident from context and from subsequent articles that this statement was intended in more qualified fashion.

occurrence of deprivation, whether or not it is likely to lead to civil violence, and the magnitude of violence when it does occur. The fundamental question, which is susceptible to a variety of empirical tests, is whether the proposed precise relationship between severity of deprivation, as determined by variables I.2 through I.5, and magnitude of violence does hold when the effects of the mediating variables M.1 through M.5 are taken into account.

DEFINITIONS AND QUALIFICATIONS

Civil violence and relative deprivation are defined above. If relative deprivation is the perception of frustrating circumstances, the emotional response to it tends to be anger. Obviously there are degrees of anger, which can usefully be regarded as a continuum varying from mild dissatisfaction to blind rage. The severity of relative deprivation is assumed to vary directly with the modal strength of anger in the affected population; the determinants of strength of anger are specified in propositions I.2 to I.5, below.

The concept of magnitude requires elaboration. Various measures of quantity or magnitude of aggression are used in psychological research on the frustration-aggression relationship—for example, the intensity of electric shocks administered by frustrated subjects to a supposed frustrater, numbers of aggressive responses in test situations, or the length of time frustrated children play destructively with inanimate objects. A consideration of theory, however, suggests that no single measure of magnitude of aggression is *prima facie* sufficient. Assuming the validity of the basic frustration-aggression postulate that the greater the strength of anger, the greater the quantity of aggression, it seems likely that strong anger can be satisfied either by inflicting severe immediate damage on the source of frustration or by prolonged but less severe aggression, and that either of these tactics is probably more or less substitutable for the other. Which alternative is taken may very well be a function of opportunity, and while opportunities can be controlled in experimental situations, in civil violence they are situationally determined. Hence neither severity nor duration alone is likely to reflect the modal strength of collective anger or, consequently, to constitute an adequate measure of magnitude of civil violence.

Moreover, there are evidently individual differences—presumably normally distributed—in the strength of anger needed to precipitate overt aggression. Hence the proportion of a population that participates in collective violence ought to vary with the modal strength of anger: discontent will motivate few to violence, anger will push more across the threshold, rage is likely to galvanize large segments of a collectivity into action. This line of argument suggests that magnitude of civil violence has three component variables: the degree of participation within the affected population, the destructiveness of the aggressive actions, and the length of time violence persists.

Frustration-aggression theory stipulates a set of variables that determine the strength of anger or discontent in response to a given frustration. Dollard and others initially proposed that the strength of instigation to aggression (anger) varies with "(1) the strength of instigation to the frustrated response, (2) the degree of interference with the frustrated response, and (3) the number of frustrated response-sequences."[33] The first of these variables, modified in the light of empirical evidence, provides the basis for propositions about characteristics of value expectations that affect the intensity of anger. The second and third variables, similarly modified, suggest several propositions about value capabilities.

Before the propositions are presented, two qualifications of the classic behaviorist conceptualization of frustration as interference with specific, goal-directed responses must be noted. First, it appears from examination of specific outbreaks of civil violence that abrupt awareness of the likelihood of frustration can be as potent a source of anger as actual interference. The Vendée counterrevolution in eighteenth-century France was triggered by the announcement of military conscription, for example.[34] A survey of twentieth-century South African history shows that waves of East Indian and Bantu rioting historically have coincided with the parliamentary discussion of restrictive legislation more than with its actual imposition. The Indian food riots in the spring of 1966 were certainly not instigated by the onset of starvation but by its anticipation.

Second, it seems evident that the sense of deprivation can arise either from interference with goal-seeking behavior or from interference with continued enjoyment of an attained condition. As an example from psychological experimentation, frustration is often operationalized by insults; it seems more likely that the insults are a threat to the subjects' perceived level of status attainment or personal esteem than they are an interference with behavior directed toward some as-yet-unattained goal. Several examples from the history of civil violence are relevant. A student of the coup d'état that overthrew the Perón regime in Argentina states that the crucial events that precipitated the anti-Perónists into action were Perón's public insults to the Catholic hier-

[33] *Ibid.*, 28.
[34] Charles Tilly, *The Vendée* (Cambridge, Mass., 1964).

archy and isolated physical depredations by his supporters against Church properties—events symbolizing an attack on the moral foundations of upper-middle-class Argentine society.[35] In Soviet Central Asia, according to Massell, the most massive and violent resistance to Sovietization followed systematic attempts to break Muslim women loose from their slavish subordination to Muslim men.[36] The two kinds of interference may have differential effects on the intensity and consequences of anger; the point to be made here is that both can instigate violence.

Consequently, analysis of the sources of relative deprivation should take account of both actual and anticipated interference with human goals, as well as of interference with value positions both sought and achieved. Formulations of frustration in terms of the "want:get ratio," which refers only to a discrepancy between sought values and actual attainment, are too simplistic. Man lives mentally in the near future as much as in the present.[37] Actual or anticipated interference with what he has, and with the act of striving itself, are all volatile sources of discontent.

VALUE EXPECTATIONS

The propositions developed here concern the effects on perceived deprivation of the salience of an expectation for a group, rather than the absolute level of the expectation.[38] The first suggestion derived from psychological theory is that the more intensely people are motivated toward a goal, or committed to an attained level of values, the more sharply is interference resented and the greater is the consequent insti-

[35] Reuben de Hoyos, personal communication.

[36] Gregory Massell, "The Strategy of Social Change and the Role of Women in Soviet Central Asia: A Case Study in Modernization and Control," Ph.D. diss., Harvard University, 1966.

[37] For this kind of approach, see Daniel Lerner, "Toward a Communication Theory of Modernization: A Set of Considerations," in Lucian W. Pye, ed., *Communications and Political Development* (Princeton 1963), 330-35.

[38] This general statement of theory is concerned with specification of variables and their effects, not with their content in specific cases; hence the conditions that determine the *levels* of expectation and changes in those levels are not treated here, nor are the conditions that affect perceptions about value capabilities. For some attempts to generalize about such conditions see Ted Gurr, "The Genesis of Violence: A Multivariate Theory of Civil Strife," Ph.D. diss., New York University, 1965, esp. chaps. 6-8. For empirical evaluation or application of the theory, it is of course necessary to evaluate in some way levels of expectation in the population(s) studied. Some approaches to evaluation are illustrated in Ted Gurr with Charles Ruttenberg, *The Conditions of Civil Violence: First Tests of a Causal Model*, Center of International Studies, Princeton University, Research Monograph No. 28 (Princeton 1967), and Ted Gurr, "Explanatory Models for Civil Strife Using Aggregate Data," a paper read at the Annual Meeting of the American Political Science Association, 1967.

gation to aggression. One can, for example, account for some of the efficacy of ideologies in generating civil violence by reference to this variable. The articulation of nationalistic ideologies in colonial territories evidently strengthened preexisting desires for political independence among the colonial bourgeoisie at the same time that it inspired a wholly new set of political demands among other groups. Similarly, it has been argued that the desire of the nineteenth-century European factory worker for a better economic lot was intensified as well as rationalized by Marxist teachings.

Experimental evidence has suggested qualifications of the basic proposition which are equally relevant. One is that the closer men approach a goal, the more intensely motivated toward it they appear to be.[39] This finding has counterparts in observations about civil violence. Hoffer is representative of many theorists in noting that "discontent is likely to be highest when misery is bearable [and] when conditions have so improved that an ideal state seems almost within reach. . . . The intensity of discontent seems to be in inverse proportion to the distance from the object fervently desired."[40] The intensity of motivation varies with the perceived rather than the actual closeness of the goal, of course. The event that inflicts the sense of deprivation may be the realization that a goal thought to be at hand is still remote. The mechanism is clearly relevant to the genesis of post-independence violence in tropical Africa. Failure to realize the promises of independence in the Congo had extraordinarily virulent results, as is evident in a comparison of the intensive and extensive violence of the uprisings of the "Second Independence" of 1964-1965 with the more sporadic settling of accounts that followed the "First Independence" of 1960.[41]

The proposition relates as well to the severity of discontent in societies in the full swing of socioeconomic change. The rising bourgeoisie of eighteenth-century France, for example, individually and collectively had a major commitment to their improving conditions of life, and great effort invested in them. Many felt their aspirations for political influence and high social status to be close to realization but threatened by the declining responsiveness of the state and by economic deprivations inherent in stumbling state efforts to control trade and raise taxes.[42]

[39] See Berkowitz, *Aggression*, 53-54.
[40] Eric Hoffer, *The True Believer* (New York 1951), 27-28.
[41] Compare Crawford Young, *Politics in the Congo* (Princeton 1965), chap. 13, with commentaries on the Kwilu and Stanleyville rebellions, such as Renée C. Fox and others, " 'The Second Independence': A Case Study of the Kwilu Rebellion in the Congo," *Comparative Studies in Society and History*, VIII (October 1965), 78-109; and Herbert Weiss, *Political Protest in the Congo* (Princeton 1967).
[42] See, among many other works, Georges Lefebvre, *The Coming of the French Revolution* (Princeton 1947), Part II.

Although much additional evidence could be advanced, the relationships cited above are sufficient to suggest the following proposition and its corollaries:

Proposition I.2: The strength of anger tends to vary directly with the intensity of commitment to the goal or condition with regard to which deprivation is suffered or anticipated.

I.2a: The strength of anger tends to vary directly with the degree of effort previously invested in the attainment or maintenance of the goal or condition.

I.2b: The intensity of commitment to a goal or condition tends to vary inversely with its perceived closeness.

It also has been found that, under some circumstances, anticipation or experience of frustration tends to reduce motivation toward a goal. This is particularly the case if frustration is thought to be justified and likely.[43] Pastore, for example, reports that when subjects saw frustration as reasonable or justifiable, they gave fewer aggressive responses than when they perceived it to be arbitrary. Kregarman and Worchel, however, found that the reasonableness of a frustration did not significantly reduce aggression and that anticipation of frustration tended not to reduce anger but rather to inhibit external aggressive responses.[44]

The low levels of motivation and the moderate nature of interference that characterize these studies make generalization to "real," collective situations doubtful. If applied to a hypothetical example relevant to civil strife—say, the effects of increased taxation on a population under conditions of varying legitimacy attributed to the action—the experimental findings suggest three alternatives: (1) that anger varies inversely with the legitimacy attributed to interference; (2) that anger is constant, but inhibition of its expression varies directly with legitimacy; or (3) that no systematic relationship holds between the two. If the sources of legitimacy are treated in Merelman's learning-theory terms, the first of these alternatives appears most likely: if legitimacy is high, acceptance of deprivation (compliance) provides symbolic substitute rewards.[45]

---

[43] Value expectations are defined above in terms of the value positions to which men believe they are justifiably entitled; the discussion here assumes that men may also regard as justifiable some types of interference with those value positions.

[44] Nicholas Pastore, "The Role of Arbitrariness in the Frustration-Aggression Hypothesis," *Journal of Abnormal and Social Psychology*, XLVII (July 1952), 728-31; John J. Kregarman and Philip Worchel, "Arbitrariness of Frustration and Aggression," *Journal of Abnormal and Social Psychology*, LXIII (July 1961), 183-87.

[45] The argument is that people comply "to gain both the symbolic rewards of governmental action and the actual rewards with which government originally associated itself" and rationalize compliance with "the feeling that the regime is a morally appro-

It may also be that the first alternative holds in circumstances in which legitimacy is high, the second in circumstances in which it is moderate. The first relationship can be formulated in propositional form, with the qualification that evidence for it is less than definitive:

Proposition I.3: The strength of anger tends to vary inversely with the extent to which deprivation is held to be legitimate.

VALUE CAPABILITIES

The environment in which people strive toward goals has two general characteristics that, frustration-aggression theory suggests, affect the intensity of anger: the degree of interference with goal attainment and the number of opportunities provided for attainment.

Almost all the literature on civil strife assumes a causal connection between the existence of interference (or "frustration," "cramp," or "disequilibrium") and strife. "Discontent" and its synonyms are sometimes used to symbolize the condition of interference without reference to interference *per se*. A direct relationship between degree of interference and intensity of strife is usually implicit but not always demonstrated. Rostow has shown graphically that poor economic conditions—high wheat prices, high unemployment—corresponded with the severity of overt mass protest in England from 1790 to 1850.[46] Variations in bread prices and in mob violence went hand in hand in revolutionary France.[47] There is correlational evidence that the frequency of lynchings in the American South, 1882-1930, tended to vary inversely with indices of economic well-being.[48] From cross-national studies there is suggestive evidence also—for example, Kornhauser's correlation of —.93 between per capita income and the Communist share of the vote in sixteen Western democracies in 1949.[49] The Feierabends devised "frustration" measures, based on value capability characteristics of sixty-two nations, and correlated them with a general measure of degree of political stability, obtaining a correlation coefficient of .50.[50]

---

priate agent of control . . ." (Richard M. Merelman, "Learning and Legitimacy," *American Political Science Review*, LX [September 1966], 551). The argument applies equally well to compliance, including acceptance of deprivation, with the demands of other social institutions.

[46] Walt W. Rostow, *British Economy of the Nineteenth Century* (Oxford 1948), chap. 5.

[47] George Rudé, "Prices, Wages, and Popular Movements in Paris During the French Revolution," *Economic History Review*, VI (1954), 246-67, and *The Crowd in History, 1730-1848* (New York 1964), chap. 7.

[48] Carl Hovland and Robert Sears, "Minor Studies in Aggression, VI: Correlation of Lynchings with Economic Indices," *Journal of Psychology*, IX (1940), 301-10.

[49] William Kornhauser, *The Politics of Mass Society* (New York 1959), 160.

[50] "Aggressive Behaviors Within Polities."

As far as the precise form of the relationship between extent of interference and intensity of aggression is concerned, the experimental results of Hamblin and others are persuasive. Three hypotheses were
tested: the classic formulation that instigation to aggression varies directly with the degree of interference, and the psychophysical hypotheses that aggression ought to be a log or a power function of interference. The data strongly support the last hypothesis, that aggression is a
power function of degree of interference—i.e., if magnitude of aggression is plotted against degree of interference, the result is a sharply rising "J-curve." Moreover, the power exponent—the sharpness with
which the J-curve rises—appears to increase with the strength of motivation toward the goal with which interference was experienced.[51] It is
at least plausible that the J-curve relationship should hold for civil strife.
Compatible with this inference, though not bearing directly on it, is
the logarithmic distribution curve that characterizes such cross-polity
measures of intensity of civil violence as deaths per 100,000 population.[52]
It also may account for the impressionistic observation that moderate
levels of discontent typically lead to easily quelled turmoil but that
higher levels of discontent seem associated with incommensurately intense and persistent civil violence. In propositional form:

> *Proposition I.4*: The strength of anger tends to vary as a power
> function of the perceived distance between the value position
> sought or enjoyed and the attainable or residual value position.[53]

Experimental evidence regarding the hypothesis of Dollard and
others that the greater the number of frustrations, the greater the instigation to aggression is somewhat ambiguous. Most people appear to
have hierarchies of response to repeated frustration, a typical sequence
being intensified effort, including search for alternative methods or substitute goals, followed by increasingly overt aggression as other responses are extinguished, and ultimately by resignation or apparent acceptance of frustration. Berkowitz suggests that most such evidence,
however, is congruent with the interpretation that "the probability of
emotional reactions is a function of the degree to which all possible

---

[51] Robert L. Hamblin and others, "The Interference-Aggression Law?" *Sociometry*,
xxvi (1963), 190-216.

[52] Bruce M. Russett and others, *World Handbook of Political and Social Indicators*
(New Haven 1963), 97-100.

[53] There is a threshold effect with reference to physical well-being. If life itself is the
value threatened and the threat is imminent, the emotional response tends to be fear
or panic; once the immediate threat is past, anger against the source of threat tends to
manifest itself again. See n. 7 above, and Berkowitz, *Aggression*, 42-46.

nonaggressive responses are blocked, more than to the interference with any one response sequence."[54]

The societal equivalents of "all possible nonaggressive responses" can be regarded as all normative courses of action available to members of a collectivity for value attainment, plus all attainable substitute value positions. Relevant conditions are evident in the portraits of "transitional man" painted by Lerner and others. Those who are committed to improving their socioeconomic status are more likely to become bitterly discontented if they have few rather than many prospective employers, if they can get no work rather than some kind of work that provides a sense of progress, if they have few opportunities to acquire requisite literacy and technical skills, if associational means for influencing patterns of political and economic value distributions are not available, or if community life is so disrupted that hearth and kin offer no surcease from frustration for the unsuccessful worker.[55] All such conditions can be subsumed by the rubric of "opportunities for value attainment," with the qualification that perception of opportunities tends to be more crucial than actual opportunities.

Much evidence from studies of civil strife suggests that the greater are value opportunities, the less intense is civil violence. The argument appears in varying guises. Brogan attributes the comparative quiescence of mid-nineteenth-century English workers vis-à-vis their French counterparts in part to the proliferation in England of new cooperatives, friendly and building societies, and trade unions, which provided positive alternatives to violent protest.[56] The first of the American Negro urban rebellions in the 1960's occurred in a community, Watts, in which by contemporary accounts associational activity and job-training programs had been less effective than those of almost any other large Negro community. Cohn explains the high participation of unskilled workers and landless peasants in the violent millenarian frenzies of medieval Europe by reference to the lack of "the material and emotional support afforded by traditional social groups; their kinship groups had disintegrated and they were not effectively organised in village communities or in guilds; for them there existed no regular, institutionalised methods of voicing their grievances or pressing their claims."[57] Kling attributes the chronic Latin American pattern of coup d'état to

[54] Leonard Berkowitz, "Repeated Frustrations and Expectations in Hostility Arousal," *Journal of Abnormal and Social Psychology*, LX (May 1960), 422-29.

[55] See, for example, Daniel Lerner, *The Passing of Traditional Society* (Glencoe 1958).

[56] Denis W. Brogan, *The Price of Revolution* (London 1951), 34.

[57] Norman R. C. Cohn, *The Pursuit of the Millennium*, 2d ed. rev. (New York 1961), 315.

the lack of adequate alternatives facing elite aspirants with economic ambitions; political office, seized illicitly if necessary, provides opportunity for satisfying those ambitions.[58]

More general observations also are relevant. Economists suggest that government can relieve the discontents that accompany the strains of rapid economic growth by providing compensatory welfare measures— i.e., alternative means of value satisfaction.[59] Numerous scholars have shown that migration is a common response to deprivation and that high emigration rates often precede outbreaks of civil violence. In a cross-national study of correlates of civil violence for 1961-1963, I have found a rather consistent association between extensive educational opportunities, proportionally large trade union movements, and stable political party systems on the one hand and low levels of strife on the other, relationships that tend to hold among nations whatever their absolute level of economic development. Education presumably increases the apparent range of opportunity for socioeconomic advance, unionization can provide a secondary means for economic goal attainment, and parties serve as primary mechanisms for attainment of participatory political values.[60] Hence:

Proposition I.5: The strength of anger tends to vary directly with the proportion of all available opportunities for value attainment with which interference is experienced or anticipated.

THE MEDIATION OF ANGER: THE EFFECTS OF SOCIAL CONTROL AND SOCIAL FACILITATION

For the purpose of the theoretical model I assume that the average strength of anger in a population is a precise multiple function of the instigating variables. Whether or not civil violence actually occurs as a response to anger, and its magnitude when it does occur, are influenced by a number of mediating variables. Evidence for these variables and their effects is found both in the psychological literature and in studies of civil violence *per se*. It is useful to distinguish them according to whether they inhibit or facilitate the violent manifestation of anger.

SOCIAL CONTROL: THE EFFECTS OF RETRIBUTION

The classic formulation is that aggression may be inhibited through

---

[58] Merle Kling, "Toward a Theory of Power and Political Instability in Latin America," *Western Political Quarterly*, IX (March 1956), 21-35.

[59] Ridker, 15; Mancur Olson, Jr., "Growth as a Destabilizing Force," *Journal of Economic History*, XXIII (December 1963), 550-51.

[60] Gurr with Ruttenberg.

fear of "such responses on the part of the social environment as physical injury, insults, ostracism, and deprivation of goods or freedom."[61] Good experimental evidence indicates that anticipation of retribution is under some circumstances an effective regulator of aggression.[62] Comparably, a linear relationship between, on the one hand, the capacity and willingness of government to enforce its monopoly of control of the organized instrumentalities of force and, on the other, the likelihood of civil violence is widely assumed in the literature on civil strife. Strong apparent force capability on the part of the regime ought to be sufficient to deter violence, and if violence should occur, the effectiveness with which it is suppressed is closely related to the likelihood and intensity of subsequent violence. Smelser states that a major determinant of the occurrence of civil strife is declining capacity or loyalty of the police and military control apparatus.[63] Johnson says that "the success or failure of armed insurrection and . . . commonly even the decision to attempt revolution rest . . . upon the attitude (or the revolutionaries' estimate of that attitude) that the armed forces will adopt toward the revolution."[64] In Janos' view, the weakening of law-enforcement agencies "creates general disorder, inordinate concrete demands by various groups, and the rise of utopian aspirations."[65] Military defeat is often empirically associated with the occurrence of revolution. Race riots in the United States and elsewhere have often been associated with tacit approval of violence by authorities.[66] Paret and Shy remark that "terror was effective in Cyprus against a British government without sufficient political strength or will; it failed in Malaya against a British government determined and able to resist and to wait."[67]

It also has been proposed, and demonstrated in a number of experimental settings, that if aggression is prevented by fear of retribution or by retribution itself, this interference is frustrating and increases anger. Maier, for example, found in animal studies that under conditions of

[61] Dollard and others, 34.

[62] For summaries of findings, see Richard H. Walters, "Implications of Laboratory Studies of Aggression for the Control and Regulation of Violence," *Annals of the American Academy of Political and Social Science*, CCCLXIV (March 1966), 60-72; and Elton D. McNeil, "Psychology and Aggression," *Journal of Conflict Resolution*, III (September 1959), 225-31.

[63] Pp. 231-36, 261-68, 332, 365-79.

[64] Chalmers Johnson, *Revolution and the Social System* (Stanford 1964), 16-17.

[65] Andrew Janos, *The Seizure of Power: A Study of Force and Popular Consent*, Center of International Studies, Princeton University, Research Monograph No. 16 (Princeton 1964), 5.

[66] See, for example, H. O. Dahlke, "Race and Minority Riots: A Study in the Typology of Violence," *Social Forces*, XXX (May 1952), 419-25.

[67] Peter Paret and John W. Shy, *Guerrillas in the 1960's*, rev. ed. (New York 1964), 34-35.

severe frustration, punishment increased the intensity of aggression.[68] Walton inferred from such evidence that a curvilinear relationship ought to obtain between the degree of coerciveness of a nation and its degree of political instability, on the argument that low coerciveness is not frustrating and moderate coerciveness is more likely to frustrate than deter, while only the highest levels of coerciveness are sufficient to inhibit men from civil violence. A permissiveness-coerciveness scale for eighty-four nations, based on scope of political liberties, has been compared against the Feierabends' political stability scale, and the results strongly support the curvilinearity hypothesis.[69] Bwy, using a markedly different measure of coerciveness—one based on defense expenditures—found the same curvilinear relationship between coerciveness and "anomic violence" in Latin America.[70] Some theoretical speculation about civil strife implies the same relationship—for example, Lasswell and Kaplan's stipulation that the stability of an elite's position varies not with the actual use of violence but only with ability to use it,[71] and Parsons' more detailed "power deflation" argument that the repression of demands by force may inspire groups to resort to increasingly intransigent and aggressive modes of making those demands.[72]

One uncertainty about the curvilinear relationship between retribution and aggression is whether or not it holds whatever the extent of initial deprivation-induced anger. It is nonetheless evident that the threat or employment of force to suppress civil violence is by no means uniform in its effects, and that it tends to have a feedback effect that increases the instigation to violence. Such a relationship is diagrammed in Figure 1 and is explicit in the following proposition and its corollary:

> *Proposition M.1*: The likelihood and magnitude of civil violence tend to vary curvilinearly with the amount of physical or social retribution anticipated as a consequence of participation in it, with likelihood and magnitude greatest at medium levels of retribution.

> *M.1a*: Any decrease in the perceived likelihood of retribution tends to increase the likelihood and magnitude of civil violence.

These propositions and corollaries, and all subsequent propositions,

---

[68] *Frustration, passim.*

[69] Jennifer G. Walton, "Correlates of Coerciveness and Permissiveness of National Political Systems: A Cross-National Study," M.A. thesis, San Diego State College, 1965.

[70] Douglas Bwy, "Governmental Instability in Latin America: The Preliminary Test of a Causal Model of the Impulse to 'Extra-Legal' Change," paper read at the Annual Meeting of the American Psychological Association, 1966.

[71] Harold Lasswell and Abraham Kaplan, *Power and Society: A Framework for Political Inquiry* (New Haven 1950), 265-66.

[72] "Some Reflections on the Place of Force."

hold only, of course, if deprivation-induced anger exists. If the modal level of collective discontent is negligible, a condition that holds for at least some small, although few large, collectivities, the mediating variables have no inhibiting or facilitating effects by definition.

The propositions above do not exhaust frustration-aggression evidence about effects of retribution. Experimental evidence further indicates that a delay in the expression of the aggressive response increases its intensity when it does occur.[73] Observations about civil violence also suggest that the effects of feared retribution, especially external retribution, must take account of the time variable. The abrupt relaxation of authoritarian controls is repeatedly associated with intense outbursts of civil violence, despite the likelihood that such relaxation reduces relative deprivation. Examples from recent years include the East German and Hungarian uprisings after the post-Stalin thaw, the Congo after independence, and the Dominican Republic after Trujillo's assassination.

A parsimonious way to incorporate the time dimension into frustration-aggression theory is to argue that in the short run the delay of an aggressive response increases the intensity of anger and consequently the likelihood and magnitude of aggression, but that in the long run the level and intensity of expectations decline to coincide with the impositions of reality, and anger decreases concomitantly. Cognitive dissonance theory would suggest such an outcome: men tend to reduce persistent imbalances between cognitions and actuality by changing reality, or, if it proves intransigent, by changing their cognitive structures.[74] The proposed relationship is sketched in Figure 2.

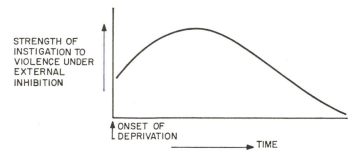

FIGURE 2. DISPLACEMENT OF INSTIGATION TO VIOLENCE OVER TIME

[73] J. W. Thibaut and J. Coules, "The Role of Communication in the Reduction of Interpersonal Hostility," *Journal of Abnormal and Social Psychology*, XLVII (October 1952), 770-77.

[74] See Leon Festinger, *A Theory of Cognitive Dissonance* (Evanston 1957).

One example of experimental evidence to this point is the finding of Cohen and others that once subjects became accustomed to certain kinds of frustration—withdrawal of social reinforcement in the experimental situation used—they were less likely to continue to seek the desired value or condition.[75] One can, moreover, speculate that the time-scale is largely a function of the intensity of commitment to the frustrated response or condition. The effects of South Africa's apartheid policies and the means of their enforcement offer an example. These policies, which impose substantial and diverse value-deprivations on non-whites, especially those in urban areas, were put into effect principally in the 1950's. Violent protests over their implementation were repressed with increasing severity, culminating in the Sharpeville massacre of 1960 and a series of strikes and riots. By the mid-1960's, when deprivation was objectively more severe than at any time previously in the twentieth century, levels of civil strife were very low, inferentially the result of very high levels of deterrence (feared retribution). Since deprivation remains severe and has affected a wide range of values, avoidance of violence in this case probably would require the maintenance of very high and consistent deterrence levels beyond the active life-span of most of those who have personally experienced the initial value-deprivation. Any short-run decline in the perceived likelihood or severity of retribution, however, is highly likely to be followed by intense violence. In propositional form:

> *Proposition M.2*: Inhibition of civil violence by fear of external retribution tends in the short run to increase the strength of anger but in the long run to reduce it.

> *M.2a*: The duration of increased anger under conditions of inhibition tends to vary with the intensity of commitment to the value with respect to which deprivation is suffered.

SOCIAL CONTROL: THE EFFECTS OF INSTITUTIONALIZED DISPLACEMENT

On the evidence, the effects of repression in managing discontent are complex and potentially self-defeating in the short run. Displacement theory suggests means that are considerably more effective. Several aspects of displacement theory are relevant for civil violence. Among Miller's basic propositions about object and response generalization is the formulation that the stronger the fear of retribution relative to the

---

[75] Arthur R. Cohen and others, "Commitment to Social Deprivation and Verbal Conditioning," *Journal of Abnormal and Social Psychology*, LXVII (November 1963), 410-21.

strength of anger, the more dissimilar will the target of aggression be from the source of interference and the more indirect will be the form of aggression.[76] With reference to object generalization, Berkowitz has proposed and demonstrated that hostility tends to generalize from a frustrater to previously disliked individuals or groups.[77] A counterpart of this thesis is that displaced aggressive responses tend to be expressed in previously used forms.

Examples of object generalization in civil violence are legion. Several studies have shown positive relationships between poor economic conditions and lynchings of Negroes in the American South.[78] An initial reaction of urban white colonialists to African rural uprisings in Madagascar in 1947 and Angola in 1961 was vigilante-style execution of urban Africans who had no connections with the rebellions. English handweavers, when their livelihood was threatened by the introduction of new weaving machines, destroyed thousands of machines in the Luddite riots of 1811-1816, but almost never directly attacked the employers who installed the machines and discharged superfluous workers.[79]

Object generalization is a crucial variable in determining who will be attacked by the initiators of particular acts of civil violence, but is only peripheral to the primary concern of the theory, the determination of likelihood and magnitude of violence as such. Most important in this regard is the psychological evidence regarding response generalization. Experimental evidence suggests that only a narrow range of objects provides satisfying targets for men's aggressive responses, but that almost any form of aggression can be satisfying so long as the angry person believes that he has in some way injured his supposed frustrater.[80]

By extension to the collectivity, insofar as adequate response displacement options are available, much anger may be diverted into activity short of civil violence. The evidence is diverse and extensive that participation in political activity, labor unions, and millenarian religious

[76] Neal E. Miller, "Theory and Experiment Relating Psychoanalytic Displacement to Stimulus-Response Generalization," *Journal of Abnormal and Social Psychology*, XLIII (April 1948), 155-78.

[77] *Aggression*, chap. 6.

[78] See n. 48 above.

[79] Rudé, *The Crowd in History*, chap. 5. The high levels of verbal aggression directed against the employers suggest that displacement was involved, not a perception of the machines rather than employers as sources of deprivation. In the Luddite riots, fear of retribution for direct attacks on the owners, contrasted with the frequent lack of sanctions against attacks on the machines, was the probable cause of object generalization. In the Madagascar and Angola cases structural and conceptual factors were responsible: the African rebels were not accessible to attack but local Africans were seen as like them and hence as potential or clandestine rebels.

[80] Some such evidence is summarized in Berkowitz, "The Concept of Aggressive Drive," 325-27.

movements can be a response to relative deprivation which permits more or less nonviolent expression of aggression. Studies of voting in the United States show that politicians in farm states are rather consistently voted out of office after periods of low rainfall and that the occurrence of natural disasters may lead to hostility against officials.[81] Extremist voting—which may be regarded as nonviolent aggression—in nine European countries during the Depression has been shown to correlate +.85 with the percentage of the labor force unemployed.[82] Studies of labor movements repeatedly document the transformation of labor protest from violent to nonviolent forms as unionization increases. Comparative and case studies similarly document the development of aggressive millenarian religious movements as a response to natural disaster or political repression, in places and eras as diverse as medieval Europe, colonial Africa, and among the indigenous peoples of the Americas and the South Pacific.[83]

This is not to imply that displacement is a sole or exclusive function of such institutions. Their instrumental functions for participants (Proposition I.5) can be crucial: peaceful political and union activism are alternative means to goals whose attainment by other means is often impaired; religious chiliasm provides hope and belief for those whose social universe has been destroyed. But insofar as men become accustomed to express discontents through such institutional mechanisms, the likelihood that anger will lead to civil violence is diminished. In propositional form:

> *Proposition M.3*: The likelihood and magnitude of civil violence tend to vary inversely with the availability of institutional mechanisms that permit the expression of nonviolent hostility.

SOCIAL FACILITATION: COGNITIVE FACTORS

Experimental, developmental, and field studies of the effects of rewarding individual aggression demonstrate that habitual aggression may be developed and maintained through intermittent rewards and may also be generalized to situations other than those in which the habits were acquired.[84] A number of experiments indicate that the pres-

---

[81] A critical and qualifying review of evidence to this effect is F. Glenn Abney and Larry B. Hill, "Natural Disasters as a Political Variable: The Effect of a Hurricane on an Urban Election," *American Political Science Review*, LX (December 1966), 974-81.

[82] Kornhauser, 161. For interview evidence on the motives of protest voting, see Hadley Cantril, *The Politics of Despair* (New York 1958).

[83] Representative studies are Cohn; James W. Fernandez, "African Religious Movements: Types and Dynamics," *Journal of Modern African Studies*, II, No. 4 (1964), 531-49; and Vittorio Lanternari, *The Religions of the Oppressed* (New York 1963).

[84] Summarized in Walters.

ence of cues or stimuli associated with anger instigators is necessary for most aggressive responses to occur. A summary proposition is that "a target with appropriate stimulus qualities 'pulls' (evokes) aggressive responses from a person who is ready to engage in such actions either because he is angry or because particular stimuli have acquired cue values for aggressive responses from him."[85]

For members of a collectivity a variety of common experiences can contribute to the acquisition of aggressive habits and the recognition of aggression-evoking cues. Among them are socialization patterns that give normative sanction to some kinds of aggressive behavior; traditions of violent conflict; and exposure to new generalized beliefs that justify violence. The literature on civil violence suggests at least four specific modes by which such experiences facilitate violent responses to deprivation. They can (1) stimulate mutual awareness among the deprived, (2) provide explanations for deprivation of ambiguous origin, (3) specify accessible targets and appropriate forms of violence, and (4) state long-range objectives to be attained through violence.

Subcultural traditions of violent protest are well documented in European history. The frequency with which Parisian workers and shopkeepers took to the streets in the years and decades following the great *journées* of 1789 is one example. At least 275 food riots, most of them similar in form and sequence, took place in rural England between 1725 and 1800 in close correlation with harvest failures and high food prices.[86] Hobsbawm points out that in Southern Italy "every political change in the nineteenth century, irrespective from what quarter it came, automatically produced its ceremonial marches of peasants with drums and banners to occupy the land," while in Andalusia "millenarian revolutionary waves occurred at roughly ten-year intervals for some sixty or seventy years."[87] Lynching as a Southern white response to Negro transgressions and the mobbing of white policemen by Negroes are comparable expressions of subcultural traditions that facilitate civil violence.

The theoretical point is that the initial occurrences of civil violence among some homogeneous group of the deprived—those events that set the pattern—tend to be nonrational responses to extreme deprivation. If violence provides a satisfactory outlet for tensions or if it motivates authorities to remedy the sources of deprivation, civil violence

[85] Leonard Berkowitz, "Aggressive Cues in Aggressive Behavior and Hostility Catharsis," *Psychological Review*, LXXI (March 1964), 104-22, quotation from 106.

[86] Rudé, *The Crowd in History*, 19-45.

[87] E. J. Hobsbawm, *Social Bandits and Primitive Rebels*, 2nd ed. (Glencoe 1959), 63-64.

tends to become a sanctioned group activity. The fact that normative support for violence thus develops does not mean that violence subsequently occurs without instigation. Deprivation remains a necessary precondition for violence; the strength of anger at which it is likely to occur is lowered.

A related source of attitudinal support for collective violence is the articulation of ideology or, more generally, what Smelser calls generalized belief among the deprived. Such beliefs, ranging from rumors to fully articulated ideologies, are said to develop in situations characterized by social strain that is unmanageable within the existing framework for social action.[88] It is evident that in many social settings relative deprivation is manifest but its sources obscure. In psychological terms, no cues associated with the anger instigator are present. The agency responsible for an unwanted tax increase is apparent to the most ignorant villager; the causes of economic depression or of the disintegration of traditional mores are often unclear even to economists and sociologists. A new ideology, folk-belief, or rumor can serve to define and explain the nature of the situation, to identify those responsible for it, and to specify appropriate courses of action.

Moreover, there usually are a number of competing generalized beliefs circulating among the deprived. Those most likely to gain acceptance tend to be those with substantial aggressive components, i.e., those that rationalize and focus the innate drive to aggression. Cohn's comparative study of the waves of chiliastic excitement that swept medieval Europe in times of plague and famine, for example, documents the fact that the heresies that most effectively mobilized the deprived were those that suited or could be molded to their states of mind: "when . . . eschatological doctrines penetrated to the uprooted and desperate masses in town and country they were re-edited and reinterpreted until in the end they were capable of inspiring revolutionary movements of a peculiarly anarchic kind."[89]

Some of these observations can be summarized in this proposition and its corollary:

Proposition M.4: The likelihood and magnitude of civil violence tend to vary directly with the availability of common experiences and beliefs that sanction violent responses to anger.

M.4a: Given the availability of alternative experiences and beliefs, the likelihood that the more aggressive of them will prevail tends to vary with the strength of anger.

[88] Chap. 5.   [89] P. 31.

SOCIAL FACILITATION: SOURCES OF GROUP SUPPORT FOR VIOLENCE

A classic subject of social psychological theory is the extent to which some social settings facilitate overt aggression. It is incontrovertible that individuals tend to behave in crowds differently from the way they act alone. The crowd psychologies of scholars such as Le Bon and Sorokin have emphasized the "unconscious" nature of crowd behavior and its "de-individuating" effects.[90] It appears more fruitful to examine experimentally identified variables that contribute to the "crowd behavior" phenomenon. From this point of departure one can distinguish at least three modes by which groups affect individuals' disposition to violence: (1) by providing normative support, (2) by providing apparent protection from retribution, and (3) by providing cues for violent behavior.

1. *Normative support.* There is good experimental evidence that individuals alone or in poorly cohesive groups are less likely to express hostility than those in highly cohesive groups. Members of highly cohesive friendship groups respond to external frustrations with greater hostility than randomly formed groups. Similarly, if individuals believe that their peers generally agree with them about a frustrater, their public display of antagonism more closely resembles their privately expressed antagonism than if they do not perceive peer agreement.[91]

Theoretical and empirical studies of civil violence repeatedly refer to the causal efficacy of comparable conditions. Social theorists describe the perception of anonymity and of universality of deprivation characteristic of riotous crowds. Hopper's classic picture of group interaction under conditions of relative deprivation in the early stages of the revolutionary process is relevant: by participating in mass or shared behavior, discontented people become aware of one another; "their negative reactions to the basic factors in their situations are shared and begin to spread. . . . Discontent . . . tends to become focalized and collective."[92] Comparative studies of labor unrest show that the most strike-prone industries are those whose workers are relatively homogeneous and isolated from the general community.[93] Some of the efficacy of revolu-

[90] Gustave Le Bon, *The Psychology of Revolution* (London 1913); Pitirim Sorokin, *The Sociology of Revolutions* (Philadelphia 1925).

[91] Representative studies include J. R. P. French, Jr., "The Disruption and Cohesion of Groups," *Journal of Abnormal and Social Psychology*, XXXVI (July 1941), 361-77; A. Pepitone and G. Reichling, "Group Cohesiveness and the Expression of Hostility," *Human Relations*, VIII, No. 3 (1955), 327-37; and Ezra Stotland, "Peer Groups and Reactions to Power Figures," in Dorwin Cartwright, ed., *Studies in Social Power* (Ann Arbor 1959), 53-68.

[92] Pp. 272-75, quotation from 273.

[93] Clark Kerr and Abraham Siegel, "The Isolated Mass and the Integrated Individual:

tionary brotherhoods and tightly knit bands of rebels in prosecuting civil violence can be interpreted in terms of the reinforcement of mutual perception of deprivation and the justification of violence as a response to it.

2. *Protection from retribution.* Groups appear capable of reducing fears of external retribution for violence in at least three ways. Crowd situations in particular provide members with a shield of anonymity. In an experimental study by Meier and others, two-thirds of subjects who were prepared to join a lynching mob said, *inter alia,* that they would do so because in the crowd they could not be punished. The same relationship is apparent in the handful of studies made of riot participants: crowd members usually feel insulated from retribution.[94]

Organized groups can provide apparent protection from retribution by acquiring sufficient force capability to prevent the agents of retribution—i.e., military and internal security forces—from effectively reaching them. Increases in the relative force capability of a deprived group may also reinforce rationalization for violence by raising hopes of success or may merely facilitate the expression of rage by providing desperate men with the means to strike at tormentors who had previously been unassailable.

A third aspect of group protectiveness is the perceived effect of hierarchical organization and the presence of highly visible leaders. Leaders of revolutionary organizations, in addition to their other manifest functions, not only foment but assume responsibility for illicit violence. Their followers tend to see such leaders as the likely objects of retaliatory efforts and hence feel less personal risk.

3. *Cues for violence.* The transition from anger to aggression is not automatic or even abrupt. Laboratory studies of imitative behavior repeatedly document the significance of aggression-releasing cues provided by social models. The act of punishing aggression itself can serve as a model for imitation by the person punished. Aggression-releasing cues need not necessarily originate with high-status persons. Polansky and others found that when frustrations were imposed on groups of children, "impulsive" but low-status children were both initiators and ready followers of aggressive behavioral contagion. On the other hand, not any aggressive model evokes aggression from angered subjects; the

An International Analysis of the Inter-Industry Propensity to Strike," in Arthur Kornhauser and others, eds., *Industrial Conflict* (New York 1954), 189-212.

[94] Norman C. Meier and others, "An Experimental Approach to the Study of Mob Behavior," *Journal of Abnormal and Social Psychology,* xxxvi (October 1941), 506-24. Also see George Wada and James C. Davies, "Riots and Rioters," *Western Political Quarterly,* x (December 1957), 864-74.

models that evoke greatest aggression are those associated with the subjects' present situation or with settings in which they were previously aggressive.[95]

Angry crowds of men also appear to require some congruent image or model of violent action before they will seize cobblestones or rope or rifles to do violence to fellow citizens. Such models may be symbolic: invocation of a subcultural tradition of violence by a leader, or articulation of a new generalized belief that is explicit in its prescription of violence. In general, however, a "call to arms" or an appeal to a tradition of violence appears less effective by itself than when accompanied by the sight or news of violence. The calculated use of terrorism by rebels can have such an effect, and so can a soldier's random shot into a crowd of demonstrators. Many specific cases of civil violence have been set off by comparable acts of violence elsewhere. "Revolutionary contagion" is evident in the 1830 and 1848 waves of European revolutionary upheavals and in the post-Stalin uprisings in Eastern Europe and Siberia. The same phenomenon is apparent in the initiation of innumerable cases of small-scale, unstructured violence. Series of riots in rural France and England have graphically been shown to spread outward from one or a few centers, riots occurring in the furthest villages days or weeks after the initial incident. Such patterning is evident, to mention a few cases, in the French Corn Riots of 1775, the "Plug-Plot" riots around Manchester in 1842, and the incidence of farmers' protest meetings and riots in Brittany in the summer of 1961.[96] The demonstration effect apparent in such series of events appears to have affected their form and timing more than the likelihood of the occurrence of strife. The people who responded to the events were already angered; they probably would have erupted into violence in some form sometime in the proximate future.

These three modes of group facilitation of civil violence can be summarized in propositional form:

Proposition M.5: The likelihood and magnitude of civil violence tend to vary directly with the extent to which the deprived occupy organizational and/or ecological settings that provide (1) normative support through high levels of interaction, (2) apparent protection from retribution, and (3) congruent models for violent behavior.

---

[95] See Walters; Norman Polansky and others, "An Investigation of Behavioral Contagion in Groups," *Human Relations*, iii, No. 3 (1950), 319-48; and Leonard Berkowitz and Russell G. Geen, "Film Violence and the Cue Properties of Available Targets," *Journal of Personality and Social Psychology*, iii (June 1966), 525-30.

[96] Rudé, *The Crowd in History*; Henri Mendras and Yves Tavernier, "Les Manifestations de juin 1961," *Revue française des sciences politiques*, xii (September 1962), 647-71.

The Forms of Civil Violence

The theoretical framework comprising the ten propositions is formally restricted to physically violent collective behavior. It is likely that it is as applicable to a still larger class of events, including those characterized by the threat of violence or by high levels of verbal aggression —for example, bloodless coups, demonstrations, and political strikes. Violent events tend to be more salient for the political system, however, and for most operational purposes constitute a more workable and clearly defined universe.

I have not discussed the propositions with reference to specific forms of civil violence on grounds that all of the variables specified are relevant to each form specified in current typologies.[97] It is nonetheless likely that the propositions are of differential weight for different forms, and it is useful to demonstrate how variations in form may be generally accounted for in the context of the theoretical model. The first question to be asked is how detailed a listing of forms one should attempt to account for. A series of factor analytic studies provide a systematic, empirical answer to that question. In each of eleven studies, data on the incidence and characteristics of various types of strife were collected and tabulated, by country, and the "country scores" (number of riots, assassinations, deaths from civil violence, coups, mutinies, guerrilla wars, and so on, in a given time period) were factor analyzed. Whatever the typology employed, the period of reference, or the set of countries, essentially the same results were obtained. A strong *turmoil* dimension emerges, characterized by largely spontaneous strife such as riots, demonstrations, and nonpolitical clashes, quite distinct from what we may call a *revolutionary* dimension, characterized by more organized and intense strife. This revolutionary dimension has two components, appearing in some analyses as separate dimensions: *internal war*, typically including civil war, guerrilla war, and some coups; and *conspiracy*, typically including plots, purges, mutinies, and most coups.[98] Events within each of the three types tend to occur together; events within any two or all three categories are less likely to do so. The implication is

[97] Representative typologies are proposed by Johnson, *Revolution and the Social System*, 26-68; Rudolph J. Rummel, "Dimensions of Conflict Behavior Within and Between Nations," *Yearbook of the Society for General Systems Research*, VIII (1963), 25-26; and Harry Eckstein, "Internal Wars: A Taxonomy," unpubl. (1960).

[98] Two summary articles on these factor analyses are Rudolph J. Rummel, "A Field Theory of Social Action With Application to Conflict Within Nations," *Yearbook of the Society for General Systems Research*, X (1965), 183-204; and Tanter. What I call internal war is referred to in these sources as subversion; I label conspiracy what these sources call revolution. My terminology is, I believe, less ambiguous and more in keeping with general scholarly usage.

that they are substantively distinct forms of strife for each of which separate explanation is required.

Two complementary approaches to accounting for these three basic types of civil violence can be proposed within the context of the theoretical model. The first is that the two major dimensions, turmoil and revolution, reflect the varying class incidence of deprivation among societies. The defining characteristic of "turmoil" events is mass participation, usually rather spontaneous, disorganized, and with low intensity of violence; the forms of "revolution" reflect organized, often instrumental and intense, application of violence. The ability to rationalize, plan, and put to instrumental use their own and others' discontent is likely to be most common among the more skilled, highly educated members of a society—its elite aspirants. Thus if the incidence of mass deprivation is high but elite deprivation low, the most likely form of civil violence is turmoil. But if severe discontent is common to a substantial, alienated group of elite aspirants, then organized, intensive strife is likely.

The forms of revolution differ principally in their scale and tactics: internal wars are large-scale, and their tactics are typically to neutralize the regime's military forces; conspirators, usually few in number, attempt to subvert the regime by striking at its key members.

The differences between internal war and conspiracy can be accounted for by several characteristics. If severe deprivation is restricted largely to elite aspirants, the consequence is likely to be "conspiracy" phenomena such as plots, coups d'état, and barracks revolts. If discontent is widespread among substantial numbers of both mass and elite aspirants, the more likely consequence is large-scale, organized violence —civil and guerrilla war. The strategic position of the discontented elite aspirants may be relevant as well. If they are subordinate members of the existing elite hierarchy, they are likely to attack the regime from within, hence coups, mutinies, and plots. If they are instead excluded from formal membership in the elite though they possess elite qualities —acquired, for example, through foreign education—they must organize violent resistance from without. These are essentially Seton-Watson's explanations for the relative frequency of conspiracy in underdeveloped societies compared with the frequency of massive revolutionary movements in more developed states. In summary, "it is the combination of backward masses, extremist intellectuals and despotic bureaucrats which creates the most conspiratorial movements."[99]

[99] Hugh Seton-Watson, "Twentieth Century Revolutions," *Political Quarterly*, XXII (July 1951), 258.

These observations are of course only the beginning of an accounting of the forms of civil strife. They are intended to demonstrate, however, that such a theoretical explanation not only is compatible with but can be formulated within the framework of the theoretical model by showing the loci of deprivation in a society. They can be stated thus in propositional form:

Proposition F.1: The characteristic form of civil violence tends to vary with the differential incidence of relative deprivation among elite aspirants and masses: (1) mass deprivation alone tends to be manifested in large-scale civil violence with minimal organization and low intensity; (2) elite-aspirant deprivation tends to be manifested in highly organized civil violence of high intensity.

F.1a: Whether organized and intense civil violence is large-scale or small-scale is a joint function of the extent of mass deprivation and the strategic access of deprived elite aspirants to the incumbent political elite.

Conclusion

I have advanced eleven general propositions about the variables operative in generating and structuring violent political unrest. They are based on the assumption that the frustration-aggression mechanism, however culturally modified, is the source of most men's disposition to illicit collective violence. The propositions do not constitute a theory of the revolutionary process or of the outcomes of strife, but of the conditions that determine the *likelihood* and *magnitude* of strife. On the other hand, the variables stipulated by the propositions are not irrelevant to revolutionary processes. Process models can be formulated wholly or partly in terms of changing patterns of weights on the component variables.

It is likely that most "causes" and "correlates" of the occurrence and intensity of civil strife can be subsumed by these variables, with one exception: foreign intervention. This exception is no oversight but simply recognition that decisions to intervene are external to domestic participants in civil strife. The effects of foreign intervention can be readily interpreted by reference to the model, however: intervention on behalf of the deprived is likely to strengthen group support (M.5) and may, as well, heighten and intensify value expectations (I.2). Foreign assistance to a threatened regime is most likely to raise retribution levels (M.1), but may also alter aspects of value capabilities (I.4, I.5) and strengthen justification for violence among the deprived, insofar as they identify foreigners with invaders (M.4).

The framework has not been elaborated merely to provide a satisfying theoretical reconstruction of the general causes of civil violence. It is intended primarily as a guide for empirical research using the techniques of both case and comparative studies. The framework stipulates the variables for which information should be sought in any thorough case study of the origins of an act of civil strife.[100] For purposes of comparative analysis it stipulates relationships that should hold among cultures and across time. Its most important objectives are to encourage empirical validation of its component propositions in a variety of contexts by a variety of operational means, and specification of their separate weights and interacting effects in those contexts.[101]

[100] For example, it has been used by Bryant Wedge to analyze and compare interview materials gathered in the study of two Latin American revolutions, in "Student Participation in Revolutionary Violence: Brazil, 1964, and Dominican Republic, 1965," a paper read at the Annual Meeting of the American Political Science Association, 1967.

[101] Studies based on this theoretical model and using cross-national aggregate data include Ted Gurr, *New Error-Compensated Measures for Comparing Nations: Some Correlates of Civil Strife*, Center of International Studies, Princeton University, Research Monograph No. 25 (Princeton 1966); Gurr with Ruttenberg; Gurr, "Explanatory Models for Civil Strife"; and Gurr, "Why Urban Disorders? Perspectives From the Comparative Study of Civil Strife," *American Behavioral Scientist* (forthcoming).

TOWARD EXPLAINING MILITARY INTERVENTION IN LATIN AMERICAN POLITICS

By ROBERT D. PUTNAM*

I. INTRODUCTION

MILITARY intervention in politics is extremely common. Outside the North Atlantic area, the armed forces are more likely than not to be among the most important power contenders in any political system, and military regimes are at least as widespread as either totalitarian or democratic ones. It is surprising, therefore, that until recently this phenomenon has attracted little attention from students of politics. Though there has been some speculation about the causes of military intervention, our actual knowledge of the subject is meager indeed.

The preeminence of the military in politics in Latin America has long been recognized, but, even in this case, as recently as 1960 George Blanksten could complain that "political studies of the Latin American armed services are sorely needed."[1] Aside from a few vague remarks about "Hispanic heritage" and "backwardness," virtually no empirically based explanations of Latin American militarism have been offered. Since Blanksten wrote, of course, Johnson and Lieuwen have undertaken excellent analyses of this topic, but both authors' works have been primarily historical studies of the development and extent of military intervention in various countries, rather than verified, general explications of the causes of this phenomenon.[2]

A study of the factors that account for the varying political role of the military in Latin America would thus be useful both for students of Latin American politics and for students of comparative politics generally. Latin America constitutes in many respects an ideal "labora-

---

* I should like to thank the following individuals for their help in the preparation of this research note: Hayward R. Alker, Jr., Karl W. Deutsch, Robert H. Dix, Richard Simeon, and Rosemary Putnam.

[1] "The Politics of Latin America," in Gabriel A. Almond and James S. Coleman, eds., *The Politics of the Developing Areas* (Princeton 1960), 502.

[2] John J. Johnson, *The Military and Society in Latin America* (Stanford 1964); Edwin Lieuwen, *Arms and Politics in Latin America* (New York 1961) and *Generals vs. Presidents* (New York 1964).

tory" for analyzing militarism. The range of military involvement is great—from "pure" military regimes, such as Argentina's present regime, to "constitutional" military regimes, such as El Salvador's, to military "protectorates," such as Brazil's, to civil-military coalitions, such as Argentina's under Perón, to regimes in which the military is merely one among numerous important "power groups," such as Mexico's, to regimes in which the military is virtually nonpolitical, such as Costa Rica's. In this "laboratory," certain independent variables are held constant—colonial background, nature of the struggle for independence, length of independence, religious background, cultural authority patterns.[3] This means that we cannot examine the impact of these constants on the propensity for military intervention, but it does allow us to focus more clearly on other possible explanations. The purpose of this research note is to investigate in this Latin American "laboratory" some of the more important speculations about the sources of military involvement in politics.

II. Theoretical Propositions

A survey of the literature on military intervention in politics discloses four broad categories of factors suggested as causes of, or conditions for, intervention or abstention: (1) aspects of socioeconomic development; (2) aspects of political development; (3) characteristics of the military establishment itself; and (4) foreign influences. I shall here present and explicate the relevant hypotheses and shall refrain from setting out the broader theoretical perspectives of the various authors.[4] In particular, I shall limit my attention to propositions that answer the question, What accounts for the varying incidence of military intervention in politics? (There are many other interesting questions in this general area, concerning the political and ideological orientations of military regimes, the political, social, and economic consequences of military intervention, and so on, but these will be ignored here.)

[3] Certain of these variables are, to be sure, not entirely constant throughout the area, but they are so nearly so as to warrant ignoring their effects.

[4] The following works were consulted in preparing this inventory of theoretical propositions: Robert J. Alexander, "The Army in Politics," in H. E. Davis, ed., *Government and Politics in Latin America* (New York 1958); Stanislaw Andrzejewski, *Military Organization and Society* (London 1954); Samuel E. Finer, *The Man on Horseback* (New York 1962); William F. Gutteridge, *Military Institutions and Power in the New States* (New York 1965); Samuel P. Huntington, *The Soldier and the State* (Cambridge, Mass., 1957); Morris Janowitz, *The Military in the Political Development of New Nations* (Chicago 1964); John J. Johnson, ed., *The Role of the Military in Underdeveloped Countries* (Princeton 1962); and the works cited in footnote 2.

One of the most common hypotheses links the propensity for military intervention with social and economic underdevelopment. Samuel Finer argues that *the propensity for military intervention is likely to decrease with increased social mobilization.*[5] The concept of social mobilization refers to such developments as urbanization, the rise of mass education and mass communications, the development of a money economy, and increased mass participation in social and political activities and associations. Social mobilization increases the number of potential political actors and diffuses increased political resources to these actors. The assumption underlying this hypothesis is that these actors will be willing and able to sustain civilian political institutions.[6]

Finer and others have also argued that *economic development, especially industrialization, diminishes the propensity for military intervention.*[7] This effect of economic development stems partly from the increased socio-technical complexity that puts public administration beyond the skills of the armed forces, partly from the civilian opportunities for social mobility which economic development opens up, and partly from greater wealth, which allows and encourages stable, civilian government.[8] Germani and Silvert have articulated a hypothesis hinted at by others, namely, that *military intervention is inhibited by the rise of middle strata in the social structure*, since these middle strata have in especial measure both the motivation and the ability to create and sustain stable civilian political institutions.[9] These same authors also argue that *the likelihood of military intervention is greater, the greater the cleavages and the less the consensus in a society.* (This proposition is related to the proposition discussed below linking military intervention and political violence.)

A second set of variables, correlated with but distinct from those involving social mobilization and economic development, may be grouped under the heading "political development." The most obvious hypothesis, as stated by Finer, is that *"where public attachment to civilian institutions is strong, military intervention in politics will be*

[5] Pp. 87-88. The term "social mobilization" (which Finer himself does not use) was introduced in this sense by Karl W. Deutsch in "Social Mobilization and Political Development," *American Political Science Review,* LV (September 1961), 493-514.

[6] Huntington's counterhypothesis linking social mobilization with *increased* military intervention is discussed later in this section.

[7] Finer, 113-15; Alexander, 158.

[8] Janowitz's attack on this proposition (pp. 18-20) is weakened by his failure to distinguish the military-civilian dimension from the democratic-authoritarian dimension and by his failure to recognize that a correlation can be important without being perfect.

[9] Gino Germani and Kalman Silvert, "Politics, Social Structure and Military Intervention in Latin America," *Archives Européennes de Sociologie,* II (Spring 1961), 62-81.

weak. . . . Where public attachment to civilian institutions is weak or non-existent, military intervention in politics will find wide scope—both in manner and in substance."[10] Though this proposition is important, it is also somewhat unsatisfying, for it fails to take our search for explanation very far from the phenomenon that we are trying to explain. A more interesting hypothesis, suggested by Finer, Johnson, and others, is that *the propensity for military intervention in politics decreases with increasing popular attention to and participation in politics.*[11] Another set of hypotheses relates military intervention to weaknesses in civilian political institutions: *military intervention decreases with increasing strength and effectiveness of political parties, of political interest groups, and of civilian governmental institutions.*[12] Huntington's theory of political development and decay stresses the importance of "the institutionalization of political organizations and procedures." "Political decay"—of which a notable symptom is military intervention—arises out of an imbalance between social mobilization and political institutionalization. Therefore, *the greater the social mobilization and the less the political institutionalization, the greater the likelihood of military intervention.*[13] A final aspect of political development that is relevant here concerns the role of violence. Lieuwen and Needler have argued that *the tendency toward military intervention increases with increasing political violence.*[14] Obviously, the military have an important advantage in a political game where violence is trump, for that is their strong suit.

The third set of hypotheses concerns the way internal characteristics of a military establishment affect its predisposition to political intervention. *"Professionalization" of the military is linked with decreased military intervention* (Huntington) *and with increased military intervention* (Finer).[15] This apparent contradiction can perhaps be resolved if we consider a few of the possible components of "professionalization." Many students of civil-military relations have suggested that *military intervention decreases with the development within the military of a norm of civilian supremacy.*[16] As with the proposition linking military

[10] P. 21.

[11] Finer, 87; John J. Johnson, "The Latin-American Military as a Politically Competing Group in Transitional Society," in Johnson, ed., *Role of the Military*, 127.

[12] Finer, 21, 87-88, 115; Alexander, 157.

[13] Samuel P. Huntington, "Political Development and Political Decay," *World Politics*, xvii (April 1965), 386-430.

[14] Lieuwen, "Militarism and Politics in Latin America," in Johnson, ed., *Role of the Military*, 132-33; Martin C. Needler, *Latin American Politics in Perspective* (New York 1963), 76.

[15] Huntington, *The Soldier and the State*, 84; Finer, 24ff.

[16] For example, Finer, 32.

abstention with the legitimacy of civilian institutions, the proposed explanatory factor in this hypothesis is "too close" to the phenomenon to be explained. On the other hand, if the hypothesis is given a historical focus, it is rather more interesting. Thus, with respect to Latin American armies it is commonly asserted that military intervention is the prevailing norm because of the Hispanic heritage.[17] Similarly, it is argued that *the propensity for military intervention increases with the habituation of the military to intervention,* or more simply, that intervention breeds more intervention.[18]

The larger and more sophisticated the armed forces, the more likely that they will have the administrative and technical skills necessary for running a government and that the military will have a preponderance of armed power over civilians. Thus, some have argued that *the size and sophistication of the military establishment are positively related to the propensity for intervention in politics.*[19] Janowitz has discussed a variety of other internal characteristics of the military establishment which he sees as related to the propensity for political involvement, such as political ideology, social and political cohesion, and career and recruitment patterns. I shall not pursue these propositions here since I do not have the data necessary to test them.

Two final factors often adduced to explain military intervention, especially but not exclusively in the Latin American context, involve foreign influences. First, it is often alleged that *military training missions from foreign nations inculcate attitudes favorable or unfavorable to military intervention in politics.* Edelmann echoes many others in arguing that "the influence of German, Italian, and certain other military missions" has been among the "most important" causes of military intervention in Latin America,[20] while Johnson argues that the effect of U.S. missions is to transmit norms of civilian supremacy along with their tutelage in military techniques.[21] Second, it is often argued that by a kind of "demonstration effect" *military intervention in one country encourages intervention by the armed forces of other countries in their own political systems,* or more simply, that coups are contagious.[22]

[17] For example, Alexander, 153.
[18] *Ibid.,* 154-55.
[19] Janowitz, 42.
[20] Alexander T. Edelmann, *Latin American Government and Politics* (Homewood 1965), 189.
[21] "The Latin American Military," in Johnson, *Role of the Military,* 129.
[22] Lieuwen, "Militarism and Politics," *ibid.,* 134.

III. Methodology

There is no dearth of suggestions about what factors are causally related to military intervention in politics. The problem is to subject this array of propositions to some kind of empirical testing. The primary method used here is correlational analysis. For each Latin American country an index is constructed representing the extent of military intervention in politics over the last decade. This is our "dependent variable." This index will be correlated with a variety of other data intended to represent or reflect some of the suggested independent variables. The strength of the empirical relationships will be summarized by the standard Pearsonian correlation coefficient r.[23]

This technique is a powerful one for testing hypotheses such as those outlined above, for it allows us to weigh and summarize all the relevant evidence. In particular, we can go beyond mere lists of illustrations and exceptions. This technique is, of course, not the only possible one— other complementary techniques are the case-study method and the comparative historical method. Nor is it without its limitations. First, the present analysis is "synchronic," rather than "diachronic"; that is, it compares information on military intervention and, for example, social mobilization at the present time in the various Latin American countries. With one important exception, we shall not compare data that would allow us to examine changes in the degree of intervention and mobilization in one country over time.

Second, as already suggested, we shall not examine all the factors that might be linked theoretically to military intervention. In particular, two classes of factors are beyond the scope of this investigation. First, we cannot examine propositions involving variables that are virtually constant throughout the Latin American area, such as religion, colonial background, length of independence, and the like. However, it is precisely these factors that could not possibly account for the wide variation among these countries in military intervention.[24] Second, a number of theoretically interesting and relevant variables must be ignored here because we lack the data necessary to test them. We lack direct information on the political allegiances of the populations, on the extent of social cleavage and consensus in the various countries, and on the

[23] See Hubert M. Blalock, Jr., *Social Statistics* (New York 1960), 273ff.
[24] Obviously, this study can consider only the range of variation in the independent variables which occurs in Latin America. For example, levels of social mobilization above or below the level achieved in Latin America might have effects on militarism which could not be detected in this study.

internal characteristics and norms of the military, such as those discussed by Janowitz. For a few of these factors we can make some
attempt to use indirect indicators, but these attempts must be especially
tentative. On the other hand, the relative success or failure of attempts
to explain military intervention with the factors for which data are
available will give us some indication of how much variation is left
to be explained by *other* factors.

Before proceeding further, the term "military intervention" must be
more precisely defined. In doing so, I shall borrow. Robert Gilmore's
definition of militarism: "The military institution is concerned with
the management and use of controlled violence in the service of the
state according to terms laid down by the state. When the military
institution veers from this role to participate in or to influence other,
non-military agencies and functions of the state, including its leadership, then militarism exists in greater or lesser degree."[25]

Obviously, the persuasiveness of this study depends on the validity
of the index of military intervention used as the dependent variable.
The heart of this index, which I shall call the "MI index," is a rating
assigned to each country for each year of the decade 1956-1965, based on
the extent of military intervention in the political life of that country
for that year. This rating is on a scale from zero to three, from least to
most intervention. Thus, for the decade, a country's MI score could
range between zero and thirty.

The ends of the scale are easiest to define. A rating of zero is given
to a country in which the armed forces were essentially apolitical, their
role restricted to that of a minor pressure group on strictly military
matters. Latin American examples of this level of intervention during
the period studied were Uruguay and Costa Rica, as well as Bolivia
during the years just after the 1952 revolution. A country that was ruled
directly by a military regime, either individual or collective, and in
which civilian groups and institutions were reduced to supplicants or
tools of the military, is rated three. Examples of this level of intervention were Paraguay and (after the coups of the early 1960's) Brazil,
Ecuador, Guatemala, Honduras, and Bolivia. Ratings of one and two
are assigned to levels of intervention falling between these two extremes.
A rating of two is given when a country was ruled by a military-civilian
coalition in which the civilian elements had some real influence, or by
civilians subject to frequent demands from a powerful military estab-

[25] Robert L. Gilmore, *Caudillism and Militarism in Venezuela* (Athens, Ohio, 1964),
4-5.

lishment, or by a dictatorship (often of a personalistic variety) based on force of arms, but not solely responsible to the armed forces.[26] Examples of this level of intervention in Latin America during the last decade were Brazil and Argentina (except for periods of direct rule by military juntas), Venezuela after Pérez Jiménez, and Nicaragua (a "familistic" dictatorship in which the armed forces played an important, but not predominant, role). A rating of one is given when a country was ruled by essentially civilian institutions, with civilian power groups preeminent, but with the armed forces still a significant political force in nonmilitary matters. Examples of this level of intervention were Mexico and Chile, and Colombia after Rojas Pinilla.

This rating method explicitly excludes from consideration certain political characteristics of related interest. I have not considered the degree of "democracy" in a country, apart from the extent of military intervention. Thus, for example, Castro's Cuba, despite its quasi-totalitarian character, is rated only one, since the available evidence suggests that the military play only a minor role in contemporary Cuban politics. Nor have I considered the ideological complexion of the military establishment; both the reactionary Paraguayan regime and the reformist regime in El Salvador are rated three.

In constructing the index I have used the literature on Latin American militarism, textbook accounts of Latin American politics, general histories of the period, and the *Annual Register* of political events. In cases of ambiguity, I have gone directly to monographic literature on specific countries. My sources are given in Appendix I, which also gives the actual year-by-year ratings for the various countries. Naturally, in a number of cases conclusive information on the precise political role of the military in a given year was lacking. In such cases I followed whatever seemed to be the preponderance of evidence, and since such cases invariably involve a difference of only a few points in the final country score, the overall effect is marginal.

This description of the construction of the MI index is some warrant for its validity, but fortunately there is an independent check on its plausibility. After the ratings had been compiled, I discovered a rather detailed classification by Martin C. Needler of the "normal political role of the military" in each Latin American country. A comparison of his rankings with my ratings will not "prove" the accuracy of

[26] In this connection it may be helpful to note Gilmore's distinction between "militarism" (as defined above) and "caudillism": "Caudillism is a political process in which violence is an essential element. . . . [It] may be defined as the union of personalism and violence for the conquest of power" (pp. 5, 47). Caudillist regimes, such as Haiti's, are rated two.

either, because both employ the "reputational" method. However, the strong concordance between the two assessments, shown in Table I, should increase our confidence in the MI index. With the exception of Needler's final category, the mean MI score for each category differs significantly from the others as it should. Moreover, the overlap in the range of MI scores between adjacent categories is, with the same single exception, one MI point at most. The only exception to this almost perfect concordance results from Needler's inclusion of Cuba and Nicaragua in the category of countries where the military are "in control," and, as I have argued above, the weight of the evidence suggests that this categorization of these two countries is misleading.[27]

TABLE I. A COMPARISON OF TWO RATINGS OF MILITARY INTERVENTION IN TWENTY LATIN AMERICAN COUNTRIES

Needler's Ranking According to "Normal Political Role of Military"	Mean MI Index Scores	Range of MI Index Scores
1. "None" $(N = 1)$	0.0	0
2. "Limited" $(N = 5)$	8.8	0-15
3. "Intervene" $(N = 5)$	21.8	20-23
4. "Veto Power" $(N = 5)$	24.4	22-28
5. "In Control" $(N = 4)$	23.2	16-30
(Category 5, excluding Cuba and Nicaragua)	(28.5)	(27-30)

SOURCE: Needler, *Latin American Politics in Perspective*, 156-57.

In sum, then, although there might be some disagreement about the exact rating for a given country, the MI score seems a fairly good measure of the extent of military intervention in the politics of each Latin American nation.

The data on the independent variables for each country are of three general types. In the first place, certain standard statistics, such as extent of urbanization, measures of economic development, and literacy rates, have been gathered from a number of statistical handbooks. Second, some variables based on rankings by informed observers have been drawn from *A Cross-Polity Survey* by Banks and Textor.[28] Finally,

[27] The fact that the differences in MI scores among Needler's third, fourth, and fifth categories are much less than the differences involving his first and second categories comports with one's intuitive notion of the "distance" between the levels of intervention indicated by the descriptions of his categories. Thus, for example, the difference between a military that habitually "intervenes" and one that has "veto power" is less than the difference between one that "intervenes" and one whose political role is "limited." Needler's ratings of individual countries are given in Appendix I.

[28] Arthur S. Banks and Robert B. Textor, *A Cross-Polity Survey* (Cambridge, Mass., 1963).

information on several dichotomous characteristics, such as the incidence of German military training missions, has been compiled from
standard treatments of Latin American politics. Sources for data on
all these variables are given in Appendix II.

The data on the independent variables involve problems of reliability
and validity. "Reliability" refers to the accuracy of the statistics in measuring whatever it is that they measure. How accurate, for example, are
the data on per capita GNP? As is well known, statistical data from
Latin America are often not of the highest quality, and the reader is
referred to the sources listed in Appendix II for discussions of this
problem in particular cases. It is important to understand that in general the effect of unreliability in measurement of variables is to *reduce*
the obtained correlation coefficients slightly below the values that would
be expected if there were no such measurement error.[29] "Validity" refers
to the accuracy of the statistics in measuring the concepts in which we
are interested. How well, for example, does per capita GNP or the
proportion of the GNP derived from agriculture indicate "socio-technical complexity"? We cannot resolve these problems; we can only use
appropriate caution in interpreting the results.[30]

IV. Results

SOCIOECONOMIC DEVELOPMENT

The correlations between the MI index and various statistical indicators of social mobilization and economic development are given in
Table II. Five variables measure social mobilization: (1) percent of
population in cities over 20,000, (2) percent of adults literate, (3) news-

[29] See George A. Ferguson, *Statistical Analysis in Psychology and Education* (New
York 1959), 289. Given the probable error margins for the data used here, reliability
coefficients in the range .8-.9 would be expected. This would mean, for example, that
an obtained coefficient of .20 understates the actual correlation by about .02-.05 and
that a coefficient of .60 understates the actual correlation by about .06-.15. For error
estimates, see Bruce M. Russett and others, *World Handbook of Political and Social
Indicators* (New Haven 1964). For a detailed analysis of GNP error and a calculation
of an approximate reliability coefficient, see Hayward R. Alker, Jr., "The Comparison
of Aggregate Political and Social Data . . . ," *Social Sciences Information,* v (September
1966), 1-18.

[30] For a few of the variables, data were not available for all twenty Latin American
countries. In some cases, I have estimated the missing data and calculated coefficients
including this "best guess" data. Unless these "guesses" are *wildly* off (and I do not
believe that they are), the error introduced by including them is probably less than the
error that would be introduced by ignoring the countries they represent. Precise data
on Uruguay, for example, are often missing; yet it would be quite misleading to ignore
the fact that this country fits many of our hypotheses remarkably well. Coefficients
based on "best guess" data are indicated as such, and in all cases coefficients have also
been presented without this "best guess" data.

TABLE II. MILITARY INTERVENTION AS A FUNCTION OF SOCIAL MOBILIZATION
AND ECONOMIC DEVELOPMENT

Variable Number	Variable Content	Correlation With MI Index
1	Percent of population in cities over 20,000	—.49
2	Percent of adults literate	—.47
3	Newspaper circulation per 1,000 population	—.57
4	University students per 1,000 population	—.45
5	Radios per 1,000 population	—.44
6	Per capita GNP (1957)	—.30
7	Percent of GNP derived from agriculture	.26 (.18)
8	Percent of labor force in agriculture	.24
9	Percent of population in the primary sector	.39
10	Percent of labor force earning wages or salaries	—.42 (—.32)
11	Percent of labor force employed in industry	—.29
12	Percent of population in middle and upper [social] strata	—.48 (—.45)

SOURCES: See Appendix II. For Variables 7, 10, and 12, the correlation coefficients are based on data including "best guess" estimates for two or three countries for which precise data are not available. Coefficients in parentheses are based on data *not* including these estimates. See footnote 30.

paper circulation per 1,000 population, (4) university students per 1,000 population, and (5) radios per 1,000 population. As one might expect, these variables are highly intercorrelated: the mean intercorrelation is .81. They are also fairly closely correlated in the expected direction with military intervention: the mean correlation is —.48.[31] To simplify subsequent analysis, I have added together each country's (standardized) scores on these five indicators to form a single index of social mobilization, or "SM index." This index represents very accurately the factor common to these five indicators—all of the intercorrelations among the five components and all of their individual

[31] There is considerable debate about whether tests of statistical significance are appropriate in cases, like the present study, in which we have not a random sample from a larger universe but a complete universe, viz., all contemporary Latin American countries. Strictly speaking, significance testing is merely a way of checking inferences from a random sample to the universe from which that sample is drawn. On the other hand, Blalock and Gold have argued that significance tests may help us sift important from unimportant findings, even when there is no question of inferring to a larger universe. See Blalock, 270, and David Gold, "Some Problems in Generalizing Aggregate Associations," *American Behavioral Scientist*, VIII (December 1964), 16-18. Gold, however, adds the qualification that when one is dealing with small N's (as we are here), "judgments of importance that can be made reasonably from the *size* of associations should take precedence over tests of significance." Keeping in mind the problems associated with significance-testing in this situation, one may find the following figures helpful: assuming a one-tailed test and an N of 20, an $r \geq .38$ is significant at the .05 level; an $r \geq .31$ is significant at the .10 level; and an $r \geq .23$ is significant at the .33 level. These significance levels are derived from the *World Handbook*, 262.

correlations with the MI index can be accounted for in terms of co-variation with the SM index. This index itself correlates —.53 with the MI index. The conclusion must be that social mobilization is fairly strongly, and negatively, related to military intervention. More than one-quarter of the total variance in the MI index can be accounted for by covariation with social mobilization. (The square of a correlation coefficient, termed the "coefficient of determination," indicates what proportion of the variance in one variable is accounted for by covaria-tion with the other. Here, for example, —.53 squared equals .28 or 28 percent.)[32]

Six of the variables are closely related to economic development: (1) per capita GNP, (2) percent of GNP derived from agriculture, (3) percent of the labor force in agriculture, (4) percent of the popu-lation in the primary sector, (5) percent of the labor force earning wages or salaries, and (6) percent of the labor force employed in industry. Again, these variables are highly intercorrelated: the average intercorrelation among them is .72. Each is moderately correlated with military intervention in the expected direction: the mean correlation of the six with the MI index is —.32.[33] As in the case of social mobiliza-tion, to make subsequent discussion simpler I have added together each country's (standardized) scores on these six indicators to form a single index of economic development, or "ED index." Like the SM index, the ED index represents very accurately the factor common to its six components. This ED index correlates —.37 with the MI index.

Before we can decide definitely on the relationship between economic development and military intervention, however, we must take into account their joint correlation with social mobilization. This procedure, in fact, produces a most remarkable result: if we remove the effect of social mobilization, economic development itself turns out to be *posi-tively*, not negatively, correlated with military intervention! The pattern of simple, or zero-order, correlations among these three variables is given in Figure 1. Since the ED index and the SM index are very highly intercorrelated, the partial correlation between economic devel-opment and military intervention, controlling for social mobilization, becomes +.26. The explanation of this finding is that the SM-MI and SM-ED correlations are so strong that they "mask" the real, positive ED-MI correlation.

[32] See Blalock, 295-99.

[33] In calculating this mean correlation and in compiling the ED index that follows, I have reversed the scoring for Variables 7-9, so that a large positive number always refers to a high level of development.

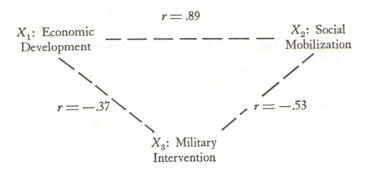

FIGURE 1. INTERCORRELATIONS AMONG ECONOMIC DEVELOPMENT,
SOCIAL MOBILIZATION, AND MILITARY INTERVENTION

A more sophisticated procedure for analyzing this pattern of inter-relations is provided by causal path analysis.[34] This technique allows us to calculate "causal weights," or "path coefficients," indicating the nature and importance of the causal relationships among a set of variables, provided (1) we are willing to posit some particular pattern of causal relations among the variables, and (2) we are willing to ignore (at least temporarily) the possible effects of variables not in-cluded in the set being considered. In our present case, the first of these conditions can be met by assuming that military intervention is a result, rather than a cause, of social mobilization and economic development. As a first approximation, this is probably true; later in this research note I shall explore this point further. (Path analysis does *not* require us to decide which way(s) the causal arrow joining development and mobilization should point.) If we can make the assumption implied in the second condition—that there is no fourth variable intruding—we can calculate from the correlation coefficients given in Figure 1 the causal weights, or path coefficients, given in Figure 2.[35] These weights

[34] The discussion that follows is not intended to be a complete presentation of the logic and methodology of causal path analysis. For introductions to this recently developed technique, see Hubert M. Blalock, Jr., *Causal Inferences in Nonexperimental Research* (Chapel Hill 1964); Raymond Boudon, "A Method of Linear Causal Analysis . . . ," *American Sociological Review*, xxx (June 1965), 365-74; and Otis Dudley Duncan, "Path Analysis: Sociological Examples," *American Journal of Sociology*, LXXII (July 1966), 1-16. For a readable and comprehensive introduction for political scientists, see Hayward R. Alker, Jr., "Causal Inference in Political Analysis," in Joseph Bernd, ed., *Mathematical Applications in Political Science*, 2nd Series (Dallas 1966).

[35] The equations for calculating the path coefficients (or p's) in this case are quite simple:

$$r_{21} = p_{21}$$
$$r_{32} = p_{32} + r_{21}p_{31}$$
$$r_{31} = p_{31} + r_{21}p_{32}.$$

This is a simple algebraic system of three equations and three unknowns. For the

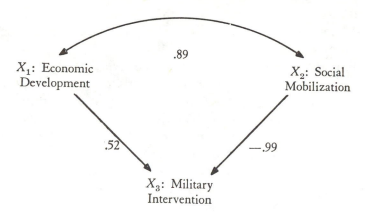

FIGURE 2. PATH COEFFICIENTS FOR RELATIONSHIPS AMONG
ECONOMIC DEVELOPMENT, SOCIAL MOBILIZATION, AND
MILITARY INTERVENTION

imply that the direct effect of social mobilization on military intervention is strongly negative and that the direct effect of economic
development on military intervention is moderately positive. Path
analysis also allows us to estimate the proportion of the variance in a
dependent variable which remains unaccounted for by a system of
independent variables.[36] Social mobilization and economic development
together account for about thirty-three percent of the variance in the
MI index, leaving sixty-seven percent yet to be explained.

The remaining hypothesis linking socioeconomic development and
military intervention refers to the rise of the middle strata. Accurate
information on the class structure of the Latin American countries is
difficult to obtain, but Germani and Silvert present data on "the percentage of the population in middle and upper [social] strata."[37] The
correlation of this variable with the MI index is —.48, supporting the
notion that the rise of the middle strata is associated with a decline in
military intervention. However, because this measure of class structure

---

general equation of path analysis, see Duncan, 5.

[36] The equation for calculating the residual variance is quite simple:

$$p_{3u}{}^2 = 1 - p_{32}{}^2 - p_{31}{}^2 - 2p_{32}r_{12}p_{31}.$$

See Duncan, 6.

[37] R. Vekemans and J. L. Segundo present numerically identical data under the
heading "Percent of population at intermediate and senior grades of employment," in
"Essay on a Socio-economic Typology of the Latin American Countries," in E. de Vries
and J. M. Echavarria, eds., *Social Aspects of Economic Development in Latin America*,
Vol. I (Paris 1963).

is almost perfectly correlated with the SM index ($r=.94$), it makes virtually no *independent* contribution toward explaining variance in levels of military intervention.

In sum, then, there seems to be good evidence that both social mobilization and economic development affect a country's propensity for military rule. Social mobilization definitely inhibits military intervention in politics, as predicted. The direct effect of economic development seems to be to encourage military intervention, although there is also a strong indirect effect linking economic development and military abstention, by way of social mobilization. The implications of this complicated pattern of findings can be brought out by several examples. Colombia and El Salvador are, in terms of the ED index, equally developed economically, but Colombian society is considerably more mobilized, as measured by the SM index. For the period under consideration, the Colombian military were much less involved in politics than were their Salvadoran counterparts. On the other hand, Venezuela and Costa Rica are about equally mobilized socially, but Venezuela is considerably more developed economically. As the preceding analysis would have predicted, Venezuelan politics in the period studied were much more subject to military intervention. Altogether the variables examined in this section account for about one-third of the total variance in the incidence of military intervention in Latin American politics.

POLITICAL DEVELOPMENT

Data on political development are much less readily available than data on socioeconomic variables. The correlations between military intervention and the political variables for which we can obtain data are given in Table III.

First, let us consider briefly the question of public commitment to civilian rule. Alexander Edelmann argues that among the most important influences counteracting military intervention in Latin America are "constitutional and legal restrictions imposed on members of the military regarding political activity. . . . Written not only on paper but also in the aspirations of liberty-loving citizens, they serve notice on the military of what their fellow countrymen expect."[38] If Edelmann is right that constitutional restrictions reflect popular norms and that these popular norms inhibit military intervention, then there should be a high correlation between constitutional restrictions and military abstention from politics. In fact, the correlation between military inter-

---

[38] Pp. 192-93.

TABLE III. MILITARY INTERVENTION AS A FUNCTION OF POLITICAL
DEVELOPMENT

Variable Number	Variable Content	Correlation With MI Index
13	Constitutional restrictions on the military	—.18
14	Percent of voting-age population voting	—.13
15	Interest articulation by parties	.04
16	Interest articulation by associations	—.19
17	Stability of party system	—.36
18	Interest aggregation by parties	—.63
19	Log_{10} ($10 \times$ deaths from domestic group violence per million population)	.20
20	Weighted Eckstein "instability" index	—.08

SOURCES: See Appendix II.

vention and constitutional limits on military political activity is only
—.18. The mean MI score for the fourteen nations that as of 1959 had
some constitutional restrictions on political activity by the military is
17.4, while the mean MI score for the entire region is 18.4. The evidence
clearly fails to confirm Edelmann's hypothesis. The explanation may
be either that constitutions and popular aspirations are unrelated or
that these aspirations do not affect military intervention.

A frequent hypothesis is that popular political participation inhibits
military intervention. The best available indicator of such participation
is the proportion of the adult population that votes in national elections.[39] Table III shows that the correlation between electoral turnout
and military intervention, though in the predicted direction, is quite
low. As a matter of fact, if we control for the level of social mobilization, the remaining partial correlation between turnout and military
intervention is virtually zero.

In assessing the hypotheses linking military intervention to the
weakness of political parties and pressure groups—the political infrastructure—we are forced to rely almost exclusively on the judgments
compiled for the Cross-Polity Survey. Four scales presented there are
relevant: (1) extent of interest articulation by political parties, (2)
extent of interest articulation by associations, (3) stability of the party
system, and (4) extent of interest aggregation by political parties. The
correlations of the two variables involving interest articulation are, in

[39] It is true that the accuracy of electoral turnout as an indicator of participation is
limited by variations in the social and institutional context of the act of voting. Voting
does not have the same meaning in the U.S. and the USSR, in the Netherlands and
Uganda. Restriction of our attention to the Latin American countries minimizes this
problem. For a fuller discussion of the problem, see Germani and Silvert.

fact, negligible, viz., .04 for parties and —.19 for associations. Judging by these statistics, strong and articulate parties and pressure groups do not necessarily inhibit military intervention, nor do weak parties and pressure groups necessarily encourage intervention.[40] The stability of the party system is somewhat more strongly related to military intervention, and the extent of aggregation by political parties is quite strongly related, with coefficients of —.36 and —.63 respectively. These figures, especially the latter one, strongly suggest that in contemporary Latin America political parties and military regimes represent mutually exclusive mechanisms for reaching political decisions. On the other hand, these relationships are hardly surprising, because they approach being tautological. In any country where a military regime was in power most experts would be likely *ipso facto* to rate as insignificant the role of parties in aggregating interests and resolving political problems.

The final proposition to be considered in this section on political development links military intervention to the role of violence in politics. Two different indices of political violence in the Latin American countries are available. Harry Eckstein compiled from the *New York Times Index* an enumeration of violent events occurring in every country in the world in the period 1946-1959 and tallied these in ten categories ranging from civil wars to police roundups. I have computed for each Latin American country an index based on five of his categories, with "warfare" and "turmoil" weighted by a factor of four, "rioting" and "large-scale terrorism" weighted by two, and "small-scale terrorism" weighted by one.[41] (These were the only categories dealing with mass violence.) The other index of political violence is based on the variable "Deaths from Domestic Group Violence per Million Population, 1950-1962" presented in the *World Handbook of Political and Social Indicators*. To reduce the skewing effect caused by the great variance in this variable (from 2,900 for Cuba to 0.3 for Uruguay), I have used a logarithmic transformation to "squash" the distribution. (Given the nature of the distribution, the effect of this transformation is to raise the correlation coefficient obtained with the MI index.) The

---

[40] Edelmann argues that one particular sort of interest group is especially likely to inhibit military intervention: "The most serious threat of all to the power of the military is that posed by the labor unions . . ." (p. 194). Actually, the correlation between military intervention and the proportion of union members is —.07. Huntington argues that political decay varies directly with the extent of party fragmentation. The comparable *Cross-Polity Survey* variable is called "Party System: Quantitative"; this correlates .23 with the MI index; controlling for social mobilization reduces this to .16.

[41] I have borrowed this weighting technique from Eldon Kenworthy, "Predicting Instability in Latin America" (unpublished).

first index of political violence, based on Eckstein, is virtually unrelated to military intervention. The second index is slightly related in
the expected direction, with $r=.20$, but this relationship disappears
when controls are introduced for socioeconomic development.

Our conclusions about the hypotheses linking military abstention
and political development must be cautious because of the limitations of
the data available. With this qualification in mind, we can conclude
that (apart from the trivial relationship between rule by the military
and rule by political parties) there is very little evidence linking
political development to military abstention in any straightforward
way. Widespread participation in elections, strong parties and pressure
groups, and freedom from political violence are neither necessary nor
sufficient conditions for military abstention.

THE MILITARY ESTABLISHMENT

Several students of military intervention have stressed the importance
of internal characteristics of the military establishment in determining
the extent and nature of military intervention. Unfortunately, data are
available for only a few, very gross, characteristics of the armed forces
of the Latin American countries. Table IV shows the relationships
between the MI index and these characteristics—military expenditures
as a proportion of GNP, military personnel as a proportion of the adult
population, and total military personnel.

TABLE IV. MILITARY INTERVENTION AS A FUNCTION OF INTERNAL
CHARACTERISTICS OF THE MILITARY

Variable Number	Variable Content	Correlation With MI Index
21	Defense spending as a percent of GNP	.55
22	Military personnel as a percent of adults	.07
23	Military personnel in thousands	—.24

SOURCES: See Appendix II.

The strong positive relationship between military intervention and
military spending is hardly surprising and is probably the result of
circular causation. Interestingly, militarism in the sense of intervention
in politics does not seem to be linked to militarism in the sense of the
proportion of men in arms. Still more interesting is the *negative* correlation between absolute size of the military establishment and extent
of military intervention. This finding directly contradicts the proposition relating intervention to the size and sophistication of the armed

forces. The finding cannot be attributed to the spurious effects of either simple population size (for the correlation between population size and the MI index is virtually zero) or socioeconomic development. Possibly the negative correlation reflects an inhibiting effect of either greater "professionalism" or lower internal cohesion in larger military establishments. Of course, the relative weight of this variable in determining military intervention is not great, for it accounts at best for only about six percent of the total variance in the MI index.

FOREIGN INFLUENCES

One of the most common explanations of military intervention in Latin America is that German military training missions during the late nineteenth and early twentieth centuries "infected" Latin American officers with ideas of military involvement in politics. As it turns out, this is a good example of a proposition that has been "tested" by time rather than evidence. The correlations between the MI index and the incidence of German, French, Chilean, and U.S. missions are given in Table V.

TABLE V. MILITARY INTERVENTION AS A FUNCTION OF INCIDENCE OF FOREIGN MILITARY TRAINING MISSIONS

Variable Number	Variable Content	Correlation With MI Index
24	German military training missions	—.20
25	French military training missions	.03
26	Chilean military training missions	.36
27	U.S. Mutual Defense Assistance Agreements	.06

SOURCES: See Appendix II.

The two most notable figures are the slight *negative* correlation between German influence and military intervention and the moderate *positive* correlation between Chilean missions and military intervention. The average MI score for the countries that had German missions is 15.2.[42] The average score for those that had French missions is 18.7, and for those with Chilean missions, 23.0. (It will be recalled that the mean score for the area as a whole is 18.4.) Neither the negative finding involving German missions nor the positive one involving Chilean missions can be attributed to spurious correlations with socioeconomic

[42] This negative finding is independent of the particular period during which the various missions were in residence. The mean MI score for only those countries that had German missions in the nineteenth century—generally the period referred to in this connection—is lower still: 13.6.

development. The explanation for the German finding seems to be simply that a plausible hypothesis has been repeatedly affirmed without adequate testing. Without more detailed information about the Chilean missions, that correlation will have to go unexplained.

The data on U.S. military missions refer to the twelve countries having Mutual Defense Assistance Agreements with the U.S. as of 1960 and are included only for general interest. The fact that the correlation of U.S. missions with military abstention is at present negligible need not imply that over a period of several decades such contacts will not affect the political orientations of the Latin American armed forces.

The other major foreign influence often alleged to affect military intervention is the "demonstration effect" of military coups in other countries. Historians of particular instances of military intervention have from time to time apparently uncovered some direct evidence of such influence, but the question to be considered here is to what extent this kind of "coup contagion" is a general phenomenon. The technique to be used is a familiar one in mathematical sociology.[43] I first listed all the successful military coups in Latin America from 1951 to 1965. The number of countries experiencing coups in each half-year period was then tallied.[44] Essentially, the technique consists of comparing the obtained distribution of coups with the distribution that would be expected if the incidence of coups were random across countries. If coups are contagious, we would expect more periods during which there were either *no* coups or *many* coups than we would expect if coups were distributed randomly throughout the fifteen-year span. Table VI compares the obtained distribution with the distribution that would be expected if the thirty-two coups of this period had been distributed randomly. (This random distribution is given by the formula called Poisson's distribution.) The evidence clearly disconfirms the contagion hypothesis. If anything, the data suggest that coups are slightly *more evenly* distributed (not less evenly, as the contagion hypothesis suggests) than chance alone would imply, although overall the differences are rather small.

[43] See James S. Coleman, *Introduction to Mathematical Sociology* (Glencoe 1964), 288-311.

[44] Attempted but unsuccessful coups were ignored, partly for the conceptual reason that the definition of an "attempted coup" is problematic, partly for the practical reason that adequate information on attempted coups is lacking. The period of a half-year is chosen as representing about the optimum length of time during which contagion might be expected to operate. An analysis using one-year intervals produced results exactly comparable to those reported. I tallied countries rather than coups so as to exclude the effects of "contagion" within a single country.

TABLE VI. NUMBER OF COUNTRIES WITH MILITARY COUPS IN
HALF-YEAR PERIODS, 1951-1965

NUMBER OF COUNTRIES	NUMBER OF PERIODS	
	Obtained Distribution	*Random Distribution*
0	8	10.3
1	13	11.0
2	8	5.9
3 or more	1	2.8
	—	—
	30	30.0

SOURCE: *The Annual Register* (London 1951-1966).

These findings conclusively disconfirm several widely repeated propositions about military intervention. Neither German military missions nor "coup contagion" can be blamed for military involvement in Latin American politics.

HISTORICAL TRENDS AND INFLUENCES

I have already described the construction of the MI index for the period 1956-1965. Exactly the same procedures were used in compiling MI scores for the periods 1906-1915 and 1951-1955 (see Appendix I). Taken together these data allow us to examine the relative incidence of military intervention at selected periods over the last half-century. Table VII gives the relevant data. The average levels of intervention

TABLE VII. THE INCIDENCE OF MILITARY INTERVENTION
IN FOUR FIVE-YEAR PERIODS

Period	Mean MI Index Per Annum
1906-1915	1.53
1951-1955	2.02
1956-1960	1.87
1961-1965	1.81

show that although the extent of intervention since 1950 has been somewhat higher than it was a half-century earlier, the general trend within the later period has been downward.[45] The intercorrelations among the scores for the most recent five-year periods, given in Figure 3, illustrate the not surprising fact that the extent of military intervention in

[45] The lower level of intervention in the earlier period probably reflects (1) the fact that after the turn of the century civilian government enjoyed a period of considerable success in Latin America and (2) my decision (see footnote 26) to distinguish "caudillism" from "military intervention."

the various countries tends to be quite constant, at least over this fifteen-year period.

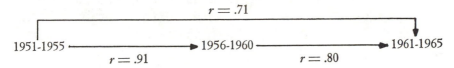

FIGURE 3. INTERCORRELATIONS AMONG MI INDICES FOR THREE
RECENT FIVE-YEAR PERIODS

Hypotheses linking military intervention or abstention to traditional norms in the military establishments imply that there will be a significant correlation between past and present levels of intervention. The simple correlation between the MI scores for the period 1956-1965 and the period exactly a half-century earlier is .47, thus moderately confirming this prediction. Perhaps, however, this correlation merely reflects the fact that the countries predisposed to military intervention by socioeconomic conditions in 1906-1915 were at the same relative level of socioeconomic development at mid-century. Perhaps, that is, continuities in socioeconomic development, rather than continuities in traditions of militarism, account for the association.

Precise information on earlier levels of socioeconomic development in all twenty Latin American countries is impossible to obtain. Fortunately, for one indicator of social mobilization—literacy—we can make some reasonable estimates. Among those seven countries for which 1910 literacy rates are available, these rates correlate almost perfectly ($r=.98$) with the 1950 literacy rates for inhabitants of sixty-five and over—the generation who were young adults in the earlier period. Relying on this fact, we can use the 1950 rates for those sixty-five and over—which can be closely estimated for all of the countries—as indicators of the levels of social mobilization a half-century ago.

Figure 4 displays the intercorrelations among our four variables: literacy in 1910 and 1960 and military intervention in 1906-1915 and 1956-1965. Of the several hundred possible causal models that might be used to fit this set of correlations, all but four can be eliminated as inconsistent with the pattern of correlations obtained or with the temporal ordering of the variables.[46] The four possible causal models are shown in Figure 5. If we assume that military intervention in 1906-

[46] This elimination process follows the technique suggested by Herbert Simon and Hubert M. Blalock, Jr. See Blalock, *Causal Inferences*, 61-94 and *passim*.

1915 could not have significantly influenced literacy rates in 1910 (even though it might have influenced *later* literacy rates), we can eliminate Models A and B. If, in addition, we assume that 1910 literacy rates do not affect 1956-1965 military intervention directly, but only indirectly through their influence on 1960 literacy rates, we can also eliminate Model C.

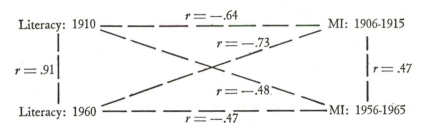

FIGURE 4. INTERCORRELATIONS AMONG LITERACY RATES, 1910 AND 1960, AND MILITARY INTERVENTION SCORES, 1906-1915 AND 1956-1965

Having decided on a particular causal model, we can apply the technique of causal path analysis to examine the interrelationships among social mobilization and military intervention for the two periods. The results of this analysis, given in Figure 6, show that both contemporary literacy rates and earlier levels of military intervention make independent contributions toward explaining present levels of military intervention. The figure also reveals that military intervention itself has a deleterious effect on subsequent levels of literacy. One implication of this pattern of findings is that part of the strong correlation earlier

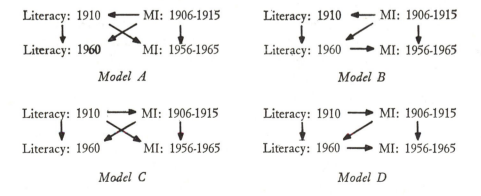

FIGURE 5. FOUR CAUSAL MODELS CONSISTENT WITH INTERCORRELATIONS SHOWN IN FIGURE 4

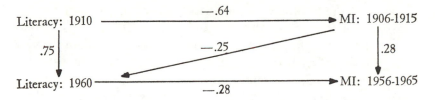

FIGURE 6. PATH COEFFICIENTS FOR RELATIONSHIPS AMONG LITERACY RATES, 1910 AND 1960; AND MILITARY INTERVENTION, 1906-1915 AND 1956-1965

noted between social mobilization and (contemporary) military intervention can be traced to the impact of earlier military intervention on both contemporary levels of mobilization and contemporary levels of intervention.[47]

Another surprising fact revealed by this historical analysis is that levels of socioeconomic development were relatively much more important determinants of military intervention a half-century ago than today. As shown in Figure 4, the correlation between 1910 literacy rates and 1906-1915 military intervention was —.64, while a half-century later the analogous correlation was —.47. In terms of variance explained, the impact of literacy on military intervention dropped from forty-one percent to twenty-two percent. We lack earlier data on the other indicators of social mobilization, but it is interesting and significant that the overall index of social mobilization for 1960 correlates —.67 with the 1906-1915 MI index, as compared to —.53 with the 1956-1965 MI index. Over the last fifty years in Latin America the political sphere has become more autonomous; that is, factors other than socioeconomic development have become relatively more important determinants of military intervention.[48]

V. CONCLUSIONS

The statistical analyses presented in this research note have answered some questions about military intervention. Social mobilization clearly increases the prospects for civilian rule. Traditions of militarism play an important role in accounting for contemporary military intervention. Neither foreign training missions nor foreign examples of successful intervention seem to have any impact.

[47] Perhaps an analogous explanation would apply to the relationship between economic development and military intervention. We lack the data necessary to carry this analysis further.

[48] Huntington argues that one aspect of political development is an increasing autonomy of politics from other social spheres. See "Political Development and Political Decay," 401-30.

But some of the findings call for further reflection and inquiry. How can we account for the fact that the direct effect of economic development seems to be to encourage, rather than to inhibit, military involvement in politics? What are we to make of recent speculations linking political institutionalization and military abstention, in the light of the present negative findings?[49] What are the implications of the declining (although still important) strength of the relationship between military intervention and levels of socioeconomic development?

Overall, the independent variables we have examined here account for somewhat less than half of the total variance in contemporary military intervention.[50] One way of beginning the search for other significant factors is to examine so-called "deviant cases," that is, countries with MI scores considerably higher or lower than would be predicted on the basis of the variables examined here. Let me illustrate this technique.

Figure 7 displays a "scattergram" of the relationship between military intervention and social mobilization. Obviously, a few countries are widely out of line with the relationship characterizing the remaining countries. Argentina has a much higher MI score than would be expected on the basis of its social development, while Bolivia and Costa Rica have MI scores much lower than would be expected. The effect of these deviant cases is to lower substantially the obtained correlation coefficients. If we remove Argentina from the analysis, the coefficient rises from —.53 to —.67, and if we remove Bolivia and Costa Rica as well, the coefficient rises to —.79. The proportion of variance explained has risen from twenty-eight percent to sixty-two percent. Similar analyses could be presented using the other independent variables discussed in this research note.

Let me be clear that the import of this discussion of deviant cases is *not* that these variables "really" explain the higher amounts of variance, for obviously we cannot "write off" countries like Argentina, Bolivia, and Costa Rica. Rather, this analysis focuses our attention on the countries that are most anomalous when analyzed in terms of the variables considered here, as well as on the characteristics that might

[49] Huntington's theory of political development (*ibid.*) implies that social mobilization leads to military rule and that civilian rule depends on strong political institutions; neither of these propositions is confirmed by the present study. It would be worth further investigation to determine whether the propositions do apply to other underdeveloped areas.

[50] Among the other independent variables considered and rejected in the present study were (1) total population ($r=.02$), (2) racial composition ($r=.16$), and (3) rates of social change (for urbanization, $r = -.18$).

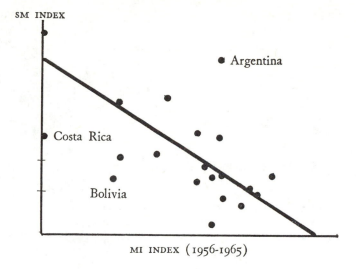

FIGURE 7. SCATTERGRAM OF RELATIONSHIP BETWEEN
SOCIAL MOBILIZATION AND MILITARY INTERVENTION

explain their deviance. In the case of Bolivia, the 1952 revolution drastically reduced (temporarily, at least) the role of the military to a level
below that which might have been expected for a country at its level
of socioeconomic development. From this perspective, the events of
1964-1965 in Bolivia might be interpreted as a "return to normalcy."
The "Argentine paradox" is a familiar one to students of Latin America; the present study graphically reveals once again the extent of this
paradox. The case of Argentina and, by contrast, the case of Costa Rica
suggest the importance of pursuing the suggestions of Germani and
Silvert that military intervention is related to the extent of cleavage
or consensus in a society.

YEAR-BY-YEAR MILITARY INTERVENTION SCORES

	1906	1907	1908	1909	1910	1911	1912	1913	1914	1915	1951	1952	1953	1954	1955	1956	1957	1958	1959	1960	1961	1962	1963	1964	1965	MI INDEX 1906-15	MI INDEX 1956-65	NEEDLER'S RANKINGS*
Costa Rica	1	1	1	1	1	1	1	1	1	1	0	0	0	0	0	0	0	0	0	0	0	0	0	0	0	10	0	0
Uruguay	1	1	1	1	1	1	1	1	1	1	0	0	0	0	0	0	0	0	0	0	0	0	0	0	0	10	0	1
Bolivia	1	1	1	1	1	1	1	1	1	1	3	1	0	0	0	0	0	0	0	1	1	1	1	2	3	10	9	1
Chile	1	1	1	1	1	1	1	1	1	1	1	1	1	1	1	1	1	1	1	1	1	1	1	1	1	10	10	1
Mexico	2	2	2	2	1	1	1	1	2	2	1	1	1	1	1	1	1	1	1	1	1	1	1	1	1	18	10	1
Colombia	2	2	1	1	1	1	2	1	1	2	3	3	3	3	3	3	3	1	1	1	1	1	1	1	1	14	15	1
Cuba	1	1	1	1	1	1	1	1	1	0	2	3	3	3	3	3	3	3	1	1	1	1	1	1	1	10	16	4
Panama	0	0	0	0	0	0	0	0	0	0	3	3	3	2	2	2	2	2	2	2	2	2	2	2	2	0	20	2
Nicaragua	1	1	1	2	3	3	2	2	2	2	2	2	2	2	2	2	2	2	2	2	2	2	2	2	2	17	20	4
Peru	1	1	1	2	1	2	2	2	2	2	3	3	2	2	2	2	2	2	2	2	2	3	2	2	2	14	21	2
Brazil	3	2	3	3	3	3	3	3	3	3	3	3	3	3	3	2	2	2	2	2	2	2	3	3	3	16	22	2
Haiti	3	2	2	2	2	2	2	2	2	1	2	3	3	3	3	3	3	3	3	3	3	3	3	3	3	30	22	3
Ecuador	2	1	2	2	2	2	2	2	3	3	2	2	2	2	2	2	2	2	2	2	3	3	3	3	3	20	23	2
Honduras	2	1	2	2	2	2	2	2	2	2	2	2	2	2	2	3	3	3	3	3	2	2	2	3	3	20	23	2
Argentina	1	2	1	2	2	2	2	2	2	1	3	3	3	3	3	3	3	2	2	2	2	3	2	3	2	10	23	3
Venezuela	2	2	2	2	2	2	2	2	2	2	3	3	3	3	3	3	3	2	2	2	2	2	2	2	2	20	23	3
Guatemala	2	2	2	2	2	2	2	2	2	2	3	3	3	3	3	2	2	3	3	3	3	3	3	3	3	20	26	3
El Salvador	2	2	2	2	2	2	2	2	2	2	3	3	3	3	3	3	3	3	3	3	3	2	2	2	2	20	27	4
Dominican R.	2	2	2	2	2	2	3	2	2	2	3	3	3	3	3	3	3	3	3	2	2	2	2	3	3	21	28	3
Paraguay	2	2	2	2	2	2	2	2	2	1	2	3	3	3	3	3	3	3	3	3	3	3	3	3	3	16	30	4

*Martin C. Needler, Latin American Politics in Perspective (New York 1963), 156-57. Rankings of "Normal Political Role of Military": 0="None"; 1="Limited"; 2="Intervene"; 3="Veto Power"; 4="In Control."

SOURCES: The Annual Register (London 1951-1966); Frank Brandenburg, The Making of Modern Mexico (Englewood Cliffs 1964); H. E. Davis, ed., Government and Politics in Latin America (New York 1958); John E. Fagg, Latin America: A General History (New York 1963); Robert L. Gilmore, Caudillism and Militarism in Venezuela (Athens, Ohio, 1964); John J. Johnson, The Military and Society in Latin America (Stanford 1964); Edwin Lieuwen, Arms and Politics in Latin America (New York 1961) and Generals vs. Presidents (New York 1964); John Martz, Central America (Chapel Hill 1959); Dana G. Munro, The Five Republics of Central America (New York 1918) and The Latin American Republics: A History, 2nd ed. (New York 1950); Martin C. Needler, ed., Political Systems of Latin America (Princeton 1964); Franklin D. Parker, The Central American Republics (New York 1964); J. Fred Rippy, Latin America: A Modern History (Ann Arbor 1958); Robert E. Scott, Mexican Government in Transition (Urbana 1959); William S. Stokes, Latin American Politics (New York 1959); Theodore Wyckoff, "The Role of the Military in Latin American Politics," Western Political Quarterly, XIII (September 1960), 745-63.

APPENDIX II. SOURCES OF DATA FOR INDEPENDENT VARIABLES

Variable Number	Variable Content	Source Number and Page
1	Percent of population in cities over 20,000	I, 228
2	Percent of adults literate (1960)	XI
3	Newspaper circulation per 1,000 population	II, 108
4	University students per 1,000 population	I, 228
5	Radios per 1,000 population	II, 118
6	Per capita GNP (1957)	II, 155
7	Percent of GNP derived from agriculture	II, 172; III, 70
8	Percent of labor force in agriculture	II, 177
9	Percent of population in the primary sector	IX, 64
10	Percent of labor force earning wages or salaries	III, 38
11	Percent of labor force employed in industry	X, 90
12	Percent of population in middle and upper [social] strata	IX, 64
13	Constitutional restrictions on political activity by military	VIII, 132
14	Percent of voting-age population voting	II, 84
15	Interest articulation by parties	V, 37
16	Interest articulation by associations	V, 33
17	Stability of party system	V, 43
18	Interest aggregation by parties	V, 38
19	Log_{10} (10 $\times$ deaths from domestic group violence per million population)	II, 99
20	Weighted Eckstein "instability" index	IV, Appendix I
21	Defense spending as a percent of GNP	II, 79
22	Military personnel as a percent of adult population	II, 77
23	Military personnel strength in thousands	III, 41
24	German military training missions	VI
25	French military training missions	VI
26	Chilean military training missions	VI
27	U.S. Mutual Defense Assistance Agreements	VII, 201
28	Percent of adults 65 and over literate (1950)	XII
29	Percent of adults literate (1910)	XIII

SOURCES: *I*. Gino Germani, "The Strategy of Fostering Social Mobility," in E. de Vries and J. M. Echavarria, eds., *Social Aspects of Economic Development in Latin America*, Vol. I (Paris 1963). *II*. Bruce M. Russett and others, *World Handbook of Political and Social Indicators* (New Haven 1964). *III*. Center of Latin American Studies, *Statistical Abstract of Latin America* (Los Angeles 1962). *IV*. Harry Eckstein, *Internal War: The Problem of Anticipation*, a report submitted to the Research Group in Psychology and the Social Sciences, Smithsonian Institution (Washington 1962). *V*. Arthur S. Banks and Robert B. Textor, *A Cross-Polity Survey* (Cambridge, Mass., 1963). *VI*. John J. Johnson, ed., *The Role of the Military in Underdeveloped Countries* (Princeton 1962), 108, 163; John J. Johnson, *The Military and Society in Latin America* (Stanford 1964), 69-71; William S. Stokes, *Latin American Politics* (New York 1959), 129-32. *VII*. Edwin Lieuwen, *Arms and Politics in Latin America* (New York 1961). *VIII*. Stokes, *Latin American Politics*. *IX*. Gino Germani and Kalman Silvert, "Politics, Social Structure and Military Intervention in Latin America," *Archives Européennes de Sociologie*, II (Spring 1961), 62-81. *X*. R. Vekemans and J. L. Segundo, "Essay on a Socio-economic Typology of the Latin American Countries," in de Vries and Echavarria. *XI*. United Nations, *Compendium of Social Statistics* (New York 1963). *XII*. *Ibid.*; United Nations, *Demographic Yearbook* (New York 1955, 1964); UNESCO, *World Illiteracy at Mid-Century* (Paris 1957). *XIII*. *Ibid.*; UNESCO, *Progress of Literacy in Various Countries* (Paris 1953).

Challenges and Changes

MODERNIZATION AND POLITICAL INSTABILITY:
A Theoretical Exploration

By CLAUDE AKE*

WHAT is the effect of the process of modernization on political
stability? That is the question I want to explore theoretically.
I will suggest that there are no plausible reasons for the expectation that
the process of modernization is destabilizing, and also that there is no
problem of political instability in transitional societies or anywhere
else. Let us begin by examining some of the arguments used to support
the thesis that modernization causes political instability.

I. ANOMIE, ROLE CONFLICT AND POLITICAL INSTABILITY

The type of argument that recurs most frequently in the literature
is the one that links modernization with anomie or with role conflict.
The substance of the argument is as follows: modernization is characterized by changes of norms and values and this causes an orientational
upheaval. The disorientation weakens societal ties and the mechanisms
of social control and creates psychological stress. These factors in turn
lead to political instability. Lucian Pye presents what is perhaps the
best known version of this argument:

> ... people in transitional societies can take almost nothing for granted;
> they are plagued on all sides by uncertainty and every kind of unpre-
> dictable behavior. In their erratically changing world, every relation-
> ship rests upon uncertain foundations and may seem to contain an un-
> limited potential for good and evil. People are not sure what they should
> get from any relationship, and so they are never sure whether they are
> getting what they should. The concepts of friend and foe become blurred.
> Above all else, the individual cannot be sure of the actions of others
> because he cannot be sure about himself.[1]

Pye draws attention to the "fragmentary" nature of the socialization
process in transitional societies. He holds that in such societies, primary
socialization and secondary socialization inculcate values which are
quite often in disharmony. This pattern of socialization makes attitudi-

* Paper presented to the International Political Science Association, IX World Congress, Montreal, September 1973.
[1] Lucian W. Pye, *Politics, Personality and Nation Building: Burma's Search for
Identity* (New Haven 1963), 54-55.

nal orientations incoherent and weakens associational sentiments. Since it is associational sentiments that make it possible for members of a society to have "considerable conflict without destroying the stability of the system," the weakening of associational sentiments renders social conflict more intense.

David Apter gives a very similar account of the political consequences of modernization. For him, modernization is the "spread of roles originating in societies with an industrial infrastructure, serving functional purposes in the industrial process, to systems lacking an industrial infrastructure." As a society modernizes, the following effects occur: (1) "the normative integration of the previous system begins to weaken, thereby widening the area of public meaning and reducing the area of prescriptive values"; (2) there are "more complex roles which need to be managed"; and (3) "there is more ambitiousness and less predictability in social action, producing greater uncertainty by individuals both of themselves and of the anticipated responses of others."[2]

For Apter, the source of the political problems and conflicts associated with modernization is the incompatibility of roles. Societies undergoing modernization are said to have three types of roles: (a) traditional, (b) accommodationist (partially new roles), and (c) new (industrial):

> In practice, the substance of modernizing politics is in large measure the result of incompatibilities between these three types of roles. The effort to adjust and modify them is particularly difficult in the absence of an impersonal dynamic mechanism such as exists in industrial countries. The modification and rearrangement of such roles, the selection of role priorities, and the use of restratification to provide possible solutions to the problems of role incompatibilities are all strategically important aspects of political policy-making. The claims put forward by competing political groups, each representing some portion of the total stratification system, are the means by which role malintegration is transformed into political conflict.[3]

Pye and Apter make an interesting and highly suggestive case. But it is not conclusive. Let us consider the point about the uncertainty of people in modernizing societies. They make a rather easy assumption here. If roles were changing on a large scale, as it appears they do in modernizing societies, then there would be some confusion over role expectations and, by implication, some uncertainty or lack of predict-

[2] David Apter, "Political Systems and Developmental Change," in Robert T. Holt and John E. Turner, eds., *The Methodology of Comparative Research* (New York 1970), 158-59.
[3] David Apter, *The Politics of Modernization* (Chicago 1965), 123-24.

ability in social life. In such circumstances some people would indeed, as Apter suggests, engage in role testing, "exploring the legitimate limits of their roles and experimenting to the point where they expect sanctions of one kind or another to be initiated."[4] The difficulty is that the expectation of uncertainty in this situation depends on a further assumption about how change is introduced. From the mere fact that a society is changing one cannot conclude that there will be more uncertainty and less predictability in regard to behavior expectations. In particular, one has to make the further assumption that change is not thoroughly planned and that those affected by change are not well socialized into new expectations. As far as I can see, Pye and Apter do not make this assumption. If they did, they would have a difficult time justifying it. If we can agree that proper planning of change and proper "anticipatory" socialization can minimize disorientations and the uncertainties associated with modernization, the question arises, why should they not be able to eliminate these disorientations and uncertainties altogether? It may well be that however thoroughly change is planned, it will cause some disorientation and make behavior expectations more confused to some degree. But this has to be demonstrated, not assumed.

Both Apter and Pye consider modernization to be a disintegrative process. Pye thinks the process is disintegrative because it weakens associational sentiments. The weakening of associational sentiments is essentially the effect of the disorientations and the uncertainty about behavior expectations which are associated with modernization. We have already seen that it is problematic to assume that people in modernizing societies will suffer from these disorientations. Let us grant, for the sake of argument, that the assumption is valid: inasmuch as people are disoriented and uncertain of role expectations, associational sentiments may be weakened. As Pye suggests, the incoherence of the world may make people not only unsure of themselves, but suspicious of other people as well.

The problem is that Pye is considering only one possibility. There is another possibility which is at least as plausible. The disorientation and confusion over roles may stimulate some forms of associational sentiments. There is a large body of literature showing that such disorientation and confusion over roles are among the conditions that give rise to charismatic leadership and mass movements. According to this literature, anxieties created by the general incoherence of the human environment can quite easily create strong if "regressive" forms of group

<hr />

[4] *Ibid.*, 125.

identity.[5] Pye needs to develop a more rigorous argument that takes account of this possibility.

Apter also finds modernization disintegrative. According to Apter, "as societies modernize the normative integration of the previous system begins to weaken, thereby widening the area of public meaning and reducing the area of prescriptive values."[6] However, this is part of a more fundamental problem, namely, the incompatibilities between roles—traditional, accommodationist, and new. Apter posits that modernizing societies (unlike industrial societies), lack a wide set of role interlinkages. As a result, "the mutually reinforcing aspects of roles do not generate a stable pattern of authority but the reverse." Apter gives the following illustration of the point: "In India, for example, the consequences of caste-fixed urban relationships, residential patterns, and factory or work place (even today) interfere with functional roles. This causes unrest, managerial uncertainty and lowered efficiency. The situation becomes a direct political problem, as well, when caste groups like the Scheduled Castes Federation take on qualities of a trade union, a caste, and a political party challenging the Congress Party."[7]

Apter is correct in saying that modernization can weaken the normative integration of the traditional system and cause role conflict. That much is obvious. However, his point does not tell us much about the consequences of modernization for the integration of society at large or for the maintenance of a stable pattern of authority. Consider the process of industrialization. Industrialization is usually associated with bureaucratic norms and bureaucratic organizations which to some extent are not in harmony with the norms and organizational patterns of traditional society. So we have a source of conflict here. However, we cannot stop with this conclusion; while industrialization generates some sources of conflict, it also has some integrative effects. Industrialization brings together (in factories, for example) people who previously had little or nothing in common. It forges links across ethnic groups, thereby possibly reducing their particularism and increasing the resiliency of social and political structures. Industrialization appears to be making African elites more homogeneous—more a self-conscious socioeconomic class and less a disorderly coalition of "opinion leaders" of tribal or ethnic groups. It is becoming increasingly difficult to make sense of what these elites are doing unless one assumes that they are acting out

---

[5] See Franz Neumann, "Anxiety and Politics" and "Notes on the Theory of Dictatorship," in Franz Neumann, ed., *The Democratic and the Authoritarian State* (New York 1957), 270-300 and 233-56; Harold D. Lasswell, "The Psychology of Hitlerism," *Political Quarterly*, IV (July-September 1933), 373-84.

[6] Apter (fn. 2), **159.**   [7] Apter (fn. 3), **132 n.**

their class-consciousness. There is no need to go into a documentation of these tendencies. For our purposes it is enough to draw attention to the logical possibility that, as the forces of production develop with modernization, the solidarity of elites and indeed their power can be enhanced.

To conclude, Pye and Apter give us some reason to believe that modernization can be disintegrative. But they have not given us any reason to believe the *process* is distintegrative.

Let us look briefly at Samuel Huntington, who also finds modernization to be disintegrative and destabilizing. He finds that rapid social and economic change "calls into question existing values and behavior patterns." It thus breeds corruption, which in turn breeds violence.[8] What does the term "corruption" mean to Huntington? "Corruption is behavior of public officials which deviates from accepted norms in order to serve private ends." According to Huntington, modernization breeds corruption, first because it entails changes in basic values; thus, "behavior which was acceptable and legitimate according to traditional norms becomes unacceptable and corrupt when viewed through modern eyes." Second, modernization creates new wealth and power whose relations to politics are undefined. Corruption occurs in the process of using wealth to secure political power or in the process of using political power to procure wealth. Finally, modernization breeds corruption because it changes and multiplies the laws by which society is governed. As the laws change, some group is put at a disadvantage and this group subsequently becomes "a potential source of corruption." What exactly is the relation of corruption to political instability? Huntington's answer is that "corruption tends to weaken or to perpetuate the weakness of the governmental bureaucracy." Corruption is at once a cause and an effect of the disorganization of political structures and authority patterns: "The functions, as well as the causes of corruption are similar to those of violence. Both are encouraged by modernization; both are symptomatic of the weakness of political institutions; . . . both are means by which individuals and groups relate themselves to the political system and, indeed, participate in the system in ways which violate the mores of the system. Hence the society which has a high capacity for corruption also has a capacity for violence."[9]

Huntington's concept of corruption—a concept clearly central to his thesis—is rather fuzzy. According to his definition of corruption, it is

---

[8] Samuel P. Huntington, *Political Order in Changing Societies* (New Haven 1968), 59-69. See also Huntington, "Political Development and Political Decay," *World Politics*, xvii (April 1965), 386-430.

[9] Huntington, *Political Order* . . . (fn. 8), pp. 59, 60, 61, 69, 63.

hard to determine whether an act is corrupt when (a) it deviates from accepted norms, (b) serves private ends, or (c) deviates from accepted norms and serves private ends. Even without going into this ambiguity, it is easy to show that Huntington's thesis is not persuasively argued. Let us consider the three points he makes to illustrate how modernization breeds corruption. The first point assumes that when modernization takes place, some forms of behavior which were not previously regarded as corruption come to be so regarded. This assumption may well be correct. But modernization cannot be said to increase corruption merely by altering the criterion of what constitutes corruption. The alteration of the criterion could conceivably decrease corruption. Huntington's second point has the same logical difficulty. He says that modernization causes corruption because it creates new groups with economic or political power who would use that power to maximize their political effectiveness or their wealth. It is conceivable that the new groups may use their wealth or power to abuse public offices for their own advantage. However, we are not told why they must necessarily act in this manner, or indeed why it is probable that they would act in this manner. Huntington's third point about the change of laws rests on two untenable assumptions. One is that modernization will lead to a multiplication of laws. It could just as easily lead to their reduction. Another is that, as laws multiply, more people are placed at some disadvantage. Why would not the changes in the laws make more people happier with the system?

Let us assume, for the purposes of argument, that modernization causes corruption. Does corruption cause political instability? To all appearances there is as yet no conclusive answer to this question. Huntington posits that corruption may weaken the bureaucracy or other governmental institutions and thereby generate political instability. On the other hand, he is also aware that corruption can be a means of enhancing political stability. Elites can use corruption to increase and consolidate their power. In admitting these two possibilities, he implicitly underlines the necessity of making a more rigorous argument. He should therefore have gone on to show us in some detail why corruption is more likely to exacerbate political instability than to enhance political stability. But he does not do it.

2. MODERNIZATION, POLITICAL PARTICIPATION, AND POLITICAL INSTABILITY

The second type of argument made to support the thesis that modernization causes political instability uses political participation as the intervening variable between modernization and political instability. Weiner and Hoselitz provide a good example of this argument. They

posit that the "political stability of many economically backward societies is the by-product of political apathy among the masses and relative isolation of persons who would form the core of potentially strong
organized groups," and that modernization, particularly economic development, "is a factor which contributes to the fairly rapid destruction
of political apathy and isolation."[10] According to Weiner and Hoselitz,
economic development improves educational facilities, creates new
groups by establishing contacts between people who were previously
isolated, and facilitates the making of demands on the government. As
economic development continues to generate new groups and demands, the political system may become more susceptible to the stresses
of demand overload.

It is not clear that economic development is likely to generate political instability just because it increases political participation. To begin
with, some forms of political participation are supportive rather than
destabilizing. From the mere fact that something increases the number
of people who can participate in politics we cannot conclude anything
about its effect on political stability. Perhaps what Weiner and Hoselitz
are saying is that unless you have political participation you cannot
have political instability, or, put differently, that economic development produces a necessary though by no means sufficient condition of
political instability, namely political participation. If this is what they
are saying, they are not refuted by showing that political participation
may also be system-supportive. However, political participation is not a
necessary condition for political instability. To govern people is to en-
join them on pain of punishment to act in certain ways and to refrain
from acting in certain ways. Either people are completely free and able
to do as they please and therefore are not being governed, or they are
being governed—in which case a limitation is imposed on their behavior. Insofar as people are being governed—that is, insofar as a political authority imposes limitations on what they can do—there is always the chance they will revolt or engage in deviant behavior or
subversion. In other words, to have political instability it is not necessary that people participate politically; it is enough if they are governed, i.e., required to obey. The mere existence of government is the
necessary condition of political instability.

3. MODERNIZATION AND THE GENESIS OF CONFLICT

I will now examine some arguments to the effect that modernization
generates or intensifies conflict in society. S. N. Eisenstadt finds that

[10] Myron Weiner and Bert F. Hoselitz, "Economic Development and Political Stability in India," *Dissent*, VIII (Spring 1961), 173-74.

modernization intensifies conflict by increasing structural differentiation: "Conflicts between various groups are inherent in any social structure, and the more differentiated and variegated the structure, the higher the extent and intensity of such conflicts; thus the very process of modernization necessarily creates a high level of conflicts."[11] The trouble with this argument is that it states only one side of the case. No one will deny that structural differentiation may generate tensions. And yet it is equally clear that structural differentiation will eliminate some sources of conflict and reduce the level of tension in some areas. For instance, it may eliminate conflicts caused by diffuse role orientations or the overlap of roles. Again, the argument needs to come to grips with the conventional wisdom that structural differentiation enhances political stability by replacing mechanical solidarity with organic solidarity.

Weiner and Hoselitz maintain that economic development magnifies some conflicts: "No matter what criteria are employed, some groups are bound to be dissatisfied. The more the capacity of government to spend increases, and the more investment decisions are made by government rather than by the private sector, the more there are likely to be conflicts over allocations between organized groups and government...."[12]

Many other people have noted that modernization creates a revolution of rising expectations which very quickly becomes a revolution of rising frustrations because of the limited capacity of the governments of transitional societies to satisfy demands for goods and services. According to Mancur Olson, one other reason why economic growth generates conflict is that it invariably creates a class of " 'nouveaux pauvres' who are much more resentful of their poverty than those who have known nothing else."[13] Once more we only have one side of the case. The expanding role of government in economic change may also be an effective instrument for enhancing the stability of the political system. It may use these powers to gain new supporters, to reinforce old ones, and to weaken opponents of the system. Olson recognizes that economic development also creates a class of "nouveaux riches." But he does not prove that, on balance, the level of governmental support will fall as a result of economic development. As for the revolution of rising expectations, it is not quite clear what it has to do with modernization. Is it in the very nature of modernization to bring about a revolution of rising expectations? Or is the revolution of rising expectations a by-

[11] S. N. Eisenstadt, "Modernization and Conditions of Sustained Growth," *World Politics*, xvi (July 1964), 584.

[12] Weiner and Hoselitz (fn. 10), 177.

[13] Mancur Olson, Jr., "Rapid Growth as a Destabilizing Force," *Journal of Economic History*, xxiii (December 1963), 533.

product of extravagant claims that elites happen to make? I do not know.

To sum up, the arguments I have examined are not successful. They are calculated to validate the proposition that modernization generates political instability. At best, they only succeed in establishing that modernization *can* generate political instability. There is a significant difference between the two propositions, "X generates Y" and "X can generate Y." The former suggests a necessary relationship between X and Y, but the latter suggests merely a possibility. The former is falsified by any instance in which X does not generate Y; the latter is not falsified by any such instance. The former is not confirmed by a single instance in which X generated Y, but the latter is fully confirmed by such an instance. If the arguments that I have examined amount to the proposition that modernization *can* cause political instability, they are telling us very little.

THE CONCEPT OF POLITICAL STABILITY

Part of the reason why no clear picture of the relation between modernization and political instability emerges is that we are rather confused about what political stability is. For the rest of this paper, I want to clarify the concept of political stability and to suggest:

(a) That misconception of political stability is a source of the belief that modernization causes political instability.

(b) That "the problem of political stability" is more apparent than real.

The writings on modernization I have reviewed conceptualize political instability, implicitly or explicitly, as violence, conflict, civil disorder, short duration of governments, lack of institutionalization, and so forth. They are typical of the conception of the phenomenon in contemporary political science. To illustrate, in *World Handbook of Political and Social Indicators*, the number of people killed in all forms of "domestic violence" is taken to be indicative of the extent of political instability.[14] Feierabend and Feierabend use aggression of groups within the political system as an indicator of political instability.[15] Jean Blondel defines political instability as lack of longevity of government.[16] For

---

[14] Bruce M. Russett and others, *World Handbook of Political and Social Indicators* (New Haven 1963), 97-100.

[15] Ivo K. and Rosalind L. Feierabend, "Aggressive Behaviors Within Polities, 1948–1962: A. Cross-National Study," *Journal of Conflict Resolution*, x (September 1966), 249-71; also, Ivo K. Feierabend, Rosalind L. Feierabend, and Betty Nesvold, "The Comparative Study of Revolution and Violence," *Comparative Politics*, v (April 1973), 393-424.

[16] Jean Blondel, "Party Systems and Patterns of Government in Western Democracies," *Canadian Journal of Political Science*, 1 (June 1968), 180-203.

Martin Needler, a country is stable if the government is chosen by free elections and if the government acts constitutionally.[17]

These conceptions of political stability do not fully reflect the fact that, properly speaking, only relations or a system of relations can be said to be stable. I would not normally describe my pen as stable or unstable. But if it is balanced on my index finger, I can properly apply the word stable—not to the pen as such but to the relation of the pen to my index finger acting as a fulcrum. The application of the term (to a relation) always suggests the possibility of change in that relation, a certain possibility of centrifugence among the elements which constitute the system. Perhaps it is the notion of possible centrifugence which restrains us from applying the term "stable" to all systems, or all systems of relations. Thus we do not usually describe the biological organism, man, as stable, though it is a system of relations, an ordered harmony of parts. In this case, the parts are very well integrated. But we readily think of alignments and political systems as being stable or unstable. The relations or systems to which the adjective stable is conventionally applied happen to be those whose centrifugence is quite obvious. For our limited purposes here, it is not necessary to go into a detailed characterization of the types of relations to which the adjective stable is applicable. It is enough to stress that only systems, or systems of relations, can properly be called stable or unstable.

We can look at this point from another angle. We say of some things that they are destabilizing and of other things that they are stabilizing. The sentence, "X is stabilizing," or "X is destabilizing," is not really fully intelligible. It is fully intelligible only when we make some assumptions about what is being stabilized or what is being destabilized. If somebody simply declares that something is destabilizing or stabilizing, that declaration invites the question, "what?" What is being stabilized or destabilized? The answer is a relation or a system. Thus, exposure of a solution to the sun may be said to be destabilizing—in the sense that it leads to the alteration of the chemical relations of the solution. It seems perfectly intelligible to say that violence destabilizes polity Y or institution T, Y and T being systems—that is, social structures or systems of roles. It does not sound quite right to say that X, for instance violence, destabilizes political socialization, a process. The implication of what we have just said is that if X is destabilizing to system S, then it is wrong to assume that it is also destabilizing to the

[17] Martin Needler, "Political Socioeconomic Development: The Case of Latin America," *American Political Science Review*, LXIII (September 1968), 889-97. For a review of the main conceptions of political stability in contemporary political science, see Leon Hurwitz, "Contemporary Approaches to Political Stability," *Comparative Politics*, v (April 1973), 449-69. I am indebted to this review essay.

system S_2, unless of course we make the prior assumption that systems S_1 and S_2 are identical. We make this type of assumption if we declare that violence, civil strife, protest, coups d'état, or failure to accept democratic procedures will destabilize political systems. The point is that what destabilizes one political system may stabilize another one and may be quite irrelevant to the stability of yet another political system. We need a definition of political stability which takes account of this elementary but important point.

Before we define political stability, it is necessary to clarify the concept of a political system. A political system is a system of acts, or more accurately, of roles. The role is a configuration of behavior expectations associated with an actor in an interactional situation. It may be convenient to think of these expectations as falling into three categories: expectations about what one ought to do (duties), about what one may do (rights), and about what one can do (capabilities). Insofar as political role expectations are the same among members of the society, and insofar as behavior corresponds to role expectations, interaction is coherent.

It is important to specify just how roles give structure to human interaction. Members of a society do not usually have a detailed knowledge of role expectations. In fact, it is more accurate to say that they hardly ever have a precise knowledge of role expectations. More often than not, what gives coherence to social interaction is knowledge of the general limits of permissible behavior. Within these limits there is some flexibility. Thus two occupants of identical roles—for example, two Supreme Court judges—may act in somewhat different ways in an identical situation. And yet, we might easily agree that each of them has fulfilled his role well. In the light of these considerations, it is perhaps more accurate to conceptualize role expectation as expectation about the general limits of permissible behavior in an interactional situation, and role fulfillment as behavior that falls within the limits of permissible behavior. Role expectations are, so to speak, obstacles limiting variability in the patterns of behavior "exchanges." By exchanges, I mean the communications and transactions of people in interaction. The structure of the social system is the system of such obstacles.

Political stability is the regularity of the flow of political exchanges. To the extent that the flow of political exchanges is irregular, the political system is unstable; to the extent that it is regular, the political system is stable. A political system is stable insofar as political actors proceed as usual—that is, confine their choice of political behavior to the general limits imposed by the role expectations of political interaction. Politically destabilizing acts are irregular exchanges; all acts which are not irregular exchanges are politically stabilizing. The irregular exchange is defined *ex post facto* from the knowledge of a political system or, what is the same thing, a particular system of political exchanges.

This definition is merely a reformulation of some current common-sense notions of political stability. When we consider the definitions which relate political instability to violence, civil disorder, etc., one striking feature of these criteria of instability is that in the context of the political systems in which they originate, they are irregular political exchanges. They fall outside permissible behavior. To illustrate the point further, if the Government of France were defeated in a constitutionally conducted national election and refused to relinquish power, we would regard the government's behavior as destabilizing. Similarly, if the President of the United States of America suddenly dissolved Congress and imprisoned the Supreme Court judges for making a decision with which he disagreed, we would again regard such behavior as politically destabilizing. In relation to the relevant political systems, these are instances of irregular political exchanges, instances of unpermitted eccentricity in the flow of political exchanges. As a rule, those things which we conventionally regard as politically destabilizing are also things which fall outside the limits of role expectations of the relevant political system. Are these acts properly described when we call them destabilizing? It seems that they are. For one thing, as their incidence increases, the political structure or the pattern of political exchanges breaks down; that is, expectations about political behavior become more and more elastic until the political order turns to its antithesis, anarchy. This is not unlike what would happen if we all simply refused to conform to conventional meanings of language: we would go into what is designated as a barber shop and find only people selling fresh vegetables; we would walk into a bakery and be asked whether we want to collect or deliver our laundry; we would go to what is advertised as a tennis match and find ourselves watching an opera. As more and more people took liberties with conventional expectations in this manner, society would become incoherent.

To ask how stable a polity is, is to seek to know the incidence of irregular political exchanges. We know this by comparing patterns of interaction or behavior with the role expectations of the polity in question. However, it is not easy to identify irregular political exchanges or destabilizing acts. For one thing, there may be some disagreement over what the expectations of certain roles are. This raises the question as to whose role expectations constitute the reference point for deciding what is an irregular political exchange or a destabilizing act. It seems to me that the solution to the problem is to take, as reference point, the role expectations sanctioned by the laws and conventions of the polity. Thus, irregular political exchanges or politically destabilizing acts are forms of behavior which violate the laws and conventions of the polity. Stabilizing acts or regular exchanges remain a residual category. This solution appears to be open to two objections. First, it contains a conservative bias because it implies acceptance of a constituted authority's notion of proper conduct. My answer to this objection is that we are interested in representing reality accurately, and this criterion appears to be the only one that reflects the reality of political life. Once we accept the premise that we decide what is irregular or destabilizing by reference to specific political systems, we have to use this criterion. Every historical political system is what it is by virtue of the laws and conventions that govern it. Whenever there is an issue as to whether someone has acted properly or not, the dispute is authoritatively resolved by reference to the laws and conventions of the polity. The choice of role expectations as a criterion is not an assertion to the effect that constituted authority is always "right." Rather, it is simply a recognition of the fact that the dominance of a particular system of laws and conventions gives the historical polity its peculiar "structure."

The second objection is that this criterion for isolating destabilizing political acts makes political acts out of all criminal acts. What is odd is not that we are making all criminal acts political, but that political scientists do not customarily draw attention to the fundamental "politicalness" of criminal acts, or indeed all acts that violate the law. Whether the effect is intended or not, all violations of the law are political acts in the sense that they defy or repudiate constituted political authority. The very essence of political authority is to command and to elicit obedience. Every crime is an instance of disobedience of the command of political authority. Hence, to commit a crime is to strike at the *raison d'état* of political authority. As more and more members within a political system commit more and more crimes, political authority weakens and the political system disintegrates.

Is There a Problem of Political Instability?

Most people who have written about modernization and political development, including the present author, have given the impression that there is a serious problem of political instability in transitional societies. The truth seems to be that this problem is more apparent than real. The problem appears to have been created by our conceptual confusion and prejudices.

One aspect of this confusion is the failure to distinguish clearly and systematically between political instability and political change. Our conventional conceptions of political stability do not pay enough attention to this distinction. When we use these conventional conceptions of political stability, we are apt to see political instability somewhat too ubiquitously. For instance, many of our conceptions of political stability contain some notion of longevity. Lipsett's conception of political stability in *Political Man* is perhaps the most famous example of this. When we build the notion of longevity into our conception of stability, we are already confusing political stability with the absence of political change. The belief that modernization is destabilizing reflects this confusion. Many of the changes associated with modernization—the decay of old roles, the creation of new roles, modifications of authority patterns, the rise of new interest groups, the erosion of certain solidaristic ties, the displacement of some primary groups by secondary groups—are too readily taken as sources or symptoms of political instability. In many contemporary modernizing societies, the executive of the state changes very frequently. This has reinforced the belief that modernization itself is destabilizing.

But these changes are not necessarily sources or symptoms of political instability. As we have seen, political stability is the regularity of the flow of political exchanges. To say that a polity is stable or that the flow of political exchanges is regular does not imply that political change is not occurring. Political change is compatible with political stability as long as the change occurs in accordance with prevailing expectations about how such change may legitimately come about. Political change therefore becomes an instance of political instability only when it violates established expectations about how that particular type of change may legitimately occur. To build the concept of longevity into the definition of political stability is to ignore the distinction between types of political change. If we work with such a notion of political stability, we will necessarily exaggerate the extent of the political instability of historical political systems.

There is another sense in which we exaggerate the extent of political instability. Polities in which phenomena such as constitutional crises, the abuse of high office, frequent changes of the executive of the state, political assassinations, and coups d'état occur frequently are usually characterized as being highly unstable.

Thus, contemporary African and Latin American polities are usually said to be highly unstable mainly because they often have coups d'état, changes of the executive, constitutional crises, etc. But do these indeed prove that these polities are highly unstable? Not really. These phenomena are forms of political interaction associated with elites. Elites constitute only a small proportion of the political population; we cannot say anything conclusive about the level of political stability by concentrating on elite interactions.

It may be argued that although elites are a small proportion of the political population, what they do is decisive for the political system, and that it is therefore necessary to pay special attention to the behavior of elites when we want to measure political stability. All the same, we cannot measure stability accurately if we give special importance to what elites do or to what happens in the elite stratum of the political system. To understand why this is so, we have to remember that political stability is the regularity of the flow of political exchanges. The assertion that a political system is highly stable or unstable ought to be based on an examination of the patterns of flow of political exchanges in the political system as a whole. In measuring political stability, we are dividing the distribution of patterns of communications and transactions into two categories. It is rather like watching the flow of traffic to determine the incidence of violations of traffic rules. Since we are interested in the extent of "regularity" of traffic behavior, we naturally do not "weight" the violations, nor do we consider the "importance" of the violators.

The more general significance of what I am saying here is that any measure of political stability which weights "destabilizing" or "irregular" patterns of political behavior misconceives what political stability is. The tendency of some studies of political stability to weight destabilizing patterns of behavior arises because of confusion of issues of measurement with issues of prediction. In measuring political stability, we are dealing with manifest behavior, and we are determining the incidence of a particular form of manifest behavior. If we are interested in predicting levels of political stability, we want to think not simply in terms of the incidence of patterns of behavior, but in terms of the balance of political forces. In those circumstances, we will have to resolve tendencies of manifest behavior into political forces by weighting them according to the resources and influence of the political actors who display them. If we avoid these confusions and remember that the level of political stability has to be a ratio of irregular political exchange to the totality of the political exchanges of the entire political population, it becomes quite clear that we have tended to exaggerate the problem of political instability.

Finally, it is pertinent to note that we take it for granted that there is a serious problem of political instability in some societies without really tackling the problem of defining critical levels of political instability. Yet it is clear that unless we can specify quantitatively what level of political instability is critical (say for the survival of the political system) we have no grounds for holding that there is a serious or even a significant problem of political instability in any political system. Is political stability something of which the more the better? Is political instability something of which the less the better? Or is there a critical or significant level of political instability? Critical for what? How is this critical level of political instability determined? Is it the same for every political system? These are questions which must be answered as part of the process of establishing the validity of the assumption that there is a significant problem of political instability in any society. It is all the more necessary to answer these questions because, to all appearances, the real and interesting problem is not how to maintain order, but how to revolutionize it.

A DYSRHYTHMIC PROCESS OF POLITICAL CHANGE

By C. S. WHITAKER, JR.*

I

WITH several notable and recent exceptions, the current literature on "modernization" in "developing countries" implicitly or explicitly assumes an inherent irreconcilability between "modern" and "traditional" values, institutions, and behavior patterns. Related to this assumption is the expectation that whenever important elements of these two social systems collide, the natural result is social convulsion.

It is typical of this literature to qualify these assumptions with the caveat, commonly employed in conjunction with the use of "ideal types," that differences between these two apparent classes of society are only relative, or that "pure" cases of either type are never manifested. Logically, however, these caveats do not contradict the assumption of a mutual exclusivity of these systems, nor can those who employ them reasonably intend that they should.[1] Thus, even those scholars who insist on a "qualified" dichotomous relationship of these systems tend to believe nonetheless that virtually the only alternatives facing people significantly exposed to modernity are atavistic withdrawal or a prolonged period of severe strain, instability, and conflict.

* A preliminary version of this paper was presented at the Princeton University Conference, "The Politics and Economics of the Emerging Nations," under the chairmanship of Sir Arthur Lewis, February 10-11, 1966.

[1] It is obvious that modifiers which indicate relative contrasts of the so-called mini-max variety must imply mutual exclusivity no less than absolute differences. Thus, if the proposition is that a given social quality necessarily conflicts with another to any degree, then maximization of both qualities in the same context is precluded. To that extent, in other words, they are mutually exclusive. Statements in connection with the use of the supposedly heuristic concepts "traditional" and "modern" typically suggest that "most people" in the one type of society behave one way with respect to certain values or activities, or that each type of society behaves as a whole in a certain way in "most instances." Indeed to claim that qualities associated with the terms "traditional" and "modern" do not diverge significantly would be to nullify the supposed significance of the terms, namely, that they identify distinguishable classes of societies.

Concerning the logical status of the Weberian "ideal-type" formulations and similar constructs, the philosopher of science C. G. Hempel demonstrated some time ago that any distinction between this sort of mental operation and a hypothesis in the strict sense is simply spurious. See American Philosophical Association (Eastern Division), *Science, Language and Human Rights; Symposium: Problems of Concept and Theory Formulation in the Social Sciences* (Philadelphia 1952), 71-134.

My study of Northern Nigeria's encounter with modernity and findings of some others elsewhere lead me to reject dichotomous conceptualizations of the nature and process of change in the so-called developing areas, at least as universally valid. Indeed, this rejection extends to the very terms "modern" and "traditional" as analytic tools.

To discuss this position fully is beyond the feasible confines of an article: my intention is to do so in a larger work. Here it must suffice merely to suggest that a full critique entails examination of (1) the comparability of Western and non-Western contexts of change, (2) the logical cogency of the premise of dichotomy, (3) the adequacy of the typology of societies associated with this premise, and (4) the predictive/explanatory value of this premise with respect to specific problems and conditions of change. The object of this article is more limited, but highly relevant to these matters. Before discussing it, however, perhaps a few more comments about the wider context are in order.

As others have noted, today's scholars of "modernization" are intellectual heirs of the most noted students of sociopolitical change in Western societies. Maine, Morgan, Weber, Tonnies, and Durkheim advanced parallel concepts of observable contrasts between historic periods—status and contract, *societas* and *civitas*, traditional and rational authority, *Gesellschaft* and *Gemeinschaft* relations, mechanical and organic solidarity. Indeed, our present conceptual understanding of sociopolitical change in general very largely *is* the work of these men, each of whom arrived at his concepts in an attempt to identify principles or norms of institutions and behavior implicit in change.

Whatever the merits of this exercise, which is not without possible controversy, in the hands of students of contemporary change in non-Western societies it has become something profoundly if subtly different. The original concepts represent abstractions derived from retrospective analysis of Western experience in terms of certain overt antagonisms of cognition, sentiment, and value, which may be shown to have accompanied sociopolitical change in the West. From an apparent soundness of these concepts in that context, today's student of "modernization" has inferred what in effect is a hypothesis about how non-Western people generally will react to the kind of institutions yielded by change in the West. This hypothesis in essence is that ultimately all non-Western peoples will either accept or reject these institutions, more or less wholesale. (This hypothesis may be called, from the point of view of the non-Western indigenous institutions, the displacement/rejection alternative.)

To reject this hypothesis is to discard the notion of "modernization." To do so in light of its pervasive influence and deep intellectual roots must at first appear foolhardy; certainly to dismiss it simply on grounds of cultural relativism seems lame and unpersuasive. To challenge the concept at the roots, however, seems to me essential if social scientists are to come to grips with important realities in at least parts of the non-Western world.

In this article, the object is to present a critique of only one of several assumptions entailed in conceptualizing the encounter of "modernity" and "traditionality" in terms of (allegedly) mutually exclusive social qualities (e.g., universalism versus particularism, achievement versus ascription, specificity versus diffuseness, and so on). For this purpose, the Northern Nigerian experience provides relevant empirical material.

Stated succinctly, the proposition to be examined here is that the process of sociopolitical change in contemporary developing societies is necessarily eurhythmic. The term "eurhythmic" is advanced because it encompasses variable connotations of several other terms more commonly used to characterize a supposed relation of various constituents in a process of change, namely, "interdependent," "complementary," "harmonious," "syndromatic," and so on. At least two such distinguishable meanings are germane to our discussion: (1) Significant change in one sphere of activity (e.g., economy) occasions corresponding and supportive change in another sphere (e.g., polity, or cult). (2) Within a given sphere of social activity, significant change in any one aspect of the activity (e.g., normative, psychological, institutional, structural) promotes consistent change in all or most other aspects.[2] The universality or necessity of a eurhythmic relation of elements in change, in either or both of the above senses, is the specific claim that this article challenges.

[2] It is important to note that the terms "eurhythmic" and "dysrhythmic" are not synonymous with "smooth" and "rough," or "peaceful" and "violent." In the present discussion, "eurhythmic" (consistent and supportive) change means *further change toward the characteristics of the society from which the original change derived.* Conceivably, both eurhythmic and dysrhythmic processes could be either smooth or rough, peaceful or violent. However, if a eurhythmic process involves the interaction of mutually exclusive qualities, then rough or violent change seems indicated. Thus it is that a combination of dichotomous and eurhythmic conceptualizations of phenomena of change have typically produced pathological characterizations of a supposed "transitional" or intermediate phase. Use of the very term "transitional" as a general category connotes unilinear direction, i.e., from one known type or class of society to another already defined one.

Before I present an account of the substance and dynamics of certain changes in Northern Nigeria which seem to disconfirm the hypothesis of eurhythmy, two assertions implied in the preceding paragraphs should be elaborated and underscored. The first is that belief in the mutual exclusivity of "modern" and "traditional" patterns is encouraged by assuming a necessary eurhythmic process; the second is that both ideas are widely held among students of contemporary social and political change in "developing countries." A third pertinent preliminary step will be to indicate some of the arguments commonly advanced in support of the view that a eurhythmic pattern of change is necessary. I shall also want to draw attention to the views of those alluded to above as "notable exceptions," whose ranks have increased significantly of late.

II

Scant reflection is needed to see the link between the two ideas. If a certain change is incapable of being isolated, contained, or counteracted as between different spheres and aspects of action, the impact of this change on the encountering society must be either transformative or abortive. To hold, in other words, that novelty is indivisible or that an innovation inevitably produces a chain reaction of mutually reinforcing consequences is to rule out the possibility of equivocal results. Innovations that come only in an "explosive package" cannot form stable mixtures or viable combinations with important elements of the encountering society. That such mixtures or equivocations are impossible is clearly the implication of postulating irreconcilability between "modernity" and "traditionality."

To speak in logical terms, eurhythmic process constitutes *a necessary condition* of irreconcilability. Eurhythmic process is *not*, however, a *sufficient* condition of irreconcilability (since, for example, change might proceed eurhythmically in an encountering society that previously contained a perfect correlative of an innovation). It follows that those who hold with dichotomous analysis are committed, willy-nilly, to the postulate of eurhythmy and that those who reject the first position must abandon the second. But the converse is not necessarily true.

III

As to my second assertion, just a partial listing of the relevant scholars indicates the currency and persuasiveness of the conceptual apparatus in question: Parsons, Levy, Hagen, Sutton, Shils, Redfield,

Riggs, Millikan and Blackmer, Sinai, the Etzionis, and (despite recent appearances to the contrary) Apter—and even this partial listing is deliberately focused only on those whose work consciously extends beyond the context of a particular case. (The number of empirical cases treated from this perspective in different branches of the social sciences is simply too prodigious to attempt their inclusion. This list also leaves aside many instances in which dichotomous formulations of change have been accepted as a feature of the analysis of problems that are related to but distinguishable from the study of change as such, e.g., much of the current literature on political integration. It also excludes certain theorists whose commitment to dichotomous schemata is less explicit and overt and therefore too hard to pin down within the limits of this article.)

Although the dichotomous analytical framework of the contemporary social scientists mentioned above is sufficiently known to make extensive elaboration of that point unnecessary here, their related attachment to the eurhythmic hypothesis does warrant special attention. Here, too, I have selected as representatives of the position only those who have most clearly articulated it. And in this company, Marion J. Levy, Jr., is conspicuous.

In a paper published in 1952 discussing what he entitled "The Vulnerability of the Structures of Relatively Non-industrialized Societies to Those of Industrialized Societies,"[3] Levy, taking for granted the validity of the mutual exclusivity idea (which he regarded as "too obvious to require elaboration") and acknowledging that his discussion is based on Parsons' pattern-variable formulation, asserts

> ... an apparent tendency of those patterns to become generalized widely through a social system if that system is to maintain its adjustment to its setting. The allocation of goods and services is only analytically separable from the allocation of power and responsibility. Highly universalistic relations in the economic aspects of action are functionally incompatible with highly particularistic ones in the political (i.e., allocation of power and responsibility) aspects of action (p. 123).

> The introduction of new patterns from one relatively non-industrialized society to another can frequently be absorbed with relatively slight changes ... [but] the highly industrialized patterns break this mold and as a minimum afford an alternative economic

[3] In Bert F. Hoselitz, ed., *The Progress of Underdeveloped Areas* (Chicago 1952), 113-25.

base for deviance not otherwise provided. In case after case the initial patterns of family organization, of production units, and of authority and responsibility have broken down (p. 124).

The net balance of subversiveness would seem to be a function of the motivation or pressures to attempt new patterns. . . . The processes [of change in the direction of highly industrialized patterns] . . . once started . . . may create stresses and strains that motivate further abandonments of the old, if only because of presentation of a functioning alternative to serve as a standard (p. 125).

Study of the prospects for long-run stability of highly industrialized systems of economic allocation combined with highly authoritarian systems of political allocation turns up extremely interesting hypotheses. They are hypotheses that, if tenable, are extremely pessimistic for long-run stability of such systems . . . (p. 123, n. 7).

In a much more recent article, Levy has reiterated the eurhythmic hypothesis underlying these paragraphs in terms that are, if anything, more explicit and, for the present purposes, most appropriate:

We are confronted—whether for good or for bad—with a universal social solvent. The patterns of the relatively modernized societies, once developed, have shown a universal tendency to penetrate any social context whose participants have come in contact with them. From many points of view it makes little difference whether these patterns penetrate at least partially by the will and preference of relatively nonmodernized peoples or whether they have the patterns thrust upon them. The patterns always penetrate; *once the penetration has begun, the previous indigenous patterns always change; and they always change in the direction of some of the patterns of the relatively modernized society.*[4]

Of particular interest in this last quotation is the deliberate dismissal (in the third sentence) of any reason to distinguish fundamentally between the historic experiences of the Western cases and those of non-Western countries currently being exposed to patterns predeveloped, as it were, in the West. In other words, one is en-

---

[4] "Patterns (Structures) of Modernization and Political Development," *Annals of the American Academy of Political and Social Science*, 358 (March 1965), 29-40. The quotation is from p. 30; the emphasis is mine. Levy's views are most recently elaborated in his *Modernization and the Structure of Societies*, 2 vols. (Princeton 1966).

couraged to disbelieve that there are any significantly different results that follow from exogenously as against endogenously induced change.[5]

It is well to reiterate that Levy has been singled out here only because he states systematically and unequivocally what many others vaguely imply. Thus, in the pertinent literature are to be readily found looser expressions, the eurhythmic purport of which is tantamount to that of the statements by Levy cited above:

"The process of modernization is a seamless web, and the strands that compose it can be analytically separated only with some loss of realism" (Millikan and Blackmer).[6] And more explicitly, ". . . In the countries in which the transition to economic growth has occurred it has been concomitant with far-reaching change in political organization, social structure, and attitudes toward life. The relationship is so striking and so universal that to assume that one of these aspects of basic social change is unrelated to the others is to strain the doctrine of coincidence beyond all warrant" (Hagen).[7] Riggs, endorsing Toynbee, strikes a similar note: "Toynbee asserts that elements in his spectrum are interdependent, despite their seeming autonomy, so that a borrower finds he cannot limit his borrowing to one element, but must go on to borrow more: 'one thing follows another.' This tends to confirm our hypothesis about the functional interdependence of institutions in our models, and the tension or disequilibrium in transitional settings where dysfunctional elements have been introduced from external sources. . . . It is only after they have borrowed the innovations that they discover they have opened their doors to a modern 'Trojan horse.' "[8]

In his more recent reformulations, Riggs develops the same theme in the context of legal and juridical innovations said to be brought by industrialization: ". . . The introduction of contract procedures and safeguards begins to transform the whole social and economic structure, all the way from the nature of the marriage vows to the emergence of associations and the reorganization of the bureaucracy."[9] Summarizing the contributions of twelve different authors on the

---

[5] Cf. Karl A. Wittfogel, *Oriental Despotism* (New Haven and London 1957), 420-21; and Eric Hoffer, *The Ordeal of Change* (New York 1964), 25-26.

[6] Max F. Millikan and Donald L. M. Blackmer, *The Emerging Nations* (Boston 1961), 44.

[7] Everett E. Hagen, *On the Theory of Social Change* (Homewood 1962), 26.

[8] Fred W. Riggs, "Agraria and Industria," in W. J. Siffin, ed., *Toward the Comparative Study of Public Administration* (Bloomington 1957), 103-4.

[9] *Administration in Developing Countries: The Theory of Prismatic Society* (Boston 1964), 47.

general topic "Processes of Change: Initiation, Diffusion, Termination," the Etzionis point out in the concluding section of their volume on social change that "underlying the analysis of most processes described in this section is the assumption that the various parts of any social system are interdependent, so that changes in one sector will be followed by strains which necessitate adjustive changes in other sectors if the social system is to maintain its viability."[10]

At the risk of tedium, it would be easy to go on culling comparable statements, varying in degree of explicitness, from other contributions to the literature; but I trust that those quoted serve adequately to indicate the currency and prevalence of the proposition under examination here.

Having deliberately lifted these statements from what are for the most part very carefully developed schemes of analysis so as to make the issues starkly clear, it is only proper for me to dispel any suggestion of unsubtleness on the part of the authors concerned. One frequently made point, for example, is the likely occurrence of a time lag in change as between different spheres or aspects of action. Since not every conceivable action or behavioral pattern is regarded as germane (though there is disagreement on what is or is not germane, e.g., cult), room is usually left for residual spheres that may be unaffected by otherwise transformative change. However, these and other exigencies are viewed precisely as complicating or limiting the scope of the eurhythmic process, not as invalidating the basic proposition. It should also be noted in this connection that the idea of inevitability of change is not *necessarily* or properly involved here; rather the crux of the argument is that *when and if* some significant element of modern Western society starts to penetrate or sustain itself in one major context of a society it always thereafter spreads, eurhythmically, to the others. Thus, some but not all of those writers cited explicitly allow for the possibility of an arrestation of change (as a whole) or for its complete reversal. Finally, it is most important to observe that while most of the scholars mentioned focus primarily on one sector or aspect of society, each nevertheless acknowledges, and some emphasize, that transformative change may also originate in any of the other sectors.

IV

Several factors are frequently cited as contributing to the necessity of a eurhythmic process of change, though these are formulated with

---

[10] Amitai Etzioni and Eva Etzioni, *Social Change* (New York 1964), 403.

varying clarity and precision in the different works of the literature concerned. (But significantly, the idea is hardly developed at all in cases where eurhythmic process is in effect deduced from the dichotomous premise.) At least four such factors or considerations may be extrapolated and summarized, in no particular rank order of incidence or salience, as follows:

1. *Psychological*. People who acquire fundamentally new habits, attitudes, or values in one major field of social activity find it necessary or desirable to conduct themselves according to the same or similar principles of behavior in the other fields.

2. *(Dys)functional*. Retention of fundamentally different cognitive and/or normative standards in different major fields of social activity would undermine the coherence of judgment and response necessary to the viability of the society as a unit.

3. *Institutional*. All the various institutions of any society are so mutually interdependent or interlocking that change is *perforce* cumulative and self-reinforcing. (This might be characterized as the "domino theory" applied to sociopolitical change.)

4. *Structural*. Significant change in one sphere of society always produces or supports persons having vested interests in that change who see to it that the change is secured through the dissemination of its spirit to every other relevant social sphere. Such persons also see to it that their ranks are elevated and swelled at the expense of persons with rival vested interests in the old order. New functions require new roles and new role occupants.

As the main object of this article is a disconfirming juxtaposition of empirical data derived from a single case with a universal claim, these propositions are suitably dealt with here in light of the relevant facts of the case. Thus, no additional effort will be made to consider as such their *internal* adequacy, except to suggest in passing that careful reflection on them individually or severally raises questions of tautological inference and necessary connection, as well as questions of sufficiency of empirical evidence. It is also very important to note that a common assumption that appears to underlie all these propositions is that in every society basic normative consensus is imperative.

V

Signs have recently appeared of a trend away from the dichotomous doctrines of "modernization" analysis. Those who have, for varying reasons (and with varying emphasis and cogency) expressed dissatisfaction include Bendix, Black, Deutsch, Eisenstadt, Hoselitz,

LaPalombara, Moore, Pye, Sanger, and Ward and Rustow. Others have come to *ad hoc* conclusions that are implicitly congenial to nondichotomous premises without formulating them as such, e.g., Levine, Friedland, and LeVine, all of whom, significantly, have been primarily concerned with African materials.[11] Of particular interest as an example in a non-African context is Lockwood's carefully un-sanguine discussion of the relationship of democratic development and industrialization in the historic Japanese experience.[12] A limited selec-tion of a few of the more explicit general statements made in recent works will again be sufficient for our purposes here:

> No society is wholly modern; all represent a mixture of modern and traditional elements. It has often been thought these elements stood in basic opposition to each other, and that there was im-plicit in the social process some force which would ultimately lead to the purgation of traditional "survivals," leaving as a residue the purely "modern" society. The preceding chapters amply document the falsity of such a thesis, at least where Japan is con-cerned, showing that the role of traditional attitudes and institu-tions in the modernization process has often been symbiotic rather than antagonistic. . . . We can, therefore, identify a quality of "reinforcing dualism" within at least some modernizing ex-periences (Ward and Rustow).[13]

> What we are suggesting is that such distinctions as ascription-achievement or consanguine-conjugal, although usually depicted as mutually exclusive alternatives useful for characterizing differ-ences between societies or groups, are more accurately viewed as conflicting principles always present (Moore).[14]

A third objection to the use of "modern" or "modernity" when dealing with problems of political systems is that the terms tend to suggest a single, final state of affairs—a deterministic, unilinear theory of political evolution. . . . The very words "modern" or

[11] Donald N. Levine, "Ethiopia: Identity, Authority, and Realism," in Lucian W. Pye and Sidney Verba, eds., *Political Culture and Political Development* (Princeton 1965), esp. 270-71. Levine's full-scale treatment of Ethiopia is *Wax and Gold* (Chicago 1965). William H. Friedland, "Some Sources of Traditionalism Among Modern African Elites," reprinted in William H. Hanna, ed., *Independent Black Africa: The Politics of Freedom* (Chicago 1964), 363-69. Robert A. LeVine, "Political Socialization and Culture Change," in Clifford Geertz, ed., *Old Societies and New States* (Glencoe 1963), 280-303.

[12] William W. Lockwood, "Economic and Political Modernization: Japan," in Robert E. Ward and Dankwart A. Rustow, eds., *Political Modernization in Japan and Turkey* (Princeton 1964), 117-45.

[13] Pp. 444-45.

[14] Wilbert E. Moore, *Social Change* (Englewood Cliffs 1963), 67.

"modernity" imply a social Darwinian model of political development. They suggest that change is inevitable, that it proceeds in clearly identifiable stages, that subsequent evolutionary stages are necessarily more complex than those which preceded them, and that later stages are better than their antecedents. What we need at this time are genuinely open models of political change that will permit us to identify the various ways in which many variables that bear on change are interrelated. . . . Systems may remain in a given stage for exceedingly long periods, and *when change does occur it may not necessarily represent a step forward*. Concern with the nature of change rather than with definition is likely to permit the development of a science of comparative politics (LaPalombara).[15]

It may be noted that a common element in these statements is the separation of economic and political definitions of modernity, a separation that would be consistent with dysrhythmic premises.

However, as might be expected in light of the depth, tenacity, and august auspices of the received concepts, the break with them has so far been halting, sketchy, and in some instances ambivalent. An example of the last difficulty is Pye, who having explicitly dissociated himself from the dichotomous analytic tradition then proceeds in its characteristic spirit to treat the case of his "transitional" Burmese bureaucrats strictly in pathological terms.[16] Furthermore, he more recently has flatly restated the eurhythmic notion, while also suggesting, curiously, the displacement/rejection choice anew.[17] Another example of less than complete liberation is Ward and Rustow's summary discussion (quoted from above) of the Japanese and Turkish experiences, which surely suggests abandonment of the term and concept of modernization in favor of the far more open-minded idea of political change. Yet unlike LaPalombara they fail to make explicit this logical implication and indeed retain the old usage and, one suspects, to a certain degree at least the definitional concept. More disappointing, this still-fledgling revolt has yet to produce anything like

[15] Joseph LaPalombara, ed., *Bureaucracy and Political Development* (Princeton 1963), 38-39, emphasis mine.
[16] Lucian W. Pye, *Politics, Personality and Nation Building* (New Haven and London 1962).
[17] "The Concept of Political Development," *Annals of the American Academy of Political and Social Science,* 358 (March 1965), 1-13. Pye states, "The politics of historic empires, of tribe and ethnic community, or of colony must give way to the politics necessary to produce an effective nation-state which can operate successfully in a system of other nation-states" (p. 7). "Although to a limited extent the political sphere may be autonomous from the rest of society, for sustained political development to take place it can only be within the context of a multidimensional process of social change in which no segment or dimension of the society can long lag behind" (p. 11).

a comprehensive and systematic examination of the issues inherent in the old tradition. Nor, to my knowledge, has an attempt been made to state explicitly and to sustain nondichotomous premises by a detailed analysis of any single empirical case, apart, if it may be demurred, from the present writer's as yet unpublished study.[18]

Most important in terms of this particular article, the theoretical role of the eurhythmic process in dichotomous schemes of analysis of change is rarely identified or appreciated. The one possible exception that I know of is Wilbert E. Moore, whose conclusions on the general subject of "modernization" at times seem close to my own. Moore certainly seems to be questioning the eurhythmic idea in asking whether "standard components of cultures and societies" may sometimes be autonomous. If a condition of relative autonomy is possible, he asserts, then "change might occur without a kind of 'systemic resistance' deriving from interlocking patterns." He adds, interestingly, that "although this line of speculation runs contrary to the major current theoretical positions in anthropology and sociology, which emphasize and possibly exaggerate systemic relations, it is consistent with rather impressive historical experience."[19]

Most serious of all, there remains a paucity of comparably developed alternative models, much less new propositions concerning specific conditions and consequences of different patterns of change. This objection should not be interpreted as a call for any immediate grand new theoretical "breakthrough" in this respect, however, for if the "modernization" model is as faulty as I believe it to be, the remedy probably lies partly in a far more substantial empirical grounding (including, especially, political history) for less grandiose generalizations about change, and this development obviously cannot take place overnight. Having expressed this reservation about hasty new departures, it is nevertheless appropriate for me simply to state, without elaborating the point here, that if the idea of a universal requisite of normative societal consensus is indeed essential to dichotomous analysis and is false, then the foundations for new theoretical perspectives may be abuilding. I have specific reference here to the concepts of social pluralism and the plural society, as exploratively formulated by Furnivall, Kuper, Smith, and Van den Berghe, whose studies challenge the premise of necessary normative consensus directly and explicitly.[20]

[18] C. S. Whitaker, Jr., "The Politics of Tradition: A Study of Continuity and Change in Northern Nigeria," unpubl. diss., Princeton, 1964.

[19] Social Change, 75. See also Moore's The Impact of Industry (Englewood Cliffs 1965).

[20] J. S. Furnivall, "Some Problems of Tropical Economy," in Rita Hinden, ed., Fabian Colonial Essays (London 1945), and Colonial Policy and Practice (London

With these observations set forth, we can turn to an account of certain concrete aspects of political change in Northern Nigeria as they relate to the proposition of eurhythmic process.

The focus of this account is the impact on the local parliamentary structure of the political system of the traditional kingdoms or emirates of Northern Nigeria, as that Region of the Federal Republic of Nigeria existed up to January 1966. At that time an assassination plot, planned and led by a small group of southern Nigerian army officers, resulted in the deaths of, among others, Sir Ahmadu Bello, the Northern Region premier and Sardauna of Sokoto, and the prime minister of the Federal Republic, Alhaji Sir Abubakar Tafawa Balewa, who was also born and politically based in that Region. This development also brought about the abolition (whether temporary or permanent is not yet clear) of civilian parliamentary government in Nigeria generally, at the direction of a new military government that has described itself as interim. Of course it is too soon to determine the implications of these events for the future of the country, and apart from two passing comments, no discussion of the events is essential to the topic here. The first comment is that the immediate context of the assassination plot was political turmoil and crisis in a southern Nigerian Region, combined with issues of interregional relations and balance, *not* the internal affairs of the then substantially autonomous Northern Region. Secondly, so far as the rise of a military government did concern the political situation within the Northern Region, this was an indication of the strength and resilience of the largely *ancien* regime there, which as we shall see had shown no signs of either regression to untrammeled "traditionality" or spontaneous growth toward true "modernity."

The discussion here proceeds with brief mention of salient features of the traditional system as it operated before and after the introduction of parliamentary forms and of the circumstances and conditions accompanying their introduction, followed by a concise synopsis of some results of change which reflect our theme.

1948). Leo Kuper, *An African Bourgeoisie: Race, Class, and Politics in South Africa* (New Haven 1965), and "Plural Societies—Perspectives and Problems" (forthcoming). M. G. Smith, who combines expertise in African and West Indian studies, has written a critical statement of his position on the premise of necessary societal consensus in the preface to his collection of essays *The Plural Society in the British West Indies* (Berkeley and Los Angeles 1965), vii-xvii. Also see his "Institutional and Political Conditions of Pluralism" and "Pluralism in Pre-Colonial African Societies" (forthcoming). Pierre L. Van den Berghe, *Africa: Social Problems of Change and Conflict* (San Francisco 1965), and "Pluralism and the Polity—A Theoretical Exploration" (forthcoming). These forthcoming papers will appear in a volume edited by Leo Kuper and M. G. Smith; they were produced for the 1965-66 Colloquium in African Studies, University of California, Los Angeles.

VI

The traditional political system of the Hausa emirates, whose begin-nings go back as far as the fifteenth century, retained its basic character throughout the colonial era, as M. G. Smith's study of one of these emirates clearly shows.[21] Thus, to a very large extent it is possible to speak of this system in continuous terms up to and including the period in which parliamentary institutions of the British type were super-imposed on it.

The major event of the precolonial era was the *jihad* of 1804-1810, which placed Fulani emirs on the thrones of most of the Hausa states, whose political (and religious) unity, with that of a few newly-founded kingdoms, thereafter centered in the Fulani imperial seat at Sokoto, whence Usuman dan Fodio had first raised the call to conquer for the sake of local purification of Islam.

The Fulani emirs, like the British colonial rulers after them, helped to assure political continuity by adapting to their own ends the main political characteristics, together with the administrative techniques and organization, of the local regimes before them.[22] (In the case of the British, it is now well known that their adaptations and adjustments were later rationalized, principally by Lord Lugard, into the now famous British colonial doctrine of indirect rule.) Though with re-spect to the structure and composition of these regimes there are im-portant variations, some of which historically, as today, have significant political implications and consequences, the major features they share amply justify their characterization as a system.

In this system, both administrative and political relations, closely entwined as these are, are centered in the emir, whose autocratic posi-tion was in practice limited originally only by recourse to extralegal sanctions, by natural exigencies, and by the dynamics and problems inherent in the nature of the system itself. Religious prescriptions politically applicable in principle have suffered from the usual embar-rassment of the classical Islamic states generally, and also, for that matter, of historic Christendom: lack of any independent machinery for enforcement and of "means of protecting against government re-prisal" for would-be defenders of those prescriptions.[23] Indeed, to the Hausa-Fulani political order, the principal impact of concern with the

---

[21] *Government in Zazzau* (Oxford 1960).

[22] See Smith, "Historical and Cultural Conditions of Political Corruption Among the Hausa," *Comparative Studies in Society and History,* vi (1963-64), 164-94.

[23] Whitaker, "Three Perspectives on Hierarchy: Political Thought and Leadership in Northern Nigeria," *Journal of Commonwealth Political Studies,* iii (March 1965), 6.

local (Maliki) version of the Islamic Shari'a, or divinely sanctioned law (at once temporal and spiritual), is the idea that disobedience to the emir or his representatives is an abnegation of faith.

The dynamics and problems engendered by the system for all Northern Region emirate regimes have stemmed in very large part from corporate organization and cleavage within the royal dynasties and other hereditary lineages, both Fulani and non-Fulani. Many of these corporate subgroups have independent and collective claims to both central and local bureaucratic offices, territorial and functional. The balance, adjudication, maintenance, and pursuit of these rival corporate claims to office at all levels of the bureaucracy have always been the overwhelming political preoccupation of members of the ruling stratum. Strictly vicariously, they are the concern of the subjugated masses of politically nonparticipant commoners as well.

This competitive feature includes the office of emir itself, succession to which is determined without benefit of primogeniture or any other automatic provision. Furthermore, Islamically sanctioned polygamy and concubinage plus cultural emphasis on maximum male progeny naturally proliferate the number of eligible persons for all hereditary offices, and this extends and intensifies the intramural competition. Severe personal tension is inherent in the system, for as Smith states about the Zaria emirate in 1950, "neither was administrative offence a sufficient ground for dismissal, nor administrative merit a sufficient ground for appointment. Political offence, defined by the system as attachment to the king's political rival, was the principal ground for dismissal; and political solidarity with the king and opposition to his rivals was the principal ground for appointment."[24] Apart from solidarity with superiors, the essential criterion of and precondition for success in this institutionalized system of competition, which in Hausa is called *neman sarautu*—the quest for offices and the prestigious formal titles that go along with them—was and is wealth and influence (largely purchased).

The ubiquitous institution of *neman sarautu* is very greatly responsible for two ostensibly contrasting sets of qualities in the system as a whole: on the one hand, political and administrative insecurity, uncertainty, instability, arbitrariness, domination, dogmatism, coercion, and restrictiveness; on the other hand, competitiveness, flexibility, mobility, calculation, inventiveness, and secular devotion to whatever the requirements and rewards of power might be. These apparently "dual" syndromes are simultaneously endemic to this system, and their copresence

[24] *Government in Zazzau,* 106.

suggests the profoundly misleading inadequacy here of a monochromatic categorization of "traditionality" as static, prescriptive, closed, and nonrational—notwithstanding the clear fact that the basis of authority and power in the system has always been fundamentally hereditary.

In terms of the supposed dichotomous antinomies, the inextricably mixed qualities of this system are epitomized by the existence of high-office-holding slaves and small numbers of commoner client-retainers who enjoy official status. Thus, the very realities that render a hereditary emir insecure and repressive also sometimes induce him to extend his official patronage to persons, such as slaves, who *because of* hereditary ineligibility are powerless to threaten legitimately the position of the emir. As such, they are highly suitable agents of autocratic and deeply personalized government. The point here, of course, is not to obscure the emphasis of the system, the approximation of which to the dichotomous model of generic "traditionality" is in many respects real, but to indicate that its more "modernistic" characteristics are equally relevant and entrenched.

Additional comment concerning the situation of the masses of commoners, or *talakawa*, is necessary here. As one government-sponsored report on the vast web of official gift-giving in cash and kind which goes hand in hand with *neman sarautu* concluded, "It is clear that in the ultimate analysis the *talakawa* pay for everything."[25] Indeed, the late prime minister of Nigeria publicly pointed out in 1950 that "much of the attraction" of holding office and title in the traditional bureaucracy or "native administration" has been the "opportunities it offers for extortion of one form or another."[26] Thus, the great majority of the largely peasant masses are not only deprived of membership and participation in this traditional political system but are systematically exploited in its behalf as well.

The one avenue of traditional political access available to *individual* commoners is clientage, a Hausa-Fulani institution that Smith defines as "an exclusive relation of mutual benefit which holds between two persons defined as socially and politically unequal, which stresses their solidarity."[27] In other words, the commoner client-participant in this system is dependent for his position wholly upon the uncertain benevolence of his overlord. Elsewhere I have stated the general function and role of the institution as follows: "The crux of the clientage relationship

[25] *Report on the Exchange of Customary Gifts* (Kaduna 1954), 6.
[26] *Northern Nigeria, Regional Council Debates*, August 19, 1950 (Kaduna 1950).
[27] *Government in Zazzau*, 8.

is that patronage, economic security, and protection may be exchanged for personal loyalty and obedience. For the *Habe* (Hausa) *talakawa*, clientage represented the principal channel of upward mobility, toward and within the ruling circle. For those who remained outside that sphere, lesser forms of clientage relationships provided virtually the only defense against such eventualities as arbitrary tax-levies, injurious treatment in judicial proceedings, discrimination in allocation of farming land or in administration of public services, to mention only the most common perils."[28]

One important final point here is that in the case of the large non-Muslim populations living under several emirate regimes, this general structure of political domination is reinforced and enhanced, in consequence of their status in the eyes of their Muslim rulers as legitimately outside the pale of any justice and security enjoined by the precepts of Islam.

VII

Whatever may be true elsewhere in Africa or even in Nigeria, the introduction in Northern Nigeria of a parliamentary structure of regional government by the British colonial authority was in essence a compromise between two not easily reconciled objectives: (1) to launch Nigeria as an independent and democratically governed national entity, and (2) to prevent abrupt discontinuity with British policy toward the emirate system which for half a century had been to preserve the Fulani regimes as instruments of law and order and as vehicles of controlled innovation along modern British social and political lines. For whatever the merits of the original policy might previously have been, once the decision was made to transfer power to Nigeria as a whole under democratic forms, the reality of past policy meant British fear that the existing foundations of social, economic, and political order and progress in the emirates would be shattered. Thus, the British perceived that their immediate responsibility in this area was to cushion the impact of change, and a British strategy of "guided democracy," as it were, therefore governed the terminal phase of colonial rule. It will be relevant and instructive to recount at this point some of the specific means through which the British contrived to manipulate change to serve the interests of continuity.

The electoral rules initially used in the Northern Region employed the hierarchy of local councils, which were almost completely composed of dependent and loyal members and clients of the emirate bureauc-

---

[28] "The Politics of Tradition," 447.

racies, as electoral colleges. These indirectly yielded the membership of the Northern parliament, the House of Assembly, which in turn chose the Northern members of the central Nigerian legislature in Lagos. As extra safeguards, emirs were given the right simply to appoint directly ten percent of the membership of the penultimate colleges, and suffrage was limited to taxpayers. These arrangements, like others, were peculiar in Nigeria to the Northern Region.

The transfer to elected Northern government ministers of executive authority over the functions of "their" ministries (and therefore of supervisory authority over many of the functions of the emirate bureaucracies) was delayed five years beyond the time of this devolution in the southern Nigerian regions. Indeed, for two years after the introduction of the nonexecutive ministers, conspicuously no minister for local government was appointed at all.

At the appropriate time, British officials helped to design substitute devices for the above measures under a new Nigerian constitution. These measures included investment of power over all matters having to do with appointment, grading, and discipline of Northern chiefs (including emirs) in an autonomous, nonpopularly elected Council of Chiefs, the small permanent membership of which included the two most important emirs (Sokoto and Kano). A constitutional provision also gave to a House of Chiefs powers that in relation to the popularly elected chamber (the House of Assembly) were coordinate, indeed, technically supreme.[29]

The ultimate power to make appointments to the higher levels of the local emirate bureaucracies legally rested with the regional government. Thus these local officials had the virtual status of civil servants. Yet, for purposes of regional and party political activity, these officials were defined as nongovernmental officials, free, under the British code of the nonpolitical civil service, to be elected to parliamentary seats, and to occupy them even while retaining local office in the traditional bureaucracies.

The British also supported the insistence, on the part of the essentially *ancien* political regime thus shored-up with the above arrangements, that the existing territorial boundaries of the North remain intact under the federal constitution. The significance of this proviso was that those boundaries politically incorporated into this region non-Muslim peoples, amounting to at least a third of the total Northern population,

[29] See R. L. Sklar and C. S. Whitaker, Jr., "The Federal Republic of Nigeria," in Gwendolen M. Carter, ed., *National Unity and Regionalism in Eight African States* (Ithaca 1966), 59.

who were historically outside the boundaries of the Fulani Empire. Their inclusion within these boundaries allowed the Fulani-dominated regional regime to dominate the minority areas, where there was strong evidence of mounting secessionist sentiment. When linked to the fact that this Northern unit as a whole contained more than fifty percent of the entire Nigerian population, the crucial contribution of the British to the policy of "One North" (and thus to the dominant political role later played by the Northern majority political party in the affairs of what became the Federal Republic of Nigeria) becomes obvious. All these constitutional and political manipulations also help explain why, under the Republic, the local emirate regimes remained safe from any unwelcome interference from Lagos.

The main point of this brief delineation of British policy in the terminal phase of colonialism is *not* that this policy alone was responsible for the actual results of political change in Northern Nigeria. On the contrary, a very good argument can be made out that those results would have occurred without British efforts. But British policy did help establish the most favorable conditions for a process that British officials in the North often approvingly called "continuity in change." A second, equally important, point here is that such compromise policies and constitutional devices made it unnecessary for either the British or their successors to reject a parliamentary structure in order to foster continuity.

VIII

The paragraphs to follow represent a compendium of selected events, facts, and relationships that indicate dysrhythmic change, i.e., examples of change in one aspect or sphere in the direction of a pattern of "modernity" which either occasioned, in another aspect or sphere, change having the effect of sustaining or reinforcing a premodern institution or pattern of behavior, or caused no significant change, in Northern Nigeria in the period 1952-1966. (Identification by the reader of what are "modern" patterns, and from the brief discussion of the emirate system above, what are "premodern" or "traditional" patterns, is assumed.)

ASPECTS OF CHANGE AND CONTINUITY

INSTITUTIONAL VS. STRUCTURAL ASPECTS

Social composition of the Northern parliament (House of Assembly). The decisive impact of traditional emirate status patterns on the composition of the Northern parliament (1956-1961) is reflected in data

derived from a careful survey using face-to-face interviews and independent sources.

Out of 103 members elected from constituencies situated in the
emirates (the total of elected members was 131), 77, or 75 percent,
belonged to the traditional ruling class, applying this term only to
members whose *fathers'* status corresponded to one or more categories
of membership in that class. Extending the definition to include those
whose own office or title or marriage relationship placed them in one
or more of these categories, the percentage of ruling-class members was
82 percent (84 members). Well over a third of the total emirate members were related to royal families and another fourth belonged to the
hereditary nobility. Twenty-four percent of the group of 77 were sons
of emirs. Out of the group of 77 belonging intergenerationally to the
ruling class, 60 held traditional titles, or *sarautu*. The 1956-1961 House
was elected on the basis of a mixed system of direct and indirect procedures (mostly the latter). All elected members of the 1961-1966 House
were elected on the basis of direct procedures and adult male suffrage.
In the expanded 1961-1966 House, 97 of 173 had not been members of
the previous House. A spot check of just under half of the new members from emirate constituencies indicated that the percentage of (inter-
generational) ruling-class members may have slightly increased, and
most certainly did not decrease significantly.

Northern Peoples' Congress party structure. The Northern Peoples'
Congress (NPC) emerged after 1952 as a party commanding the support of the overwhelming majority of the Northern Nigerian electorate.
It won by increasingly wide margins in the elections of 1954 (federal),
1956 (regional), 1961 (regional), and 1964 (federal).

Prior to 1952, when parliamentary government was established, the
NPC was controlled by a majority whose occupations, traditional social
status, and political attitudes placed them outside the sphere of traditional elite membership and loyalty. It could be described as a party of
"moderate radicals."[30] After 1952, control of the party passed to persons
loyal to and dependent upon the emirate bureaucracies. An important
impetus for this shift was the advantage to the party in having the
apparatus of the traditional bureaucracy double as the organizational
machinery for the party. Having gained control of the party, the new
dominant faction voted in 1957 to "freeze" the slate of elected party
officers, and no further voting was ever held. Indeed, after 1957, no open

[30] P. C. Lloyd, "Traditional Rulers," in James S. Coleman and Carl G. Rosberg, Jr.,
eds., *Political Parties and National Integration in Tropical Africa* (Berkeley and Los
Angeles 1964), 400.

congresses of the party were held, all decisions being taken by the *parliamentary* party in the name of the party as a whole.

In 1952, the presidency of the party passed to Ahmadu Bello, Sardauna of Sokoto (a traditional title) and a member of the Sokoto Fulani imperial dynasty; first-round balloting had indicated a majority preference for Abubakar Tafawa Balewa, a commoner and an outspoken critic of traditional bureaucratic administration. The consideration leading to the second-ballot election of the Sardauna was the desire to secure the backing and influence of the emirs and their supporters.

After 1952, NPC party nominations for parliamentary seats were monitored by and subject to the approval of the emir in whose domains constituencies were located. In effect, membership in the legislature became a *sarauta* in the patronage of the emir.[31]

Majority-minority relations. Control of the regional legislature accomplished what historic Fulani ambitions had previously failed to achieve: extension of Fulani jurisdiction over unconquered tribes and enclaves (e.g., notably, the Tiv people). As elsewhere observed, "even such formerly independent Muhammedan Chiefdoms as Habe Abuja have been forced by this situation to follow the Fulani lead in order to avoid isolation."[32]

The political solidarity of kingdoms that were historically and ethnically divided, i.e., Bornu and the Sokoto Empire as a whole, was stimulated by the need to mobilize support for the perpetuation of the ruling elites in the emirates against (1) radical, commoner-oriented opposition parties operating within the emirates (e.g., the Northern Elements Progressive Union and the Bornu Youth Movement), (2) opposition parties based in the minority areas or Northern "Middle Belt" (e.g., the United Middle Belt Congress), and (3) nationalistic and radical socialist-oriented parties based in the southern regions of Nigeria, which were naturally attempting to gain support in both majority and minority areas of the Northern Region. The roles of the Sardauna of Sokoto as regional premier and of Shettima Kashim (previously Waziri or Vizier of Bornu) as (constitutional) governor of the Northern Region appropriately expressed this development. This solidarity, achieved "at the expense" of incorporating new non-Fulani elements into the dominant political structure, facilitated Fulani preponderance.

Dual membership in the traditional bureaucratic structure and the

[31] R. L. Sklar and C. S. Whitaker, Jr., "Nigeria," in Coleman and Rosberg, 609.
[32] Smith, *Government in Zazzau,* 250.

parliamentary structure. Those who were simultaneously members of a modern legislature and office-holders in one of the traditional emirate bureaucracies enjoyed enormous and reciprocal advantages, both personal and political, over others. Salaries starting at £720 per annum (before a national "austerity" cut in 1961 the figure was £860) were often invested in the pursuit of promotion in the local bureaucracy, while chances of success in this, the ubiquitous traditional institution of *neman sarautu,* were enhanced considerably by command of the various resources that legislative membership provided. This relationship is reflected in the successful "dual" careers of numerous legislators.

As ministerial office in the regional government required such officials to reside in Kaduna, the regional capital, ministers (unlike rank-and-file legislators) could not simultaneously hold bureaucratic office (though they usually retained the status of "on leave without pay"). They could, however, pursue higher title without office, and at least eight ministers succeeded in elevating their positions in this respect while in office. Even more significant, no fewer than ten Northern ministers of government (including here both regional and federal ministers) *resigned* office to accept prestigious posts in their local emirates after enjoying remunerative terms of office at Kaduna or Lagos.

These reciprocal advantages had important implications for the balance between rival dynasties and lineages in the ruling hierarchies of the emirates. One implication was that a parliamentary contest involving members of such rival traditional corporate groups sometimes exacerbated those corporate cleavages and solidarities in the context of the local native administration. In several instances, dismissed local office-holders (members of rival dynasties or lineages) compensated for their loss of office by winning a parliamentary seat, thus recapturing status.

INSTITUTIONAL VS. NORMATIVE ASPECTS

Secular promotion of Islam. In 1959 the Sardauna proclaimed in the Northern House of Assembly: "As long as [my] party, the NPC, is in power in the Region, it . . . [will] not legalize what God has forbidden."[33] This attitude was reflected in various ways in and through the new political institutions. Symbolically, the official motto of the Northern government was "Work and Worship"; green, the color of dan Fodio's flags of investiture of authority in the *jihad,* and strongly evocative generally of Islam, was the official color both of the government (e.g., it replaced "Westminster black" in the robes of the Speaker

[33] *Daily Times of Nigeria,* September 3, 1959, 3.

of the House of Assembly) and of the NPC, whose women supporters, especially, duly displayed it on all appropriate occasions.

Conspicuously frequent trips to Mecca on pilgrimage (Islam *requires* only one) by the Sardauna and his prominent and favored colleagues in both regional government and native administration served to emphasize the role of the new political leaders as vehicles of the faith, as did a series of Muslim convocations convened by the Sardauna in Kaduna between 1960 and 1966.

Under the Northern Nigerian Penal Code introduced in 1960, drunkenness is a criminal offense (Section 401), as is drinking of any amount of alcohol by a Muslim (Section 403—punishable by one month's imprisonment, five pounds, or both). Adultery is punishable by two years' imprisonment, a fine (maximum unspecified), or both. In homicide cases there has been an attempt to capture the spirit of the orthodox Islamic law of talion (Sections 393, 394). Several other provisions approximate authoritarian Islamic standards of relations between bureaucratic officials and the public (especially Sections 136, 137, 138, and 10).

A persistent and highly inflammatory NPC campaign theme has been the duty of true Muslims to follow Muslim political leadership, or to reject, in other words, that of non-Muslim or "nonorthodox" southern Nigerians. In the cause of this NPC doctrine of religious obligation to follow its lead as the great protector of traditional authority, the conservative *mallamai*, or religious teachers, have been very active and most effective.

Secular promotion of hereditary rule. Apart from the more or less spontaneous reinforcement of traditional norms implicit in the preceding sections on dual membership and secular promotion of Islam, the regional government sought to strengthen the position of the native administration structures in many ways. It vested them with legal authority and responsibility to maintain law and order generally, to regulate and determine issuance of permits for political party meetings, assemblies, and so on, and to serve as officials for the conduct of popular (parliamentary) elections. In the case of the larger emirates, it confirmed the judicial functions of (otherwise executive) emirs, extending in some cases to the power to try capital cases. It devolved much of the responsibility for the administration of public services onto native administrations, such that virtually every important government amenity in rural areas was distributed through these units. It utilized the local bureaucracies, as had the British, as tax-assessing and tax-collecting agencies. It made available to them considerable financial aid through grants, loans, and retention of tax revenues, and allotted them a significant role in capital or economic-development projects and expenditures (by 1960 over ten percent of the total regional funds were so allocated). While the composition of the central executive councils of the emirates was generally liberalized to include representatives of nontraditional ruling elements, in the great emirates (especially Sokoto, Kano, Bornu, and Zaria) such reforms went no further than a shift from autocracy to oligarchy. Thus, measures strengthening "local government" in the North were in effect bolstering hereditary rule.

NORMATIVE VS. STRUCTURAL AND INSTITUTIONAL ASPECTS

NEPU's use of traditional influences in an effort to effect radical change. The objective of the opposition NEPU (Northern Elements Progressive Union) was structural transformation, i.e., abolition of the traditional bureaucracies; secular government; popular participation in, and effective control of, governmental institutions, local and regional. Particularly after 1956, probably out of frustration at its failure otherwise to attract mass support, NEPU not only emphasized the traditional cleavages between *talakawa* and *sarakuna* (ruling-class members), but also utilized religious symbols and themes in its own appeals and propaganda to counter NPC strategy. It accepted dissident traditional elements into its fold and sought to exploit their residual prestige and influence, e.g., most revealingly in the 1959 federal election, when two of NEPU's candidates were deposed emirs seeking to recover lost glory. In a number of situations involving local dynastic or lineage rivalries, NEPU sought to take part to its own advantage. In sum, NEPU, which ostensibly represented a revolutionary political force working contrary to the traditional structure, in practice was to a significant extent obliged to rely tactically on "premodern" and to some degree "antimodern" tendencies.

SPHERES OF CHANGE

ECONOMY VS. POLITY

The traditionally oriented regime working in the cause of economic development. The social and political characteristics of the parliamentary regime described above evidently were no deterrent to its serious pursuit of economic development, including industrial projects.

A 1963 study conducted under the auspices of the Northern Ministry of Trade and Industries, with the cooperation of British industrial consultant firms, boasted findings as follows: "Factories built in Northern Nigeria during the period 1960-63 produce a variety of products and the total investment in industrial development in this short time approximates £20,000,000 of which about £5,000,000 is from Northern Nigerian sources." And, "Within the Federal national income growth Northern Nigeria has shown the most rapid growth. From 1950 to 1957 the national income of the North increased more than twice as fast as that of either of the other two Regions. Since 1957, Northern Nigeria has at least maintained her share of the Federal total so that by 1960 her national income had risen to a total of about £560 million, at 1960 prices—an increase of 68 percent over the decade compared with 47 percent increase in Federal national income."[34]

Admittedly, some of the impressiveness of these figures results in part from the relatively backward base from which the North began its growth compared with that of the South, but the figures do indicate that the regime neither was indifferent to nor did it seek to inhibit economic development. In fact, the regime assiduously sought to publicize the advantages offered by a "disciplined" society for purposes of economic growth.[35]

Economic development in the service of traditional interests. As in the other regions of Nigeria, government-created and government-controlled marketing boards in the Northern Region purchased the main export crops from producers at fixed prices for sale abroad, the difference between prices paid to the producer and received from abroad yielding a surplus. These surpluses were used to fund statutory development corporations, which undertook projects aimed at development and, through subsidiary loan boards and finance corporations, made loans and grants to local government authorities, private firms, and individuals. As might be expected, high-status persons in traditional roles who benefited through participation, indirect or direct, in such projects and new enterprises were numerous. Suffice it to say that like the perquisites of parliamentary membership, wealth generated through the process of economic development was also available for "reinvestment" in traditional institutions and structures. Moreover, it was hardly a secret that private foreign firms, confronted with the copious legal and practical powers at the disposal of native administrations, found it convenient to grant to the more influential local officials substantial favors.

EDUCATION VS. POLITY

Achievement sustains ascription. Striking as the hereditary origins of

---

[34] Northern Nigeria, Ministry of Trade and Industries, *The Industrial Potentialities of Northern Nigeria* (Kaduna 1963), 13, 16.

[35] *Ibid.,* 30; also see *Provincial Annual Reports* (Kaduna 1953-1964), *passim.*

the Northern parliamentarians are, the fact is, too, that they constituted
an elite in terms of Western education as well. My survey of the 1956-
1961 members showed that in a general population of which less than
two percent were literate, these parliamentarians enjoyed an average
of 7.5 years of formal, Western-type schooling. The average for Northern ministers (regional and federal combined) was 10.6 years. The
relatively high modern educational attainments of this traditional elite
group were directly attributable to the initial British view that, as one
governor put it, "If indirect rule is to be truly tribal [in Northern
Nigeria], we must educate from the top down, and not as in Southern
Nigeria from the bottom upwards."[36]

Although the percentage of children at school in Northern Nigeria
doubled between 1959 and 1965, the percentage in 1965 was still strikingly low in the great emirates (e.g., Kano, 4.9 percent, Bornu, 4.1
percent, Sokoto, 3.2 percent), suggesting that, despite the fact that
Western education is officially now open to all, its result in those areas
continues to be that it further sets the established ruling classes apart
from the ordinary masses of subjects.

CONCLUSION

It will be noted that the illustrations above omit explicit consideration of important combinations of variables. One of these, the spheres
of polity and cult, was left out because it seems unnecessary to elaborate
the obvious lack of parallel between how they are thought to have
been related in the historic Western experiences of change and how
they have interacted in the Northern Nigerian situation. Clearly, that
situation has not conformed to any model of political change involving a shift from sacred to secular political institutions and values.
Lack of hard data dictated no special attention to the relationship of
psychological to other aspects of change, though here, too, it seems an
obvious inference that psychic stress has hardly characterized the condition of those called upon to play dual roles. More generally, it might
be noted that the illustrations tend to stress simple continuity at the
expense of the occurrence of change short of the model of "modernity,"
though again this latter result represents merely an implicit variation
on the theme of what is presented.

In any case, the illustrations seem quite sufficient to indicate the
unacceptability, so far as the Northern Nigerian experience is concerned,
of the proposition that "once the penetration [of modern patterns] has
begun, the previous indigenous patterns always change; and they always

[36] Whitaker, "The Politics of Tradition," 408.

change in the direction of some of the patterns of the relatively modernized society."[87]

Three likely objections to this attempted disconfirmation may be anticipated. One is that the patterns involved were not "truly" or sufficiently modern to provide a fair case; the second is that there was not enough time (fourteen years) for an inherent eurhythmic process to unfold; the third is that the Northern Nigerian experience in this period was unique. To the first and second objections, there are essentially two pertinent rejoinders. One, if certain quantitative degrees or levels of "modernity" are necessary to the eurhythmic hypothesis, then this quantification must be incorporated in it, which evidently has not heretofore been done. Indeed, we have been encouraged to believe that the process will obtain under virtually any magnitude of stimulus. The same point holds true for the matter of time span: the operative amount will have to be included in the proposition. Secondly, even if an operative time span is indicated and such elusive qualities as "achievement," "universalism," and "specificity" were quantifiable for operational purposes, significant phenomena resulting from "low" or "subthreshold" conditions must nevertheless be taken into account in any valid general theory of the process of change. As for the third objection, it may be suggested, apart from the fact that a single counterinstance is sufficient to disconfirm the hypothesis as presently stated, that any apparent "uniqueness" of the Northern Nigerian case may well be an effect of the prevalence of the hypothesis rather than a sign of its general validity.

In the absence of a revised formulation of the hypothesis of eurhythmic process, three general counterpropositions to the present version seem to be suggested by this discussion of the Northern Nigerian case:

1. Significant change in one important sphere or aspect of social activity may ramify in other aspects or spheres; however, such ramifications are not always consonant with the character and direction of the initial change.

2. Change may offer novel opportunities for those adversely subjected to that change to defend, recoup, reaffirm, augment, or facilitate antecedent activity or value, notwithstanding that such activity or value is manifestly or latently inconsistent with the character and direction of the initial change.

3. Subjected to potentially transformative political change, a society previously characterized by political domination presents special oppor-

[87] Levy, cited n. 4.

tunities for "manipulative response" that limits the impact of that change.

None of the fine points of this analysis should be allowed to obscure the deeper general significance of the Northern Nigerian case, however. The analysis reveals that the general factors (as outlined in Section IV) which allegedly contribute to a necessary eurhythmic process of change are at best special occurrences. We have seen, moreover, how a "traditional" system may include important features that are as close to the modern model as to the traditional one, and how agents of "modernity" may simultaneously act in defense of "tradition." Furthermore, many of the points of convergence between "traditional" and "modern" elements in the Northern Nigerian case seem highly functional and systematically viable. They point to the possibility of those very symbiotic combinations of qualities which dichotomous and eurhythmic conceptions would preclude. As a general proposition, in other words, analytically or normatively antithetical social elements may in actuality be quite compatible under certain conditions. If so, the occurrence of a dysrhythmic process of change, as described in this article, ultimately indicates the need for hypotheses about political change which are at once more limited and more inclusive than the concept of modernization allows.

TOWARD A FRAMEWORK FOR THE STUDY OF POLITICAL CHANGE IN THE IBERIC-LATIN TRADITION:

The Corporative Model

By HOWARD J. WIARDA*

INTRODUCTION

IN the early 1960's a great deal of "scare" literature was produced concerning Latin America. The titles and subtitles of many of the books and articles written during the period help bear this contention out: "The Eleventh Hour," "Reform or Revolution," "Evolution or Chaos."[1] The concern of scholars and public officials, stemming principally from the Cuban revolution, was that Latin America was about to explode in violent upheaval, that unless democratic reforms were quick in forthcoming, the Latin American nations would soon be the victims of Castro-Communist takeovers. The "one-minute-to-midnight" mentality shaped not only a great deal of official thinking and policy with regard to Latin America during the 1960's, but also permeated,

* Prepared for delivery at the annual meeting of the American Political Science Association, Chicago, September 1971. This paper is part of a larger study which seeks to develop a general framework for the analysis of socio-political change in Latin America. Some of the ideas presented here have previously been explored in preliminary fashion and in different contexts in the author's "The Latin American Development Process and the New Developmental Alternatives: Military 'Nasserism' and 'Dictatorship with Popular Support,' " *Western Political Quarterly*, xxv (September 1972); "Law and Political Development in Latin America: Toward a Framework for Analysis," *American Journal of Comparative Law*, xix (Fall 1971); and "Elites in Crisis: The Decline of the Old Order and the Fragmentation of the New in Latin America," in Jack M. Hopkins, ed., *Political Ethics of Latin America* (New York, forthcoming). For efforts at applying the model, see also the author's "The Catholic Labor Movement in Brazil: Corporatism, Paternalism, Populism, and Change," in H. Jon Rosenbaum and William Tyler, eds., *Contemporary Brazil* (New York 1972); and *Dictatorship, Development, and Disintegration: The Political System of the Dominican Republic* (forthcoming). A preliminary version of the paper was presented at the Mershon Center, Ohio State University, Columbus, Ohio. Useful commentaries on the earlier draft and on some of the ideas presented have been provided by Kenneth Erickson, Abraham F. Lowenthal, Terry L. McCoy, Keith Rosenn, Philippe C. Schmitter, Ronald M. Schneider, and Iêda Siqueira Wiarda. The responsibility for the views expressed, however, rests solely with the author.

[1] These titles and subtitles are familiar enough in the literature that there is no need to provide the full references. In any case, these examples are cited only as illustrations of a larger *genre* of literature in which similar themes are expressed.

in varying degrees of sophistication, the large body of development literature dealing with the area.

More recently the counter-arguments have gained prominence. Latin America, in the words of John Mander, is an "unrevolutionary society," a seemingly inherently and permanently conservative region.[2] The peasants, the workers, and the students have not proved very revolutionary; revolutions and guerrilla movements have achieved neither widespread support nor great success; the old-time Communist parties are by now outdated and tired bureaucracies; the traditional structures and institutions have not collapsed but have demonstrated remarkable resilience; and the profound social revolution predicted for the area has not occurred and probably will not.[3] Midnight has not tolled—or if it has, little has happened; the choice of reform or revolution has proved to be a false, or at least not an all-inclusive, choice. In Washington, this interpretation of the essentially conservative nature of Latin America, and particularly of the absence of threatening Castro-like movements, has been reflected in a new period of official neglect and indifference.

None of these scenarios, or models, accurately delineates the nature of the Latin American development process. The eleventh-hour theme is probably useful for arousing student interest in the area, for securing aid funds from a reluctant Congress, and for raising the level of public concern regarding Latin America; but it does not reflect the sociopolitical realities of or main forces at work in the Latin American countries, or in Spain or Portugal. Moreover, the scare tactics and verbal overkill that accompanied this era have now produced the inevitable reaction in the form of public and official unconcern and a body of literature that, in seeking to correct past misinterpretations, overcompensates by focusing solely on the static, conservative aspects of Latin American development. Unfortunately, this approach does as much injustice to the complexities involved as does the earlier one of reform-or-revolution. These interpretations have not only inaccurately portrayed the Iberic-Latin development process but, in so doing, they have

[2] Mander, *The Unrevolutionary Society: The Power of Latin American Conservatism in a Changing World* (New York 1969).

[3] See especially the two volumes edited by Claudio Véliz, *The Politics of Conformity in Latin America*, and *Obstacles to Change in Latin America* (London 1967 and 1965, respectively); Luis Mercier Vega, *Roads to Power in Latin America* (New York 1969); Harry Landsberger, "The Labor Elite: Is It Revolutionary?" in Seymour M. Lipset and Aldo Solari, eds., *Elites in Latin America* (New York 1967), 256-300; and Joan Nelson, *Migrants, Urban Poverty, and Instability in Developing Nations* (Cambridge, Mass. 1969).

rendered a disservice to our better comprehension of this culture area.[4]

This brief critique of some of the conventional wisdom regarding Latin America serves as the point of departure for the main theme of the paper: that there are some unique aspects to the process of socio-political change in the Iberic-Latin tradition that do not correspond to the models ordinarily used to analyze national development. These nations are not particularly well served by Rostow's "stages of growth" analysis, by Easton's and Almond's systems theory and the functionalist development literature, or by class analysis and the "power elite" paradigm.[5] Rather, because of their peculiar tradition and antecedents, the Iberic-Latin nations are subject to special imperatives and interpretations and have evolved some distinctive developmental patterns that seldom find expression in our studies of the history of political thought or the literature on social and political change. Indeed, it may well be that the Iberic-Latin tradition represents a "fourth world of development," a peculiar way of managing the great transformations of modern times, that has not yet received the attention it merits.[6] It is toward

[4] For the argument that Spain and Portugal should be included as part of a single Iberic-Latin culture area, see Lawrence S. Graham, "Latin America—Illusion or Reality: A Case for a New Analytic Framework for the Region" (unpub., University of Texas 1969); also, the numerous writings of Kalman H. Silvert regarding what he terms the "Mediterranean ethos," discussed and cited in full below.

[5] Wiarda, "Elites in Crisis" (introductory note). For some additional critiques of the literature of development as it applies to Latin America, see Alfred Stepan, "Political Development: The Latin American Tradition," *Journal of International Affairs*, xx, No. 2 (1966), 223-34; Milton I. Vanger, "Politics and Class in Twentieth Century Latin America," *Hispanic American Historical Review*, xlix (February 1969), 80-93; Mercier Vega (fn. 3); Véliz, *The Politics of Conformity in Latin America* (fn. 3), Introduction; Juan Marsal, *Cambio Social en América Latina: Crítica de Algunas Interpretaciones Dominantes en las Ciencias Sociales* (Buenos Aires 1967); Susanne J. Bodenheimer, *The Ideology of Developmentalism: The American Paradigm —Surrogate for Latin American Studies* (Beverly Hills 1971); and N. Joseph Cayer, "Political Development: The Case of Latin America" (unpub. Ph.D. diss., University of Massachusetts 1972).

[6] The development literature of the last decade has largely ignored or dealt only uncomfortably with the place of Latin America in these various schemes. The nations of Latin America can hardly be called "new states"; they are not "non-Western"; they do not often identify or think of themselves as a part of the "Third World"; and there is considerable doubt as to whether they are "emerging" or "developing." For an argument parallel to the one offered here—that Latin America should be regarded "as something of a Fourth World, with characteristics of its own which entitle it to be studied in its own right and not forced to conform to whatever generalizations can be made about the Third"—see J. D. B. Miller, *The Politics of the Third World* (London 1967), Introduction. See also John D. Martz, "The Place of Latin America in the Study of Comparative Politics," *Journal of Politics*, xxviii (February 1966), 57-80; Merle Kling, "The State of Research on Latin America: Political Science," in Charles Wagley, ed., *Social Science Research on Latin America* (New York 1964), 168-213; and Martin C. Needler, "Political Development and Military Intervention in Latin America," *American Political Science Review*, lx (September 1966), 66.

the explication of the Iberic-Latin developmental model that this paper is directed.

The Traditional Structure of Iberic-Latin Society

The Iberic-Latin nations were largely bypassed by the great revolutions associated with the making of the modern world. The Protestant Reformation, the rise of capitalism, the scientific revolution, the rise of socially more pluralistic and politically more democratic societies, the Industrial Revolution and its many-faceted ramifications—all of these had little effect on the nations of the Iberic-Latin culture area. They remained cut off and isolated from these modernizing currents, at the margin of the ideological trends and socio-political movements taking place elsewhere in Europe, fragments and remnants of a peculiarly Iberic-European tradition dating from approximately 1500, with a political culture and a socio-political order that at its core was essentially two-class, authoritarian, traditional, elitist, patrimonial, Catholic, stratified, hierarchical, and corporate.[7] Given the times and the circumstances, it should not be surprising that the Latin American region should also be structured on the model and as an extension of the Iberic metropoles; what is remarkable is the durability and perseverance of this structure into the present. For despite the recent accelerated onslaught of modernization, the traditional political culture and institutions have proved permeable, accommodative, and absorptive, bending to change rather than being overwhelmed by it, and thus in many respects retaining their traditional essence even under the strains and currents set loose during this century. Since the weight of history and the past is still so heavy in virtually all the Iberic-Latin nations, and since what seems to have evolved is a unique, peculiarly Latin mode of coping with the process of change, let us examine this traditional structure in detail.

THE THEORETICAL DIMENSION

One looks in vain in the standard works on political theory for more than brief mention of the Iberic-Latin tradition. They treat of medieval Christian thought; but, aside from Machiavelli, once in the modern era attention turns to the Northern and more dynamic developing areas of Europe: Locke and the Anglo-American experience, Rousseau and

---

[7] See Louis Hartz and others, *The Founding of New Societies* (New York 1964), especially the essay, "The Heritage of Latin America," by Richard M. Morse, 123-77.

the Revolution, the Germans Kant and Hegel. By the nineteenth century the focus has become even more circumscribed, treating of English utilitarianism and liberalism, Socialist thought, and the ideological concomitants of rising nationalism and industrialization. Later, we may trace the evolution of democratic thought, the varieties of socialism, and the ideological underpinnings of modern totalitarianism. All of these are peculiarly Western conceptions, however, conceptions born of a particular part of Western Europe. The point merits further elaboration, but it seems likely that part of the bias and ethnocentrism that pervades the literature of development stems from this conception of the evolution of political thought in the West and from our selectivity as to which themes and movements are worthy of mention and support, and which are not. In structuring attention along these lines, however, we miss an important thread of thought that remains dominant in the Iberic-Latin nations, that lies at the heart of their peculiar national histories and development processes, and that, because we ignore or reject it out of hand, contributes to our miscomprehensions concerning the area. As Morse suggests in explaining the deficiencies of Latin American studies in the United States, ours has been a Protestant and is now a pluralist nation, and our academic disciplines are of an increasingly secular and scientific orientation, with the result that we are "insensitive and vaguely hostile to the *sociological* and *psychological* foundations of a Catholic society."[8]

If modern political analysis in the Northern European and Anglo-American tradition was to lead to the glorification of the accomplished fact and of political pragmatism, to materialism and the success theory, and to a unilinear, stage-by-stage conception of development, which was also derived principally from the experiences of these nations, then Iberic-Latin culture can surely claim as its basis a moral idealism, a philosophical certainty, a sense of continuity, and a unified organic-corporate conception of the state and society. This conception derives from Roman law (one can still profitably read Seneca for an understanding of the Iberic-Latin tradition), Catholic thought (Augustine, Aquinas), and traditional legal precepts (the *fueros* or group charters of medieval times, the law of the *Siete Partidas* of Alfonso the Wise). In comprehending the Iberic-Latin systems, one must think in terms of a hierarchically and vertically segmented structure of class and caste stratifications, of social rank orders, functional corporations, estates,

---

[8] Richard M. Morse, "The Strange Career of Latin American Studies,'" *Annals of the American Academy of Political and Social Studies*, CCCLVI (November 1964), 11; emphasis in original.

juridical groupings and *intereses*—all fairly well defined in law and in terms of their respective stations in life—a rigid yet adaptable scheme whose component parts are tied to and derive legitimacy from the authority of the central state or its leader. The foundations for these systems lie in what Morse has called the "Thomistic-Aristotelian notion of functional social hierarchy,"[9] and they find their major expression in the political thought of Spain's Golden Century.

In pursuing paths other than those of Protestant or secular thought, such thinkers as Vitoria, Soto, Suárez, Molina, and Mariana, the chief intellectual architects of the sixteenth-century Spanish state and of the transfer of its essential features to the New World, laid the foundations of a modern theory of Christian society.[10] In contrast to the separation of politics and morality, which dates from Machiavelli and which we usually take to be the beginning of modern political analysis, the integration of the ethical and the social remained the ideal of Spain. Empirical facts had to show the credentials of logic, rightness, and relation to abstract justice. From the modern, secular viewpoint, such scholasticism shackled Spanish thought and removed the Iberic-Latin nations from the mainstreams of modern history. But perceived in another, less utilitarian light, it helped give Spanish life its firm moral pattern, its philosophy of behavior and dominant political culture, and its peculiar mode of adjusting to the pressures of modernization.

Vitoria and Suárez stand as the great system builders on which the Spanish empire and Iberic-Latin society were constructed. Their genius lay in fusing the older Thomistic conception and the system of juridical estates derived from Spanish customary law with the newer concept of absolute, state-building royal authority. There were important differences among the several writers mentioned, to be sure,[11] but what is more striking are the common, unifying themes. All assume an ordered universe, all adopt the Thomistic hierarchy of laws, and all base their theories of state and society on Christian assumptions. All share, furthermore, a disdain for the common man; what they mean by popular government is feudal and aristocratic, based upon a restoration of the privileges or *fueros* of the Middle Ages, the power of the traditional estates, dominated by "natural" elites, and without popular suffrage.

---

[9] Morse, "Recent Research on Latin American Urbanization: A Selective Survey with Commentary," *Latin American Research Review*, 1 (Fall 1965), 41. See also John Henry Merryman, *The Civil Law Tradition: An Introduction to the Legal Systems of Western Europe and Latin America* (Stanford 1969); and Wiarda, "Law and Political Development" (introductory note).

[10] The argument here follows that of Mariano Picón-Salas, *A Cultural History of Spanish America* (Berkeley 1968), 39-40.

[11] Bernice Hamilton, *Political Thought in Sixteenth-Century Spain* (Oxford 1963).

Their view of society and the state is an organic one—that government is natural, necessary, and ordained by God for achieving harmony among men. This conception is an almost inherently conservative one. In contrast to contract theory which, except in Hobbes, is individualistic, democratic, liberal, and progressive, organic theory subordinates human law to natural and divine law, is more tolerant of authority, slights the individual in favor of group "rights" or a superior "general will," accepts and justifies the status quo, reserves extensive powers for traditional vested interests, and leads inherently toward a corporate system which subordinates man to some allegedly higher end and unity.[12]

The best form of government therefore is an enlightened monarchy or an all-powerful executive; there can be no "separation of powers" or "checks and balances" on the U.S. model. Rather, a monistic structure is required to keep peace and maintain the "natural" order. Extensive powers are also reserved for such corporate entities as the Church, the municipalities, the landed and commercial elites, the guilds, the military hierarchy, and other vested and chartered interests. Organic theory in both Church and state rejects liberal individualism and the materialistic and secular conceptions that accompanied development in northern Europe. Although this repudiation does not *necessarily* follow from the organic, Catholic, and scholastic premises, it certainly has a powerful basis in them.[13]

It is not surprising that this view of the proper ordering of socio-political relations should be articulated and strongly established in sixteenth-century Spain, Portugal, and their colonies in the New World; what is surprising is that it should endure so long. In the metropoles, with their conservative, non-revolutionary traditions, it persisted through the decline of Spanish power in the seventeenth century, the Bourbon reforms of the eighteenth, the divisive currents of the nineteenth, and the period of challenge and conflict in the twentieth—only to be re-established in almost pristine form in the Spain of Primo de Rivera and Franco, and the Portugal of Salazar and Caetano. In Spanish-Portuguese America it not only survived some three centuries of colonial rule but also, in slightly reordered and rebaptized form, the separations from the mother countries in the early nineteenth century, the tempestuous histories that followed (in which *restoration* of the Spanish system often remained the operating ideal), and on into

---

[12] See especially the analysis in Guenter Lewy, *Constitutionalism and Statecraft During the Golden Age of Spain: A Study of the Political Philosophy of Juan de Mariana, S.J.* (Geneva 1960), 49-50.

[13] *Ibid.* See also Hamilton (fn. 11), Introduction and Conclusion.

the period of accelerated industrialization, social change, and ideological challenge of the present. Despite these newer pressures—discussed in greater detail later on—one still finds powerful echoes and manifestations of the earlier corporate-organic framework in virtually all contemporary regimes and institutions in Latin America and in their underlying political-cultural foundations. As Newton comments, sixteenth-century Spanish political theory endowed the state "with a remarkable stability, a stability achieved through the delicate balancing of opposing and ultimately antagonistic forces, . . . a system admirably designed, out of very disparate components and different traditions, for the preservation of the status quo."[14]

Space does not permit elaboration of all the nuances and challenges to this dominant tradition. The Laws of the Indies, derived from both the *Siete Partidas* and the newer sixteenth-century concepts, provide a remarkable early example of and bulwark for this tradition, albeit modified and reinterpreted many times over. In the eighteenth century, the newer ideas of empiricism and the Enlightenment began to have their impact, but their influence was superficial, limited chiefly to a small circle of royal advisers and an occasional daring intellectual.[15] In the early nineteenth century came the break with Spain and Portugal, but in the New World this implied mainly a redefinition and reformulation of the classic Iberic-Latin tradition, not its repudiation. Historians have long argued that the Wars of Independence were not true social revolutions because the fundamental nature of society remained largely intact; now, as the research of Dealy has demonstrated, we know there was also precious little change in the political order.[16] The constitutional forms were representative and democratic, but in substance the non-democratic, elitist, corporate, hierarchical, authoritarian heritage was retained almost intact. The direction of political thought in Latin America maintained a remarkable continuity both before *and* after 1810.

By now, however, the commercial success of the English, the growth of the natural sciences and technology, the inspiration of representative rule in North America, the glitter and glory of France, and the ideals of the Revolution, together with the restlessness for change on the part of the Latin American creoles themselves, had begun to have their

[14] Ronald Newton, "On 'Functional Groups,' 'Fragmentation,' and 'Pluralism' in Spanish American Political Society," *Hispanic American Historical Review*, L (February 1970), 12.

[15] Arthur P. Whitaker, ed., *Latin America and the Enlightenment* (Ithaca 1961).

[16] Glen Dealy, "Prolegomena on the Spanish American Political Tradition," *Hispanic American Historical Review*, XLVIII (February 1968).

impact. New, agonizing questions were asked: Who are we? Spanish? New World? What? What shall be our relations with North America, Europe, Spain, or Portugal? How did we become what we are, and what is our destiny as a continent and as a people?[17] In the absence of restraints imposed by the Spanish Crown on the questioning of established truths and as a result of contact with the outside world, the dominant tradition was subjected to the increasing challenge of new ideas and conceptions. In Spain and Portugal, this was also a period of unprecedented challenge to established ways and frequently one of bloody conflicts. In both the Iberian Peninsula and Latin America, subsequent intellectual history would hence be written in terms of the dialectical interplay between the prevailing organicist-corporatist framework and the gradually more numerous adherents of alternative systems.

Throughout the nineteenth century, liberalism was the foremost challenger in the attack on corporate privilege.[18] Its impact varied from country to country, but one can safely say that liberalism was seldom very successful and nowhere dominant. Positivism, with its emphasis on order and progress, was accommodated and assimilated within the prevailing tradition. Later, the ideologies of socialism, communism, nationalism, social democracy, Christian democracy, populism, developmentalism, Third-Worldism, and others also made their presence felt. Except in rare, probably unique circumstances, however, such as Cuba and possibly now Chile, the older tradition has been able to maintain its paramountcy even in the face of these challenges. It has done so by absorbing that which is useful from the newer currents and rejecting the rest. Much of the traditional, organic-corporatist philosophy has thus been retained, albeit in somewhat diluted form, while its challengers have been repeatedly thwarted or co-opted. This is what Anderson means by his characterizing Latin America as a "living museum,"[19] for in the absence of any genuine social revolution in all but two or three of the Iberic-Latin nations (which would have resulted in the discarding of the older structures), virtually all the systems of society that have ever governed men's affairs continue to coexist— a blend of Thomism, divine-right monarchy, feudalism, autocracy, republicanism, liberalism, and all the rest.

[17] These questions form the common threads in the writers considered in W. Rex Crawford, *A Century of Latin American Thought* (New York 1966), Introduction.

[18] Charles A. Hale, *Mexican Liberalism in the Age of Mora, 1821–1853* (New Haven 1968).

[19] Charles W. Anderson, "Toward a Theory of Latin American Politics," Occasional Paper No. 2, Graduate Center for Latin American Studies, Vanderbilt University (February 1964); incorporated into his book, *Politics and Economic Changes in Latin America* (Princeton 1967), chap. 4.

This discussion of the dominant Iberic-Latin ideological tradition has up to now portrayed it as a generally conservative, reactive, closed ideology that has shut out those currents it could not usefully absorb. This, however, is only partially true. As a set of what we might term traditional and non-revolutionary beliefs, the Iberic-Latin heritage has indeed often been a reactive one, filtering out (albeit quite selectively) the "dangerous," heretical ideas of Protestantism, empiricism, the Enlightenment, rationalism, liberalism, socialism, and the like. But, beginning in the mid-to-late nineteenth century there began to be articulated in the Iberic-Latin nations a new developmental ideology, uniquely attuned to their own tradition, positive, progressive, and serving as the Iberic-Latin counterpart to the modernizing ideologies that had evolved elsewhere. This tradition remains almost wholly ignored in our intellectual histories, but it is crucial for an understanding of Iberic-Latin development.[20]

Spain, Portugal, and their former new-world colonies had by then begun to be affected by industrialization, urbanization, accelerated social change, and the newer ideological currents of that period. Their major thinkers—such as Donoso Cortés, Balmes, Menéndez, Antonio, Unamuno, Maeztu, Ortega, to cite only some of those most prominent in the Spanish tradition—began to grapple with the same fundamental questions that concerned Marx, Durkheim, Weber, and other, more well-known writers. The Iberic-Latins built upon the new and reformist currents emanating from the Church and also drew upon their own historical tradition. Still within the corporate-organic mold, they sought to fashion a framework for thought and action blending the traditional regard for order and hierarchy with the newer imperative of change and modernization. They attempted, for instance, to deal with the phenomenon of mass man by erecting corporate structures that provided for class harmony rather than conflict, structured participation rather than rootlessness and alienation. Representation was generally to be determined by functions (labor, business, agriculture, religion, etc.) rather than through divisive interest groups and political parties. The state was to regulate and harmonize the entire process. In this way, the Iberic-Latin nations sought to face up to modern realities, but without sacrificing the organic-corporate structures of the past.[21]

[20] See the discussion by the editor, Kalman H. Silvert, in *Expectant Peoples: Nationalism and Development* (New York 1967), 360.

[21] The literature is remarkably extensive even though much of it is largely ignored. For Spain, see the flawed but useful study by Francis G. Wilson, *Political Thought in National Spain* (Champaign, Ill. 1967), as well as the original writings of the authors mentioned. For Portugal, there are also numerous historical writings, some of the best

By the third and fourth decades of this century these ideas had been diffused widely, not only in Spain and Portugal, but also throughout Latin America. They helped give rise to a variety of at least semi-modernizing movements—the corporate state of Portugal, the *Falange* in Spain, the *Estado Novo* in Brazil, integralism and Christian Democracy in a variety of countries, *Peronismo* in Argentina, the MNR in Bolivia, the PRI in Mexico, and numerous others. Despite the significant differences that marked these regimes and movements, the common ingredients were at least equally impressive: a common historic and philosophic tradition, some agreed-upon assumptions about the way the socio-political order ought to be arranged, new but similar social and political forces to be dealt with, and a shared predisposition not to destroy the old order but to inherit it, bending it sufficiently to accommodate the newer forces while maintaining inviolate the essential corporate, hierarchical, and elitist structures. With World War II, many of these movements and corporately organized schemes suffered ignominy and were discredited; some were overthrown, others rebaptized under different names, still others continued much as before. It matters little what labels are applied, however; the important fact is that the same fundamental and historical conception of the state and society still remains, powerful and almost all-pervasive, finding contemporary expression in the ideology and actions of old-style *caudillos* and new-style military "Nasserists," in the evolving structure of the PRI, in the traditional authoritarian regimes and in the newer "syndicalist republics," perhaps even in revolutionary Cuba and Chile. There is obviously room for considerable variation within this framework, but there can be no doubt that it remains crucial for a proper understanding of the Iberic-Latin tradition.[22]

More work remains to be done in this area—a project in which the present writer is currently engaged. However, it should be stressed that

---

written by the present premier, Marcello Caetano. The literature for the Latin American nations is also extensive; see, among others, Picón-Salas (fn. 10); Crawford (fn. 17); and Harold E. Davis, ed., *Latin American Social Thought* (Washington, D.C. 1963). A volume that shows the parallels and continuities in these various national traditions is Fredrik B. Pike, *Hispanismo* (Notre Dame 1971).

[22] For the relationship of this Iberic-Latin heritage to contemporary political movements, see especially Charles W. Anderson, *The Political Economy of Modern Spain: Policy-Making in an Authoritarian System* (Madison 1970). For some early and formative efforts, see Howard J. Wiarda, *Dictatorship and Development: The Methods of Control in Trujillo's Dominican Republic* (Gainesville 1970); Wiarda, *The Brazilian Catholic Labor Movement: The Dilemmas of National Development* (Amherst 1969); and Philippe C. Schmitter, *Interest Conflict and Political Change in Brazil* (Stanford 1971). For some intriguing comparisons, see Roland Sarti, "Fascist Modernization in Italy: Traditional or Modern?" *American Historical Review*, LXXV (April 1970), 1029-45; and Henry Ehrmann, *Politics in France* (Boston 1968), chaps. I and II.

the movements mentioned here were and are by no means all wholly reactionary or "fascistic"; they often represented and continue to represent forward-looking, dynamic efforts at achieving modernization. They attempted to evolve a uniquely Iberic-Latin ideology and mode of action, one which sought to deal with contemporary pressures while preserving those traditional features that are considered valuable in their own heritage. It is this strand of thought which our studies of political theory and of social change have neglected but which must be recognized if we are to comprehend the Iberic-Latin development.

There is, thus, a distinctively Iberic-Latin model and political tradition of development whose complex dimensions fail to accord with our more familiar developmental paradigms and whose functioning these other models are, by themselves, incapable of fully explaining. Some aspects of this framework may be ideologically distasteful to us, but as scholars and/or developmentalists we ignore what is probably the still-dominant conception within the Iberic-Latin tradition at the cost of continuing to misinterpret fundamentally the experience and present-day realities of the nations that are a part of this culture area. What is required, therefore, is a counterpart volume for Iberia and Latin America of, say, Hartz's *The Liberal Tradition in America*, a study which traces and analyzes these dominant political-cultural variables and provides us with that integrative view of the whole Iberic-Latin tradition that is so sorely needed.[23]

THE SOCIO-POLITICAL DIMENSION

The Iberic-Latin socio-political tradition goes hand in hand with the religio-cultural tradition. Again, a good starting point for the discussion is to picture the Iberic-Latin nations as structured horizontally in terms of distinct and fairly rigid layers and vertically in terms of a number of corporate elites and *intereses*, with the Crown or the central state apparatus controlling and guiding its various components. Historically, each corporate entity as well as each "class" in the hierarchy had its own responsibilities, status, and special privileges (*fueros*), corresponding to natural law and to God's just ordering of the universe. Men were expected to accept their station in life; there could thus be little ques-

---

[23] The reference is to Louis Hartz, *The Liberal Tradition in America: An Interpretation of American Political Thought Since the Revolution* (New York 1955). Various fragments for a similar study of Latin America may be found in the work of many of the scholars cited here: Adams, Anderson, Dealy, Graham, Hale, McAlister, Morse, Newton, Silvert, Véliz, and others. Many of these writings and ideas are brought together in Howard J. Wiarda, ed., *Political Development: The Latin American Experience* (tentative title, forthcoming).

tioning of the system and little mobility. Little change could or did take place. The Crown rested at the apex of the socio-political pyramid, regulating, through its power over financial affairs and its authority to grant charters and legal recognition, the corporate and group life that swirled about it. These units related to each other through the central administration, rather than directly or across class lines. The Iberic-Latin model of political authority is thus essentially a traditional-patrimonialist one, where the wealth of the realm, its subjects, etc., are all a part of the ruler's own domain.[24]

The institutions of the two metropoles—a corporate and hierarchical social order, an authoritarian-patrimonialist polity, an exploitive, "milk-cow," semi-feudal–early-capitalist, "colonial trader" economic system, a fixed and immutable religion and law—all formed part of the structure that Spain, and in a more easy-going form Portugal, first established at home and then transplanted to the New World.[25] Institutions that would soon be anachronistic and dying in the rest of Europe and North America remained largely intact in the Iberian peninsula and in Latin America, where they not only received a new lease on life but thrived and persisted. This, of course, is not to say that no change took place within the prevailing structure, but that changes were generally accommodated within the prevailing system. As Newton concludes, "the social and political patterns and juridical legitimation of the corporate regime remained substantially intact to the eve of independence."[26]

Though the separation from the mother countries in the early nineteenth century brought on a severe politico-administrative legitimacy crisis, no sharp changes occurred in the basic structure of society. Indeed, the wars of independence were largely conservative movements, designed to preserve corporate privilege and elite, centralized rule against the revolutionary, democratizing currents then at work. The apex of the pyramid had been lopped off, but the underlying base and the governing mores and institutions remained intact. Once the legitimacy vacuum created by the withdrawal of Spanish and Portuguese authority had been filled by the creole aristocracies, *caudillos*, and

[24] Patrimonialism was one of Weber's forms of traditional authority. See Reinhard Bendix, *Max Weber: An Intellectual Portrait* (Garden City, N.Y. 1962), 334-60. For a fascinating application to the Portuguese-Brazilian tradition, see Raymundo Faoro, *Os Donos do Poder: Formação do Patronato Político Brasileiro* (Pôrto Alegre 1958). See also Ronald Glassman, *Political History of Latin America* (New York 1969).

[25] Magali Sarfatti, *Spanish Bureaucratic-Patrimonialism in America* (Berkeley 1966); and L. N. McAlister, "Social Structure and Social Change in New Spain," *Hispanic American Historical Review*, XLIII (August 1963), 349-70.

[26] Newton (fn. 14), 26.

armies, the traditional structure reasserted itself. New institutional arrangements were grafted on; but in essence the hierarchical patterns of class and caste, the system of *fueros* and corporate privilege (now extended to include the national armies), the seigneurial system of *patrón-clientela* relations, the power of the Church and of a preeminently Catholic religio-political culture, the patrimonialist political structure—all these elements of the Iberic-Latin tradition were mainly unaffected by independence.[27]

The nineteenth century was characterized by the attempts to create nations out of the disparate, fragmented factions that made up society. This was the classic era of Latin American caudilloism, of rival men on horseback vying for national power and galloping in and out of the National Palace with frequent regularity. By the 1880's and 1890's, the long quest to restore order and unity had largely succeeded in virtually all the Latin American nations; power had been consolidated in the hands of the oligarchic interests, the merchant-entrepreneurial elements that were closely bound up with them, and a new breed of order-and-progress *caudillos*. A period of stability, prosperity, and national infrastructure-building ensued. These changes helped stimulate the economic "take-off," gave rise to a greater variety of social groups than had existed in the old stratification system, and provided new escalators of social mobility. But again, these changes—and those that followed in the twentieth century—were accompanied by little fundamental reordering of the basic structure of power and society. Through the techniques of adaptation, accommodation, and co-optation, the two-class, corporate-patrimonialist system remained unaltered except in peripheral ways. The established groups adjusted readily to the shift from the self-sufficient *hacienda* to the capitalistic plantation or commercial enterprise; and usually they were able to co-opt the rising merchant-business elements into their own system of dominance—or to go into these activities themselves, thus welding the older and the newer basis of wealth and power.[28]

Later, the franchise was extended to the rising middle sectors, greater respect was paid to the classic nineteenth-century freedoms, and a variety of new middle-class associations and parties emerged. From roughly the 1920's onward, new pressures were felt upon the traditional elitist structure, and in several countries the new bourgeois parties and

[27] Dealy (fn. 16); William H. Beezley, "Caudillismo: An Interpretive Note," *Journal of Inter-American Studies*, XI (July 1969), 348; and Orlando Fals Borda, "Marginality and Revolution in Latin America, 1809–1969," *Studies in Comparative International Development*, VI (1970–71), 63-89.

[28] Warren Dean, *The Industrialization of São Paulo, 1880–1945* (Austin 1969).

movements came to power. But the pervasiveness of the dominant political culture and legacy remained strong: the new middle sectors lacked any sense of class consciousness, they aped and imitated elitist ways, and, once in power, they acted in much the same way as had the traditional elites. Eventually they forged an alliance with these elites or were fused into the dominant elitist structure so as to preserve the privileges and place in the system that they had recently won against the rising pressures from the awakening masses.[29] A number of new corporate interests were thus accommodated and some new institutional pillars grafted on, but the basic order of society and polity remained largely intact.

More recently some other interests have begun to make their presence felt. From the 1930's on, organized labor, usually incorporated in the form of official, government-controlled syndicates, directed and often organized by the elitist and middle-sector ruling groups, was assimilated into the prevailing structure. Now, albeit in the same paternalistic fashion, it has become the peasants' turn. The extension of the labor laws to the rural areas, the enactment of agrarian reform laws, the structural innovations in the countryside being carried out in Peru and elsewhere provide ample illustration of this. Frequently these changes in labor's or the peasants' position have been introduced as a result of structured violence, or the threat of violence, emanating from the workers and rural masses themselves; but more often than not they have come about through the action of the ruling elements who were seeking to ensure their hegemony and control of the change process. Moreover, once these techniques of structured violence and frequently revolutionary posturing have helped the labor and peasant leaders to secure their place in the system, the tendency has been for them also to become conservative and guard their positions against new encroachments.[30]

Change in the Iberic-Latin context, as Morse states, has been not so much a matter of "fundamental" change in the European or North American sense (that is, implying a revolutionary transformation, the substitution of one ruling class for another, or the obliteration of the past) as it has been the mediating and gradual accommodating of the accoutrements and rallying cries of industrial civilization to a political

---

[29] Jane-Lee Woolridge Yare, "Middle Sector Political Behavior in Latin America," (unpub., University of Massachusetts 1971).

[30] This phenomenon may help to explain the differences between Henry Landsberger, who today proclaims Latin American labor to be conservative, and Víctor Alba and Robert J. Alexander, who, drawing their evidence from an earlier period before labor had consolidated its position, proclaim it to be revolutionary.

culture that remains in its essence Ibero-Catholic, creole-feudal, and patrimonialist.[31] A number of adjustments were made, but the basic pattern of ownership and wealth was perpetuated, the fundamental two-class structure of society was continued, past values and behavioral norms were preserved, the system of *fueros*, patronage, and privileges was retained, and the structure of power and society has remained hierarchical, elitist, authoritarian, and corporative. Some new social groups were assimilated, but this has generally been accomplished under the tutelage and containment of the older ruling groups and norms. These latter elements have also been the chief beneficiaries of development. Thus, as an ECLA study has concluded, the "traditional structure" of Latin America, "far from having been rigid and impenetrable, has had sufficient permeability for a good many of its component parts to be modernized, without this having implied a swift and radical process of 'modernization.' "[32]

THE PROCESS OF CHANGE

We have been considering the religio-theoretical aspects of Iberic-Latin political culture and have provided an overview of the socio-political system and its modifications, but we have not so far addressed ourselves explicitly to an analysis of the process of change.

In keeping with the Catholic-Thomistic conception, society and the state in the Iberic-Latin context are thought of as an organic whole with a profoundly moral purpose. Attempts are thus made, through personal and family ties, the *compadrazgo*, and personal identification with the leader, to construct various linkage mechanisms so that a sense of "belonging" is engendered and all are integrated into the prevailing structure. Branches, associations, and official syndicates now exist for nearly everyone. The national system is often conceived of in terms of the family metaphor—implying strong, benevolent leadership, assigned, accepted duties, privileges, status, and a purpose greater than the sum of its individual parts. It is now the state, replacing the Crown, that serves as the instrument of national integration, incorporating diverse groups, guilds, and interests, and functioning as the regulator and filter through which the legitimacy of new social and political forces is recognized and through which they are admitted into the

[31] Morse (fn. 9), 41; see also Morse's essay in Hartz (fn. 7), and his "Toward a Theory of Spanish American Government," *Journal of the History of Ideas*, xv (1954), 71-93.
[32] Economic Commission for Latin America (ECLA), *Social Development of Latin America in the Post-War Period* (United Nations, April 15, 1964), 6.

system. Power tends to be concentrated in the executive and in the bureaucratic-patrimonialist state machinery; the President is viewed as the personification of the nation with a direct identification with and knowledge of the general will of his people. The bureaucracy serves to dispense the available goods, favors, and spoils to the deserving. The traditional *patrón*-client relationship thus remains strong, with the government and its many agencies playing the role of national *patrón*, replacing the *caudillos* and local *hacendados* of the past. The same paternalistic *clientela* system persists, dressed up in new and more "modern" forms, but retaining its traditional substance and mode of operation.[33]

The same traditional hierarchical, corporative, elitist, and authoritarian orientation and structure is also still present today, modified by twentieth-century changes but by no means destroyed by them.[34] Politics still centers around the old, hierarchically organized and vertically compartmentalized system of corporate *intereses* and elite groups, now expanded and broadened somewhat to include the newer elements, but still authoritarianly controlled from the top and linked together directly through the government. The "corporative framework" thus refers to a system in which the political culture and institutions reflect a historic hierarchical, authoritarian, and organic view of man, society, and polity.[35] In the corporative system the government controls and directs all associations, holding the power not only to grant or withhold juridical recognition (the *sine qua non* for the group's existence) but also access to official funds and favors without which any sector is unlikely to succeed or survive. Group "rights," or *fueros*, hence take precedence over individual rights; similarly, it is the "general will" and the power of the state that prevail over particular interests. The government not only regulates all associations and corporate bodies, but also seeks to tie those that have earned their place in the existing system into a collaborative effort for integral national development. Obviously the system works best where the number of interests is small

[33] See Claudio Véliz, "Centralism and Nationalism in Latin America," *Foreign Affairs*, LIXVII (October 1968), 68-83, and John D. Powell, "Peasant Society and Clientelist Politics," *American Political Review*, LXIV (June 1970), 411-25.

[34] The analysis here draws heavily on the excellent discussion of corporatism in James Petras, *Political and Social Forces in Chilean Development* (Berkeley 1969), esp. pp. 5, 199-203, 209-19, and 247-48. See also the Introduction in John J. Johnson, ed., *Continuity and Change in Latin America* (Stanford 1964).

[35] The definition used here is derived from Faoro (fn. 24), and Kenneth P. Erickson, *Labor in the Political Process in Brazil: Corporatism in a Modernizing Nation* (unpub. Ph.D. diss., Columbia University 1970).

and within a context of shared values, but it is not necessarily incompatible with a growing pluralism of ideologies and social forces.

In the virtually inherently corporative systems of the Iberic-Latin nations, the effort is made to ameliorate social and political conflict—to deal with it bureaucratically rather than to provoke divisiveness and breakdown. Administration supersedes politics in both theory and practice; thus, society is represented functionally, in terms of its component segments, and organized bureaucratically, with the government seeking to maintain the proper balance between the various interests and to coordinate them into the state apparatus.[36] Political issues are dealt with more through the process of elite integration and the granting of access to the spoils and privileges that accrue with acceptance into the system, rather than through program enactment and implementation. The greatest need is social and political solidarity; there can be no room for divided loyalties, autonomous political organizations, or challenges to the system's fundamental structure. The personnel of government may shift, new groups and ideas may be assimilated, and the elites may rotate in power (thus giving the appearance of change more than its substance); but the essentials of the socio-political order and the base on which it rests must remain steadfast.[37] The newer groups may be co-opted, but they cannot challenge or seek to topple the system *per se*. Those that do are likely to be crushed—unless their goal is merely the limited one of trying to demonstrate a power capability and the right to be admitted as a bargaining agent in the larger system. This kind of limited and usually carefully-orchestrated violence may be tolerated, even accepted; a movement aimed at toppling the entire structure, in contrast, can expect to and will probably be suppressed.[38]

Considerable change can and does take place within the corporative system, but it usually comes from the top downward rather than as a result of grass roots pressure from below. A culturally-conditioned form of "democracy" may be established, as in Venezuela, Colombia, Uruguay, Chile, or Costa Rica, but its structure is that of a tutelary or guided democracy directed from above. The state system is founded on a structure of institutionalized popular movements. An attempt is thus made to transfer the traditional elitist values to the rising newer groups through example and education. First the business-commercial

[36] See Michel Crozier, *The Bureaucratic Phenomenon* (Chicago 1964).

[37] The concepts of the "ruling class" and "circulation of elites" are derived from the Italian sociologists, Mosca and Pareto. See also Fals Borda (fn. 27).

[38] See James L. Payne, *Labor and Politics in Peru* (New Haven 1965).

elements were "civilized" in this way, then the rising middle sectors, and now the lower or popular classes. That helps explain the persistent presence, in the Iberic-Latin context, of government-supported and -run trade unions, political parties, peasant leagues, professional associations or "colleges," etc. Through these agencies, which often are bureaucratic appendages of the state, the prevailing systems have sought to institutionalize and thus contain the rising social forces. Middle- and now lower-class elements are offered marginal benefits and a stake in the system as a means of defusing discontent and of putting them directly under the paternalistic direction of the state. "Agrarian reform," for example, has become more an instrument of social control than of social change. In this way the dominant elements have skillfully managed the historic unfolding of the development process, channeling it in preferred directions and either co-opting or snuffing out new challenges to their power and way of life.[39] Through adaptation, the traditional order, instead of being overwhelmed or discarded as development has gone forward, has profited from it, proving to be remarkably resilient and even strengthening itself in the process.

It is the duty of the state and its *líder* to organize public opinion and maintain the proper societal equilibrium through the delicate balance of domestic interests and, increasingly in the 1960's, foreign pressures. Decisions are usually made by a cadre of elite-group representatives, linked by formal and informal ties to the administrative hierarchy and centering, ideally, in a single individual who personifies the national values, knows the general will, and is the best and most qualified leader. The United States Ambassador and the various U.S. mission heads may at times also be included in this coterie. Traditionally, patronage, status, favors, and access to the channels of influence and wealth, rather than concrete benefits, have served as the chief media of political currency; now, however, at least lip service (and sometimes more than that) must be paid to program enactment and implementation. Patronage, privileges, even programs are doled out by the state to groups and individuals who might otherwise attempt organized opposition, in exchange for support and acquiescence to official policies.[40] Thus, the public service becomes a huge "social security" system, a haven for friends, relatives, party hacks, and dissident oppositionists, as well as for a large part of the middle class and now increasingly the labor and peasant leaders, who are in effect "bought off" by being

---

[39] Petras (fn. 34).
[40] Erickson (fn. 35), chaps. I-II; James L. Payne, *Patterns of Conflict in Colombia* (New Haven 1968).

put on the public payroll. Effective program implementation is difficult by a bureaucracy for which this has traditionally been a secondary function.[41]

The corporate framework helps maintain the traditional structure while concurrently providing for limited change through the co-optation of new social and political units into the administrative apparatus of the state system. Corporate structures, reinforced by a political culture grounded on hierarchy, status, and patronage, enable the traditional socio-political forms in the Iberic-Latin tradition to hang on so tenaciously. The corporative framework helps preserve the status quo, but it also provides for the gradualist, incremental accommodation to newer currents. It helps keep the pressures for change in check by minimizing the possibilities for disruption and full-scale revolution.[42] The corporative state may thus respond to modernization and adopt those "modern" aspects that are useful and can be controlled; but in seeking at the same time to preserve certain traditional attitudes and institutions, it may reject the social and political concomitants that ordinarily accompany the modernization process.

It should be emphasized that corporative structures and value systems are nothing new in either Spain, Portugal, or Latin America. They did not originate in the 1920's and 1930's when the corporative states and certain "integralist" ideologies acquired self-consciousness, power, and a full-blown statement of political philosophy, but stretch back for centuries to ancient and medieval political theory and organization and were later transferred to the New World by the metropoles. In the warp and woof, the dialectic of Iberic-Latin development, they have been reformulated and updated many times, but the basic organic-corporate-elitist structure of the socio-political system has remained steadfast.

In the Iberic-Latin political systems new social groups and political forces, new ideas and new institutional arrangements may be appended in a continuous fusion-absorption process; but, owing to the absence of genuinely revolutionary transformations in that tradition, old ones are seldom completely discarded.[43] Only in Mexico, Cuba, and perhaps Bolivia and Peru have there been sharp breaks with the past which destroyed the power of the traditionally privileged elites; in the rest of

---

[41] See Lawrence S. Graham, *Civil Service Reform in Brazil: Principles versus Practice* (Austin 1968), and Robert E. Scott, "The Government Bureaucrats and Political Change in Latin America," *Journal of International Affairs*, xx, No. 2 (1966), 289-308.

[42] Erickson (fn. 35); Faoro (fn. 24).

[43] The argument here and in the following paragraph is derived from Anderson (fn. 19), Morse (fns. 7, 8, 9), and the ECLA study (fn. 32).

the countries, and even in some of those that have had revolutions, the traditional structures remain strong. In the socio-political structure as well as in the theoretical base, one is reminded of Anderson's "living museum" concept. Organizational forms that have died off or have been discarded elsewhere in the West continue in the Iberic-Latin context to exhibit a remarkable durability and viability, adapting and coexisting with the newer currents spawned by industrialization and modernization.

As a result of the tenacity of these traditional socio-political institutions, there has been limited "development" in the Iberic-Latin nations in either a Marxian or an Almondian sense. The Iberic-Latin political process has involved not the transcendence of one "class" or "stage" over another, but the combination of diverse elements—rooted in distinct historical periods—in a tentative working arrangement. The question has been not so much one of "development" or "modernization" but of reconciling, in Morse's words, the static and vegetative features of the older, patrimonial-corporate state with the imperatives of a modern, urban, industrial order. The traditional order has not been as rigid as is usually pictured, but flexible, permeable, and capable of absorbing a variety of newer currents—without undermining the traditional structures in the process. It has assimilated those features of modernity that were necessary and could be controlled, but it has rejected the rest. As the newer elites and social forces have been absorbed into the dominant system, the number of participants has slowly increased, but the system itself has changed little. Hence, in virtually all the Iberic-Latin nations there has grown up a series of layers of distinct social and political forms, each superimposed upon the other, with new elements continuously being appended and adapted to an older tradition, but without that older tradition being sloughed off or even undergoing many fundamental transformations. These distinct but overlapping layers originate in different historical eras, but in the Iberic-Latin tradition they have been combined and blended. It is the genius and ongoing challenge of politics and politicians in these nations that they have been able to function and accomplish anything at all of a developmental sort, given the heterogeneous, frequently crazy-quilt political systems in which they must work.

In seeking to explain these aspects of the Iberic-Latin process of change, Richard Adams has fashioned a theory of what he terms "secondary development."[44] Secondary development refers to the course

---

[44] Adams, *The Second Sowing: Power and Secondary Development in Latin America* (San Francisco 1967).

development takes when it enters an area that was previously an isolated hinterland of the industrial revolution and of the modern world. Development in Latin America does not *follow*, as a matter of successive stages, the development patterns of Western Europe and North America, but involves the *adaptation* of an older order to some newer forces. This is a process of derivation, assimilation, and reorganization, not of innovation. Secondary development, in Adams' formulation, implies the importation and adaptation of more modern social and political organizations and techniques and their superimposition on an already established socio-political order, rather than the replacement of the one by the other.

In Anderson's terms,[45] the key dilemma in the politics of these nations is and has been to find a formula for reaching agreement among various "power contenders" whose power is unequal and whose interests and life-styles are almost totally incompatible because they emerged from and pertain to quite different historical epochs. Characteristically, the political process involves manipulation and almost constant negotiation among these several power contenders, for elections are tentative and but one means to power, and they do not carry the definitiveness they do in the Anglo-American context. The shuffling and reshuffling of the delicate power balance is almost an every-day preoccupation. The distinctive flavor of the change process is that new power contenders may be accommodated and admitted to the system if they accept and conform to its rules, but old ones are not eliminated. However, because these various elites and *intereses*— including landowners, businessmen, the Church, the army, middle sectors, students, labor, peasants—emerged from different eras, with distinct expectations and uneven bases for their power and legitimacy, the attempt to fashion an accommodation among them is exceedingly difficult. The job of the President, who must juggle and reconcile these contending forces and maintain the equilibrium between them, is complex and uncertain.

One comes to think, writes Newton, in terms of "multiple currents of cultural evolution moving at different rates to uneven rhythms, regressing as well as advancing, submerging as well as predominating, intersecting and interacting fortuitously within the framework of a given metropolis, a given institution, or indeed, a given personality structure."[46] Some modernization is possible within this context, but only within circumscribed limits. Politics, Anderson says, thus involves

---

[45] Anderson (fn. 19).
[46] Newton (fn. 14), 27.

the capacity to combine heterogeneous and incompatible power contenders and capabilities in a conditional and continuously shifting
coalition. Frequently these efforts involve what to North Americans
appear to be some incredible marriages of convenience, alliances that
defy not only all "reason" but also our conceptions of ideological consistency, or the stretching or interpretation of the law and constitution
so as to render them all but meaningless. Yet it is precisely these features—the application of a little "grease" here or a little "cement" there,
a delicate compromise, accommodation, or favor, the exercise of patronage and mutual obligation—that help account for the distinctive
flavor of the process of development in these countries, and that give
them their dynamism and capacity to respond. If we wish to understand this process, the focus of scholarly inquiry ought also to be
toward this direction: Rather than seeking to bring to bear categories
and concepts derived from a different tradition and to apply them to
societies where they do not fit, scholars must try to comprehend the
Iberic-Latin systems on their own terms and in their own context,
the way traditional institutions have been modified to meet the exigencies of modern times as well as how the modernizing groups have
used traditional institutions to further their own ends.[47] These mechanisms, which lie at the heart of the Iberic-Latin change and development
process, frequently bear little correspondence to the paradigms and
grand theory in the literature of political sociology and political
economy.

Kalman Silvert's analysis of what he terms the "Mediterranean
ethos" or "syndicalism" also closely parallels the present framework.[48]
This ethos is founded upon a value system dedicated to hierarchy,
order, and absolutes. The urge toward corporatism provides another
manifestation of this ethos, since the organization of men by functions
is in accord with the historical tradition and actualizes the love of
order and hierarchy, serves to contain divisive class conflict, and avoids
the hated liberal and materialistic values. It also provides for the slow
and at least partial adaptation of traditional, patrimonial society to
urbanization, industrialization, and modernization. An effort is made
to bring into harmonious coexistence those characteristics venerated

[47] This is the special merit of Erickson's study (fn. 35), and of Schmitter (fn. 22).
[48] See Silvert's "National Values, Development, and Leaders and Followers," International Social Science Journal, xv (1964), 560-70; "The Politics of Social and Economic Change in Latin America," in Paul Halmos, ed., The Sociological Review Monograph: Latin American Sociological Studies (Keele, Staffordshire, February 1967), 47-
58; Expectant Peoples (fn. 20), 358-61; The Conflict Society: Reaction and Revolution
in Latin America (New York 1966), chaps. 1, 2, and 17; and Man's Power (New York
1970), 59-64 and 136-38.

from the past and those considered valuable in the modern world. The good society is still pictured as one in which each individual is rooted and secure in his life station, where representation is determined by functions and status and not as the result of mere citizenship, where decision-making is centered in the hands of corporate, sectoral elites who are harmonized and coordinated into an organic whole, and where the state exercises firm but benevolent authority over the whole scheme. The "City of God" still takes precedence in many respects over the "City of Man," but since a modern society can no longer exist on this simple bi-institutional basis, the Iberic-Latin response has been to erect new institutionalized pillars to accommodate the changes taking place. Each pillar remains highly striated by social class, with recruitment into the upper levels still largely a function of social position. As Silvert concludes, "The major social purpose of the syndicalist approach is to find a way of subsuming the new class complications of modernization to hierarchy, preserving a kind of Latin 'Führerprinzip,' leaving inviolate the privileges and power of the traditional, and thus escaping the secularization and, to their eyes, immorality of the nation state."

The Crisis of the Traditional System

What we have termed the corporative framework for the analysis of socio-political change in Iberia and Latin America has exhibited remarkable staying power. At present, however, the traditional system is experiencing a crisis of major proportions which may sweep away the regime of hierarchy, elites, and special privileges once and for all.[49]

We may use as our point of departure Bernice Hamilton's assertion that "the fabric of natural law of the 16th century could only remain unshaken in a homogeneous, fairly static society with no major cleavage on moral principles, or in a primitive community which had little disturbing contact with the outside world."[50] These conditions obviously no longer apply in the Iberic-Latin nations. They are no longer homogeneous or static; major cleavages have emerged as to the proper way of ordering society and polity; and contact with the outside world, as well as deep foreign involvement in their internal affairs, has helped break down the traditional isolation. Since World War I particularly

---

[49] The discussion here is derived from Wiarda, "Elites in Crisis" (introductory note), 25-30 and 50ff. For further evidence, see the documents and essays collected in James Petras and Maurice Zeitlin, eds., *Latin America: Reform or Revolution?* (New York 1968), and in Irving L. Horowitz, Josué de Castro, and John Gerassi, eds., *Latin American Radicalism* (New York 1969).

[50] Hamilton (fn. 11), 158.

(to use an arbitrary and approximate cut-off date), the pace of change has been accelerated, new social forces have emerged, the older basis of legitimacy has been increasingly challenged, and the foundations on which the ancient order rested have been progressively undermined.

The older power bases—and the religious, social, behavioral, and economic foundations on which they rested—are in decline.[51] These include the village community, the *hacienda*, the Church, caudilloism, the extended family, the landed oligarchy, the traditional cadre-type parties, and so on. Meanwhile, new power bases have emerged, including the educated *técnicos* and professionals, organized labor and peasants, mass-based political parties, more professionalized and development-oriented militaries, the "new" Church, and the like. The situation is complicated by the presence of various external influences—principally that of the United States, but also encompassing that of a myriad of international agencies and other foreign pressures —in the domestic politics and social programs of these countries. This is a factor with which the neatly patterned system of adding new pillars and power contenders, as described by Silvert and Anderson, does not adequately come to grips. The fact that new interests have emerged who have organized themselves around principles not previously considered the only right or legitimate ones for the society, that the old interests and corporate units are themselves undergoing transformation, that new values and organizing principles are competing for men's minds, that government is being called upon to perform services that it had never provided before, that foreign pressures and influences have multiplied—all these and other changes have added a new, complex, and increasingly conflicting dimension to the Iberic-Latin potpourri.

Politics has become progressively more class-, issue-, and interest-oriented. The traditional mechanisms for accommodating and adapting to change have also begun to break down. The Brazilian *jeito*, for instance, which may loosely be translated as "grease," and which has traditionally served as a many-faceted means to ease the cumbersome turning of the wheels of government, is no longer, under conditions of "no-nonsense" military rule, quite the effective instrument that it was before. The pace of change is becoming so rapid and its extent is so great that the traditional techniques of adjustment, accommodation, and co-optation are proving inadequate. The participation crisis is reaching revolutionary proportions, the level of new demands and expectations has far outstripped the capacity of

[51] See the discussion in Adams (fn. 44).

the political systems to cope with them, and the older corporate-elitist structures are proving incapable of handling the new pressures that have suddenly been thrust upon them. The present Iberic-Latin political panorama has tended to become a profoundly fragmented and unstable one, marked by the absence of any single consensus, by the tenacious attempt of the traditional elements to hang on to their wealth and power, by the rising revolutionary sentiments of the newly mobilized, and by the weakness and ineffectiveness of those who might occupy the middle ground. We are witnessing the erosion and at least partial eclipse of the old order—without the emergence of a sufficiently strong or legitimized new order to take its place.

It is difficult to maintain the ideal of the nation as an organic "family" when the common basis of understanding on which the older solidarity was based no longer exists, when the earlier idea of the "harmonization" of classes is giving way to class conflict, when the number of interests or pillars in the corporate structure has multiplied beyond the capacity of the traditional mechanisms to control them, when issues are no longer confined to small elitist coteries but reach further down into the social pyramid and now involve the early stirrings of mass-mobilizationalist politics, when new educational and ideological formulas are replacing the paternalism and accepted truths of the past, and when increased national divisiveness and polarization have set in. A framework of order and stability has increasingly been superseded by a philosophy of change. New ideologies, new interests, and new institutional forms organized internally, coupled with new pressures from the external environment, have combined to provoke a challenge of unprecedented proportions to the older, established institutions.

In spite of all these changes, the traditional organic-corporate-elitist-patrimonialist order in the Iberic-Latin nations remains remarkably strong and viable. With one or two exceptions, it is probably still the dominant mode throughout the countries of this culture area. Moreover, its capacity for weathering the present crisis and challenge, as it has weathered others in the past, should not be underestimated. There is considerable evidence of the capacity of the dominant elites to continue mobilizing workers and peasants into official appendages of the traditional corporate structure and thus to defuse mass discontent and maintain their own privileged positions, to manage the pressures from the United States and other external influences chiefly to their own advantage, to articulate new developmental ideologies and to erect new institutional arrangements that provide more the appearance of change than its substance, to continue to direct and control the essentials of the entire process of change and moderniza-tion. Though, as committed "developmentalists," we may prefer other forms of change, and though our scholarly analyses, often exhibiting what we might call wishful political sociology, may focus on those groups and institutions that seem to offer the best hope for rapid modernization or democratization, it is the older and still venerated tradition that remains dominant, whose structure and methods of adaptation and assimilation have not been adequately studied, but which we ignore at the risk of our continued misunderstanding of the Iberic-Latin nations.

Conclusion and Implications

The first part of the 1960's saw a great outpouring of books and articles which offered a generally hopeful and optimistic view of the development process in emerging nations; in the later 1960's there was considerable disillusionment with this view and more and more questioning of the assumptions and biases on which the model rested. By this time, we are safe in concluding that, for all the fresh per-ceptions and stimuli to research which the general development literature has provided, it has subjected not only Latin America but much of the so-called Third World to too hasty interpretation and over-generalization. The echoes of Marxian and Weberian theory, both based on the common assumption of the dissolution of tradi-tional societies before the onslaught of industrialization and mod-ernization, have reverberated widely, too widely, far beyond the examples of those nations, principally of Western Europe, on whose developmental experience these two paradigms were essentially based. The assumption of both of these models is that traditional societies are hardened shells, capable only of remaining obdurately unyielding or else shattering into pieces. The fact is, however, that many traditional societies, and particularly those of the Iberic-Latin nations, have proved to be remarkably permeable and flexible, assimilating at various points more "modern" and more "rational" elements, but without thereby losing their characteristic features.[52]

Granted that much of the work in comparative political develop-

[52] J. P. Nettl and Karl von Vorys, "The Politics of Development," *Commentary*, xlvi (July 1968), 52-59. One cannot help but be reminded of Japan, where many tradi-tional patterns have similarly been retained at the same time that more modern features have been absorbed. See also Lloyd and Susanne Rudolph, *The Modernity of Tradition* (Chicago 1967).

ment provides new and sometimes perceptive insights, the proposition presented here is that the Latin American nations, as well as their two mother countries, Spain and Portugal, are subject to special imperatives as offshoots of a Catholic, Iberic, patrimonialist, semi-feudal Europe *circa* 1500. Until recently these nations had never experienced the full force of the great revolutionary movements that we associate with the rise of the modern era; moreover, their traditional institutions, because of their capacity for accommodation and assimilation, have not been swept away under the impact of the process of contemporary change, but have remained largely intact and, indeed, quite viable even to this day. It is time to put away the concept of a unilinear path to development, to re-examine the narrow and frequently ethnocentric models on which these interpretations are based, to begin to study the Iberic-Latin nations on their own terms rather than through the lenses of some universal scheme that, upon close inspection, turns out to be far less comprehensive than its advocates have posited.[53] In the Iberic-Latin context the issue may even now be not the either/or one of reform or revolution, of tradition versus modernity, but of adjustment, adaptation, accommodation, and continued muddling along. This remains not so much a matter of class conflict, in a Marxian sense, or of transcendental development, from a North American point of view, but of reconciling, largely on an *ad hoc* basis, the conflicting currents—traditional and modern—that continue their interplay within the Iberic-Latin culture, and of assimilating those desirable features of the modern, industrial world to a way of life that retains much of its traditional essence.[54] Perhaps it is appropriate here to suggest something of a *verstehen* approach to the study of these foreign areas, for it is clear that future developments in comparative politics are not likely to take place at the level of grand, universal theory-building, but at a lower level and by culture areas.[55]

The framework employed here implies that the process of change in the Iberic-Latin tradition has been and remains a fairly, but by no means wholly, conservative one. The corporative structure tends to serve the interests of the dominant elites by subordinating the rising social forces to the authority of the elite-dominated central state apparatus. The characteristically Iberic-Latin model of development seeks to preserve as much as possible of the traditional order by structuring

[53] These questions are explored in Wiarda, "Elites in Crisis" (introductory note).
[54] The interpretation here is derived from Morse (fn. 31).
[55] For a somewhat parallel argument, see Kenneth L. Johnson, "Causal Factors in Latin American Instability," *Western Political Quarterly*, xvii (September 1964), 432ff.

the participation of these new power contenders under its control and direction.[56] But although the change that takes place within this mold often seems inordinately slow and circumscribed, one should not assume that no change at all is possible. Change in the Iberic-Latin context, we have emphasized, has occurred through a special and often unique process, usually gradually and incrementally, through adaptation and assimilation, within a framework that combines and seeks to reconcile traditional and modern elements, rather than implying the transcendence of one over the other, or of one "class" or "stage" over another. In the past, change in Latin America has mostly come discontinuously and usually not as the result of any major quantum leaps forward, or even through much purposeful action. Change has come, ordinarily, by fits and starts, through the repeated crises and alternations of government that Latin America is popularly known for, through shifting coalitions, cabinet changes, barracks revolts, new re-alignments, and the circulation of elites. In all of these changes some subtle shift in the balance of power is usually implied—the accommodation of new groups and new ideas, the demonstration by a new power contender of its power capacity and hence of the legitimacy of its claim to be incorporated into the dominant corporate power structure. Change takes place not so much as the result of any great or glorious revolution, but through continuous shifts in the constellation of socio-political forces, through disintegration and *ad hoc* rebuilding, from various forms of structured and unstructured violence that seldom reach the dimensions of a full-scale revolution. This may not, by North American standards, be a very "rational," ideologically consistent, or model-conforming way to achieve development, but it is development nevertheless, cumulative and thus eventually of a structural sort.[57] Moreover, it does seem to correspond, more realistically than the models that have often been employed in the past, both to the peculiar nature of the historic Iberic-Latin development process and also to the present realities of power and society in these nations.

One final consideration merits mention, and that involves the outcome of the process we have described. At this point, based on the analysis and conclusions presented, we might well arrive at a fairly hopeful and at least modestly optimistic prognosis for the future development of the Iberic-Latin nations. Up to a point, indeed, some

---

[56] Erickson (fn. 35), 3, 26, 98, 339; Mander (fn. 2).

[57] See especially Douglas A. Chalmers, "Crisis and Change in Latin America," *Journal of International Affairs*, XXIII, No. 1 (1969), 76-88; Anderson, *Politics and Economic Change in Latin America* (fn. 19); and Albert O. Hirschman, *Journeys Toward Progress: Studies of Economic Policy-Making in Latin America* (New York 1965).

optimism may be justified, but only up to a point. For, as the process we have been describing unfolds, as new ideologies, new frames of reference, and new power contenders are constantly added on without the older and anachronistic ones being cast off, there comes a time when a kind of saturation and national paralysis set in, when the number of corporate interests and ideologies becomes so large and divergent that they are no longer manageable or reconcilable, when, therefore, in the absence of any common consensus or of a dominant ruling coalition, the national fabric begins to unravel, when crisis becomes a constant and virtually everyday fact of life, when an almost Hobbesian war of all against all ensues, and when national politics becomes a situation of seemingly permanent disintegration and conflict. The future of the Iberic-Latin nations lies not in Bolivia or even Cuba, and probably not in those others that have been mentioned as possible developmental models, but more likely in Argentina or perhaps Uruguay, by all indices among the most "modern" of the Latin American nations, but which, precisely because they are so socially differentiated and with such a wide variety of groups and interests competing in their political arenas, have also progressed further along the path to virtually permanent national breakdown.[58] The result of the process of change in Latin America is unlikely to be the final triumph of a new order and epoch over the old one, nor a more-or-less peaceful transition from traditional to modern. More probably it will entail a series of eruptions and blockages, a continuation of the present system coupled with a deterioration of its capacity to manage and accommodate to change in the traditional fashion, a rise in tension and society-wide praetorianism, and a long-term condition of spiraling discord, institutional paralysis and decay, and recurrent breakdowns.[59]

[58] It is not coincidental that Kalman H. Silvert's title, "The Conflict Society," stems chiefly from his research in Argentina. On the same theme, see also Kenneth L. Johnson, *Argentina's Mosaic of Discord, 1966–1968* (Washington 1969), and Roberto Ortigueira, "La disintegración, estado normal de países en desarrollo," *Journal of Inter-American Studies*, v (October 1963), 471-94, also based on the Argentine example. One is also reminded of Ortega y Gasset's perceptive *España Invertebrada*, published in 1922. The Italian experience may provide an additional example of this syndrome.

[59] On praetorian societies, see Samuel P. Huntington, *Political Order in Changing Societies* (New Haven 1968), chap. 4. For an application to Latin America, see Riordan Roett, "The Quest for Legitimacy in Brazil: The Dilemma of a Praetorian Army," paper prepared for the 1970 Annual Conference of the Midwest Association for Latin American Studies, University of Nebraska, Lincoln. A good general discussion is S. N. Eisenstadt, "Breakdowns of Modernization," *Economic Development and Cultural Change*, xii (July 1964), 345-67; also see his *Modernization: Protest and Change* (Englewood Cliffs, N.J. 1966).

SUPPORTIVE PARTICIPATION WITH ECONOMIC GROWTH:
The Case of Japan

INTRODUCTION

THE simultaneous advancement of economic development, socio-economic equality, and democracy in terms of broad-based political participation is a difficult goal for political elites because these three variables are not readily compatible. According to Huntington and Nelson, political elites in developing countries must choose between two conflicting paths in the later phase of development: the technocratic model and the populist model.[1] On the first developmental path, political elites repress political participation in order to promote economic development; as a result, economic inequality may increase. On the second path, the elites allow more political participation, promoting economic equality through governmental programs that aim at economic redistribution; the rate of growth, however, may be slowed down. These classifications of developmental paths raise the question of whether broad-based political participation and economic equality are necessarily incompatible with economic growth.

After World War II, Japan followed a developmental path that was at variance with both of those suggested by Huntington and Nelson. In the wake of rapid economic growth, it experienced a narrowing of income inequality.[2] Moreover, Japanese participatory opportunities have opened widely since the war. The Japanese experience suggests that the relationships among rapid growth, economic equality, and the expansion of political participation are not necessarily zero-sum games. Still, several

* Research for this study was supported by a Harvard Yenching Institute Junior Fellowship for 1977–1979 and the Japanese Ministry of Education's Grant-in-Aid for Scientific Research for 1982–1983. I am grateful to Sidney Verba, Edwin O. Reischauer, and Samuel P. Huntington (Harvard University) and Ichiro Miyake (Doshisa University) for their comments on my Ph.D. dissertation on which this paper draws, and also to Terry E. MacDougall (Harvard University) for his comments and encouragement.

[1] Samuel P. Huntington and Joan M. Nelson, *No Easy Choice: Political Participation in Developing Countries* (Cambridge: Harvard University Press, 1976), 17-29.

[2] Martin Schnitzer, *Income Distribution: A Comparative Study of the United States, Sweden, West Germany, the United Kingdom, and Japan* (New York: Praeger, 1974), 232.

important questions remain unanswered: What is the role of political participation in determining this unique pattern of development? More specifically, what was the structure of political participation in Japan during the period of rapid growth? Did participation matter in reversing a natural tendency toward increased income inequality in the rapid-growth stage of the economy? Why did the expansion of political participation not deter political elites from promoting economic development?

Although we may assume that the expansion of political participation promotes income equality, previous studies of the effect of participation on economic equality have suggested that the former has little effect on the latter.[3] Jackman did find a significant bivariate relationship between democracy and socioeconomic equality; but he discovered this relationship to be spurious because economic development was positively related to *both* socioeconomic equality and democratic performance.[4] Jackman's index of democratic performance places the emphasis on the expansion of democratic rights such as the right to vote, competitiveness of the party system, electoral regularity, and freedom of the press. Why is democratic performance, when measured in this manner, not related to socioeconomic equality?

Verba and Nie suggest an explanation. Their fundamental assumption is that the socioeconomic hierarchy of a society corresponds with its political hierarchy.[5] Under this assumption, the expansion of political rights will not automatically result in economic equality because the have-nots simply do not exercise their participatory opportunities as much as the haves. "Equal rights to participate are just that: rights, not obligations."[6] In other words, Verba and Nie suggest a positive relationship between equality and income neutrality in participation, but not between equality and the expansion of democratic rights *per se*. Income neutrality in political participation refers to the extent to which the economically disadvantaged groups in a society reveal their preferences in the political system through various political acts, while the other conditions of democracy—such as the right to participate in politics, electoral regularity, freedom of the press, and the competitiveness of the party system—are held constant. The basic hypothesis of the

[3] Irma Adelman and Cynthia Taft Morris, *Economic Growth and Social Equality in Developing Countries* (Stanford, Calif.: Stanford University Press, 1973); Robert W. Jackman, *Politics and Social Equality: A Comparative Analysis* (New York: Wiley, 1975).

[4] Jackman (fn. 3), 68-89.

[5] Sidney Verba and Norman H. Nie, *Participation in America: Social Equality and Political Democracy* (New York: Harper & Row, 1972).

[6] *Ibid.*, 335.

present study is that there was little income bias in political participation during Japan's period of rapid growth, and that this income neutrality in participation is related to an equitable income distribution in the course of economic development.

The specific objectives of this essay are:

1. To analyze the structure of Japanese political participation during the country's rapid-growth stage. To what extent is the participatory structure income-neutral, and what social and demographic variables reinforce income neutrality in political participation?

2. To relate the participatory structure to the postwar trend in income distribution. What is the role of participation in determining an equitable growth pattern, and how are the expansion of political participation and rapid economic growth compatible?

3. To discuss the findings in a comparative perspective.

THE STRUCTURE OF POLITICAL PARTICIPATION

Our first task is to analyze the structure of Japanese political participation. The present analysis is based on data collected in 1966, at the height of Japan's period of rapid economic growth, by the Cross-National Program in Political and Social Change headed by Sidney Verba.[7] Table 1 presents a comparison of the extent of income elasticity in different modes of political participation for seven countries.

The indices of different modes of political participation are the same as those constructed by Verba, Nie, and Kim.[8] The income figure is based on the respondent's family income before taxes. Relatively speaking, the structure of participation in Japan is quite income-neutral. Income elasticity in voting, campaigning, and communal activities is 0.06, 0.13, and 0.36 respectively. Income elasticity in voting is lower in Japan than in five of the other countries; it is lower still for Austria and India. Not only is the coefficient small; it is also not statistically significant at an 0.05 level. Japan's income elasticity in campaign activity is the lowest of the seven countries; in communal activity, it is comparable to India, lower than the United States, the Netherlands, and Nigeria, and higher than Yugoslavia and Austria.

The income elasticity shown in Table 1 neglects the influence of politically relevant subpopulations. In the situation shown in Figure 1-

[7] For the nature of the program and sampling design, see Sidney Verba, Norman H. Nie, and Jae-On Kim, *Participation and Political Equality: A Seven-Nation Comparison* (New York: Cambridge University Press, 1978), xi-xxi, 349-75.

[8] *Ibid.*, 340-48.

TABLE 1

INCOME ELASTICITY IN THREE MODES OF POLITICAL PARTICIPATION IN
YUGOSLAVIA, U.S.A., JAPAN, INDIA, AUSTRIA, NIGERIA, AND THE
NETHERLANDS

	Voting	Campaign Activity	Communal Activity
Yugoslavia	0.19	0.57	0.17
	(24)	(81)	(8)
U.S.A.	0.50	0.47	0.48
	(121)	(94)	(90)
Japan	0.06	0.13	0.36
	(1)	(4)	(32)
India	0.03	0.52	0.34
	(1)	(152)	(71)
Austria	− 0.06	0.28	0.29
	(1)	(11)	(22)
Nigeria	0.23	0.42	0.42
	(9)	(28)	(28)
Netherlands	0.19	0.25	0.54
	(4)	(7)	(31)

Note: The term "income elasticity" indicates the percent change in the rate of political participation for every percent change in income. It was estimated by a simple regression model in the log-log form. The figure in parentheses is an F-ratio which provides a testing of the significance of the coefficients. If the F-ratio is more than 4, it is statistically significant at an 0.05 level of significance.
Source: Survey data collected in 1966 by the Cross-National Program in Political and Social Change.

A, subpopulation X clusters around the upper left-hand side of the income-participation dimension.

The positive slope line, I, shows the effect of income on participation independent of subpopulation X (hereafter referred to as partial income elasticity). The main feature of subpopulation X is that the mean level of income is low, whereas the mean rate of political participation is high. Because of the presence of subpopulation X, the left-hand side of line I is pulled up so that the observed regression line is much flatter (i.e., it indicates a smaller income bias).

The location of subpopulations is not limited to the upper left-hand corner. Figure 1-B shows alternative locations of subpopulations. Subpopulation A pulls up the right-hand side of line I, while subpopulation B pulls it down. Subpopulation A reinforces income bias in participation because both the mean of income and the rate of participationn are

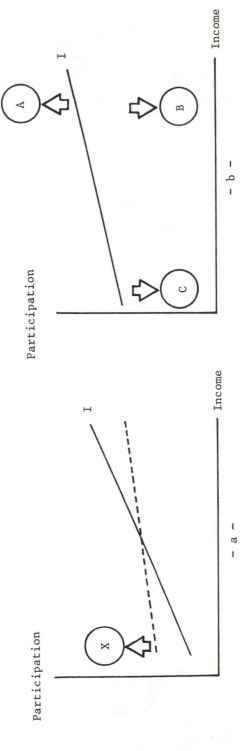

FIGURE 1

THE RELATIONSHIP BETWEEN PARTICIPATION AND INCOME
AS AFFECTED BY DIFFERENT SUBPOPULATIONS

high; the combination steepens line I. Subpopulation B neutralizes income bias in participation, whereas subpopulation C reinforces the bias. Thus, the figures in Table 1 represent the combination of effects of income and other sociological variables.

A diagrammatic presentation of sociological sources of income bias in participation can be described by statistical equations.[9] The log-linear relationship between t's political participation (P_t) and income (I_t) can be shown as

$$\ln P_t = \alpha_o + \alpha_1 \ln I_t + u_t \tag{1}$$

where α_o, α_1, and u_t indicate a constant, income elasticity of participation, and a residual, respectively. We assume that u_t is not correlated with $\ln I_t$. However, P_t is not only dependent on I_t, but is also related to the set of other sociodemographic variables denoted by S_t.

$$\ln P_t = \beta_o + \beta_1 \ln I_t + \sum_{j=2}^{k} \beta_j \ln S_{jt} + \epsilon_t \tag{2}$$

The income bias in participation (α_1) defined in equation (1) is related to the behavioral parameters defined in equation (2) by

$$\alpha_1 = \beta_1 + \sum_{j=2}^{k} \beta_j \gamma_j \tag{3}$$

where γ_j is the elasticity of a sociodemographic variable with respect to income. Equation (3) thus states that the extent of income bias in participation is the combination of:

1. the partial income elasticity of participation, β_1;
2. the elasticity of participation with respect to sociodemographic variables, β_j; and
3. the elasticity of sociodemographic variables with respect to income, γ_j.

By estimating β_1, β_j, and γ_j individually, we are able to ascertain sociological sources of income bias in participation.

[9] I learned a great deal from Martin S. Feldstein, "Wealth Neutrality and Local Choice in Public Education," *American Economic Review* 65 (March 1975), 75-89, for constructing the following model. For purposes of estimation, it is convenient to replace equation (3) by the more explicit system of equations $\ln S_{jt} = \alpha_j + \gamma_j \ln I_t + u_{jt}$, $j = 2, \dots k$, where error terms u_{jt} are assumed to be mutually independent and each independent of ϵ_t in equation (2). By differentiating each of these equations with respect to income, one may readily verify that each γ_j is precisely the elasticity of S_{jt} with respect to I_t. Hence these equations together with (2) are equivalent to (1), (2), (3), and are seen to define a *recursive* system of linear equations within which the parameters β_1, β_2, $\dots$ β_k and γ_2, $\dots$ γ_k can be consistently estimated by ordinary least squares. See Phoebus J. Dhrymes, *Econometrics: Statistical Foundation and Application* (New York: Springer Verlay, 1974), 307.

This approach is very similar to that of Verba and Nie.[10] In Part II of *Participation in America*, their analysis begins with the standard socioeconomic status model of political participation—i.e., the higher the socioeconomic status of citizens, the more they participate in politics. The authors go on to ask what variables would neutralize this socioeconomic status bias in the United States. Their approach to assessing the magnitude of the neutralizing force of the variables involves the following questions:

1. What is the effect of a particular variable on the rate of political participation, independent of socioeconomic status?
2. Is this impact greater for citizens of lower socioeconomic status or for citizens of higher socioeconomic status?
3. How accessible is this variable to citizens of lower socioeconomic status?
4. What is the total effect of this variable on socioeconomic status bias in political participation?

Obviously, Verba and Nie's standard socioeconomic status model of political participation is comparable to β_1 in our model; their first, third, and last steps are comparable to β_j, γ_j, and $\beta_j \gamma_j$ of the income bias model, respectively.

So far, we have not defined sociodemographic variables (S_t) relative to the income bias model. We hypothesize that income, education, organizational involvement, urbanism, and *Sokagakkai* membership are related to the income bias model.[11] The educational figure is based solely on the last grade in school completed by the respondent: since we assume that college graduates behave differently from the rest of the population because they have different social training, in the model this variable is independent of the educational dimension. The organizational involvement index is based on a scale of 1 for respondents who are not members of any organization; 2 for passive members; and 3 for active·members, regardless of the number and kind of organizations to which respondents belong. Urbanism is measured by the size of the community in which the respondent lives. Although Japan is essentially a homogeneous society with little ethnic and religious conflict, *Sokagakkai*, the lay association of the *Nichiren Shoshu* sect of Buddhism, grew rapidly after World War II in the urban areas, drawing its members mainly from the lower socioeconomic section of the population. We expect *Sokagakkai* mem-

---

[10] Verba and Nie (fn. 5), Part II.

[11] We included age and gender variables in equation (2), but excluded them from equation (3) because they were assumed to be unrelated to family income. Empirical estimation of the correlation between age and family income was -0.04, and that between gender and family income was -0.05, respectively. Neither was statistically significant at an 0.01 level.

bership to be an important variable in relation to the income bias model, neutralizing in its effect. Table 2 presents the estimates of coefficients of the income bias model.

The total income bias in political participation at the bottom of Table 2 is obtained by adding up the figures in the $\beta_i\gamma_i$ columns. When F-values of both γ_i and β_i are greater than 4, the figures are in a box; thus, figures in a box imply that they are statistically significant at an 0.05 level.

The data show that the largest component of income bias in partic-ipation is a partial income elasticity (β_1). The partial income elasticities in voting, campaign activity, and communal activity are 0.11, 0.16, and 0.32 respectively.

Education tends to reinforce income bias in political participation, except for voting. There is a significant positive relationship between income and education, and the independent effects of education on campaign and communal activities are positive; the combination rein-forces income bias in these modes of participation. The educational effects on campaign and communal activities are not statistically sig-nificant, however, and are even negative in the case of voting. A similar tendency operates with respect to college graduation. Graduation from college might be expected to reinforce income bias in participation, but the results run counter to our expectations. The relationship between income and this variable is significantly positive, but the independent effects of college graduation on voting and communal activity are not statistically significant; on campaign activity, they tend to be negative.

These findings are not consistent with the generalization that educated people participate more in politics than others.[12] Highly educated persons generally participate more in politics because they are more interested in politics, have more information about politics, and think themselves capable of influencing the government. A separate analysis shows that the elasticities of political interest, political information, and political efficacy with respect to education were 0.59, 0.55, and 0.30, respectively.[13] These findings suggest that highly educated persons are more likely to express high civic attitudes, but these attitudes do not necessarily mobilize the Japanese to participate. According to Milbrath and Goel, a higher level of education does not lead to greater patriotism and system affection in some societies; this negative feeling toward the political system is part

[12] See Lester W. Milbrath and M. L. Goel, *Political Participation*, 2d ed. (Chicago: Rand McNally, 1977), 98-102, for a summary of literature on this subject.

[13] Ikuo Kabashima, "Political Participation and Income Distribution in Growing Econ-omies," Ph.D. diss. (Harvard University, 1979).

TABLE 2

THE SOCIOLOGICAL SOURCES OF INCOME BIAS IN THREE MODES OF POLITICAL ACTIVITY IN JAPAN

Variables	γ_i	Voting		Campaign		Communal	
		β_i	$\beta_i\gamma_i$	β_i	$\beta_i\gamma_i$	β_i	$\beta_i\gamma_i$
Income	1.00	0.11 (3.8)	0.11	0.16 (5.6)	0.16	0.32 (23.0)	0.32
Education	0.22 (248)	-0.01 (0.0)	—	0.11 (0.8)	0.02	0.12 (1.0)	0.03
College graduate*	0.10 (129)	0.04 (0.1)	—	-0.03 (0.0)	—	0.28 (2.2)	0.03
Organization	0.04 (8)	0.61 (44.8)	0.02	1.22 (123.6)	0.05	1.38 (165.2)	0.06
Urbanism	0.52 (59)	-0.13 (51.7)	-0.07	-0.18 (68.9)	-0.09	-0.15 (51.4)	-0.08
Sokagakkai*	-0.02 (11)	0.29 (2.3)	-0.01	0.41 (3.2)	-0.01	-0.39 (3.0)	0.01
Total income bias			0.05 (0.06)		0.13 (0.12)		0.37 (0.36)

Note: Figure in parentheses is an F-ratio. Figure in parentheses under total income bias is the income elasticity estimated by equation (1).
*The coefficients of these variables measure the percentage of change in dependent variables due to one unit of change in independent variables.
Source: Survey data collected in 1966 by the Cross-National Program in Political and Social Change.

of the reason why highly educated people in Japan do not participate more in politics.[14] It is beyond the scope of the present study to seek the reason for the lack of a significant positive relationship between education and participation in Japan.

Among various sociological variables, the most important one that reinforces income bias in political participation is organizational involvement (OI). Organizational involvement significantly reinforces income bias in all modes of participation, accounting for approximately 18, 31, and 19 percent of the partial income elasticity in voting, campaign, and communal activities, respectively. The significant biasing effects of OI derive more from the high independent effect of this variable on participation than from the relationship between income and organizational involvement. This finding leads us to the proposition, similar to one made by Verba and Nie, that OI is an important "potential" source of narrowing the participation gap between the haves and the have-nots.[15] Since the elasticity of OI is great, a small change in the OI/income relationship could significantly alter the effect of OI on the extent of income bias in participation. If the OI/income relationship were to be negative (e.g., recruiting the have-nots to organizations), OI could neutralize income bias in participation. The next variable, *Sokagakkai* membership, does in fact play this role.

As already mentioned, the *Sokagakkai* recruits its members mainly from the lower socioeconomic sectors of the population. Hence, our data reveal a negative relationship between membership in this organization and income level. *Sokagakkai* is successful (though this is not statistically significant) in mobilizing its members in voting and campaign activities. But it does not mobilize people to participate in communal activities. Consequently, *Sokagakkai* tends to play a neutralizing role on income bias in voting and campaign activity, but a reinforcing role on income bias in communal activity.

A notable variable in the income-bias model is the degree of urbanism. It neutralizes income bias in all modes of political participation in Japan, registering 63, 56, and 25 percent of the partial income elasticity in voting, campaign, and communal activities, respectively: while there is a positive relationship between income and city-dwelling, there is a negative relationship between city-dwelling and participation. This result is counter to some cross-cultural findings with respect to the relationship between urbanism and participation. A possible explanation for the significant negative relationship between urbanism and political ac-

[14] Milbrath and Goel (fn. 12), 101.
[15] Verba and Nie (fn. 5), 208.

tivity in Japan is that rural residents are mobilized to participate in politics because they live in dense social and geographical networks and abide by authoritarian traditions requiring deference to leaders.[16] To explore why rural residents in Japan participate more in politics than urban ones, and to provide an alternative explanation, is, again, beyond the scope of the present study. Rather, in the next section we will examine the consequences of this rural bias in participation in relation to the pattern of income distribution accompanying economic development.

A summary of our analysis up to this point and an explanation of its implication for the forthcoming analysis are in order. Thus far, we have shown that the extent of income bias in participation in Japan is considerably lower than in the other countries included in our data. As we hypothesized, income bias in Japan is based on a combination of (1) an independent income effect and (2) various income-biasing and neutralizing effects of sociological variables. Among different sociological variables, OI, the most important one, reinforces income bias around 20-30 percent of the partial income elasticity in participation. The biasing effect of OI is reversed by high political participation from rural residents who benefit inadequately from economic development. Another factor making the Japanese structure of participation income-neutral is that highly educated citizens do not necessarily participate more in politics than those who are less well educated; in fact, they even withdraw from some forms of political activities.

What are the implications of this Japanese pattern of political participation for income distribution and economic development? Clearly, the effect of the place of residence on the extent of income bias in participation is important in the analysis of the role of political participation in achieving equitable growth. Previous findings indicate that increased income inequality accompanying economic development is closely related to the widening of intersectoral inequality between the rural and urban sectors.[17] If there is a negative relationship between urbanism and the rate of participation (implying that rural citizens participate more in politics in this stage of growth), we would expect a significant redistribution of income from the urban sector to the rural sector through the political system. Consequently, rural bias in participation overshadows the widening of intersectoral inequality, resulting in equitable growth. This is the main hypothesis to be tested in the next section.

[16] Bradley M. Richardson, "Urbanization and Political Participation: The Case of Japan," *American Political Science Review* 67 (June 1973), 433-52; Joji Watanuki, *Politics in Postwar Japanese Society* (Tokyo: University of Tokyo Press, 1977), 65-76.

[17] Simon Kuznets, "Quantitative Aspects of Economic Growth of Nations: Part VII, The Distribution of Income by Size," *Economic Development and Cultural Change* 11 (January 1963), Part 2.

The Effect of Rural Bias in Participation
on the Pattern of Income Distribution

Available theories and empirical evidence suggest that the relationship between economic development and income inequality is bell-shaped.[18] In the growing stage of economies, the intersectoral inequality between the urban (modern) sector and the rural (traditional) sector becomes wider. Consequently, overall income inequality widens. However, as economies continue to grow, income inequality is narrowed because (1) income inequality within the urban sector narrows and (2) intersectoral inequality between the urban and rural sectors narrows.

In their empirical study, Adelman and Morris conclude that the increase in GNP per capita tends to widen income inequality at the lower level of development while economic growth narrows inequality at the higher level of economic development. Thus the relationship is nonlinear.[19] The hypothesis that the relationship between economic development and income inequality is bell-shaped seems plausible, but the question is whether this pattern continues indefinitely. Empirical investigations of the relationship over time in the United States suggest that there is a limit to the extent to which economic development influences the pattern of income distribution.[20]

On the basis of the above theories and findings, we expect the functional form of the relationship between economic development and income inequality to be nonlinear: in the early stage of developing economies, the relationship is convex, whereas for substantially developed economies, it gradually becomes horizontal, as shown by curve A in Figure 2.

We expect the path of Japanese income distribution accompanying economic development to deviate from this general pattern and to appear as line B. The main difference is that line B skips the bump in an income inequality/economic development relationship. Since the positively sloped portion of curve A is closely related to the widening of intersectoral inequality following rapid economic growth, a significant redistribution of income from the urban sector to the agricultural sector through the political system should reverse the natural tendency of the widening of

[18] *Ibid.*; also see Jerry Cromwell, "Income Inequality, Discrimination, and Uneven Capitalist Development," Ph.D. diss. (Harvard University, 1974); Adelman and Morris (fn. 3).
[19] Adelman and Morris (fn. 3), 165.
[20] T. Paul Schultz, "Secular Trends and Cyclical Behavior of Income Distribution in the United States: 1944-1965," in Lee Soltow, ed., *Six Papers on the Size Distribution of Wealth and Income* (New York: N.B.E.R., 1969); Barry R. Chiswick and Jacob Mincer, "Time-Series Changes in Personal Income Inequality in the United States from 1939, with Projections to 1985," *Journal of Political Economy* 80 (May/June 1972), 34-73.

FIGURE 2

HYPOTHETICAL RELATIONSHIP BETWEEN INCOME INEQUALITY
AND ECONOMIC DEVELOPMENT

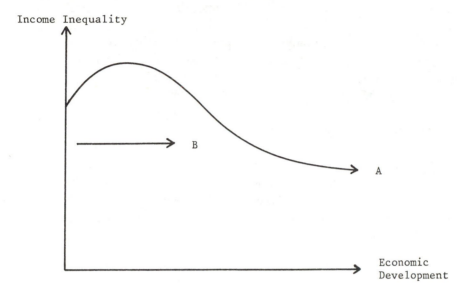

intersectoral inequality. The above hypothesis is shown in the following causal diagram.

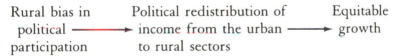

| Rural bias in political participation | → | Political redistribution of income from the urban to rural sectors | → | Equitable growth |

We will test the above explanation of causality in reverse order by asking the following questions:

1. Did the Japanese inequality/economic development line skip the bump (i.e., achieve equitable growth)?
2. Was skipping the bump a result of narrowing intersectoral inequality?
3. Was the narrowing of intersectoral inequality a result of the redistribution of income from nonagricultural to agricultural sectors through the political system?
4. Do farmers participate more in politics than do other occupational groups?

Figure 3 answers the first question. The x- and y-axes of the figure indicate the extent of income inequality measured by GNP per capita and the Gini coefficient, respectively. Scales differ for the global pattern and Japan, since the former is an aggregate. The scale under the x-axis is for the global pattern; the one above it is for Japan. The global curve is obtained by computing the Gini data from 62 countries (excluding the communist states).[21] The global trend line shows a relatively small income inequality in the very early stage of development; it peaks with a per capita income of $200-400. The curve then begins to decline, at first rapidly, then gradually. The Japanese inequality/economic development curve does not skip the bump completely.[22] There is a clear tendency toward a widening of income inequality between 1956 and 1962. After 1962, however, this tendency is reversed quickly. As a consequence, there is only a small bump in the inequality/economic relationship in Japan as compared to the global pattern.

Figure 3 also illustrates that the rate of economic development is very high during this period. Between 1956 and 1971, the increase in per capita income in Japan is almost tenfold in nominal terms. Previous studies have shown that the relationship between economic development and income inequality is negative in the long run, but that the rate of growth is positively related to income inequality.[23] This generalization is partly true and partly false for Japan: the progression of income inequality in the early period of development is reversed even though the country was still experiencing high economic growth. What, then, are the sources of such a pattern of income distribution? If our hypothesis is correct, the narrowing of intersectoral inequality should be an important source of overall income equality.

To test the above hypothesis, we divided the Japanese population into two sectors: agricultural and nonagricultural. Figure 4 shows that there is a basic lack of variability across time in income inequality for each sector.

In the nonagricultural sector, we do find a minor decline in income inequality from a Gini ratio of 0.33 in 1959 to one of 0.27 in 1969. Mizoguchi suggests several reasons: (1) diminishing profit differentials between big plants and small plants; (2) a shortage of young workers in the labor force, increasing the incomes of young people; and (3) diminishing earnings inequality among cities of different sizes.[24] The

---

[21] The income distribution data and GNP compiled by Shail Jain, *Size Distribution of Income* (Washington, D.C.: World Bank, 1975), include a relatively large number of countries in both the communist and noncommunist countries. We used income distribution data based on distribution of family income sampled from the national population between 1960 and 1970.

[22] The Japanese income distribution data used here are from Toshiyuki Mizoguchi, "Sengo Nihon no Shotoku-bunpu to Shisan-bunpu" [The Distribution of Income and Wealth in Postwar Japan], *Keizai-Kenkyu* 25 (October 1974), 360.

[23] Adelman and Morris (fn. 3); Jackman (fn. 3).

[24] Mizoguchi (fn. 22), 355.

FIGURE 3

THE RELATIONSHIP BETWEEN GINI RATIOS
AND THE LEVEL OF ECONOMIC DEVELOPMENT,
GLOBAL AND JAPAN

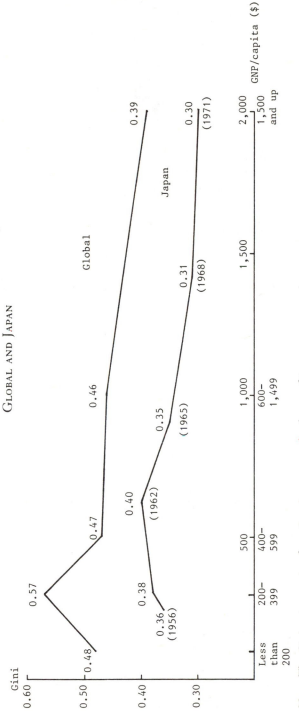

Note: The Gini ratio, ranging from 0 to 1, measures the degree of income concentration
in the population. The greater the ratio, the greater the inequality.
Source: Jain (fn. 21), for global data; Mizoguchi (fn. 22), 360, for Japanese data.

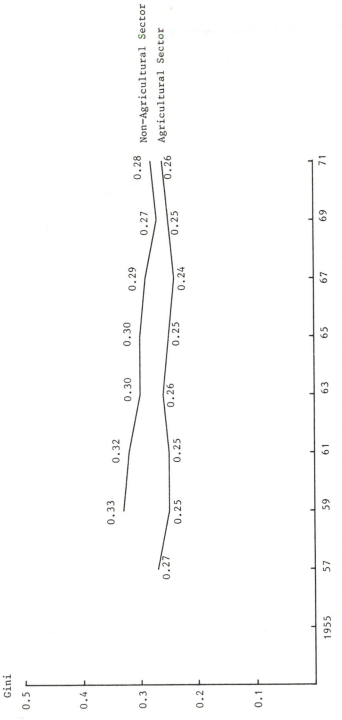

FIGURE 4
TRENDS OF INCOME DISTRIBUTION
IN THE AGRICULTURAL AND NON-AGRICULTURAL SECTORS,
JAPAN, 1957–1971

Gini

Non-Agricultural Sector

Agricultural Sector

Source: Keizai Kikaku Cho, *Shotoku oyobi Shisan Bunpai no Genjo to Mondai-ten* [Status and Problems of Income and Wealth Distribution] (Tokyo, 1975), 203, 210.

degree of variation and the direction of change of income inequality within the agricultural sector are not significant or clear.

The extent of the decline in income inequality within each sector does not explain the decline of overall inequality from 1962 to 1971. The overall decline in the Gini ratio is 0.1, while for the nonagricultural sector alone, it is 0.05. An increasing urban population during this period should increase overall inequality, because inequality in the urban sector is greater than in the rural sector. Moreover, neither the change in income inequality within the nonagricultural sector nor the change within the agricultural sector corresponds with the progression of overall income inequality between the late 1950s and the early 1960s.

Turning to an analysis of the intersectoral inequality between the agricultural and nonagricultural sectors, we should expect a change in intersectoral inequality that corresponds to the change in overall income inequality.

TABLE 3

INTERSECTORAL DIFFERENCES IN THE GROWTH OF
MEAN HOUSEHOLD INCOME

	Workers' Households	Farmers' Households	Intersectoral Differences
1955	$ 973	$ 995	$ − 22
1957	1,089	946	143
1959	1,229	1,035	194
1961	1,504	1,276	228
1963	1,776	1,374	402
1965	2,171	1,832	339
1967	2,624	2,951	33
1969	3,255	3,127	120
1971	4,152	4,056	96
1973	5,228	5,985	− 757
1975	7,871	8,844	− 973

Note: Unit is U.S. dollar based on the exchange rate in 1965 ($1.00 = 360 Yen).
Source: Sorifu Tokei Kyoku (Bureau of Statistics, Office of the Prime Minister of Japan), *Kakei Chosa* [Family Income and Expenditure Survey] (Tokyo: 1977), 7.

Table 3 illustrates the intersectoral differences in the growth of household income between workers' households and farmers' households. In 1955, ten years after the end of the war, the income of workers' households was lower than the income of farmers' households, reflecting the fact that the industrial production bases in the urban areas had not fully recovered from the total destruction of the war, and the agricultural sector was more productive at that time. With the beginning of postwar economic development after 1955, the income of workers increased rapidly, overtaking that of farmers; as a result, the intersectoral inequality between workers' and farmers' households increased sharply. This progression of the intersectoral inequality between 1955 and 1963 corresponds with the progression of the overall inequality shown in Figure 3. After 1963, intersectoral inequality declined rapidly, corresponding to the diminishing of overall inequality. The expansion of farmers' income proceeded more rapidly than that of workers' income, with the former eventually outstripping the latter. What made the farmers' income increase so rapidly as to overshadow the widening of intersectoral inequality in the early stage of the postwar economic development?

One possible explanation for the rapid expansion of farm income is that agricultural productivity expanded and eventually outstripped that of wage earners. This explanation fails intuitively as well as empirically. Both the absolute level of productivity and the rate of growth in productivity of the manufacturing sector are higher than those of the agricultural sector in the postwar period.[25]

Another possible explanation is the increase in the number of part-time farmers. Economic growth caused an insufficient supply of labor, resulting in the mechanization of agriculture, and giving farmers an opportunity to work part-time in industry while continuing to farm. The large number of part-time farmers among the agricultural population partially explains the growth of farm income, which derives to a significant extent from the growth of wage income. However, it is still puzzling that the mean income of the agricultural sector has outstripped the mean income of the urban sector: in view of the part-time nature of nonfarm occupations taken by farmers, the growth in part-time wages should not exceed the growth in wages of full-time workers.

The most probable reason for the rapid increase in farm income is that, while the income from farming remains comparable to that of wage earners, farmers utilize the spare time available to them through the mechanization of agriculture to earn *extra* income from part-time employment. This is possible because the size of the average farm in Japan is only approximately 2.5 acres. The question then becomes, what makes the income from farming—with farmers spending little time on their small farms—comparable to wage income?

[25] Norin Tokei Kyokai, *Nogyo Hakuso* [Agricultural White Paper] (Tokyo, 1978), 29.

The income of farmers has been affected by politics. In order to raise the income of farmers, the government has maintained high price supports for agricultural products and has heavily subsidized the improvements that have made the mechanization of agriculture possible. Donnelly describes the situation as follows:

A major issue concerning Japanese economic policy in the 1960's involved the extraordinary rise in prices paid by the government to rice producers. Beginning in 1960 producer prices doubled in eight years from 10,405 yen to 20,640 yen per 150 kilograms of unpolished rice. This rise was far greater than that in price paid by consumers which were also officially determined.[26]

In addition, in order to improve the economic situation of farmers in the long run, it was necessary to adopt new technologies. Since small farmers in Japan had neither the capacity to finance large investments in agricultural machinery nor a way to make the land suitable for modern machinery, the government of Japan has subsidized them heavily. Table 4 illustrates the share of government spending that serves the farming population in Japan (the amount above any general services offered by other ministries of the government) and governmental expenditures on agricultural price support programs, as compared to those on defense and social welfare.

Table 4 demonstrates the following:

1 In 1955, 11 percent of the national expenditure was allocated to the agricultural sector. The fact that this ratio remained at the same high level throughout the 1950s and 1960s is particularly significant in view of the fact that the number of farm households declined drastically over the same period.

2. The expenditure on the agricultural sector is disproportionately high in comparison to defense spending; in 1973, the former was twice that of the latter.

3. The expenditure on social welfare programs has grown significantly since 1961. It is possible that this has contributed to the decline in overall inequality.

4. A significant portion of the government's total expenditure on agriculture is allocated to the price support program for rice and other agricultural commodities.

Table 5 shows governmental spending on the agricultural sector in Japan to be disproportionately high in comparison to the United States,

---

[26] Michael W. Donnelly, "Setting the Price of Rice: A Study of Political Decisionmaking," in T. J. Pempel, ed., *Policymaking in Contemporary Japan* (Ithaca, N.Y.: Cornell University Press, 1977), 146.

Table 4

The Structure of Governmental Expenditures in Japan: 1955-1975 (Unit = 100 million yen)

	A Total Expenditure	B Agriculture		B-1 Agricultural Price Supports		C Defense		D Social Welfare	
	Amount	Amount	(B/A)	Amount	(B-1/A)	Amount	(C/A)	Amount	(D/A)
1955	10,133	1,113	(.11)	—		1,347	(.13)	1,038	(.10)
1957	11,846	1,183	(.10)	150	(.01)	1,430	(.12)	1,161	(.10)
1959	15,121	1,512	(.10)	0	(0)	1,556	(.10)	1,480	(.10)
1961	20,074	2,296	(.11)	660	(.03)	1,835	(.09)	2,454	(.12)
1963	30,568	2,984	(.10)	740	(.02)	2,476	(.08)	3,891	(.13)
1965	37,447	3,981	(.11)	1,205	(.03)	3,054	(.08)	5,458	(.15)
1967	52,034	6,158	(.12)	2,415	(.05)	3,870	(.07)	7,396	(.14)
1969	69,309	8,244	(.12)	3,530	(.05)	4,949	(.07)	9,743	(.14)
1971	96,590	11,452	(.12)	2,601	(.03)	6,935	(.07)	13,418	(.14)
1973	152,726	18,709	(.12)	5,380	(.04)	9,790	(.06)	22,196	(.15)
1975	212,888	21,768	(.10)	7,520	(.04)	13,273	(.06)	39,269	(.18)

Source: Ōkurashō [The Ministry of Finance of Japan], *Kuni no Yosan* [The National Budget] (Tokyo: 1960, 1965, 1970, 1975).

TABLE 5
AGRICULTURAL EXPENDITURES AS A PERCENTAGE OF
TOTAL GOVERNMENTAL EXPENDITURES IN MAJOR COUNTRIES
1971–1977

	1971	1974	1975	1976	1977
Japan	12.0	10.5	10.0	8.8	7.9
United States	2.0	0.8	0.5	0.7	1.4
Britain	—	4.0	3.2	2.1	1.5
West Germany	3.8	1.6	1.4	1.2	1.1
France	3.3	3.8	3.8	3.7	3.7

Source: Ōkurasho [Ministry of Finance], Zaisei no Genjō to Tenbō [The Status and Future of Public Finance], unpub. internal mimeo., 1980.

England, West Germany, and France. In the latter countries, agricultural support as a share of total spending amounts to between 2 and 4 percent of the national budget, whereas in Japan it is 8 to 12 percent. The evidence suggests that in Japan, a redistribution of income occurs from the nonagricultural to the agricultural sector through the political system.

Finally, we examine the proposition that political participation will be higher in the agricultural sector than in other occupational groups. Table 6 compares the rate of political participation among different occupational groups, again based on data collected by the Cross-National Program in Political Change. The participation score in the table was standardized so that the average score for the entire population is zero, and one standard deviation above and below the average is 100 and − 100, respectively. The figures in Table 6 are consistent with our hypothesis. The rate of participation of farmers in voting, campaign, and communal activities is approximately 0.1 to 0.2 standard deviations higher than the average. It is plausible that, because of this higher level of participation, farmers can apply strong pressures on the government and are able to communicate their preferences to governmental decision makers.

The analysis thus far has shown that high political participation from the rural sector has reversed a natural tendency toward widening inequality between the rural and urban sectors during the period of rapid growth. The question as yet unanswered is why high political participation by the rural sector in the growing stage did not undercut the rate of growth.

TABLE 6
COMPARISON OF THE RATE OF POLITICAL PARTICIPATION AMONG OCCUPATIONAL GROUPS IN JAPAN

	Voting Activity	Campaign Activity	Communal Activity	N
Service	− 1.7	− 6.8	− 16.0	148
Factories and Mines	− 2.9	− 10.8	− 17.7	598
Transportation and Communication	0.9	9.3	− 12.4	127
Agriculture	9.1	21.0	13.9	529
Sales	3.6	1.0	3.8	186
Clerical	− 8.2	− 14.0	− 6.0	375
Professional	6.6	− 2.8	20.0	168
Top Management and Administration	− 2.6	16.3	35.4	100

Note: Participation score is standardized so that the average score for the entire population is zero, and one standard deviation above and below the average is 100 and − 100.
Source: Survey data collected in 1966 by the Cross-National Program in Political and Social Change.

TOWARD A NEW MODEL OF DEVELOPMENT:
A MODEL OF SUPPORTIVE PARTICIPATION

Huntington and Nelson postulate technocratic and populist models for the later phase of a country's economic development. The technocratic model

> assumes that political participation must be held down, at least temporarily, in order to promote economic development, and that such development necessarily involves at least temporary increases in income inequality

as this

> widening gap between rich and poor, combined with governmental efforts to repress political participation, build[s] up stresses and pressures and lead[s] eventually to a "participation explosion"[27]

as illustrated in the diagram on page 331.[28]

[27] Huntington and Nelson (fn. 1), 23.
[28] Ibid., 24.

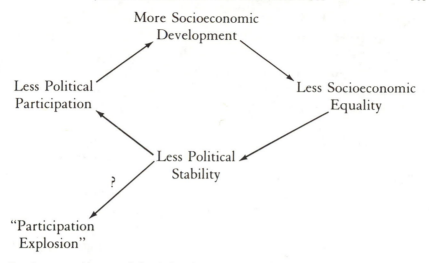

In the populist model of development,

high and increasing levels of political participation go with expanding
governmental benefits and welfare policies, increasing economic equality,
and if necessary, relatively low rates of economic growth. The logic of
this pattern of evolution leads toward increasing social conflict and the
polarization of society, as more groups become participant and attempt
to share in a stagnant, or only slowly growing, economic pie.

Eventually, this may lead to "participation implosion,"[29] as shown in
the following diagram.[30]

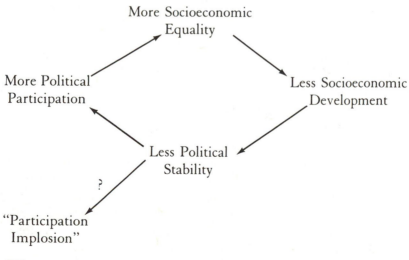

[29] *Ibid.*, 23.   [30] *Ibid.*, 25.

Japan has followed a developmental path that varies from the two suggested by Huntington and Nelson. In its development, Japan has not only traveled a path of equitable growth, but has done so very rapidly. How are we to reconcile equality, rapid growth, and broad-based political participation after the war? The answer seems to rest on the phenomenon of rural participation as supportive participation.

Several factors account for Japan's rapid economic development after World War II. Among the most important are (1) a high rate of savings, permitting rapid capital formation; (2) the high quality of the labor force, which is educated, motivated, and diligent; and (3) effective technology transformation. While these economic and social factors were important in achieving rapid economic development, political factors were no less so. Huntington and Nelson imply that a technocratic government is best suited to rapid economic growth because political elites need to make authoritative decisions in order to initiate and carry out effective economic policies. Moreover, stability and continuity in government are required to implement economic plans.

In Japan, this stability and continuity has been attributed to the dominance of the Liberal Democratic Party, which has been in control of the government literally since the Democratic Party and the Liberal Party merged to form the LDP in 1955. By their overwhelming support for the party, farmers have played a significant role in maintaining this dominance. More accurately, the LDP has depended heavily on farmers for votes and on businessmen for political contributions.

Table 7 presents data on party support by occupational groups during the period of rapid growth. It is clear from the table that farmers and top managers and administrators constitute the largest group of supporters of the LDP. Approximately 71 percent of those farmers who supported any party, and 75 percent of all managers and administrators, supported the LDP. This fact, combined with the high level of political participation of these groups, has made governmental decision makers extremely sensitive to the demands of farmers and economic elites.

Table 7 suggests an explanation of why substantial redistribution policies in Japan are compatible with rapid economic growth. Governmental policies favoring high economic growth (through industrial development) naturally meet the expectations of economic elites. But the achievement of high economic development requires a certain continuity in government and consistency in policy; the economic elites alone are not a sufficient base of support for the ruling party in Japan. Although the Liberal Democrats have managed to broaden their base of support considerably during the years of economic growth, it was the farmers

TABLE 7

PARTY SUPPORT BY OCCUPATIONAL GROUPS IN JAPAN
(Percentages)

	Liberal Democrats	Socialists	Democratic Socialists	Communists	Komeito	N
Service	55.0	29.4	6.4	4.6	9.2	109
Factories and Mines	35.9	49.9	5.6	1.9	6.4	373
Transportation and Communication	27.8	59.7	8.3	1.4	2.8	72
Agriculture	70.8	23.5	3.1	0.5	2.0	391
Sales	63.3	28.8	5.5	0	5.5	128
Clerical	45.9	43.0	8.3	1.2	1.7	242
Professional	35.1	58.6	5.4	0.9	0	111
Top Management and Administration	74.6	16.4	4.5	1.5	3.0	67

Source: Survey data collected in 1966 by the Cross-National Program in Political and Social Change.

who continued to back the party by a consistent and crucial margin. This is particularly true because—despite the rapid decrease in the farm population—rural areas remain overrepresented, and most electoral districts in Japan's lower house retain a small but critical agricultural component. In return for their support, farmers receive preferential treatment through the budgetary system, which substantially equalizes the intersectoral inequality that might otherwise result from rapid growth.

Supportive rural participation is also related to political culture. Almond and Verba maintain that democracy requires a certain balance between the power of political elites and the responsiveness of these elites to the people.[31] However, the promotion of economic development often requires a shift in balance in the direction of increased power to the elites in order for them to carry out effective economic policies. Since rural participation tends to be "passive, uninvolved, and deferential to elites,"[32] it does not undercut authoritative decision making by the elites. Rather, supportive rural participation, in the period shortly after Japan allowed broad-based political participation, softened the intensity of divisiveness and tension among social groups and the demands for radical change that accompanied economic development.

Moreover, supportive rural participation during the country's period of rapid growth was based to a significant degree on village solidarity that was institutionalized through various intermediate groups. As Watanuki has pointed out, the

> need for cooperation in the control of water for irrigation, common worship of village Shinto gods, common ties to the same Buddhist temple, concentrated physical location of houses in a narrow area, networks of extended family ties and other conjugal ties, and the administrative practice of utilizing the village as an administrative unit ... created a high degree of village solidarity.[33]

Although in the prewar and immediate postwar years local influentials played a dominant role in relating these local social networks of the village to political processes at higher levels, administrative amalgamations of local governmental units in the 1950s and early 1960s created the need for intermediate organizations on a broader scale. Agricultural cooperatives filled this role on one level; on another, conservative politicians organized constituency-wide individual support groups (*Koenkai*). These organizations have become the principal means for mobilizing rural voters and distributing governmental benefits. The intense

---

[31] Gabriel A. Almond and Sidney Verba, *The Civic Culture* (Boston: Little, Brown, paperback ed., 1965), 1-35, 337-74.

[32] *Ibid.*, 344.   [33] Watanuki (fn. 16), 82.

concern of rural voters with improvement of local conditions has made them particularly receptive to politicians from the party in power, who can respond with governmental largess.[34]

The pattern of combining supportive participation with substantial redistribution was further reinforced by the policy-making style developed in Japan since the 1870s: elite bureaucrats have dominated policy making, and parties have acted as agents of outsiders pressing claims against the bureaucracy. In contrast to the bureaucrats' efforts to concentrate resources, party politicians have had a strong redistributive orientation. Since 1955, the power elite has been composed of senior leaders of the LDP, senior bureaucrats, and representatives of big business who are interested in achieving rapid economic development.[35] Members of the Diet, on the other hand, have lobbied heavily with the bureaucrats to promote rural development (and, hence, redistribution) in order to win rural support for their reelection.

The success of rural voters and politicians in disseminating government funds to their rural districts is of course partly dependent on the availability of these funds. Economic growth and the subsequent increase in government revenues have made massive resources available for redistribution to the rural sector. According to Campbell, the average yearly growth in governmental revenues between 1954 and 1974 was 14.4 percent in constant prices; this increase is attributable to the progressive tax system which has allowed governmental revenues to grow more rapidly than GNP.[36] In 1955, total governmental expenditure amounted to barely one trillion yen; by 1975, it had increased to approximately 21 trillion yen. (See Table 4.) Since the ratio of agricultural expenditures to total governmental spending remained constant during this period while the number of farm households declined drastically,

[34] To please these supportive groups, the LDP government often uses the policy of giving subsidies to them. As a result, the share of governmental subsidies in the national budget is much larger in Japan than in other countries. For example, the subsidies in Japan's budget amount to around 32 percent whereas in England and France, they are 4 to 6 percent, in the United States 8 to 10 percent, and in West Germany 18 to 20 percent. Approximately 14 percent of the total is allocated to the agricultural sector in Japan; of 1,500 items, 474 go to the agricultural sector. See Michisada Hirose, *Hojokin to Seikento* [Subsidy and the Party in Power] (Tokyo: The Asahi, 1981), 76, 98. Hirose also discusses the mechanisms by which subsidies are apportioned.

[35] The triumvirate model is popular among political scientists in Japan. See Haruhiro Fukui, "Studies in Policymaking: A Review of the Literature," in Pempel (fn. 26), 23-59. See also Joji Watanuki, "Kodo Seicho to Keizai Taikokuka no Seiji Katei" [Political Process of Japan's High Economic Growth and her Emergence as an Economic Giant 1955-1977] *Nihon Seijigakkai Nenpo* [Annuals of the Japanese Political Science Association] (1977), 141-92.

[36] John Creighton Campbell, *Contemporary Japanese Budget Politics* (Berkeley: University of California Press, 1977), 3.

the absolute amount allocated to individual farmers increased substantially. This increase in agricultural spending through rapid economic development reinforced supportive participation. Hence, the Japanese pattern may be called a *model of supportive participation in development*, as summarized in the following diagram.

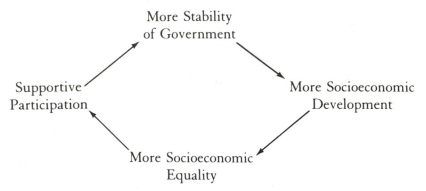

The dynamics of the model of supportive participation are summarized as follows:

1. The greater the supportive participation by less privileged groups, the more continuity and stability in government.
2. The greater the continuity and stability in government, the greater the economic development while other economic factors are held constant.
3. The greater the economic development, the greater the opportunity for redistributing income from the more privileged to the less privileged.
4. The greater the redistribution, the more supportive participation and stability in government.

It should be obvious, therefore, that the model of supportive participation is more stable than the two models suggested by Huntington and Nelson.

SUMMARY

This paper provides a basis for improving our understanding of postwar politics in Japan and the implications of the Japanese experience for models of development. In analyzing the structure of Japanese political participation and the relationship between the structure of participation and the pattern of income distribution accompanying economic development, we found that there was little income bias in political participation in Japan during its period of rapid growth. This low level may be attributed to the following factors: (1) the independent effect of income on participation was relatively low; (2) the independent effect of education on participation was at a minimum; and (3) there was a rural bias toward political participation that substantially corrected any possible income bias in participation. The rural bias in political participation was especially important for the determination of income distribution that accompanied economic development.

Economic development narrowed the size of income inequality in the long run, but this relationship was not linear. In the early stage of growth, there was a positive relationship between economic development and income inequality; this trend was reversed after peaking at a per capita income of $200-400. As the economy grew further, the inequality curve declined—at first rapidly, then more gradually. We assumed that this gradual decline was closely related to the widening of intersectoral inequality between the rural and the urban sector. (This was in fact true in Japan.) Examination of the Japanese case revealed a rural bias in political participation that resulted in a significant redistribution of income from the urban to the rural sector through the political system; this redistribution was of sufficient scale to overshadow the widening of the intersectoral inequality that had accompanied the earlier stage of growth.

High political participation from the rural sector which benefited inadequately from economic development did not undercut the rate of economic development because it was supportive participation. Stability and continuity of government is an important political source of growth; the rural sector in Japan enhanced this continuity and stability by its overwhelming support for the incumbent government, the Liberal Democratic Party. In return, farmers received preferential treatment through the budgetary system, which substantially equalized the intersectoral income distribution.

Although the present paper examines only the Japanese developmental path, it offers some implications for future studies in political development. Previous inquiries have suggested that broad-based participation in democracy is not necessarily positively related to economic equality when the level of economic development is controlled. The present findings suggest that high political participation by those who benefit inadequately from a growing economy has resulted in greater economic equality, at least in Japan. This finding tends to support Verba and Nie's proposition that socioeconomic neutrality in participation is positively related to economic equality, though not to expansion of democratic rights *per se*.

This case study of Japan offers more than just a test of the hypothesis that political participation has a significant impact on the pattern of income distribution. Its primary implication for theories of development is that political participation by the have-nots is not *necessarily* a cost to economic development, as Huntington and Nelson have argued.

Is the Japanese case unique? This essay has emphasized domestic factors that govern the relationship among economic growth, income equality, and political participation. Analysts of comparative politics may wish to determine whether the domestic preconditions for fudging the trade-off are present in other societies. The present study has not emphasized international factors that may have affected the relationship across growth, equality, and participation. The U.S. occupation, aid programs, and asymmetric access to the American economy may have been important permissive factors during the period treated. Analysts of international politics may wish to determine whether present international circumstances permit developing nations to depart from the two paths identified by Nelson and Huntington. Nonetheless, participation by have-nots, rapid growth, and economic equality *can be* compatible with each other, as the Japanese case suggests.

Agenda for Future Study

THE IDEA OF POLITICAL DEVELOPMENT:

From Dignity to Efficiency

By HARRY ECKSTEIN

FROM one point of view, the study of political development is a
major area of achievement in recent political inquiry; from another, which matters more, it is a conspicuous failure.

What has been achieved is great and rapid growth. The study of
political development, in contemporary form, started barely two
decades ago.[1] In short order, an extraordinary boom occurred in publications on the subject. By 1975, a standard overview listed over two
hundred pertinent works. Accretion became especially rapid after 1964,
though it seems to have "peaked out" (at a high level of production)
in 1970-1971.[2]

The negative side is that the result is mostly muddle. The study of
political development has all the traits of too-rapid, jerry-built growth,
and of its concomitant, "decay."[3] The muddle is especially pronounced
where it does the most harm: in regard to the very meaning of political
development. Even scholars who were conspicuous in pushing the
boom along are now viewing the matter of definition with dismay.
Thus, Huntington and Domínguez start their review of the literature
with remarks about loaded and wishful definitions—an "alarming
proliferation" of them—and the consequent "superfluity" of much
work on political development.[4] It stands to reason that, if a concept
is encumbered with many meanings, theories using it also will vary
alarmingly, because they are not about the same thing.

---

[1] The salient exploratory works are Rupert Emerson, *From Empire to Nation*
(Boston: Beacon Press, 1960), and Gabriel Almond and James S. Coleman, eds., *The
Politics of the Developing Areas* (Princeton: Princeton University Press, 1960). Among
the pioneers, two others also stand out: Karl W. Deutsch, "Social Mobilization and
Political Development," *Political Science Review*, Vol. 55 (September 1961), 493-514,
and Lucian W. Pye, *Politics, Personality, and Nation Building* (New Haven: Yale University Press, 1962).

[2] Samuel P. Huntington and Juan I. Domínguez, "Political Development," in Fred
I. Greenstein and Nelson W. Polsby, eds., *Handbook of Political Science*, III (Reading,
Mass.: Addison-Wesley, 1975), 98-114.

[3] The term decay is used in Huntington's sense, as an antonym to "order." See
Samuel P. Huntington, *Political Order in Changing Societies* (New Haven: Yale
University Press, 1968), chap. 1. Earlier, Huntington had used "decay" as an antonym
to "development"; see "Political Development and Political Decay," *World Politics*,
XVII (April 1965), 386-430.

[4] Huntington and Domínguez (fn. 2), 3.

The study of political development thus is at a critical juncture. One can let it decay further or, not much different, choose to abandon it—Frank Lloyd Wright's prescription for what to do about Pittsburgh (and, I think, Huntington's for political development). Or one can try a project in conceptual and, through it, theoretical renewal. In this essay, I develop a basis for renovation. Abandonment might, of course, be the wiser course. But the present conceptual muddle in studies of political development seems to me due to avoidable causes; the early explorers of the subject were getting at something worth getting at—if it was attainable.

CRITICAL ANALYSIS OF THE CONCEPT OF POLITICAL DEVELOPMENT

The reasons for the muddle about the meaning of political development start with a strange inversion of the proper and usual relations between concepts (labels), objects, and subjects.

Normally, one begins with observations or ideas (or both). Concepts are used to make statements about them: "messages" that convey information. In making statements, difficulties may arise. More or less misinformation, or "noise," may be conveyed. Unless conventional language has been seriously abused, the fault can hardly lie in the words. Messages will be unclear to the extent that observations or ideas are crude or fuzzy. To achieve greater clarity, it is usually not to the point to revise the definitions; the obvious remedies are more exact observation and more lucid thought. The exceptions that call for abandonment are concepts that turn out to be vacuous because they label ignorance itself—like "phlogiston" or "having the vapors."

If, then, one asks what a concept means, the answer ought simply to be that it means what it is intended to mean. If disputes about the labels we ourselves have devised concern meaning as such, one can be sure that something went wrong at the first move. But, in point of fact, nothing is more discussed and debated among specialists in the study of political development than what the concept means. Huntington and Domínguez put their finger on the reason in pointing out that scholars first became concerned with a "thing" called political development, and that this concern "naturally" (sic) led them to try to define what the thing is.[5] Trying to find a proper bottle to attach to a label had a predictable result: the "alarming proliferation" of meanings mentioned earlier. One sees this best in overviews of the literature on

---

[5] Ibid.

political development which generally present lists of meanings—lists that tend to be lengthy as well as different from one another.[6]

Why this topsy-turvy procedure of putting concepts before meanings? The explanation seems to me apparent in the actual unfolding of studies of development since the early fifties. At first, the term "development" became fashionable policy language for describing economic differences between Western (and other) societies and the assumed aspirations of Third World countries. In the economic sense, the concept was reasonably informative: it referred to levels of material abundance and processes of raising the levels. When political scientists appropriated the label, they also referred to assumed aspirations in the Third World, and differences between it and the West; they then searched for a special content for the concept. Since "political abundance" has no immediately apparent meaning, the results were bound to be odd and eclectic.

The search for a political version of abundance is most evident in attempts to define political development in terms of capabilities—levels of them; "crises" regarding them; changes in them; various capabilities (as in Almond and Powell); or some particular kind (as in Organski).[7] This tack, however plausible, turned out, at best, to be problematic. Capabilities being potential, it is intrinsically difficult to be precise about them. More important, the notion of capability only removes the problem of definition by one step. We now ask: Capability to do what, and how?

In most cases, the definition of the "thing" called political development was sought in a manner even more likely to lead to conceptual entropy. From the outset, development was, as stated, a norm-laden concept, distinguishing "us" from "them," Western achievements from non-Western aspirations—much like the earlier, less euphemistic word civilization. The difficulty here is not just parochial bias, but the tendency to conceive political development simplistically—as what exists in the West and had gone on in its history (especially its recent history), and what was sought to be replicated, or was bound to occur, in "backward" societies. Since a great many things have gone on in Western history, scholars were virtually compelled to choose for emphasis some aspect, or aspects, of Western history. They could—

[6] A prototype (ten definitions) is in Lucian W. Pye, *Aspects of Political Development* (Boston: Little, Brown, 1966), 33-45.

[7] Gabriel A. Almond and G. Bingham Powell, *Comparative Politics: A Developmental Approach* (Boston: Little, Brown, 1966), 28-29, 190-212; A.F.K. Organski, *The Stages of Political Development* (New York: Knopf, 1965), 7.

perhaps had to—choose by opinion. And so we get eclectic catalogues of meanings, which, taken altogether, simply spell Western history.

Thus, political development has been especially associated with increasing "democratization"; with growing "bureaucratization"; with the professionalization of politics (what Weber called living "off," not "for" politics);[8] with the "formalization" of politics (actions based on explicitly prescribed legal rules); with the decline of "ascription" and the rise of "achievement" in political roles; with the growing "clarification" and "resolution" of political jurisdictions (the gradual vanishing of parallel or overlapping functions, like those of the Church, principalities, and other traditional corporations, and the clearcut rank-ordering of roles and structures, contrasted to the messy lack of hierarchy produced by infeudation).[9] The very fact of the building of nation-states has also been equated with political development ("nation-building" once was the most common meaning), as has the increased "penetration" of societies by governmental authorities, and the increase in "redistributive" policies. The list can easily be extended. History is enormously multifaceted.

Granted, development is not a sensible concept unless used in a historical sense. But if the concept remains closely tied to concrete history, there is no need for it. We already have a more intelligible concept for development *as* history: namely, history. Development must surely stand for something more abstract and "ruleful" (theoretical)—something that is manifested *in* histories (plural).[10]

Why not, then, simply abandon the idea of "political development"? In the first place, the present literature on political development simply does not represent "developmental" inquiry properly. In fact, little but the label itself (plus some other, mostly misused, concepts culled from developmental thinkers) links that literature to genuine developmental thought. The state of the literature, consequently, is irrelevant to assessing the utility of theories of development, properly constructed. (It might be added that the disjunction of the label from the theorizing it represents is ironic, because developmental thought occurs at the

---

[8] Max Weber, "Politics as a Vocation," in *From Max Weber: Essays in Sociology*, trans. and ed. by H. H. Gerth and C. Wright Mills (New York: Oxford University Press, 1946), 84-86.

[9] Robert T. Holt and John E. Turner, *The Political Basis of Economic Development* (Princeton: van Nostrand, 1966), 57-58.

[10] Although Binder surely was right in writing about political development that "it cannot be expected that Western scholars could wholly escape the influences of their own political cultures," there is no evidence at all for his views that this need not "eventuate in a narrow parochialism" or that a "general theory of political development" can "emerge from a specific history." Leonard Binder and others, *Crises and Sequences in Political Development* (Princeton: Princeton University Press, 1971), 67.

very origin of modern social science in the 19th century, and was devised to deal with its core issue: what it is to be "modern.") Secondly, the core issue that gave rise to developmental thought has hardly been transcended by later history. It remains obtrusive and urgent, and is still very much a puzzle. Finally, the potential of developmental thought for unravelling the puzzle it was meant to solve has hardly begun to be realized. The failure is the result of misunderstanding its intention. Very summarily, this intention was to understand our own societies (and, by extension, others) by finding their location in social time as a critical theoretical dimension.

THE NATURE OF DEVELOPMENTAL THOUGHT

SOCIAL TIME AND THE PUZZLE OF MODERNITY

Societies exist in, and "move" through, history—and social history differs from other sorts of history. Obviously, then, social theories must somehow come to grips with the nature and significance of "social time." One issue that is thus posed is how to think of the flow of history: whether to treat history annalistically, as a continuous thread, or as passing through distinct phases—as Geertz puts it, "a medium through which certain abstract processes move."[11] A further issue arises if the latter tack is chosen: how to think of history as an abstract medium. For the most part, that question has been dealt with via picturesque metaphors, above all that of organic growth and decay.[12] Developmental thought is preeminent in trying to transcend mere imagery in the treatment of social time,[13] as well as in the extent to which such time is treated as a puzzle and a key to understanding.

The context in which developmental thought appeared had much—perhaps everything—to do with its animus. Developmental theories

---

[11] Clifford Geertz, *Negara: The Theatre-State in Nineteenth-Century Bali* (Princeton: Princeton University Press, 1980), 5.

[12] The standard work on this subject—and, surprisingly, the only history of thought centered on conceptions of social time—is Robert A. Nisbet, *Social Change and History: Aspects of the Western Theory of Development* (New York: Oxford University Press, 1969). Nisbet's work treats at considerable length, and splendidly, what I discuss very tersely in this section. His book can elucidate anything that seems obtuse here. I have drawn a great deal on his study, as anyone writing about social and political development must. But I differ from Nisbet in some respects, one of which is especially important. Nisbet holds that all Western thought is developmental. Different theoretical accounts of social change in history seem to him to be only variations on a continuing theme, already present in classic myth. I think this argument is forced and impedes understanding of the idea of development. Theories of social development, it seems to me, are more notable for their novelty than for anything they have in common with previous thought.

[13] This, *pace* Nisbet, is a fundamental aspect of its novelty.

began, simplistically, early in the 19th century and attained their apogee early in the 20th. Roughly, the period runs from Comte, the first volume of whose *Cours* appeared in 1830, to Durkheim and Weber; this period was, as we know, one of rapid, tumultuous, broad-scale, and above all almost wholly unprecedented changes, in scope and in kind, in the West. The changes need no elaboration. They include the spread of industry; the rapid growth of science and tech-nology; the "disenchantment" of the world, as Weber called it, through rational perceptions and behavior; growing bureaucratization; democ-ratization and its many concomitants (the appearance of political parties, changes in the composition of elites, and so on); nationalism and the emergence of new states; vastly increased social mobility; great cities; transformed networks of transport and communications; revolutions; reaction; and much else. Such extraordinary changes, especially while still novel, were bound to pose profound puzzles. They were also bound to unhinge established ideas about the nature of societies' movement through time. And they were, at the least, likely to make the proper understanding of historical process appear funda-mental to all worthwhile social understanding. The belief in the critical significance of social time, and of the location of particular societies in it, emerges most categorically in Durkheim's sociology. For Durkheim, all was time-bound and, therefore, culture-bound: not just social facts, but even the "epic" issues of moral philosophy (because moral im-peratives are senseless out of their historical context) and those of validity and truth (because no universal mind exists, only particular cultural *consciences collectives*).[14]

Thus, the core problem of developmental thought was the puzzle of modernity. That puzzle had numerous related facets. Where were Western societies on the continuum of history? How did they get there? What forces had moved them from some long-past primal con-dition to the present? Where was historical process taking them? These questions differ from the way the problem of modernity is put now. In its earlier version, the subject was Western society: "we" rather than "they"; modernity rather than achieving modernization. Comparisons with pre-modern societies might, of course, help in finding solutions, but "we" were the problem. It follows that developmental theories could hardly have conceived of modernity in terms of the general

---

[14] This much misunderstood concept is the foundation of the most profound at-tack on all moral and epistemological absolutes. Nevertheless, Durkheim is nothing if not a moral philosopher and believer in verities. The paradox is resolved by Durk-heim himself in the preface to his first masterpiece, *The Division of Labor in Society* (New York: Macmillan, 1933).

condition, or selected facets, of "advanced" societies. Their first task was to diagnose that condition itself, in contrast to other conditions of societies.

In order to come to grips with the problem of modernity, and with the more general problem of passage through social time, the developmental theorists devised a mode of theory as unprecedented as the social conditions that they tried to understand—a change in thought perhaps as momentous as the appearance of Newtonian mechanics and cosmology in the physical sciences. To understand their mode of theorizing, it is particularly necessary to grasp two things at the outset. One is that the developmental theorists tried, in essence, to find patterns in pervasive novelty and seeming flux—to get bearings in a world devoid of all fixity and precedents. The second involves the nature of conceptions of social time available for them to find such patterns— conceptions they rejected as inadequate for their task. Discussion of these earlier conceptions should help to clarify the nature and novelty of developmental thought by contrast; and discussion of perceived shortcomings in the conceptions should clarify the animus of developmental theory—and thus also the traits such theory should possess.[15]

NONDEVELOPMENTAL THOUGHT

Universal-abstract theory. The strict antithesis of developmental theory is a body of social thought not far removed from it in history, and still its chief competitor. For want of a conventional label, I will call it universal-abstract thought. In such thought, there is no temporal dimension at all, or at least none that matters.

Although societies and polities exist in history, it is possible to theorize about them as if they did not. Many social and political issues are universal. In politics, the manifest universal issues are those of authority and subjection: the origin or basis of governmental authority, its proper domains, the obligations and rights of subjects and princes, the nature of justice, and so on. Since these issues arise wherever a polity exists, it may seem simple logic to seek their solutions independent of contexts, including temporal contexts. Before the 19th century, sociopolitical theory was addressed chiefly to such "universal" issues and aimed at such atemporal solutions.[16]

[15] The subject of predevelopmental conceptions of social time, plus critical analysis of them, no doubt deserves a full essay, or—as in Nisbet—most of a considerable book. In an earlier version of this essay, the part that follows was, in fact, a sizable article. I have severely reduced it, since my purpose is not to write a history of thought, but to work toward a renovated theory of political development.

[16] I do not mean to say, of course, that noncontextual theorizing ceased in the 19th century. It has remained with us—during the 19th century chiefly in Utilitarianism

If issues are not tied to contexts, it will seem plausible to seek solutions by methods that also ignore contexts. The systematic method of abstract thinking thus is deduction, and, in fact, the prototypical method of universal-abstract thought was social geometry. One invoked axiomatic truths and deduced theorems (mostly to serve as normative imperatives) from them. Both the axioms and deductions often were odd, and hardly involved tight geometric reasoning. Sometimes, to be sure, premises were stated as explicit postulates, as in the opening of the Declaration of Independence. More often, they made apparently empirical assertions, especially about human nature: that human life is "nasty, poor, brutish, and short," or that people have a "natural identity of interests." Or they postulated some alleged primordial sociopolitical event—usually a social and/or governmental "contract." At best, the links between the postulates and theorems also were quasi-mathematical; but the spirit of universal-abstract theories certainly was geometric.

Geometry, of course, is wholly abstract. It is a tool for imposing logical exactness on understandings of experience. If geometry as such is made into theory, the world that is theorized about will necessarily seem static, timeless, ahistorical, and noncultural. The universal-abstract theories of Hobbes or Locke (among many others) do seem to pertain to a sort of clockwork social universe. Time exists in it; but societies move in time like planets through their orbits.

Such a theoretical world can only be plausible if one's sense of social life is fundamentally one of fixity. Surely this at least partly explains the historical location of sociopolitical geometry. It postdates the upheavals of the Renaissance and the Reformation. It played a major role in the *philosophie* of the *ancien regime*. It was, in short, the characteristic thought of embryonic "modernity" not yet become mysterious and perceived as a sort of permanent, if still youthful, maturity. Therefore, developmental thought should be understood, above all, in counterpoint to universal-abstract social and political theories. To repeat, Durkheim insisted on temporal answers even for the seemingly timeless issues of such theories.

Of course, there existed, alongside universal-abstract thought (indeed, long preceding it), modes of social thinking in which time does play a role, sometimes a considerable one. It would be strange if this were not the case. None of these modes of thought, however, could

---

and its derivatives (including modern Economics) and, not quite so clearly, in Idealist thought.

be suited to the goals of developmental theory—though one came close in time and traits, and may be considered its flawed precursor.

Social time in classical and Christian thought. In Greek and Roman philosophies, as in the early myths which the classic philosophers rationalized,[17] all time is cyclical: the myth of Demeter made into rational philosophy. The cycle manifestly is fundamental to political philosophy in Aristotle ("the same opinions appear among men infinitely often") and underlies history in Polybius. It was perhaps inevitable that early thought about social time should use the imagery of cycles. The obvious reason is that the perception of time as a cycle surely is the most immediate experience of our personal time as organisms, and of the organisms all about us, in the recurrence of germination, growth, withering, and rebirth.

The idea of organic *growth* is not incompatible with developmental thought. Perhaps it even is the prototype of all developmental thinking, as Nisbet argues.[18] Growth and development have always been inseparable ideas. But this does not apply to the notion of organic *cycles*. The idea of cycles, after all, is close to being atemporal: it involves infinite repetition—changeless change. The idea may be a useful *deus ex machina* for historical explanation: things happen, as they often do in Polybius, because the time is ripe for them; or they do not happen because their season is not yet. But the notion obviously will not do if the *explanandum* is considered unprecedented. In fact, when the Greeks and Romans thought of the emergence of their own civilization, they used a quite different imagery: that of a gradual trajectory, so to speak—from an age of childish ignorance and contentment to philosophic wisdom and serenity.[19] The inconsistency can be explained by the fact that the classical philosophers, quite unlike the developmentalists, knew their historic place: despite imperfections and corruption, they considered themselves to be at the end of "advancement"—certainly not on a novel journey to an unknown destination.[20]

The conception of history as a trajectory, essential in developmental thought, is, of course, the basis of the Christian idea of social time. The

[17] See Mircea Eliade, *Cosmos and History: The Myth of the Eternal Return* (New York: Harper Torchbooks, 1954), chaps. 2-3.

[18] Nisbet (fn. 12), chap. 1.

[19] The alternative to thinking in terms of cycles and trajectories is used in Theodor Gomperz, *Greek Thinkers*, I (London: John Murray, 1901), 141.

[20] I agree here with J. B. Bury, *contra* Nisbet, that the Greeks had no (philosophic) idea of "progress." See *The Idea of Progress* (New York: Macmillan, 1932), 19.

Christian trajectory is a pilgrim's progress. This is especially explicit, before Milton, in St. Augustine: "The education of the human race . . . has advanced . . . through certain epochs or, as it were, ages, so that it might gradually rise from earthly to heavenly things."[21] The pilgrim's advance, though, was gloomy, as befit the time of Alaric's sack of Rome; it was an advance through corruption toward apocalypse. Such a vision could hardly speak to thinkers in a hopeful age. But, more important, what makes the Christian idea of history irrelevant to developmental thought is, again, what is most basic in the latter: puzzlement over social time as a variable. The Christian (and especially the Augustinian) thinkers also knew their historic place: at the nadir of time, when an old world had died and a new one had not yet germinated. It is difficult to think of anything less appropriate to the mystifying ferment and burgeoning of the developmental theorists' world.

Progress theory. A considerable, and familiar, body of thought that lies much closer to developmental theory certainly does not share Christian gloom, nor does it envisage the apocalyptic transformation of a dying world: progress theory. The nature of theories of progress (from Fontenelle and Leibnitz, through the greater intricacies of Kant, to the detailed "sketch" of Condorcet, and beyond) surely needs no discussion here. Progress theory is one of the staples of academic political education.[22] What does need discussion, and a fair amount of it, is why progress theories do not measure up to the developmentalists' task, and therefore differ from developmental thought.

We must be especially careful to distinguish progress theories from developmental theories because it is common to think of progress theory as an early version of developmental thought. No doubt there are continuities and resemblances. They occur contiguously in time, and the line of division between late progress theory and early developmental thought (like Comte's) is blurred. But, seen whole, progress theory differs from developmental thought in crucial ways—especially in ways that are important for dealing with modernity as a puzzle.

Most significant, neither the future nor the past really were treated as a puzzle in progress theory in the first place; consequently, the present also was considered to be transparent to clear minds. Even if any specific location on the path of history might be hard to fix exactly, the path itself was known. It was, typically, defined by the continuous growth of human knowledge, not least through the waning

---

[21] *The City of God* (New York: Random House, 1950), Book X, 14.
[22] The recognized *summa* on the subject is Bury's *Idea of Progress* (fn. 20).

of superstition and magic. Such a belief seemed plausible, even obvious, when only the lighter side of modern secular history was in evidence.[23] Although in most progress theories, the future was a vague, poetic vision, the theories at least were of paradise glimpsed, if not yet gained. In any case, paradise was certain.

To be sure, there were, as always, thinkers of skeptical disposition (like Hume and Voltaire) who did not so much dissent as abstain; there were also the gloomy-minded. But it was not until the French Revolution and its aftermath that the simplistic, sunny theory of progress wobbled. In the context of developmental theory, pretty visions of constant progress toward Utopia were as out of place as doomspeaking. The world was growing richer, more knowledgeable, busier, more secure. But much of what was novel also was patently ugly, and novelty coexisted with reaction.

Also important was the belief of progress theorists in a certain fixity in change itself. That is why some progress theorists fit well into the category of abstract-universal thought. Fixity existed especially in "human nature"; history was the social realization of that nature over time. In retrospect, we ourselves can discern a considerable temporal puzzle here. But that the theorists of progress did not do so is evident in their tendency to write what has been called "conjectural history," the prototype of which is the *Discourse on the Origin of Inequality*. It is still more evident in their searches for the essence of their own refined identity in rude or savage peoples. (Adam Ferguson's *Essay on the History of Civil Society* is the outstanding case in point).

Surely there is all the difference in the world between theories that profess to understand the present through the remote past and those in which the nature of the trajectory from past to present to future consists of deeply sensed mysteries. Granted that developmental thinkers, like theorists of progress, made much of rudimentary societies and did so in order to understand themselves and their own times. But developmental theory did not seek the sophisticate in the savage. Rather, like Melville, developmental theorists stressed contrast. Above all, where progress theorists wrote with certainty about the flow of social time, developmental thinkers puzzled and theorized.

DEVELOPMENTAL THOUGHT

We can now outline the essential traits of developmental thought (its "form"), in contrast to earlier treatments of social time.[24] Each trait

---

[23] Nisbet (fn. 12), 105.

[24] It should be noted that developmental theories fall into two fairly distinct subtypes. One comprises what we generally identify as social evolutionary theory. Comte,

can be related to some facet of the puzzle of modernity. And, in each case, the point can be substantiated that contemporary work on political development represents developmental thought inadequately.[25]

Inherent change. The foremost trait of developmental thought is that it proceeds from the premise that change is inherent in society. Thus, social statics and dynamics coincide, and the dichotomy between order and change is false; order, as Comte said, is order-in-change.[26] All other traits of developmental theories follow from the first in some fashion. The sheer scope and obviousness of change in the context in which developmental theories were formulated demanded that change be regarded as inherent, and thus ubiquitous, in social life.

What is most important theoretically about the premise of inherent change is that it involves an explicit choice at the fundamental dividing line between all theories; the primary branchpoint at which alternative theories occur. I have made this argument extensively elsewhere,[27] so I will be sketchy about it here. In explanation, the matter to be explained can be considered inherent or contingent. If contingent, it occurs because of abnormal (literally aberrant) conditions that happen fortuitously. If inherent, it occurs ineluctably, unless impeded or diverted by chancy conditions. (Thus, our deaths are inherent, our illnesses contingent.) Everything in theory depends on the choice made at this branchpoint. As a familiar example, I would cite the fatefulness of the change from the Aristotelian conception of motion, which was contingent, to the Galilean, in which motion is considered to inhere in matter. Developmental theory was, potentially, just as revolutionary.

How does the premise of inherency set developmental thought apart from other modes of socio-temporal thinking? First, in early ideas of social time, change was inherent in society only as changeless change, as repetition; or else, necessary change was a "one-shot" apocalyptic transformation. Even in progress theories, the trajectory

---

Spencer, and Morgan, among others, are members of the earlier species, not yet quite liberated from progress theory; note, for instance, Comte's vision of a "final" positive-industrial Utopia. Nisbet calls the other subtype "neo-evolutionism" (fn. 12, 223-39). It includes, roughly, Ferdinand Toennies's *chef d'oeuvre* of 1887, *Gemeinschaft und Gesellschaft*, Durkheim, Simmel, and Weber. One might simply call this species mature developmental thought—less simplistic, and with the tendentious and ambiguous aspects of the earlier species cleaned up.

[25] For distilling the general traits of developmental thought, Nisbet's treatment of the "premises" of socio-evolutionary theories is invaluable (fn. 12, 166-88). I draw on him—though not on his vocabulary, for reasons not really necessary to spell out here.

[26] *Ibid.*, 166-67.

[27] Harry Eckstein, "Theoretical Approaches to Explaining Collective Political Violence," in Ted Robert Gurr, ed., *Handbook of Political Conflict* (New York: Free Press, 1980), 138-42.

of social time always came, inherently, to rest—and rest was never far off.

In all thought before developmental theory, then, social motion was Aristotelian. It tended toward a *telos*: a literal end. Also (Thucydides is typical), the events of concrete history tended to be explained largely by manifestly contingent causes: by the particularities of acts, contexts, wise or unwise choices, and the like. Historical philosophy and explanation were bifurcated and inconsistent. In the former, cyclical necessity prevailed; in the latter, accidents. This bifurcation is still evident even (or especially) in Marx as a philosopher of history and interpreter of particular events.

The first task of developmental thought, then, is to formulate a really general theory of social time; the next is to apply it, as explanation, to particular cases at particular points in particular histories. "Really general" means abstract theory regardless of time, place, and circumstance—theory that spans the whole of history, from primal origins to modernity. Clearly, the contemporary literature on political development does not come close to discharging that task. In much of it, even our own development seems to have begun only in the 19th century, or not long before.[28]

Dimensional change. It is necessary in developmental theory to construct what Simmel called "abstract grammars"[29] with which to make sense of the immensely complex actual flow of social time, and to locate concrete cases in such time. These grammars, in Kantian terms, are forms of history that fit the contents of particular histories. If social change is regarded as inherent, that flow must be along a continuous dimension—although aberrant conditions might slow down movement, or produce apparent rest, on the dimension.

To define such a dimension, developmental theorists had to characterize its poles: the nature of the primal and of the fully advanced conditions of society—the latter not really "final," but a vision of the future that could link with present and past. Only in this way could developmental theorists hope to find their own place in history, in relation to the remote past and the uncertain future. The polar conditions seem simplistic, and indeed they are so, intentionally. Maine, for instance, considered the poles of the continuum of history to be relations based on status and on contract; he explicitly called them formulas—abstract

---

[28] Huntington is an exception: he goes back all the way to the Tudors. (See fn. 3, 1968, 122-39.)

[29] Kurt Wolff, transl. and ed., *The Sociology of Georg Simmel* (Glencoe, Ill.: Free Press, 1950), 22.

tools for constructing "the law of progress."[30] The polar types of Toennies were community (*Gemeinschaft*) and association (*Gesellschaft*): abstract concepts constructed to correspond to "external" (viz., concrete) association; to describe old and new; and to find underlying themes in familial, economic, political, religious, aesthetic, and scholarly life.[31] Durkheim's orienting concepts referred to polar modes of social solidarity, the mechanical and organic;[32] these concepts, again, were used as highly abstract forms to make sense of concrete cultures, by a theorist preeminently aware of their variability. Weber's poles were traditional and rational systems of action: pure types that were useful for describing and explaining impure (concrete) cases.[33]

In regard to the construction of such continuous dimensions, the contemporary literature on political development again falls dismally short. Writers tend to take positions on modernity (as we saw, simplistically), but not explicitly on pre-modernity, and least of all on the primal conditions from which development flows. Huntington just tells us that traditional political systems vary.[34] And Lerner, typically, says no more than that traditional systems lack modern traits.[35]

Growth and stages. If social change is dimensional, all cases fall between minimal and maximal poles. Historic flow along a dimension thus involves changes in degree, or quantitative growth. Throughout the corpus of developmental thought, change in scale in fact played a major role. In Toennies, for example, *Gemeinschaft* involved small-scale units (household, kinship, village, neighborhood, town); *Gesellschaft* was associated with large entities (city, nation, cosmopolitan life, markets, industries, scientific fields). In Durkheim, organic solidarity was associated with growth in the sheer "volume" of society and in "moral density": the number and variety of interactions in which people participate. "Lower" societies were spread out sparsely, lacked cities, had few and slow modes of communication and transport; "higher" ones had the opposite traits, and, above all, denser networks of interaction as a result.[36] In Simmel, the quantitative element played a critical role even more explicitly. Virtually the whole of Sim-

[30] Sir Henry Sumner Maine, *Ancient Law* (London: Murray, 1861).
[31] Ferdinand Toennies, *Community and Society*, trans. by Charles P. Loomis (New York: Harper Torchbooks, 1963), 231-32.
[32] Durkheim (fn. 14), 70-132.
[33] Max Weber, *Economy and Society*, I (Berkeley: University of California Press, 1972), 24-26, 215-20.
[34] Huntington (fn. 3), 148.
[35] Daniel Lerner, *The Passing of Traditional Society* (New York: Free Press, 1958), esp. chap. II and pp. 85-89.
[36] Durkheim (fn. 14), 275-80.

mel's thought was based on a distinction between two-person (dyadic) and three-person (triadic) relations. This distinction was, for Simmel, a metaphor for small and large—a basis for showing that even a change merely from a relation of two to three would have enormous consequences.[37]

An essential premise of developmental thought, nevertheless, is that not just change (singular) is inherent in societies, but also changes (plural). The developmental conception of social change is typological.[38] Just as the premise of inherent changes responded to the obtrusiveness of change in the developmentalists' social world, so the positing of qualitative changes accommodated their sense of novelty—of new species being originated. Size and growth do matter, but chiefly as bases of generic changes. Durkheim's distinction between mechanical and organic solidarity clearly was typological; but the long process by which organic solidarity replaces the mechanical type results from quantitative change. At the outset, there is a growth of what Durkheim called "moral density"—of the volume of interactions (and hence of regulative mores). As this occurs, conflicts increase—if only through proximity, like conflicts among animals living off the same parts of a tree. The chief mechanism available for reducing conflicts caused by proximity is a kind of distancing: the division of labor separates people and, as a bonus to harmony, makes them more mutually dependent. In this way, a generically quite different kind of solidarity replaces that of early societies. In the latter, solidarity results from the sameness of their parts; in advanced societies, its source is just the opposite: differentiation.[39]

If social change is *both* quantitative and typological, an obvious issue arises: how to reconcile the two. The developmentalists' solution (the only solution possible) was to think of the flow of social time as involving stages: critical thresholds at which growth in degree generates changes in kind. Comte posited three such stages: theological, metaphysical, and positive. Spencer considered social change to be more obviously continuous, but also to involve typological change: from homogeneous to heterogeneous societies.[40] Obviously such change is quantitative, but Spencer himself referred to the result as "transformations."

The idea of social stages, essential in developmental thought, sharp-

[37] Wolff (fn. 29), 145-69.
[38] Nisbet (fn. 12), 162.
[39] Durkheim (fn. 14), 256ff.
[40] Herbert Spencer, *Essays Scientific, Political, and Speculative* (New York: Appleton, 1891), 60.

ly distinguishes such thought from progress theories.[41] In theories of progress, change is the growth of some desirable aspect of society (typically, rational knowledge) and a concomitant zero-sum decline in its obverse (superstition or ignorance). Progress theorists thus could, and did, envisage a final resting place for society: in the elimination of its defects. If, on the other hand, the inherency of typological changes is posited, social time must be open-ended. A historical process not conceived in simple monotonic, zero-sum terms can hardly arrive at absolute completion. The resulting theory is gloomier, appropriate to a time of puzzlement about society.

Again, contemporary work on political development has virtually nothing to say about how quantities (and which quantities) flow through political time and become converted into generic transmutations at critical stages. The imagery of developmental thought is much used: for instance, "takeoff." So is terminology that seems typological —above all, the labels "traditional" and "modern." I have already commented on the vacuity of both. If the polar types are vacuous, it follows that "takeoff" and intermediary types (e.g., transitional society) also must be mere imagery. The essential task of developing a theory of political stages—linking changes in degree and kind—remains unfulfilled.

Ruleful, necessary change. One way to orient thought to a world inherently in transmutation, in which all is perceived as time-bound and culture-bound, is to treat all cultures as having "meaning" only in themselves. In that case, understanding consists merely of interpretation. It is no accident that *Kulturwissenschaft* and the method of *Verstehen* came into being when developmental thought also flourished. As universal-abstract thought best represents the perception of underlying social fixity and uniformity, so interpretative sociology—"thick description," or cultural aesthetics—is one major response to the perception of social flux and variability.[42]

Cultural science, however, provides no orientation to the general flow of history, and offers no solution to the puzzle of modernity. Changes (and differences) may be inherent in societies, but no account of the process of change is provided. The alternative—and the fundamental difference between social science and cultural interpreta-

[41] This is said *pace* Condorcet. It seems to me that in the *Sketch* the notion of stages is simply a literary convenience.
[42] I consider Clifford Geertz to be its outstanding present practitioner. See *The Interpretation of Cultures* (New York: Basic Books, 1973)—especially 3-30 (on "thick description") and 412-53 (on the social meaning of Balinese cockfights).

tion—is to proceed from the premise that societies pass through the stages of social time in a ruleful manner. In that case, modernity—as a stage or passage to a stage—may become comprehensible, in comparison to other cultures, as a particular location on a general and necessary socio-temporal continuum. Also, in this way, comfort can be provided in a still ugly, unfinished world. The tumult of early modernity may be regarded as the onset of a higher stage in which, as in any pure type, all will at last fit coherently. At the same time, the naive optimism of believers in finality can be avoided.

Thus, again, it is a critical task of developmental theory to construct a comprehensive theory of history—one that identifies distinct stages in a continuous flow of social time which links primal to modern society. Such abstract history must, of course, especially describe and explain how changes on the dimension of time have produced whatever is qualitatively distinct about modernity.

As we have seen, though, the puzzle of modernity did not just involve location in historical time. It also involved questions about how we arrived at our temporal location and others at theirs, and about where history was taking us and them. A related task of developmental theory, then, was to identify, alongside uniform motion, the uniform forces pushing societies ineluctably along the continuum of history—especially forces inherent in societies. Only thus was it possible to see the necessity of what had occurred since primal times, and only thus can one have a sure sense of direction in looking ahead— orientation to present, past, and future.

All developmental theories posit such an underlying moving force (and special forces at different stages) that pushes societies through time. Specifying such a force—describing historical gravity, so to speak —is, needless to say, a very difficult task. What force could possibly do what was theoretically needed? Obviously, it had to be absolutely fundamental—something "essential" in the very nature of societies, and thus always present as a dynamic force, through qualitative changes. The early evolutionists saw the problem, but they tended to circumvent it, because they wanted a quick fix to make sense of change. Their circumventions involved truisms—resort to unspecified "properties of our species," as Comte put it[43]—that is, to human nature. But as evolutionary thought itself evolved, the solutions became less vacuous. In Spencer, for instance, the driving force behind social change was the desire for social efficiency, which Spencer equated with complexity of structure. In Durkheim, it was something even more obviously

[43] Auguste Comte, *The Positive Philosophy*, II (London: George Bell, 1896), 229.

essential: social existence as such—the need for solidarity among the elements of society.

Here, once more, contemporary theorists of political development fail dismally to live up to the form of developmental thought. Not only is their continuum of political time truncated, but the force supposedly driving underdeveloped societies is, generally, little more than an unexplained urge to be more developed. At bottom, this is a truism *à la* Comte; it involves an assumed intrinsic "property of our species," reinforced by the extrinsic accelerator of cultural diffusion. What is absent, above all, is a theory of the fundamental force, or forces, that brought "us" to our political condition, and continues to push us through political time.

Conclusion. It should be obvious that the mysteries of modernity, as I said above, still are very much with us. For a long time, in contemporary political inquiry, they were shifted to the Third World. But now, again, they arise in reference to ourselves: e.g., in the concerns with the nature and future of postindustrial societies, and their governability. Developmental thought was itself developed to deal with these puzzles. Surely, it is uniquely suited to do so; thus, it is sensible to take such thought seriously—that is, to try to construct developmental theory properly. Hence this section, as groundwork for the next.

The quintessential developmental theorist, Durkheim, best summarized the spirit of the developmental mode of thought:

> Every time we explain something human, taken at a given moment in history . . . it is necessary to go back to its primitive and simple form, to try to account for the characterization by which it was marked at that time, and then to show how it developed and became complicated little by little, and how it became that which it is at the moment in question.[44]

I propose now to do this, in broad strokes, for the political aspect of human experience.

SKETCH FOR A REVISED THEORY OF POLITICAL DEVELOPMENT

The passage from Durkheim succinctly describes what is needed to renovate the idea of political development. A more detailed agenda of questions to be dealt with follows from the summary of the traits of developmental thought:

[44] Emile Durkheim, *The Elementary Forms of the Religious Life* (Glencoe, Ill.: Free Press, 1947), 3.

(1) What conception of continuous growth can plausibly describe the long passage from primal to highly advanced polities?

(2) What is the essential nature of polity in its "primitive and simple" form?

(3) What forces make the "advancement" of primal polities toward "higher" forms ineluctable (or at least highly probable)?

(4) What distinctive stages lie along the trajectory of political time? In what ways do these stages involve both quantitative growth and change in kind?

(5) What forces move polities from stage to stage?

(6) What do the answers to these questions imply for polities that are at present less developed, and for "advanced," modern polities?

1. What Conception of Continuous Growth Describes the Passage from Simple to Highly Advanced Politics?

I have argued that contemporary theories of political development are historically myopic. Even in Georgian England—hardly remote history—the traits now most widely associated with political development were still embryonic. Democratization was certainly not far advanced. The suffrage was severely restricted; leaders (e.g., M.P.s) either were nobles and gentry or their handpicked clients, bound to serve their patrons' interests.[45] In regard to bureaucratization, administrative and judicial roles remained entangled, nationally and locally; recruitment was highly ascriptive; specialization and formalization were elementary.[46] Among the more familiar conceptions of political development, only the "clarification" of societal authority was mature, for the messiness of corporate jurisdictions had certainly been cleared up by the 18th century.

How, then, can one characterize a continuum of political time on which the Georgian polity itself belongs to a rather advanced period? Recall that such a continuum must involve quantitative growth, and must be a "form" that can contain much variable content. Moreover, the dimension involved must be anchored in time by minimal and maximal poles, one corresponding substantially to rudimentary cases, the other a vision that links perceptions of modernity to its remote and nearer past and, still more important, to an approximated future.

I suggest that the most serviceable way to characterize such a

[45] Samuel H. Beer, British Politics in the Collectivist Age (New York: Knopf, 1962), 22-31.
[46] D. L. Keir, The Constitutional History of Modern Britain (London: Adam & Charles Black, 1938), 292-320.

continuum is also the simplest: *what grows in political development is politics as such*—the political domain of society. Through political history, political authority and competition for politically allocated values have continually increased. Using Durkheim's terminology, we might regard this as growth in "political density," perhaps as a special aspect of a growing "moral density." More and more political interactions occur, overall and in place of nonpolitical interactions.

To avoid confusion about what is being argued here, a conceptual distinction must be made. One can think of "the political" as any relations that involve, say, legitimate power, or conflict management, or the regulation of social conduct, and the like. In that case, "politics" may simply exist throughout society and not be located in any clearly defined social domain or institution. Or one can think of "politics" as the functions and activities of such a concrete domain: that of the heads of societies, the princes, chiefs, or kings (for, in its modern sense, politics is associated with government, and government and social headship are synonymous). What I argue is that, through political time, the "princely domain" has constantly grown—increasingly penetrating society. And, in conjunction, political activities and relations in the less concrete sense have also grown. Expropriation by "princes" and expansion of political activity occur in conjunction.

One pole of the dimension of political time thus might be called the *social polity*. In the social polity, as a pure type, there exists a "princely" domain: some institution of headship of society, chieftaincy, firstness. That domain, though, is little differentiated from others, in the sense of having separate organizations and administrative staffs; it is anything but a subsociety—neither a "machine" nor a "system" in itself. Above all, next to nothing is done by princes, at least as we understand political activity: there is almost no active princely management of society. The society is virtually all and the polity virtually nothing. Relations of power exist, regulations of conduct and of conflicts occur; but they do so throughout society, not in special relation to chieftaincy.

At the other pole is *political society*. In political society as a pure type, "private" relations have been wholly preempted by the "public" domain of the chiefs. The institutions of that domain are highly differentiated and separately organized; governmental officers and staffs constitute a large subsociety. That subsociety is a complex system in itself, while at the same time it permeates social life.

The passage from social polity to political society can be described summarily: The domain of princes, who at the outset do virtually nothing, has great, indeed irresistible, potential for growth: power resources. Over a long period, these power resources are gradually realized. The chiefs of society convert headship into primacy, and primacy into actual control—at first very slowly, then with gathering, ultimately runaway, momentum. The momentum results from the fact that, as power resources are converted, they are not used up, but in fact increase. As this process unfolds, growth in degree corresponds, at specifiable periods, to transmutations of type. In our own modern period, we approach a condition in which the distinction between polity and society has again become blurred—not because the public realm is minimal, but because it has virtually eliminated all privacy. This, though, is not an end, but itself a stage in a continuing process. The political society generates its own dynamics; and we should at least be able to discern the forces likely to move it, even if not yet where it is destined to go.

This conception of political time has been anticipated by other theorists. It parallels Durkheim's view of more general social development. The minimal pole of the continuum is grounded in the anthropologists' notion of "stateless" societies.[47] The conception of political development as expropriation is in Weber: the emergence of the modern state was, for Weber, a process of continuous expropriation by princes of "autonomous and 'private' bearers of executive power," resembling the expropriation by large capitalist enterprises of small, independent economic units.[48] In his publicist essays written shortly after the Russian Revolution, Weber envisaged the further, accelerating, and continuous expropriation by the political domain of economic life, and then also of the more intimate, and the scientific and cultural, spheres—a remarkable prevision. The idea of "total" politics now also is a recurrent theme in works on modern democratic states. Sharkansky, for example, refers to runaway governmental growth "in response to incessant demands for more services," and repeatedly alludes to the erosion of the "margins" of formal government as a consequence.[49] The vision of political society informs especially the critiques of modern governments by perspective (if also hotheaded) "libertarians": Hayek, Oakeshott, Ellul, Nisbet, and others.[50]

[47] See, for instance, Lucy Mair, *Primitive Government* (Harmondsworth, Middlesex: Penguin Books, 1962), Part I—especially the chapter on "Minimal Government" (61-77).

[48] See Gerth and Mills (fn. 8), 82.

[49] Ira Sharkansky, *Whither the State?* (Chatham, N.J.: Chatham House, 1979), throughout.

[50] See, for example, Kenneth S. Templeton, Jr., ed., *The Politicization of Society* (Indianapolis: Liberty Press, 1979).

2. What Is Polity in Its "Rudimentary" Form?

To sustain the thesis that what grows and changes in political development is the political domain *per se*, one must, first of all, characterize that domain in its "primitive and simple form," from which advancement proceeds. None of the many structural or functional notions that political scientists have used to define the essence of polity seem to make sense for its very early forms.[51] What seems distinctive and universal to the princely realm in its simplest form is that its occupants and practices represent the very fact that society exists. Chiefs, khans, liegelords "embody" society. They are figures through whom societies personify themselves or sometimes (much the same) the ideal order of things imperfectly reflected in social order. They stand for the fact that a common, thus moral, life exists, and they celebrate the common life and make it compelling.

Surely that is fundamental in society, if anything is, because societies are nothing if not collective entities with which members identify— that is, define themselves. Thus, ceremony and symbolism—what Bagehot called the dignified parts of government—are not to be regarded as mere pretty trappings of power; nor are consummatory (expressive) and instrumental polities,[52] or "sacred" and "secular" ones, distinctive types at all developmental stages. At the "simple" stage (thus, perhaps, always), symbolism is the very nature of the princely, not a guise. That is why, to us, the primal political domain seems empty. Primal "symbolic politics" does not stand for "real politics." It stands for society.

The evidence suggesting that primal politics is symbolic[53] is considerable. For instance, in Schapera's study of sub-Saharan tribes[54] the following points emerge: The chiefs, as heads of societies, do not do much at all; they are simply marked out from others (e.g., in costume), exalted (in special rituals), subjects of rejoicing and of eulogies.[55]

---

[51] For a catalogue of such notions, see Harry Eckstein, "Authority Patterns: A Structural Basis for Political Inquiry," *American Political Science Review*, Vol. 67 (December 1973), 1142.

[52] These are Apter's terms; see David E. Apter, *The Politics of Modernization* (Chicago: University of Chicago Press, 1965), 24ff.

[53] I do not use the term entirely as does Murray Edelman in *The Symbolic Uses of Politics* (Urbana: University of Illinois Press, 1964). Edelman considers political symbolism to be an aspect of political practices that "condenses" them (and thus evokes emotions) or provides simple "references" to complex facts (his example is accident statistics). At times, Edelman comes close to what I mean by symbolic politics; see, for instance, 16-17. This is not to say that his use of the notion is wrong. It is different—mainly, much more diffuse.

[54] I. Schapera, *Government and Politics in Tribal Societies* (London: Watts, 1956).

[55] *Ibid.*, chap. 4. Varying "powers" are associated with chiefliness (102ff.). I will refer to the most common below. But simply being "chiefly" is clearly the heart of the matter.

Tribes are often defined simply by identification with chiefs, not by territoriality or even kinship. Sometimes no abstract tribal name exists, only that of the chief. Often, tribal names are the inherited names of the ancestors of chiefs, and at times chiefs are named by the tribal name. In some cases, any injury done to a member of a tribe is regarded as an injury to the chief (as we talk about crimes against society). In short, the collective and the personal are thoroughly joined in the chief's personage. Much the same comes out in Lucy Mair's studies of primitive governments and African kingdoms.[56] Mair argues, indeed, that the substantive wielding of "power over the conduct of public affairs" generally is not so much the chief's or the court's function as that of lesser figures, for whom kings are mouthpieces.[57] Lowie's work on North American Indian tribes makes a similar point.[58]

More important from the developmental point of view, we find this to be true also in the primitive condition of a prototypical advanced society—English society. (England may be considered as a good concrete approximation of an idealized case of continuous development: something close to an experimentally contrived universe—free of uncontrolled, deceiving contingencies—which any theory of sociopolitical development should fit closely.)

Anglo-Saxon society approaches the extreme of what I have called social polity.[59] If a "public sector" existed in that society, it could only have been that of king, *folkmoot*, and *Witan*. The king was principally a source of social identity, as were all lesser chiefs of the English tribes. His one significant activity was leadership in the common enterprise of making war, and practically no other common enterprise was engaged in. The *folkmoot* originally was not a council, but simply a local muster of warriors. By 900, local moots had pretty much been displaced by the *Witan*, a "national" council of "wise men." But the *Witan*'s essential function simply was to advise the king on the nature of "unchanging custom." Here the primacy of society is espe-

[56] Mair, *Primitive Government* (fn. 47), and *African Kingdoms* (Oxford: Clarendon Press, 1977).

[57] *Ibid.*: *Primitive Government*, 63, 69; *African Kingdoms*, 107-8.

[58] R. H. Lowie, "Political Organization among American Aborigines," *Journal of the Royal Anthropological Institute*, Vol. 78 (February 1948), 1-17.

[59] Dating poses difficulties here, but a sensible point in time for looking at the Anglo-Saxon polity surely is circa 900 A.D. A sense of an English society had crystallized out of the diverse identities of Teutonic tribal invaders and become personified in a single chief, Edward of Wessex. *Beowulf* remains the best primary source for understanding Anglo-Saxon life. See also J.E.A. Jolliffe, *Constitutional History of Medieval England* (New York: Norton, 1967), Parts I and II; Sir Frank Stenton, *Anglo-Saxon England* (Oxford: Oxford University Press, 1943); Dorothy Whitelock, *The Beginning of English Society* (Harmondsworth, Middlesex: Penguin Books, 1952).

cially evident: while the king embodied its consciousness of itself, the *Witan* kept him honest, as the guardian of its mores.

Much the most perceptive study of primal politics as I conceive it is Geertz's magnificent book on the 19th-century "theatre-state" in Bali, *Negara*.[60] Geertz alone seems to have grasped fully the critical significance of political ceremony and ritual: of the "poetics" of power as against its "mechanics"—as Bagehot alone discerned that the dignified parts of English government were not mere vestigial histrionics, but essential to its "efficiency." Geertz does temporize between regarding theatre as essential in polities as such and considering Bali an exotic alternative to politics as efficient power.[61] But, at least in Bali, "power served pomp, not pomp power."[62]

3. What Forces Make the Growth of Primal Polity Ineluctable?

Chieftaincy in primal polities is much indulged and rewarded, with awe and with goods. But that does not immunize chiefs (much less their retainers) against the appetite for mundane power; and, perhaps just because the chiefs are symbolic figures—awesome rather than powerful—power struggles are pervasive in primal societies.[63] For the purpose of developmental theory, it is necessary to show next that in such struggles the princely domain has overwhelming resources for subduing rivals and enlarging its effective control over society. What, then, are its power resources?

By itself, the representation of societies is an essential resource for power—perhaps the one seed that is capable of growing into political society. Societies are requisites of personal identity, safety, the satisfaction of material needs. But, though necessary, they are highly intangible. They are complex even when they are rudimentary. Seeing them as networks, or complexes of roles, or fields of interaction, or patterns of exchange—these are major feats even for modern professionals. Even if the task of abstract understanding were less difficult, such understanding would hardly move affections, which surely are needed for identification and legitimacy. So the personal symbols of society derive potential from the fact that they perform the most necessary of societal functions: making society appear "real."

It is true that there are other ways of making societies tangible. Primal societies, in fact, are always personified in their gods, through

---

[60] Fn. 11.   [61] *Ibid.*, 127, 135.

[62] *Ibid.*, 13. (Geertz's book appeared some months after I wrote the first draft of this paper for the NSF Conference on Economic and Political Development, Wayzata, Minnesota, October 1980.)

[63] E.g., *ibid.*, 24.

rites and magic. Thus, priests and magicians are the logical (and actual) main rivals of the chiefs for principal power. But the chiefs themselves are generally presumed to have special links to the supernatural, magical world—for instance, as rainmakers, healers, invokers of prosperity, possessors of sacred objects (fishing spears and the like), and as wielders of curses.[64]

These links to the supernatural not only reinforce secular symbolism (or make it sacred), but also associate chiefliness and "potency," for the magical world is a world of fateful powers. Chiefs are also considered especially potent figures in the material sense of prowess. All societies have collective business of some sort—in primal societies, for instance, moving camp and herds.[65] The function of making decisions about societal business naturally tends to be lodged in the locus of collectiveness. The one universal collective business of rudimentary societies is warfare: in defense against predatory others, for conquest (slaves, tribute, etc.), or, often, simply as a ritual.[66] So chiefs, though they have rivals in heroes,[67] generally are the main loci of potency as prowess. This accounts for the strange duty of chiefs in some tribal societies to be in good health, as well as for the use of wars of succession (in which the strongest survive), and for the frequent use of the phallus as a symbol of chieftaincy.

To exist, and to carry out collective enterprises, societies must, of course, be harmonious in some degree. Conflicts must be managed, quarrels mediated, crimes avenged. There is a universal social need for adjudication, and, again, a "natural" tendency to associate that necessary function with society's embodiments. The actual management of conflicts and deviance tends, in fact, to be decentralized and dispersed in primal societies—a matter of self-help in feuds, revenge, and exacting reparations. But the chief always has at least some vague special responsibility in regard to justice. For instance, we are told by Traill that a basic function of the Anglo-Saxon kings was to go about the kingdom putting down "evil customs." Traill's catalogue of judicial duties actually is a list of things kings could *not* do; and it seems evident that kings were little more than especially prestigious "oath-helpers."[68] Still, justice and chieftaincy had special, even if largely hortatory, links.

[64] See Mair (fn. 56): *Primitive Government*, 65, 66, 76; *African Kingdoms*, 39. Geertz (fn. 11) considers the link to the supernatural order the very basis of Negara: see pp. 17-19, 104-5.
[65] Schapera (fn. 54), 211ff.   [66] Geertz (fn. 11), 24.
[67] See, for example, Daniel Biebuyck, *Hero and Chief* (Berkeley: University of California Press, 1978).
[68] H. D. Traill, ed., *Social England*, I (New York: Putnam, 1894), 134.

The moral, surely, is evident. The primal princely domain is ages removed from the monopoly of legitimate power. But where could there be greater potential for eventual monopoly than in a domain standing for society itself; for potency, military, and magic; and for justice? "Dignity" and "efficiency," granted, are obverse faces of politics—but also interchangeable resources.

4. What Are the Stages of Political Time?

The fact remains that in primal polities, whatever the chief's potential, one can barely detect an active public core. Our own political world could hardly differ more. At "our" location in political time, as stated, it is difficult to find anything that is clearly private. I am not referring to "totalitarian" polities, or only to those, but (less categorically) to the other typically modern form of polity: popular democracies. (Modern democracies, in historical perspective, simply are the gentler twins of totalitarian rule, mitigated by open competition, free communications, and a sense of rights and liberties—which, compared to earlier times, no longer really divides the public from the private, but is a sense of political decency.)

I have described the extraordinary pervasiveness of political authority in contemporary British society elsewhere, and need not dwell much on details.[69] To convey the flavor of the matter, suffice it to say the following: (1) The national government (as in other modern democracies) now directly controls about half of GNP, and indirectly plans, guides, and channels most of the remainder. (2) Parliamentary sessions, once convened only occasionally, fill up the whole available legislative work-year, and even this at the cost of large omissions—uncontrolled "executive legislation," and a severe decline in the role of private members. (3) The Cabinet has virtually disappeared; as I wrote in 1958:

> Cabinet functions have become dispersed to an almost unfathomably complex administrative and deliberative machinery. Decisions once made collectively in the Cabinet are now made by cabinet committees, by individual Ministers, bureaucrats, the Treasury, official committees, party machinery, and even private associations; and, most often, by interaction among all of these bodies. If power is concentrated anywhere in the British machinery of government it is concentrated not in the Cabinet but in this complex framework of decision-making.[70]

One can argue that what mainly mitigates the darker aspects of fully

[69] See Samuel H. Beer and Adam Ulam, eds., *Patterns of Government*, 2d ed. (New York: Random House, 1962), chap. 10.
[70] *Ibid.*, 235.

politicalized society is the very inability to control such a concentration of functions, due to sheer diversity and overload. The gentle myths of liberal rule surely help, but perhaps not as much as the fact that monolithic authority itself is too large to manage. Privacy, in political society, is found in the interstices of authority; it is, perhaps, itself mainly a product of the structure of the public realm.

How did this transmutation to something close to "political society" come about? What lies beyond the primal polity's potential for growth? This is an enormous question, and we have not even the beginning of a plausible answer. As such a beginning, I suggest a six-stage process. The process is "logical" in that each stage manifestly is a condition for the next. The stages also make sense in the context of the English polity—our standard case for observing gradual, evolutionary "unfolding" (the literal meaning of *développer*) in politics. For this reason I will use English history—in gross summary—to exemplify the stages.

The politics of primacy. I have already treated the first stage, primal polity, using Anglo-Saxon England to illustrate its nature. The second stage involves what might be called the struggle for, and achievement of, primacy. The forces that push polities to and through that stage (and later stages) will be discussed presently. Here, it must suffice to say that nothing in political development can possibly come before the clarification of a distinct public domain that, in regard to "efficient" functions, is minimally *primus inter pares*. Without this, there is nothing that may grow. One may suppose that the establishment of a realm of substantive primacy—one that involves more than symbolic headship—will not be a tranquil process, but will involve stubborn conflicts over domination and autonomy. Aside from chiefs, there are others who have politically convertible resources: religious, economic, and military. But, as we have seen, the chiefs generally have much weightier resources for providing political goods—not least, safety, in a context of continuous struggle among social domains: Hobbes's good, and no doubt the fundamental value.

This general stage fits, in England, the period of *feudal monarchy*, say of the 12th century. The feudal monarchy certainly was quite different from the Anglo-Saxon, despite the fact, generally agreed, that the Conquest caused no sharp break. The domain of the Angevin and early Plantagenet princes, to be sure, remained mainly on the level of symbol and pomp; its practical authoritative functions were sparse. What is most conspicuous about the period is struggle for "dominion" as such. The histories portray incessant turmoil. But the tumult was not about policy, in our sense. It involved competition about spheres of autonomy and subjection; and the fundamental source of that struggle was a lack of clarification and resolution of the functions of the great and small corporations of society—all authoritative in their own domains, and constantly striving to expand or protect them.

Corporate boundaries now, though, mattered for more than symbolic reasons. They mattered because the princely domain had begun to acquire a critical function: material extraction—a condition of all effective action, and thus an obsession in feudal monarchy. The Treasury preceded all other political institutions in development. The classic account of 12th-century royal "administration" is FitzNeal's *Dialogue on the Exchequer*, the exchequer being its one great administrative creation. It regularized the royal revenues, and the great pacification under Henry II was, at heart, a matter of reestablishing the central revenues in face of embezzlement by the barons. Extraction increased political "density," and the latter changed institutions.

Still, Henry's charter upon his coronation was little more than an assurance of liberties, grants, and customs. Petit-Dutaillis' study of feudal monarchy tells us that the King's *concilium* attended to "all sorts of business";[71] but, as to particulars, he lists only personal issues (e.g., marriages) and familiar matters of peace, war, loyalty, treason, and the administration of justice.

The last is important, however. Judicial activities now were much enlarged and wholly reorganized—coequal with pomp and war as the core of royal primacy. Indeed, aside from finance and war, the whole royal establishment now looked like a sort of national judiciary. The King's "prime minister" was the Chief Justiciar; the Curia had become a "normal court" for the kingdom, not just an occasional tribunal; the judicial circuits, administering Common Law, had been established; and central justice had largely expropriated the seignorial jurisdictions, of which only "a few islets" remained.[72]

The feudal monarchy thus achieved, gradually, a considerable legal and extractive permeation of society, as a material basis for primacy. Contestation persisted for a long time, but in an increasingly muted, one-sided way. The nascent monopoly over extraction, the increasing practical responsibility for the management of conflicts, and the emergence of specialized institutions to handle these functions, real-

---

[71] Ch. Petit-Dutaillis, *The Feudal Monarchy in England and France* (London: Adam & Charles Black, 1948), 128.

[72] *Ibid.*, 138.

ized a potential already present in the primal polity; but, more important, all this added to the growth potential of the prince's domain.

The "prophylactic" polity. Substantive primacy, especially when added to symbolic headship, is both gratifying in itself and a supremely valuable resource for acquiring additional resources. Once it is established, struggles for its possession inevitably occur. One of the fundamental tasks of politics is to institutionalize such struggles in order to defuse them—a basic function, for instance, of competition among political parties. But institutionalization is always gradual—a sort of subtheme of development. Early on, contestation for possession of the domain of primacy must involve—in greater or lesser degree—unregulated, brutal conflicts. Lacking institutionalization (or the transformation of real and deadly conflicts into ritualized competition) damage can be limited only by prevention: prophylaxis.

In the prophylactic polity, the overriding objective of the prince is to detect and disarm usurpation, while that of others is to seize or control principality. To protect principality, it is functional to place it in a tangible physical domain and to draw potential usurpers into that domain. Hence, the identification of primacy with the prince's court. It is there that the game of trying to get and keep primacy and its perquisites is played; politics turns inward.

To a degree, however, prophylactic politics must also reach out into society, further than before. Courtly politics cannot be wholly isolated, because the discontents of society might play into the hands of usurpers. Therefore—rather than for altruistic reasons—the princely domain begins to furnish something else that is valuable to society: a degree of controlled social order, as prophylaxis in everyday life against society's *misérables*. The result is both a qualitative change in the nature of politics and the increased penetration of society by its political domain.

In England, *the era of the Tudors* illustrates the stage. The late medieval and Renaissance political struggles in England increasingly had a flavor different from those of feudalism. They were epitomized, and pretty much ended, by Tudor rule, for which "absolutism" is an egregious misnomer. Nothing really was absolute. Rather, the Tudors —especially Elizabeth—successfully coped with conspiracies *within* the realm of princely authority. If anything authoritative was absolute it was courtly absolutism, which transformed Lords into mere courtiers. Concomitantly, political competition was courtly competition—scheming within the firm.

Nevertheless, one can discern a threshold in the permeation of society by authoritative policy. Outside of the royal palaces, authoritative regulation was still sparse; but before the Tudors (conflict management and extraction aside), authoritative space, outside its royal core, had been virtually empty. A good many histories refer to an abundance of "proclamations" by the Crown, and subservient parliaments and courts, in Tudor times.[73] Elizabeth's parliaments did indeed pass 429 bills. The figure is often mentioned to impress. Actually, it brings out only the limitations of policy making. Elizabeth's reign lasted 45 years; nowadays, British legislative output runs to about a hundred bills a year. Much of Elizabethan "legislation" had to do with issues of diplomacy, foreign intrigues, war, and extraction. Some of the regime's authoritative activities, however, involved a novel extension of authority into society: the systematic maintenance of roads and bridges, the licensing of alehouses, controls over wages, the mobility of labor, entry into trades, dealings in commodities, interest rates, and—most familiar —a uniform law to care for the poor.

Growing political density surely is evident, especially since this reaching out into society supplemented unprecedented ceremonial activity (royal equipages and pageantry) and an even greater increase in foreign adventurism, war, and defense. The primacy of feudal monarchy clearly was now being put to use as a generalized resource. Perhaps this was a response to much-increased "social density": the manufacturing revolution in textiles, mining, iron-making, and petty trades (perfumery, barbering, etc.)—a response, in general, to a busy society of promoters, speculators, patentees, dramatists, composers, astronomers, astrologers, physicians, surgeons, alchemists, sorcerers, explorers. What Black calls "the chaos of society,"[74] however, did not engender policy as an attempt to impose any sort of rational order. Rather, the point of authoritative "outputs" seems to have been an extension of the defusing of courtly intrigues: the prevention of social discontents and marginality that were potentially threatening to the security (and isolation) of the courtly domain. The increased permeation of society under Tudor rule aimed, above all, at prophylaxis: controlling vagabonds, dealing with food riots, limiting speculators, usurers, and drunkards. The Poor Law and the relentless pursuit of religious recusants are all of a piece in this effort. A valuable resource was now being hoarded—though not yet much used for additional gain.

[73] Keir (fn. 46), 98.
[74] J. B. Black, *The Reign of Elizabeth: 1558-1603* (Oxford: Clarendon, 1936), 217.

The polity of interests. When principality no longer needs to be pre-occupied with usurpation, but has been institutionalized at least in accepted rules of succession, politics can turn outward for reasons other than prophylaxis. The primacy of a social domain above other domains and, even more, the "distancing" of courts from societies, inevitably lead to a conception of princely power and social order (not "order-liness") as being somehow unrelated. The initial extroversion of the princely domain thus can hardly be concerned with such matters as engineering social harmony or just distribution. In introverted politics, these are matters for natural order or divine ordination. When politics turns outward from the court, then, the purpose is initially not so much to manage society as to exploit primacy as a safe resource: the gainful use of primacy by privilege. In the polity of interests, competition overshadows majesty. Though it in no sense involves democratization, the arena of politics as competition becomes much enlarged and structurally altered. It still takes place in the court, but now also in institutions associated with the court (e.g., parliament) and, to a degree, in society. Through the "outputs" sought by patrons and their clients, the polity, as Durkheim would say, markedly "condenses." Royal administrative and judicial institutions become a rather complex "machinery" government.

In England, such acquisitive exploitation of established primacy—and through it the much enlarged penetration of society—is the essence of the *Georgian period*.[75] One sees the scope of the 18th-century British polity best in the activities of its local officials. The Justices of the Peace were broadly charged with collecting and delivering revenues; assuring the proper practice and flow of trade; looking after the poor, the food supply, prices, and wages; licensing brewers and drinking-houses; supervising gaols; establishing asylums and confining lunatics; seeing to the lighting of streets, their paving, policing, and cleaning. All this required at least an embryonic differentiation of political labor—though bureaucratization had hardly yet begun. There were now distinct judicial and administrative sessions, distinct highway and licensing councils, as well as individual specialists, like road surveyors and constables. Late in the century, new statutory authorities, with special duties, appeared: for instance, turnpike trusts, corporations for

[75] The great work on the Georgian polity is Sir Lewis Namier, *The Structure of Politics at the Accession of George III* (London: Macmillan, 1957); the standard history is J. Steven Watson, *The Reign of George III: 1760-1815* (Oxford: Clarendon, 1960); and the best concise political perspective on the period is provided by Samuel H. Beer, *British Politics in the Collectivist Age* (New York: Knopf, 1965).

administering relief to the poor, and, above all, a growing number and variety of improvement commissions.[76]

This expansion of activities, and of organizations for performing them, was not intended to manage society. The overriding trait of the Georgian polity was that it was a marketplace of influence and spoils. The central level did not really manage society, yet there was extraordinary jockeying among parliamentarians and, as a result, ministerial instability. According to Namier, men went into parliament partly out of a sort of "predestination" (men of "political families"), but even more as clients looking after patrons' interests: as placemen and as purveyors and receivers of favors (there was, says Namier, a "universal . . . plaguing of Ministers on behalf of friends and relations");[77] to advance themselves in the military and administrative services or reap rewards from service; to obtain contracts, jobs, subscriptions, loans, and remittances. The Enclosure Acts and what Beer calls "canal politics" epitomize this extraordinary politics of interests.

The politics of incorporation and of incumbency. When the domain of politics is used chiefly for acquisitive purposes by privileged groups, other groups will try to become incorporated into the game as players, rather than be excluded from it as passive victims. As the stakes grow (that is, the spoils increase) so, one may suppose, does the appetite for shares. Certainly the pervasive theme of early modern (19th-century) British politics is democratization. Tilly depicts the process as one in which excluded subjects first become "challengers," and then, through challenge, incorporated "members" of the polity:[78] voters, of course, and eligible to hold office. The transformation of challenge into membership occurs because the challengers have resources of their own that can be effectively mobilized—such as strikes, violence, and the like.

As the polity's membership expands, and thus becomes more diverse in interest, the political penetration of society necessarily grows rapidly in scope; when "civic incorporation" is virtually total, so is the politicization of social life—but not just in the sense of universal citizenship. Two other processes occur that rapidly transform social into political space. One is familiar: as new members are incorporated, the volume of political demands grows, and with it, the volume of outputs; with outputs, the network of committees, agencies, departments, boards,

---

[76] Keir (fn. 46), 312-16.   [77] Namier (fn. 75), 76.
[78] Charles Tilly, *From Mobilization to Revolution* (Reading, Mass.: Addison-Wesley, 1978).

to define and deliver them; and, with such organizations, their own demands: "withinputs," as David Easton calls them.

Perhaps this chain reaction sufficiently explains the rapid development of political society out of acquisitive politics. I would suggest, though, that a second process supplements the demand-response relation, and perhaps is more consequential. It bears at least a vague resemblance to the Tudor preoccupation with political prophylaxis. To put it starkly: political primacy in the modern polity clearly is more than ever worth possessing and keeping in possession; however great the resources of princes before, they were puny compared to the fully realized monopoly over legitimate power. The theater of political struggle, though, is no longer confined to the small stage of the court; it comprises society as such. Thus, the modern counterpart of coping with conspiracy in order to retain control over the princely domain is either mass suppression or the search for mass support (plus the special support of the more powerful, better organized interests). Mass support is elicited, at least in part, by going *beyond* responsiveness: by "redistributive" policies that make large public groups into clients— collective placemen. The unparalleled scale both of repression in authoritarian modern polities and of the political provision of all sorts of goods in welfare states serves the maintenance of incumbency. No doubt welfare policies and other distributions of benefits result from good intentions; but surely, they also provide benefits, in the form of political support, for their providers. At any rate, here is a parsimonious explanation of the substantial consensus on social policy in the contemporary British welfare state. The politics of incorporation leads logically to that of incumbency.

"Political density" during these stages grows rapidly toward its maximal pole. The vastness of the business done by the machine of government requires, as Durkheim realized, more and more internal complexity of structure, in large part just for keeping things sorted and coordinated; it requires the development of a political "system,"[79] which is not at all the same as a machinery of government. Structures of political competition also become highly organized and institutionalized networks of organizations. In gist, the pomp of primal chiefliness virtually disappears within the systems and networks of the polity.[80]

[79] I use "system" here in the manner of general and political systems theorists; the latter seem to me pertinent only—or anyway, chiefly—to "modern" polities. See, for instance, James G. Miller, "Living Systems: Basic Concepts," *Behavioral Science*, x (July 1965), 193-237; David Easton, *A Systems Analysis of Political Life* (New York: Wiley, 1965).

[80] The elevation of the leader in totalitarian polities can certainly be regarded as a reaction against the fathomless sobriety of typical modern political systems. It is,

Two important questions should be raised about the abstracted stages to determine whether they indeed constitute a general developmental sequence. First: Do the stages occur, *mutatis mutandis*, in other longitudinal political processes, and do they furnish a good typology for the "cross-sectional" classification of polities in the present? If so, we can assert (in the manner of early exponents of the "comparative method" —Ferguson, Comte, Tylor, Morgan)[81] that typological differences among polities are basically developmental: viz., that there is history, not just histories. Second: Would a schematic treatment of political functions, goals, and structures by stages indeed show qualitative distinctions in each class, along with the quantitative growth of the political domain? These questions cannot be treated briefly; they are posed here as items on an agenda to follow up this essay.

5. *What Forces Move Polities from Stage to Stage?*

In the preceding section, I have tried to show sequential connections between stages of political development: how the earlier stages are preconditions for those that follow, and how these, in turn, are latent in preceding stages. (An important, familiar issue for *praxis*— too large to be tackled here—is raised by the question whether stages can be skipped, without the occurrence of pathologies, and without regression.) This demonstration, though, says nothing about the forces that propel polities from stage to stage. We need at least a summary answer to complete our sketch for a theory of political development.

In developmental theory, one wants, ideally, to identify a general motive force that operates throughout developmental time (akin to physical inertia) and also special forces, generated in each earlier stage, which similarly lead to each later stage.

The general motive force at work in the sequence of stages I have described is surely the drive for the direct and indirect benefits of "efficient" primacy in and over society—the direct benefit of social elevation and indirect perquisites, such as material goods. That drive characterizes most directly the transformation of primal, ceremonial polity. The maintenance of primacy for getting other values follows in the polity of interests, and leads to the challenges that incorporate excluded groups in the domain of primacy. The possession of higher positions—primacy in the domain of primacy—animates political motion in the most advanced stage.

---

of course, more satanic than sacred. And surely the "system" uses the leader, perhaps more than vice versa.

[81] Nisbet (fn. 12), 189-208.

Although primacy-seeking is the essence of the initial developmental transformation of polities, it is clear that struggles for establishing an "efficient" principal domain are only resolved when an urgent societal need for such resolution arises. In the West, that need arose from the differentiation of society into distinct but overlapping "corporations" in virtually continuous collision. One may surmise, more generally, that an initial locus of efficient primacy will emerge when it is functionally critical to social integration that this occur—that is, when the integrative force of "mechanical solidarity" no longer works. The theatrical chiefs are destined to win struggles to perform the integrative function, and to reap its benefits.

If there is such a thing as "pure" power politics, it occurs when struggles for primacy have been resolved. Pure power politics is about possessing primacy, not about establishing it. Once the domain of the prince itself is safe, a different propulsive force emerges; we might call it resource conversion.[82]

The results of converting political into other goods now come to pose a quite different, but again functionally critical problem of integration: not of society but of the political domain itself, for the sake of its effective operation. The need for political integration has two facets. As new groups are incorporated into the polity, the plethora of interests and demands they generate must be coordinated: in Almond's terminology, a need exists to aggregate interests, so that demands may be effectively pressed and responded to. More important, as society is greatly politicalized through processes of civic incorporation, the machinery of government grows into a complex system; as a result, efficient management of the system itself must increasingly become a *sine qua non* of political goals, even exploitative ones. Without efficient political management, social life itself is imperiled, precisely because the polity pervades it; and, without such management, power itself is a chimera. In this way, we can see in political development a diminution, if not a metamorphosis, of pure power politics—and still avoid the "fault" of tendermindedness.

Thus, while struggles for primacy propel politics throughout developmental time, at each stage they take different forms and are reinforced by special forces: forces of greed and, more important, forces generated by collective functional needs. These themes of politics—primacy-seeking, power-seeking, greed, and integration—are familiar.

[82] Or, in language that used to be familiar in political science, turning political "base values" into other "scope values." See Harold D. Lasswell and Abraham Kaplan, *Power and Society* (New Haven: Yale University Press, 1950), 83-92.

What is not familiar is the special roles they play at different stages of political development.

The process of political development moved by these forces is monotonic in two senses. I have stressed one—the politicalization of society. The long trajectory from social polity to political society can also be considered a modulation from "dignity" to "efficiency" (the most fundamental qualitative social change conceivable), and each stage of the process can be treated as a changing balance between the two. In parallel, polities change structurally from personage to court, to machine, to system.

Conclusion

The idea of political development, then, seems to me capable of renovation along the lines sketched. What I have tried to present is a design along proper "developmental" lines. The design is, and must continue to be, far from a completed theoretical structure. But if it proves to have merit, it helps to answer the final question raised above. It has important implications precisely for the issue that a developmental theory should illuminate: the puzzle of our own modernity. I will mention one such implication for a critical problem in modern political life.

We have lately heard much about a crisis of authority in highly advanced societies. The evidence is overwhelming that there is at least a malaise about authority. Strangely, that malaise seems to exist concurrently with the progressive growth of what people supposedly (and no doubt actually) want authority to be: decent, down to earth, participant, lenient, concordant, open to achievement. Might not the solution of this riddle lie in the "disenchantment" of theatrical politics (which moves affections), by rationally effective but too-drab systems? After all, society and polity remain intangible mysteries; the social sciences are devoted to their understanding. They have become all the more mystifying as they have grown in scale, density, and differentiation. At the same time, dignity has waned in relation to efficiency. More and more, our representative figures are capable but plain, managers but not princes: Fords, Carters, Wilsons, Heaths; in our families, schools, and workplaces, authority increasingly also has derogated rank. We want this, and it seems good; but can we live with it?

Perhaps that is what Weber saw when he forecast a political "polar night of icy darkness and hardness." Perhaps, too, the tension between the needs for what Weber called matter-of-factness and devotion is the force propelling us into the future of political time.

REQUIEM OR NEW AGENDA FOR THIRD WORLD STUDIES?

By TONY SMITH

THANKS to the vigor of the dependency school's attack on the established "developmentalist" framework for studying change in the Third World, debates going on today in development studies are perhaps the most interesting and important in the field of comparative politics. The debates are interesting because, both methodologically and substantively, a wide range of new issues has been raised in a field that by around 1970 had become relatively moribund. They are important because, in the Third World especially, the mainstream developmentalist models earlier formulated in the United States—such as those sponsored by the Social Science Research Council (SSRC)—have been angrily discarded by many in favor of politically explosive explanations of underdevelopment that lay the manifold problems of these areas squarely at the feet of Western imperialism (and, in the case of the Latin Americanists heading this school, at the doorstep of Washington in particular). Thus, there are acutely perceived moral and political dimensions to this clash of paradigms for the study of Third World development, beyond the intellectual, or academic, interest that such controversy is sure to excite.

No matter how interesting and important these debates, it should be apparent that the field of Third World studies is in a state of crisis. For if the old-time religion preached by the American academic establishment has been found wanting in many respects, the new fundamentalism represented by the dependency school offers scant reassurance that a compelling new intellectual vision, with a broadly accepted set of assumptions as to what questions should be asked and how they might be answered, will soon become widely accepted. To be sure, many of the Old Guard, as well as the Young Turks writing from the dependency perspective, will deny that a crisis exists; and the continued pursuit of traditional concerns in Third World studies—ranging from the analysis of alternative paths of economic development to that of different forms of political legitimacy—may provide the appearance that they are correct, that a healthy field of development studies continues to flourish whatever (and perhaps because of) the rivalries between the dependency and developmentalist paradigms. But for those outside these charmed circles, it seems evident that the emperor wears no clothes; that no matter how vital the debate over particular topics may indeed remain, a broad, relatively unified field of comparative study focused on the Third World no longer exists in satisfactory form. The question, then, is whether the current crisis will open the door for a fresh synthesis of work in the area, a new agenda in comparative studies, or whether instead we had better write a requiem for the effort to see the Third World in terms of any meaningful whole, having by now become rightly suspicious of the intellectual baggage accumulated by 30 years or more of "grand theory."

The first three sections of this essay lay out in schematic form the character of the current crisis; the fourth discusses what form a new agenda for the field might take.

I. THE DEVELOPMENTALIST MODEL

The field of development studies, which has always been dominated by American academics, was founded in the first years after World War II, when the United States assumed leadership of a ravaged world in which the problems of containing the Soviet Union and dealing with national liberation movements throughout much of Asia and Africa were the country's top foreign policy priorities. From the beginning, the divisions among the academic disciplines and the avowedly eclectic concerns of many working in the field made it difficult to label developmentalism a "school." Area specialization constituted one line of differentiation among these scholars, but formal training in economics and political science—as well as in anthropology, sociology, psychology, and history—tended to create other distinctions in interest and method as well. And yet, a field of study certainly existed. Formal mechanisms such as the SSRC pulled these analysts together as a group, but more informal ties also held them together: their familiarity with each other's work through their association at the country's leading universities, and their conscious effort in a larger sense to see their work as complementary, each cultivating a different vineyard for the sake of a common harvest. Thus, while economists laid out models of how productivity in the late-industrializing world might be stimulated, sociologists and social psychologists studied the group dynamics of change, and political scientists devoted themselves to the problems of state and nation-building. Whatever the rough edges, the result was indeed a unified and cumulative agenda for Third World studies, a "whole" of intellectual discourse both theoretically and empirically.

The life span of the school might be variously dated, but there seems to be some agreement that it began after 1945, that it had what might be called its "Golden Decade" for economists in the 1950s and for political scientists from the late 1950s until the late 1960s, and that it ran out of steam in the early 1970s. Writing in 1975, Samuel Huntington and Jorge Dominguez, two political scientists, professed to find nothing particularly surprising about the fact that "in the early 1970's the initial surge, which had emerged about 1960, in the study of political development had about run its course." It was the fate of any theoretical paradigm, they maintained, to go through a set stage of phases (note the usage even here of a developmentalist style of reasoning) where an "initial surge" was typically followed by a "pause," "redirection," and a "new surge."[1] In 1983, Gabriel Almond, one of the fathers of political developmentalism, attributed the school's stagnation more to the motivation of those working in it: "Over time as the new and developing nations encountered difficulties and turned largely to authoritarian and military regimes, the optimism and hopefulness faded, and along with it interest, productivity, and creativity abated."[2] The developmentalist economist Albert Hirschman voiced a similar lament in 1980: "As an observer and long-time participant I cannot help feeling that the old liveliness is no longer there, that new ideas are ever harder to come by and that the field is not adequately reproducing itself."[3] Hirschman's explanation of the school's failure was more self-critical than those of his colleagues in political science (reflecting perhaps a professional difference: economists frequently pride themselves on being mavericks, while political scientists are more likely to think of themselves as team players). Trying to explain the end of the earlier "easy self-confidence" and the rise of "self-doubt," Hirschman looked not only at the disappointments that developmentalists faced in dealing with the increasingly intractable problems of the South, but also at the weakness of the theoretical models they had used in their efforts to explain and influence events:

> The story of development economics ... tells of progress on condition that intellectual progress is defined as the gradual loss of certainty, as the slow mapping out of the extent of our ignorance, which was previously hidden by an initial certainty parading as paradigm.[4]

[1] Samuel P. Huntington and Jorge I. Dominguez, "Political Development," in Fred I. Greenstein and Nelson W. Polsby, eds., *Handbook of Political Science*, Vol. 3: *Macropolitical Theory* (Reading, MA: Addison-Wesley, 1975), 90.

[2] Gabriel Almond, "Comparative Politics and Political Development: A Historical Perspective," Joint Seminar on Political Development, Harvard - Massachusetts Institute of Technology, October 26, 1983, p. 7.

[3] Hirschman, *Essays in Trespassing: Economics to Politics and Beyond* (New York: Cambridge University Press, 1981), 1.

[4] *Ibid.*, 59.

Yet the early objectives of the developmentalist school were sensible enough, even if ambitious. They sought first to specify general categories which, despite their universality, would allow analysts to distinguish essential elements of the chief social processes that interested them; or, alternatively, to differentiate various types of social organization and stages, or sequences, in their development. These general categories were to be heuristic tools, "metatheoretical" classificatory schemes, promoted most successfully by Talcott Parsons along the lines of Max Weber's ideal types. Such models or paradigms of social action were labeled "structural-functionalism" in sociology and political science, and were intended to be both basic and comprehensive enough to provide the vocabulary and concepts allowing any society to be described in comparative terms. Thus the individuality and the specificity of the various forms of social life in Africa, Asia, and Latin America would be respected, while these lands would at the same time be recognizable comparatively (in terms of the advanced industrial countries as well as of each other).

Hirschman may have been correct when he maintained that "the compulsion to theorize . . . is often so strong as to induce mindlessness."[5] But the effort in question must be understood to lie at the heart of the social sciences, concerned as they are to establish general verifiable explanations of human action. Led particularly by sociologists like Parsons, and working on the basis of earlier men of genius such as Durkheim, Toennies, and especially Weber, the developmentalist school was deliberately doing what whas expected of it. And, as we shall see presently, the Marxists in their efforts to offer a better analysis of the Third World than that of the developmentalists were engaged in a strikingly similar heuristic undertaking.

Although the descendants of Weber and Marx were alike in their concern with establishing a general framework for comparative historical analysis, the similarity ended there. For, whereas the Marxists held to a single analytical category in their belief that the force of the class struggle swept all else before it, the followers of Weber were more avowedly eclectic in the variety of theoretical tools they brought to an understanding of the Third World. General heuristic categories provided a common vocabulary, a common set of problems, and the promise of readily exchangeable information, so that an integrated, cumulative understanding of the Third World could proceed; developmentalism intended to apply insights or theories developed independently by the

---

[5] Hirschman, "The Search for Paradigms as a Hindrance to Understanding," *World Politics* 22 (April 1970), 329.

various social sciences to explain the logic of social action in the South. The general categories did not, then, claim the status of scientific theories, but acted instead as intellectual guidelines that assured some connect- edness to the host of empirically verifiable theories that were anticipated. The result was a proliferation of books written by teams of specialists, often from different backgrounds or dealing with very distinct issues, whose unity presupposed or confidently anticipated commonly shared models—for instance, Talcott Parsons and Edward Shils, eds., *Toward a General Theory of Action* (1951); Clifford Geertz, ed., *Old Societies and New States* (1963); Max F. Millikan and Donald L.M. Blackmer, eds., *The Emerging Nations* (1961).

In retrospect, it is difficult not to empathize with the excitement of those years. Scholars anticipated not simply a better understanding of the Third World, but the growing unification of the social sciences around their increasingly common understanding of a set of particular issues. The various "cultures" of sociology, anthropology, economics, history, political science, and psychology might keep their separate iden- tities, but their interdisciplinary pursuits would allow them to draw strength from one another, to pull them away from their narrow (often parochial) concerns, to the level of the wholeness of social life. One might even say that a bit of American pluralism was involved here, for no single discipline (much less theorist) was expected to have the answer to the entire puzzle (although some surely came to think they did); instead, the truth would emerge as the result of the collaborative efforts of quite dissimilar kinds of work. The outcome would be a unified social science able not only to criticize but finally to replace Marxism.

The obvious question we must ask of this approach today is whether the products of its labors were at the level of its ambitions. Without denying the importance of some of the work, the answer must surely be negative—even in the minds of those most active in the field. Today, it is rare indeed to see any of these books cited other than critically; library shelves are invariably fully stocked with the numerous (unused) copies of each volume that were once the standard fare of graduate students the country over.

In my opinion, there are two principal reasons developmentalism failed in its efforts, reasons that at first glance might appear contradictory. One problem was that the models in many cases were so formal and abstract that they proved too stifling, too tyrannical, and ultimately too sterile for the empirical work they sought to organize. The other problem was that the models were too loose, too incoherent, and too incomplete to act as adequate guidelines assuring the interconnectedness of research. Let us look at each of these shortcomings in turn.

The most frequently heard, and the bitterest, charge against the developmentalist paradigm is that it was "unilinear" or "ethnocentric" in its concept of change; that is, it projected a relatively inflexible path or continuum of development in which social and political forms would tend to converge, so that the developmental path of the West might well serve as a model from which to shed light on transformations occurring in the South. As a result, developmentalism might be accused of being too "formalistic" in the sense that it sought to reduce the histories of the various countries of Asia, Africa, and Latin America to the terms of models or ideal types and jargon that distorted the true logic of social change in these areas. Thus, although Gabriel Almond adamantly denies that the charge that developmentalist literature was unilinear can "survive even a casual reading" of its authors, his own evocation of this school of thought at its inception indicates otherwise:

> The "new," the "emerging," the "underdeveloped" or "developing" nations, as they were variously called, challenged the classificatory talents and theoretical imaginations of Western social scientists. They brought to this effort to illuminate the prospects of the Third World the ideas and concepts of the enlightenment and 19th century social theory which at an earlier time had sought to make sense out of European and American modernization. What had happened in Europe and North America in the 19th and early 20th centuries was now, more or less, about to happen in Latin America, Asia, and Africa. The progress promised by the enlightenment—the spread of knowledge, the development of technology, the attainment of higher standards of material welfare, the emergence of lawful, humane, and liberal polities, and the perfection of the human spirit—now beckoned the Third World newly freed from colonialism and exploitation, and straining against its own parochialisms.[6]

In cases where the West was not self-consciously posited as a model of the future the South might come to enjoy, the heuristic models of "modern" and "traditional" societies performed much the same function. Here the work of Talcott Parsons proved to be particularly influential— especially his so-called pattern variables, with their assumption that cultural values are of a whole with economic, social, and political systems in such a fashion that social organization should be conceptualized as a self-reinforcing unity. This kind of thinking resulted in the unfortunate tendency throughout much of developmentalism, first, to exaggerate the congruence of elements within a given social organization (a preference for static equilibrium models which often classified contradiction and change as "dysfunctional"), and second, to separate "traditional" from "modern" societies as if such a dichotomy made not only heuristic but empirical sense.

[6] Almond (fn. 2), 2.

The models that emerged were too confining to be of much use in actual empirical investigation. When the past of the West or the model of traditional society was projected onto the Third World, too much disappeared from sight. The formalism of these paradigms often turned out to be as reductionist as Marxism—a turn of events developmentalism had hoped to escape by virtue of its avowed disciplinary eclecticism. There is, then, some justice to the charge leveled by many radical as well as by some conservative writers who felt that the reality of the Third World was simply not being grasped. Reinhard Bendix, for example, formulated some of these charges quite early; Howard Wiarda has stated more recently:

> The critique of the Western model as particularistic, parochial, Eurocentric, considerably less than universal and hopelessly biased, as not only perpetuating our lack of understanding regarding these areas but also of wreaking downright harm upon them, seems to this observer devastating, valid, and perhaps unchallengeable.[7]

Yet if formalism of the sort described above was a real problem with developmentalism—as the work of Daniel Lerner, Cyril E. Black, and W. W. Rostow suggests[8]—it was not a completely endemic disease. I think there would be wide agreement, for example, that the two most influential books by political scientists on development were Gabriel Almond and James Coleman's *Comparative Politics of Developing Countries* (1960) and Samuel Huntington's *Political Order in Changing Societies* (1968). True, in his introductory essay, Almond favorably mentions Parsons' pattern variables, but he also disputes the notion that there are such things as "all modern" or "all primitive" societies; he favors seeing political systems as more complexly "mixed." Moreover, the volume was written by a group of area experts whose primary accomplishment was their ability to match a rich sensibility toward local Third World issues

---

[7] Wiarda, "Toward a Non-Ethnocentric Theory of Development: Alternative Conceptions from the Third World," paper presented at the meeting of the American Political Science Association, September 1981, p. 25. For a more accessible version of this position, see Wiarda, "The Ethnocentrism of the Social Sciences: Implications for Research and Policy," *The Review of Politics* 42 (April 1981). For an earlier statement of this view by a Weberian, see Reinhard Bendix, *Embattled Reason: Essays on Social Knowledge* (New York: Oxford University Press, 1970), esp. 268 ff., and *Nation Building and Citizenship: Studies of Our Changing Social Order* (Berkeley: University of California Press, 1964), chap. 8.

[8] For example, in the 1964 Preface to *The Passing of Traditional Society: Modernizing the Middle East* (Glencoe, IL: The Free Press, 1958), Lerner writes: "The 'Western model' is only historically Western; sociologically it is global . . . the same basic model reappears in virtually all modernizing societies of all continents of the world, regardless of variations of race, color or creed" (pp. viii-ix). Two other well-known examples from an abundant literature are Rostow, *The Stages of Economic Growth: A Non-Communist Manifesto* (New York: Cambridge University Press, 1960); and Black, *The Dynamics of Modernization: A Study in Comparative History* (New York: Harper & Row, 1966).

with more general, theoretical questions of change and development. Although the classificatory schemes proposed to each of these area specialists appear to do little more than to give them a common vocabulary with which to work—no empirically verifiable "science" of political development is forthcoming—it would be quite unfair to accuse these contributors of ethnocentrism or formalism. For its part, Huntington's book rests on such an explicitly damning criticism of a unilinear approach to the study of history that on this account alone it deserves to be seen as one of the classics of political science during the period. In economics, there is equal agreement that Alexander Gerschenkron's *Economic Backwardness in Historical Perspective* (1962) is a classic statement on the development process similarly free of formalistic bias. In short, some excellent comparative historical work has been free of the problems of formalism. Moreover, it is important to insist that formalism as a reductionist mode in the social sciences must not be confused with the effort to establish general theoretical frameworks for the understanding of change in the fashion of Weber or Keynes. This latter enterprise is the hallmark and the promise of the social sciences; it must not be repudiated simply because some of its practitioners have given it a bad name.

Indeed, rather than lambasting developmentalism for models that were too rigid and writers who were overly concerned with methodology, we might complain that it did not generate stronger general categories to integrate research and that it did not concern itself adequately with producing a set of robust "middle-range" theories of development, or general analytical propositions established empirically, that could serve to organize the field. At the time, prominent developmentalist writers certainly seemed to sense the problem. Thus James Coleman admitted in 1960 that, "Given the array of disparate systems ... it is only at the highest level of generalization that one can make statements about their common properties."[9] In 1963, Harry Eckstein offered a much more biting commentary. While he welcomed the return to fundamental questions of comparative study as a healthy event, he nonetheless complained of the "bewildering variety of classificatory schemes" his colleagues had produced, whose "disconcerting wealth" was "almost embarrassing": "The field today is characterized by nothing so much as variety, eclecticism, and disagreement ... particularly great in regard to absolutely basic preconceptions and orientations."[10]

[9] Gabriel A. Almond and James S. Coleman, eds., *The Politics of the Developing Areas* (Princeton: Princeton University Press, 1960), 535.
[10] Eckstein, "A Perspective on Comparative Politics, Past and Present," in Harry Eckstein and David Apter, eds., *Comparative Politics: A Reader* (Glencoe, IL: The Free Press, 1963).

Why was the modeling not better? The quickest answer is that no theorist emerged of the status of Weber or Durkheim, a person of genius who could pull the entire field together into a coherent whole. Brave attempts may be cited—the work of David Apter, for example—but they proved unable to impose themselves intellectually on the community of developmentalists. Instead, there was a kind of happy anarchy, where writers seem to have labored to invent jargon and classificatory schemes in the manner of a Freud or a Durkheim—as much to ensure their professional standing as to advance the discipline. And here the highest accolades would be reserved for the theorist who could establish a "general theory of action," to recall the title of a book Talcott Parsons and Edward Shils edited in 1951. Or, as Shils put it in 1965:

> There is at present no systematic, dynamic general theory of society of universal comprehensiveness; nor is there, as yet, any analytical or empirical comparative theory of society. . . . We exist at present in a middle ground in which the general theory has begun to reveal its main lines and in which empirical comparative analysis, influenced by this theory—and influencing it—has begun to show how it is going to develop.[11]

It would be an error to explain the limitations of developmentalism by placing too much emphasis on the skills of the individuals involved. The striking shortcoming of the school was its inability to articulate a unified model of comparative political economy, just as it lacked any broad-based comparative historical perspective into which the problems of mid-20th-century development could be placed. It must be emphasized that the obstacle was not individual mediocrity, but institutional and ideological impediments best studied in terms of a sociology of knowledge. Two sets of factors emerge as important in this respect: the structure of the social science disciplines in American universities, and the place of the academics concerned with it in American political life.

Whatever the attraction, rhetorically, of interdisciplinary studies in the United States, the various fields of the social sciences jealously insisted on their autonomy, on an identity based on a body of theoretical propositions over whose integrity they stood guard. In this context, development studies represented virgin territory, not only for the unification of the social sciences, but more immediately for the carving out of new, discrete domains of analysis. Thus, Gabriel Almond proudly declared in the introduction to *The Politics of the Developing Areas*, "This book is the first effort to compare the political systems of the 'developing'

[11] Shils, "On the Comparative Study of New States," in Clifford Geertz, ed., *Old Societies and New States: The Quest for Modernity in Asia and Africa* (Glencoe, IL: The Free Press, 1963), 18.

areas, and to compare them systematically according to a common set of categories. . . ." He considered it to be "a major step forward in the nature of political science as science."[12] From the viewpoint of political science, economics in particular represented a threat, for it had an apparent sophistication as a science that many political scientists longed to duplicate. For this reason, for example, the Harvard-M.I.T. Joint Seminar on Political Development, founded in 1963, has always deliberately excluded economists from its membership. The ambition, then, of political scientists was to elaborate the logic of political processes in a manner that would establish their analytical independence and their social importance. At the same time, they would strike a blow against Marxism, which had constantly sought to reduce political factors to reflections of more decisive socioeconomic processes. One can exaggerate the extent or the impenetrability of these barriers between academic disciplines; these scholars knew each other's work and felt themselves to be engaged in a collaborative enterprise. And one can fail to do justice to the cogent reasons that underlay the decision to draw these distinctions in the first place; a genuine flowering of an understanding of political processes may be said to have occurred in part *because* of this divorce. In any case, many of the crucial issues of Third World development continued to be ignored simply because they fell outside the purview of the subject as it was perceived from its many different angles.

To derive at a different sociological explanation for the lack of adequate modeling, one may look at the place of the American academics involved in Third World studies in terms of American political life. For example, Irene Gendzier has recently suggested that many of these scholars intended their writing to be policy-relevant, and that their interests included fostering the spread of capitalism and an elitist brand of democracy in the South while blocking the expansion of communism. These concerns limited the agenda and biased the arguments of many developmentalists in a way unappreciated at the time.[13]

I see no reason to quarrel with this argument so long as it is not presented as the sole explanation of the logic of developmentalism. It is not persuasive even as a primary explanation. Too many Americans who were the products of this school emerged as harsh critics of American imperialism; one has only to recall Henry Kissinger's repeated complaints about all the regional specialists who knew nothing of the require-

---

[12] Almond and Coleman (fn. 9), 3, 4.

[13] Gendzier, *Managing Political Change: Social Scientists and the Third World* (Boulder, CO: Westview Press, 1985). For a powerful early attack along these lines, see Noam Chomsky, *American Power and the New Mandarins* (New York: Pantheon Books, 1969).

ments of "geopolitical equilibrium" to realize that the school cannot be understood this easily.

In view of the ideological and institutional concerns of those working in developmentalism, it is difficult to see how, as a group, they might have sponsored the kind of work in comparative history or political economy that at one and the same time would have ensured more broad-range model building at the level of heuristic typologies and more robust constructions of theories at the level of aggregate empirical analysis. Take, for example, the volume that most North American specialists (including this writer) would agree to be the finest work in developmentalism by a political scientist—Samuel Huntington's *Political Order in Changing Societies* (1968). The book has little economic perspective. True, "participation" is on the upswing; "mobilization" is taking place. Yet the forces of the industrial revolution, even those of agricultural development, go virtually unmentioned. Sections of the book may deal with the urgency of land reform, but there is not a clue as to why this problem has arisen now and not a century earlier; any number of key questions ranging from productive effectiveness to distributive justice are deliberately avoided. Though class conflict is implied at times, the topic is never systematically addressed. Nor does the impact of foreign actors on events in the Third World get much of a hearing. Indeed, the hypothesis that military interventions in the politics of these areas are linked to foreign penetration and encouragement is specifically discounted (chap. 4). Certainly the book's sense of political institution building is masterful in scope and nuance, assuring it the status of a classic in modern political literature. Yet the fact that the intricacies of this process occur in a world of class struggle and imperialism finds no recognition here. Countries have self-contained histories, and political problems have political explanations. Period. Albert Hirschman reports that a similar narrowness of focus typified most of the developmentalist work done by economists.[14]

Developmentalist paradigms were, then, loose and incomplete at a heuristic level on the one hand, and deficient in genuinely interdisciplinary empirical propositions at the level of comparative theory on the other. Since there was no intellectual center of gravity holding together all the disparate undertakings that characterized the field, specialization proliferated, spin-off leading to spin-off, with some perhaps holding Shils's happy illusion that eventually it would all add up to a unified movement. Instead, however, the focus shifted increasingly to more

[14] Hirschman (fn. 3), 24.

modest and manageable models targeted on particular issues or areas. In many of these instances, a deeper understanding of the process of change did occur. But as the field became more complex, questions of its unity became more difficult; memories of the common origin of it all, in the Big Bang of trying to establish order amid the chaos of the postwar world, grew increasingly dim. An essential reason for the stagnation of the field around 1970, therefore, was what was coming to be seen as its chaotic diversity. If developmentalism's *formalism* (the reductionist tyranny of its models) was a real problem, it was relatively minor. The major cause of its debilitation lay in its *fragmentation* (the weakness of its models).

This fragmentation emerged as an acute problem when it became evident to many that developmentalism was impotent in the face of many of the terrible trials through which the Third World was passing. The growth of poverty and the attendant human misery; the spread of repressive, authoritarian regimes; the waste and suffering caused by wars both civil and regional—all combined to disillusion those working in the field, especially as the realization began to grow that in fact there was no theoretical, commanding height from which to make sense of these awful realities. The fragmentation made it difficult to get more than a partial understanding of the range of forces at work in the South.

The disillusion grew more acute in the mid- and late-1960s with the growing realization that American foreign policy had a tremendous influence on the course of events in the Third World; this influence had seldom been explicitly addressed by developmentalism and now could not be dealt with satisfactorily. To be sure, many developmentalists opposed American imperialism in Latin America and in Southeast Asia; but that is not the point. It is rather that developmentalism no longer had anything particularly interesting to say about the conduct of American policy one way or another. Thus, it is far from accidental that this school of thought entered into crisis just as American policy with respect to the Alliance for Progress and the Vietnam War proved so wanting. Although there were those like W. W. Rostow or Samuel Huntington who never felt this to be a problem, and who indeed explicitly intended to make their work an instrument of American foreign policy, a more general feeling was one of impotence—or betrayal. For here, at a critical juncture in the international life of the United States, the school of study most intimately concerned with the character of the Third World had fallen silent. It was, most felt, the bankruptcy of the field. The fact that the point is seldom candidly admitted today shows that the wound is still festering.

With "emotion recollected in tranquility," one can certainly see that such an observation should not lead to an across-the-board condemnation of developmentalism's achievements. As we shall see in section IV, it is possible to recognize the professional sophistication that characterized much of the field and to learn from its insights. Yet one should not expect that the field will recover, either from its conceptual fragmentation or from its loss of innocence. The vigor it experiences at present is much like that of Medieval Europe—a vitality that was scattered, slow in germination, but real—after the fall of the Roman Empire: by analogy, after the heyday of grand theory, as it existed in the 1950s and 1960s, has become a thing of the past.

II. THE DEPENDENCY PERSPECTIVE[15]

For many, the void left by the demise of developmentalism as a unified theory of change in the Third World was filled in the 1970s with the analytical categories provided by the dependency perspective. The term "dependency" grows out of writing on Latin America; related works dealing with Asia and Africa have until recently been more comfortable using the term "neocolonialism" to describe the world that concerns them. Whatever the preferred nomenclature, these *dependencistas*, if we may use their Latin American name, share the view that the power of international capitalism setting up a global division of labor has been the chief force responsible for shaping the history of the South. Originally as mercantilism, then as free trade, later as finance capital, and most recently under the auspices of the multinational corporation, capitalism over the last five centuries has created a world economic system. The profound changes this process has generated in every part of the world offer, then, a common historical experience that is the basis of a *unified comparative* model of social life in the Third World. Dependency literature is therefore properly viewed as a subset of the so-called "world system" approach, whose terms have become increasingly prominent in the United States in the field of international relations. To be sure, as in any broad-based intellectual movement, debates within the dependency school are many and sharp. The clear dominance of Marxism within the literature has not prevented fierce differences over such far-ranging matters as how to establish the identity of classes in widely disparate settings; what degree of autonomy to accord the state as a political

---

[15] The discussion here draws on my contribution on dependency thinking in Howard Wiarda, ed., *New Directions in Comparative Politics* (Boulder, CO: Westview Press, forthcoming 1985).

institution charged with providing coherence in circumstances typified by rapid domestic change and extensive foreign penetration; and how to argue for typologies of stages or degrees of dependency. However acute these differences, they are overshadowed by the common allegiance of the writers in this school to an approach whose roots run back to the 1920s, even if it was not until the 1970s that the dependency perspective made itself felt in force within American academia. And the fundamental premise of this approach—the uncontested proposition on the basis of which all this writing has been constructed—is that, to understand the chief forces of change in the Third World (or "on the periphery"), one must see them ultimately as a function of the power of economic imperialism generated by the capitalist "core" of world affairs.[16]

Indeed, it is the emphasis on imperialism that constitutes a recognition on the part of many *dependencistas* themselves that their approach cannot claim the status of a theory. For dependency literature studies the *effects* of imperialism, not the *nature* of imperialism itself. Its focus is therefore on a part and not on the whole—the latter providing the "totality" of experience on which sound theory can be based. Traditional matters, such as the character of capitalist accumulation with its "anarchy of production" combined with such modern forces as the logic of multinational corporate competition, must ultimately escape the purview of the dependency approach (only to fall into the domain of the related world system analysis); the primary agent of change in the South thus escapes direct study. As explained by Fernando Henrique Cardoso and Enzo Faletto in a book that has found a wide audience throughout the Americas, "it seems senseless to search for 'laws of movement' specific to situations that *are dependent*, that is, that have their main features determined by the phases and trends of expansion of capitalism on a world scale."[17] Relying on a theory of imperialism proposed by their colleagues doing world system analysis, dependency writers content themselves with explaining the logic of capitalist expansion on the periphery. The result is a powerful, unified theory of imperialism: the

---

[16] For the debates within the dependency camp, see, among others, Fernando Henrique Cardoso, "The Consumption of Dependency Theory in the United States," *Latin American Research Review* 12 (No. 3, 1977); Richard R. Fagen, "Studying Latin American Politics: Some Implications of a *Dependencia* Approach," *Latin American Research Review* 12 (No. 3, 1977); and Ronald H. Chilcote, ed., *Dependency and Marxism: Toward a Resolution of the Debate* (Boulder, CO: Westview Press, 1981). The most influential writer on world system analysis in the United States is Immanuel Wallerstein; see his *The Modern World System: Capitalist Agriculture and the Origins of the European World-Economy in the Sixteenth Century* (New York: Academic Press, 1974), and *The Modern World System II: Mercantilism and the Consolidation of the European World-Economy, 1600-1750* (New York: Academic Press, 1980).

[17] Cardoso and Faletto, *Dependency and Development in Latin America* (Berkeley: University of California Press, 1979), xxiii.

world system analysts establish the logic of the "whole" or core of historical change while the dependency scholars lay out the working of these forces on the periphery.

In this undertaking, their most important conceptual tool is the analysis of the dual economy. The notion of the dual economy itself did not originate with these writers, but in their hands it has acquired a character particular to their analysis.[18] In brief, the argument is that—as capitalist penetration has occurred successively in Latin America, Asia, and Africa under the impetus of northern imperialism—one part of the local economies of these regions has come to be a modern enclave. By virtue of these historical origins, the basis of the modern sector is export trade (even if subsidiary manufacturing or service interests grow up to sustain it). Here capital accumulates, skills are learned, and class interests are formed whose innermost needs tie them tightly to foreign concerns. The culture of the modern enclave may be of the periphery; but its economic and political character make it a child of the international system. Root and branch, it is dependent.

Alongside this modern economy, there exists a subsistence sector— whence the term *dual* economy. To some extent, the technology, culture, and social institutions of the subsistence sector are inherited from the past. But this is not a simple traditional world slumbering in a millenary torpor, as writers from the developmentalist school have so often depicted it. Today as yesterday, the modern sector is constantly at work disintegrating this subordinate sector, try as the latter may to preserve its integrity. Thus, cheap manufactured goods destroy the traditional artisanry; the expansion of plantation agriculture displaces large numbers of peasants, forcing them onto poorer land; and elites in the subsistence area invest such capital as they possess in the modern enclave, thereby intensifying the lack of investment funds for projects that might directly benefit the poor. Through the linkages between the two sectors, the modern acts like a leech on the body of the subsistence economy—ever increasing the difficulty of life there, while by its very exploitation it consolidates its own power. In short, the terrible misery of so much of the Third World derives not from a locally generated, traditional resistance to modernity—for example, the lack of appropriate skills, attitudes, or resource endowments of the poor, where developmentalist

[18] For an indication of the history of the concept, see Benjamin Higgins, *Economic Development: Principles, Problems, and Policies*, rev. ed. (New York: W. W. Norton, 1968), chaps. 12 and 14. For a comprehensive application of the notion of the dual economy in dependency terms, see William W. Murdoch, *The Poverty of Nations: The Political Economy of Hunger and Population* (Baltimore: The Johns Hopkins University Press, 1980), chaps. 8 and 9.

economics had us look—but from the operating forces of modernity itself, as it has historically implanted itself on the periphery. The misery of the many and the affluence of the few have their common origin in an international division of labor spawned and maintained by the forces of capitalist imperialism.

As the foregoing account implies, economic forces do not live in a social vacuum, but express themselves in class formations on the periphery. Here the key development is the modern sector, where class interests form in symbiosis with the interests of international capitalism. A class alignment thus takes shape in the South wherein the power of the dominant groups derives from their role as intermediaries between the international order run by imperialism and the local peoples over whom they must secure their rule. Although this collaborating class may have local concerns, its reliance on the world economic system ultimately decides its conduct. At different times or in different countries the character of these elites may vary, but their common identity lies in their dependence on the rhythms of the international economic order to ensure their survival as a class. There is an international political dimension to this as well. These local bourgeoisies have struck the main political bargains that concern their well-being not with domestic forces, but with foreign capitalists. The result is that the collaborating class is not only particularly exploitive in historical terms, but it is particularly weak at home as well. For these reasons, it is subject to being overthrown by local revolutions when those in the subsistence sector try to save themselves through force of arms. It is at this point, of course, that the United States intervenes today by suppressing such uprising in the name of anticommunism, when its real interest is to preserve a certain established form of economic organization locally as well as globally. Just as poverty in the Third World must ultimately be understood in terms of the international division of labor, so authoritarian governments there must in the final analysis be seen as products of foreign imperialism.

From the preceding discussion it should be apparent that the dependency school's primary intellectual debt is to Marxism (which is not to say that all Marxists subscribe to this view). First, the division of labor is seen as the prime social reality, the engine of change that drives all else before it. The originality of dependency writing lies in its tying the dynamic of economic life on the periphery into that of the world system beyond; to see it as *dependent*, that is. The dependency approach thus works on an ambitiously large canvas, linking the pace of life on the periphery to movements at the core. Second, political activity is understood to take place through social groups or classes antagonistically related to one another around ownership of the means of production. In this respect, the originality of dependency writing lies in its capacity to seize on the function of the collaborating class and to plot the changes in its conflicts and alliances over time, including those that link it to political forces abroad. Finally, the dependency approach shares with Marxism a bias against certain other considerations: that ethnic rivalries may have a life quite their own (hence, for example, the denigration of the term "tribe" in relation to groups in Africa); that the state may play a relatively autonomous and enormously significant role in the process of great historical transformations; and that, in foreign affairs of powerful states, balance-of-power considerations are a primary calculation of leaders at critical historical junctures. To be sure, there are individuals who are not Marxists who have contributed to this school: John Gallagher and Ronald Robinson with their idea of the "informal empire" of "free trade imperialism"; Gunnar Myrdal with his descriptions of how dual economies create "backwash effects" that systematically disadvantage the traditional sector; Raúl Prebisch with his work concerning the way in which unequal exchange in international trade acts to handicap the South.[19] Such ideas are not held eclectically by the dependency school, however. They have been adopted because they strengthen the tools of analysis of an approach that enjoys a fundamental unity of orientation through a reliance on Marxist analysis.

The foregoing sketch of the dual economy was too brief to suggest certain crucial refinements that have added enormously to the sophistication of the dependency approach during the last decade. Three relatively new conceptual qualifications are of particular importance. The first is the argument that the dual economy is not actually as rigid as was once believed. Spurred on especially by the work of Cardoso, many dependency writers have come to see the abundant evidence that a genuine industrial base is being laid in parts of the South, and that economies there are becoming far more diversified, integrated, and advanced than earlier spokesmen of this persuasion had thought possible. For, although both Marx and Lenin had anticipated that the worldwide spread of the industrial revolution would take place under capitalist auspices, the first generation of *dependencistas* talked of "growth without development" and of the way the southern countries would forever be, in their favorite cliché, the "hewers of wood and drawers of water" of

---

[19] Gallagher and Robinson, "The Imperialism of Free Trade," *Economic History Review*, 2d series, 6 (No. 1, 1953); Gunnar Myrdal, *Economic Theory and Underdeveloped Regions* (London: Gerald Duckworth, 1957). On Prebisch, see Joseph L. Love, "Raúl Prebisch and the Origins of the Doctrine of Unequal Exchange," *Latin American Research Review* 15 (No. 3, 1980).

the world economic system. But facts are a hard thing, and in due course, dependency analysts had to face the mounting evidence that heavy industry was growing in the Third World; that the manufacturing component of exports was steadily mounting there; and that internal, integrated markets were beginning to pulse with a life of their own. Indeed, statistics are readily at hand to show that the vigor of economic growth in large parts of the Third World is substantially greater than in the North. As Peter Evans describes it, "classic dependency" is giving way to "dependent development."[20]

A second (and related) conceptual innovation made by dependency writers during the last decade lies in their new emphasis on the crucial role of the state in this changing order of things. Whereas *dependencistas* had previously viewed Third World politics as little more than an auxiliary function of the international economic system, they have now begun to argue (and here the work of Guillermo O'Donnell is especially important) that the growing complexity of class and economic relations locally as well as internationally calls for more assertive action on the part of the state on the periphery. As the diversity and integration of these local economies grow, new groups arise that have to be controlled politically, just as some old groups must be divested of their power or find ways to reconstruct it. In a parallel manner, foreign actors have come to be more closely supervised than before. Their investments have been made a part of local plans involving the creation of backward and forward linkages, and their action has increasingly been harmonized with more fine-tuned domestic fiscal and employment measures. In a word, the growing complexity of local economies calls for new demands for a more competent state. In conceptual terms, the result is that the dependency literature now possesses a far richer political vocabulary that has substantially expanded its range of analysis.

The two preceding conceptual refinements in turn prepare the ground for a third: the recognition of the diversity of Third World countries and a growing appreciation of the significance of local factors in determining the pattern of long-term development processes. Not all countries on the periphery are industrializing, and not all have states aggressively determined to promote domestic interests. Different natural resource

---

[20] Evans, *Dependent Development: The Alliance of Multinational, State and Local Capital in Brazil* (Princeton: Princeton University Press, 1979). An early and especially strong statement on this matter can be found in Bill Warren, "Imperialism and Capitalist Industrialization," *New Left Review* 81 (1973). See also Fernando Henrique Cardoso, "Dependent Capitalist Development in Latin America," *New Left Review* 74 (1972), and Cardoso, "Associated-Dependent Development: Theoretical and Practical Implications," in Alfred Stepan, ed., *Authoritarian Brazil: Origins, Politics, and Future* (New Haven: Yale University Press, 1973).

endowments, preexisting lines of class or ethnic group conflict or coalition, political culture and the structure of inherited political institutions—all of these are acquiring a new relevance in analysis. As a
consequence, stages or degrees of dependency may now be discussed,
whereas previously not much more could be said than that a country
was or was not dependent.

As we have seen, then, the dependency perspective is not only coherent
and complex, but it is capable of conceptual self-criticism and development. In the wake of the demise of developmentalism, it offers an
alternative paradigm of study. The fact that it has not only survived
sharp internal dispute, but that it has actually grown in conceptual
acuteness as a result, is the most conclusive evidence that as a school of
thought the dependency approach has come of age. It should come as
no surprise, therefore, that its core argument is appearing in other
intellectual activities. We find Edward Said, for example, criticizing
longstanding Western cultural interpretations of the East:

> Taking the late eighteenth century as a very roughly defined starting
> point, Orientalism can be discussed and analyzed as the corporate insti-
> tution for dealing with the Orient—dealing with it by making statements
> about it, authorizing views of it, describing it, by teaching it, settling it,
> ruling over it: in short, Orientalism as a Western style for dominating,
> restructuring, and having authority over the Orient.[21]

At this point, the reader may well anticipate the final trump in the
dependency deck: the charge that developmentalism itself was the ideological handmaiden of imperialism and the ruling elites in the Third
World. For even if the charge were only implied, it was frequently
enough asserted that the very categories with which American academics
analyzed the South were—as the quotation from Edward Said suggests—instruments in the subjugation of Africa, Asia, and Latin America.

Such an argument might be constructed along the following lines. In
its "classic" form, economic developmentalism posited a modern sector
acting as a pole of development from which the industrial revolution
would eventually diffuse out to the rest of Third World society. Although
the modern sector might initially be in league with the international
system, it would invariably turn toward the local market—first for food
and labor, later for intermediate manufacturing products, and finally as
a source of demand for larger-scale manufacturing. Eventually, an integrated local economy should form, still a part of the world economy

---

[21] Said, *Orientalism* (New York: Random House, 1978), 3.

producing in line with comparative advantage, but reflecting throughout the characteristics of economic modernity, including a generalized modern skill structure. Where obstacles to development occur, they should be understood as having a nonmarket origin: inadequate resource endowment; a population base that is too small or growing too rapidly; inept governments unable to oversee capital formation because of weakness or corruption, or misguided notions about the merits of state planning; inherited ethnic prejudices making the free mobility of economic factors especially difficult.[22] In this light, the job of political development becomes more comprehensible. It is to engineer solutions to these obstacles to economic diffusion through the use of force or by the building of consensus, so that institutions are ultimately created that can make the process of change self-sustaining.

From a dependency perspective, the problem with this diffusionist approach is that it fails to recognize that its alleged solutions to problems in the Third World—the intensification of market relations there—are in fact at the origin of all the difficulties. That is, political instability in the Third World comes not so much from the recalcitrance of the traditional world in the face of change as from the brutality of change inflicted on the traditional world. When peasants are dispossessed of their land and herded into urban slums; when traditional artisans find their means of livelihood destroyed; when old patterns of power that provided at least some security are removed and the nuclear family is left to determine its fate as best it may—then one may indeed expect conflict. But it is modernity, not tradition, that is at the origin of the struggle. From the dependency perspective, therefore, the authoritarian governments typical of a large portion of the Third World are perceived as a necessary concomitant of capital exploitation rather than as the inevitable response to traditional backwardness. As we have seen, the fragility of these authoritarian regimes may be understood in terms of the weakness of the local classes they represent. Since these classes are the product of international economic forces and not the consequence of indigenous development, the political pacts they have made at home are relatively flimsy. The result is a ruling class ideologically unsure of itself ("denationalized") and only shallowly rooted in local social forces. The governments that represent the interests of such classes will of necessity be particularly reliant on the use of force to ensure their rule.

---

[22] For a standard neoclassical economics text, see Higgins (fn. 18). For a more current restatement in particularly sharp language, see the writings of P. T. Bauer, most recently *Reality and Rhetoric: Studies in the Economics of Development* (Cambridge: Harvard University Press, 1983). For a standard dependency critique of such an approach, see Michael Todaro, *Economic Development in the Third World*, 2d ed. (New York: Longman, 1981).

In this undertaking, such Third World governments can usually count on the support of the United States. For just as the international economic system lays down the social bases of much of southern development, so the international political system will attend to shifts in the political balance of power. Where the International Monetary Fund cannot travel, we might say, there the Marines will tread. From a dependency perspective, then, the consistently counterrevolutionary cast of American foreign policy is entirely in line with what one would expect. When the power of collaborating states in the Third World proves unequal to the task of containing the enormous pressures released by capitalist economic development in these areas, Washington will aid them in repressing popular uprisings and so protect the international economic system from the challenge of socialist economic nationalism.

It should thus be understandable that, in the eyes of the *dependencistas*, developmentalists in the United States were responsible for much more than inadequate model building with respect to affairs in the Third World. This very "inadequacy" was nothing more than an ideological smokescreen behind which North American imperialism freely operated. Developmentalist economists presented models of the beneficent spread of the industrial revolution throughout the world and denounced obstacles to such progress as being caused by backwardness. Their colleagues in political science presented institution building as one of organizational techniques, and often sanctioned the establishment of military governments for periods of "transition." The separation of economics from politics was not an artificial, but rather a logical, expression of the needs of advanced capitalism. So was the developmentalists' failure to credit imperialism with the force it has had. In their work, the developmentalist intelligentsia of American universities had given the lie to all their protestations of academic freedom and value-free or progessive theorizing, revealing instead their true character as apologists for the established international division of wealth and power. The attack was now complete: the dependency school not only had established a paradigm for the study of the Third World, but it had provided an explanation of its rival, developmentalism, powerful enough to complete the latter's disintegration.

The self-confidence of the dependency perspective is now so firmly rooted that we find fairly well-known social scientists writing vulgarizations of the approach for mass audiences—books in which the central methodological premises of the school are taken as needing no further discussion. Thus, L. A. Stavrianos opens his book *Global Rift* declaring:

The Third World emerged in early modern times as the result of a fateful social mutation in northwestern Europe. This was the rise of a dynamic capitalist society that expanded overseas in successive stages, gaining control over widening segments of the globe, until by the nineteenth century it had established a world-wide hegemony. ... What were the roots of this European expansionism? ... This central question in Third World history [comes from] analyzing the dynamics of European expansionism.[23]

In the same vein, Eric Wolf begins his study *Europe and the People without History* by stating:

The central assertion of this book is that the world of humankind constitutes a manifold, a totality of interconnected processes, and inquiries that disassemble this totality into bits and then fail to reassemble it falsify reality. Concepts like "nation," "society," and "culture" name bits and threaten to turn names into things. Only by understanding these names as bundles of relationships, and by placing them back into the field from which they were abstracted, can we hope to avoid misleading inferences and increase our share of understanding. ...[24]

The coherence, complexity, flexibility, and self-confidence of the dependency approach should be clear. When we add the important consideration that it can serve as a powerful political force uniting Marxism ideologically with Third World nationalism—as is clear in the case of Liberation Theology in Latin America—we must recognize that dependency thinking has established itself as an intellectual force with which we must reckon. Quite unlike developmentalism—which lives on in the wide variety of studies it spawned earlier, but which today lacks a center of gravity in a well-anchored, broad-based theory of change—the dependency school is in its prime.

III. CHALLENGING THE DEPENDENCY APPROACH

It is no easy matter to determine from where critical assaults on dependency thinking should come. Because of the fragmentation of the field described in section I, developmentalism by the 1970s lacked the conceptual unity and vigor to mount an attack. Without a broad historical perspective and an integrated study of political economy, what serious hope was there that this school could rally, particularly after a fuller verdict on the Alliance for Progress and the engagement in Viet-

[23] L. A. Stavrianos, *Global Rift: The Third World Comes of Age* (New York: William Morrow, 1981).
[24] Eric Wolf, *Europe and the People without History* (Berkeley: University of California Press, 1982).

nam had become available? No wonder, then, that no one closely related with developmentalism has demonstrated an ability to do more than thumb his nose ineffectively at the *dependencistas*.

One possibility is that, like developmentalism, the dependency perspective will over time breed its own undoing. As this approach becomes increasingly sophisticated in its insights and broad in its applications, there is the chance of divergent or rival lines of analysis, or of an adulteration of the basic unity of view that characterized its literature throughout the 1970s. Consider the possible fate of the three recent refinements in the dependency approach discussed in the preceding section: the importance of local factors in determining the course of change in the South; the critical role of the state in development there; and the genuine gains in economic strength that have become apparent there over the last two decades. Could these factors be persuasively combined to suggest that a situation of dependency no longer exists (if indeed it ever did)? Looked at more closely, are these refinements not simply restatements of a version of the diffusion/political modernization models reviewed earlier as the hallmarks of developmentalism? If genuine growth *is* taking place, if the shape and pace of this change *do* reflect in good measure local economic and social circumstances, and if the state *is* especially responsible for how these events transpire, then one quite plausible inference would be that the ability of imperialism to make these areas "dependent" is declining, and that therefore the cardinal reference point of the dependency approach is fast losing its utility as a lodestar. Ironically, then, *dependencia* as a perspective may be spreading just as the situation that gave rise to it is coming to an end, and the very sophistication of its method can be used as its own cannons turned against itself. Surely to a Marxist there should be nothing paradoxical to such a situation, as the doctrine teaches that ideas reflect the material world around them, usually with a time lag. The judgment of other historians may be more severe; they may hold that dependency theorizing reflected on a transitory moment in the process of Third World change, and that its major contribution was not to give insight to events there, but to be the ideological representation of a triumphing nationalist consciousness in these areas. It might even appear in retrospect that dependency writing represented only the narrow and short-term perspective, while the developmentalist approach proved better able to explain the course of change in the Third World over the long haul. What greater irony than for the dependency school to reaffirm, as the result of its own labors, the established verities of developmentalism!

Intriguing as such speculation may be, there is little reason to think that the dependency approach will founder for these reasons. As we have seen, dependency writing is not a simple-minded affair. It is no surprise, therefore, to learn that it has already generated concepts that enable it to pull back into line any potentially fissiparous tendencies leading toward apostasy.

A key argument in this respect is that the dramatic changes occurring on the periphery essentially leave untouched both the central characteristics of political life in the South and the predominance of northern power in shaping development there. For instance, industrialization to build up import substitution, through which southern countries attempted to become more self-reliant, led to the costly purchase of plants and equipment from abroad, the increased penetration by multinational corporations of local tariff barriers, and the development of ventures that catered largely to the ruling class. On the other hand, export-led industrialization also relied (as its very name suggests) on foreign know-how, markets, and financial institutions. In either case, the rich continued to monopolize the benefits of growth on the periphery and to depend on authoritarian governments to keep the masses in their place.

At the same time, foreign actors retained their paramount positions. *Dependencistas* point out that, while the periphery may be developing economically, the leading sectors of industry there—the "commanding heights" or the "pace-setters"—are owned overwhelmingly by Americans, Europeans, and Japanese. Moreover, because the local economy is now far more integrated than it was previously, it has also become far more sensitive to economic fluctuations abroad, as the current Third World debt crisis with its extreme vulnerability to interest rates in the United States so dramatically illustrates. As a result, the international system has maintained its grip on the periphery despite the real economic changes that have taken place there. And with this grip, its various agents—from multinational corporations to the International Monetary Fund—are able to create an environment suitable for the unimpeded accumulation of capital: a docile, cheap work force to exploit; favorable taxing regulations for private enterprise; and a fiscally "responsible" state (i.e., one that does not engage in "excessive" social service expenditures). Once again, the consequences have entailed the impoverishment of a substantial portion of the population and the need for an authoritarian regime to keep the discontented in line: the dependency relation itself may even have been strengthened.[25]

According to the *dependencistas*, the economic modernization of the

---

[25] See, for example, discussions along this line in Evans (fn. 20), and Murdoch (fn. 18).

periphery has also affected the international order; but here, too, the continuity of imperialist control lies beneath the apparent change. As countries in the South come to diversify and integrate their economies, they may leave the periphery—but not to join the core, since neither their financial nor their technical infrastructure is autonomous enough to play a part in controlling world economic affairs. Instead, because of their continued dependence, these countries come to play the part in the world system that their middle class plays domestically. That is, they have little real power, but the demonstrable privileges they enjoy relative to those beneath them on the periphery (in part because of their ex-ploitation of those less well placed) obligates them to do their part to keep the system operating. So those on the "semi-periphery" (sometimes called the "newly industrializing countries" or NICs) become junior, collaborating members of the international trading, investment, and financial system—their very gains serving only to reinforce the system that binds them to its will. If in appearance the international economic system is undergoing change, in reality the power of capitalism and the dominance of the northern imperialists have never been more effective.[26]

Thus, however much the dependency school may seem to possess within itself arguments that could lead to its own destruction, such a forecast takes no account of the ways in which the doctrine can maintain its stability despite the changes it is undergoing. Like other coherent ideologies, the dependency perspective has self-protecting concepts to deflect all manner of threat and preserve the doctrine's integrity. More than just an ideology is at stake here; there are other forces in operation assuring the doctrine's stability. The dependency perspective is an ide-ological "united front" in the Leninist sense: it binds together Marxists and Third World nationalists in their mutual hatred of imperialism. Just as *dependencistas* maintain that developmentalist ideas are "ideolog-ical" in the sense of serving political interests, so there is a political urgency to the dependency case as well. In short, for practical political, as well as doctrinal, reasons, we should expect the dependency approach to remain assertive. It will not be undone, as was speculated above, by its own hand.

An adequate criticism of the dependency school must simultaneously provide an account of British and American imperialism since the late 18th century and an account of change in the late-industrializing world.

---

[26] While the term "semi-periphery" appears to have been coined by Immanuel Wallerstein, the earliest use of the concept of which I am aware occurs in the idea of "go-between countries" as explained by Johan Galtung, "A Structural Theory of Imperialism," *Journal of Peace Research* 8 (No. 2, 1971).

It must demonstrate that economic interests constitute but one motive to imperialism (and not necessarily its most important), and it must establish that the form development has taken in Africa, Asia, and Latin America is only partly (and usually not primarily) the result of imperialism's influence; instead, it represents the outcome of local forces at work. Any such undertaking will confront fully and directly the core propositions of the dependency school: that imperialism works fundamentally to accumulate profits for capitalists, and that the power of this enterprise over the last several centuries has been so great that it has literally molded the economic, social, and political profile of the Third World. One cautionary note: piddling criticism of the dependency school is a waste of time. A perspective as supple and complex as that of *dependencia* will have no trouble explaining away as irrelevant, or as understandable in its own terms, relatively minor points about change in the core, the periphery, or the international system, or demands that its claims be made quantifiable and so readily testable. One must instead go to the heart of the matter, exploding dependency's myth of imperialism at the same time as its myth of the logic of change on the periphery. This is not to say that imperialism does not continue to be of influence in the South, or that Marxism is without its insights into the human condition. It is indeed possible to accept dependency interpretations of history where they seem appropriate. But that is not good enough for the advocates of dependency; like proponents of any holistic ideology, they are intensely suspicious of eclecticism. For the unity of the movement to be irredeemably shattered intellectually, it is not necessary, in short, to maintain that dependency is always and everywhere mistaken, but only that it is no better than a partial truth.[27]

The extremeness of the dependency model, its holism, and the way it comes to rest on a few simple premises constitute its source of unity and strength, and at the same time its point of greatest vulnerability. Consider, for example, its enormous emphasis on the character of the collaborating class in the Third World context. This group, born of imperialism and serving its interests locally through the power to manage affairs on the periphery, is predominant thanks to its international connections. But if it can be maintained that, for a specific time or place,

---

[27] See Tony Smith, *The Pattern of Imperialism: The United States, Great Britain, and the Late-Industrializing World since 1815* (New York: Cambridge University Press, 1981), chaps. 1 and 2. Strong attacks on world system analysis—which is the cornerstone of dependency theory—include Theda Skocpol, "Wallerstein's World Capitalist System: A Theoretical and Historical Critique," *American Journal of Sociology* 82 (March 1977); Aristide R. Zolberg, "Origins of the Modern World System: A Missing Link," *World Politics* 33 (January 1981); and Patrick O'Brien, "European Economic Development: The Contribution of the Periphery," *The Economic History Review*, 2d series, 35 (February 1982).

this class is only one among many, and that other factors, such as inherited political institutions or ethnic cleavages, are equal or even more significant in determining the course of events, the claim that the country is dependent loses its essential meaning. Through the insertion of a collaborating class in the South, imperialism must dominate life there; it is not enough that this be one force among the many, or only triumphant at certain intervals. If it were not dominant, then the country would no longer be shaped primarily by the force of economic imperialism. The tie with world system analysis would snap, the claim to a unified approach to the study of the Third World would be invalid, and the militant accusations that the class struggle and the national struggle in the South are one would be more difficult to sustain. One may find that some countries, at some times, correspond more closely to the dependency model than do others; so it clearly has its value as a paradigm for analysis. But the suggestion that the paradigm is useful only sometimes would be unacceptable to this school. Its ambition requires far more. And, though this ambition is an undeniable source of the dependency movement's strength, it is likewise the point at which the arms of criticism may be used most devastatingly against it.

There is no reason to believe that attacks on the dependency approach will weaken the convictions of its advocates. Like the proponents of any strong model, these writers have ways of deflecting attacks and maintaining their conceptual unity. And, as we have seen, the political interests served by such an ideology will insist on the veracity of this way of understanding the world whatever the objections.

IV. New Agenda for Third World Studies?

One ready answer to the serious problems caused by inadequate model-building for Third World studies is to avoid comparative studies in favor of the traditional historical method, where the intelligibility of events is assumed to flow from the unfolding of unique constellations of circumstance. I believe that this is what Hirschman was suggesting when he contrasted the occasional weakness of the comparative method with the richness of John Womack's *Zapata and the Mexican Revolution* (1970). Similarly, Clifford Geertz has emphasized the value of understanding social orders from within, citing Roy Mottahedeh's *Loyalty and Leadership in an Early Islamic Society* (1980).[28] Although these two works have no explicitly comparative ambitions, they produce such insights on

[28] Hirschman (fn. 5); Geertz, "Conjuring with Islam," *The New York Review of Books*, May 27, 1982.

the interested reader in much the manner a good novel may work, with a message far exceeding the historical limits actually set by the work of art.

In fact, however, there is no need to contemplate abandoning the comparative method as a serious remedy for the shortcomings in Third World studies bequeathed us by the descendants of Marx and Weber. Despite our inability to come up with a "general theory of action," or our reluctance to believe that virtuoso applications of class analysis will unravel all the complexities of development, work is going ahead on a variety of important questions whose analytical manageability is proof of the enduring worth of the comparative method.[29] *Social Origins of Dictatorship and Democracy* by Barrington Moore, Jr. (1966) and *Economic Backwardness in Historical Perspective* (1962) by Alexander Gerschenkron are examples of the kinds of comparative work that may serve as models in the field. As long as worthwhile problems are posed that have the possibility of empirical analysis on the basis of well-formulated theories not hostage to some hidden agenda and drawing from the domains of the social sciences combined, it would be premature indeed to announce the field of study closed. Certainly the interest is there. The proliferation of problems studied and the range of approaches used to deal with them, combined with a sense of the moral and political seriousness involved and their close relationship with questions of American foreign policy, make the field particularly dynamic even if there is no single center of gravity pulling everything together.

In future undertakings there is no need to repudiate the important insights provided by either the developmental or the dependency approaches. For whatever the shortcomings of their general categories of analysis as such, each has provided useful empirical and theoretical tools for Third World studies which should on no account be abandoned. Freed of the agendas set by their paradigms, we may nonetheless borrow from their labors.

The problem with developmentalism was that it was too fragmented; with *dependencia*, that it is too holistic. Is it nonetheless possible to promote some kind of cross-fertilization that breeds the strengths of each into a new synthesis while leaving the deadwood behind? If we have catalogued the failings of each school, what of their positive le-

---

[29] For interesting reflections on the comparative method, see Neil J. Smelser, *Comparative Methods in the Social Sciences* (Englewood Cliffs, NJ: Prentice-Hall, 1976), esp. chaps. 6 and 7; Theda Skocpol and Margaret Somers, "The Uses of Comparative History in Macrosocial Inquiry," and Victoria E. Bonnell, "The Uses of Theory, Concepts and Comparisons in Historical Sociology," both in *Comparative Studies in Society and History* 22 (No. 2, 1980).

gacies? Is some kind of "postmodernist" borrowing possible that moves us forward?

Thanks in good measure to the dependency perspective, those in the "mainstream" must now think more broadly and complexly about the Third World than before, while moral advocacy is no longer taboo in the name of an "objective" social science. We must think more broadly because the dependency approach obliges us to analyze Third World development globally and historically on a far larger scale than before. We must think more complexly because *dependencia* obliges us to see the interconnectedness of things—especially in the realm of political economy. And we must think in a more normative manner because of the dependency school's insistence that the terrible human problems of change can simply not be put to the side. Indeed, it should be possible to take the dependency lesson one step further, not only by extending its methods to new areas, such as the study of Soviet imperialism in Eastern Europe or examining the ways in which relations with the South actually debilitate and undermine the great powers involved (witness the multinationals exporting jobs and selling the technological patrimony of the West for a pittance), but by expanding our sensitivity to the range of influences apart from the economic that the United States in particular may use to shape the Third World in basic ways. In its greatly exaggerated emphasis on the economic motivations of the United States and the earlier imperialist powers, the dependency school has completely overlooked the political logic of imperialism, both as a reason for American policy and as an active agent of change in the South. Thus, for all its warnings of the threats that imperialism poses to the late-industrializing world, dependency thinking has neglected, ironically enough, one of the chief avenues by which northern influence is exercised.

By contrast, the major accomplishment of developmentalism lies in the variety of analytical tools it brought to the study of change, and in the care with which it used them. The focus of this school was essentially on working out the logic of different social processes in their own terms—political, economic, social, and psychological. If God is in the detail—that is, if excellence is apparent in the mastery of nuance and technique—if it is the specificity, the concreteness of social life that brings us closest to understanding it, then developmentalism still has a great deal to teach us by example. It is from developmentalism that we can come to appreciate, for instance, the "laws of motion" of discrete domains; in politics, there are the rich studies done on bureaucracies, parties, and matters of legitimacy, for instance. Eclecticism is sometimes thought of negatively, as if it had an *ad hoc*, superficial character that is of little use analytically. But if eclecticism is thought of instead as the effort to bring a variety of insights to bear on a problem in a patient manner that respects the complexity of the problem studied, then the various analytic tools offered by the social sciences today can continue to have the utility that the developmentalists originally hoped they would have. Thus, current topics—such as ethnicity as a source of solidarity or conflict in development, the character of the state and its role in change, and the varieties of religious cultures and their impact on change—were all subjects of interest to developmentalists a good quarter of a century ago.

From dependency thinking, we may learn a breadth of vision (even if most of these writers used this vantage point to violate the integrity of individual cases). From developmentalism, we can learn how a variety of theoretical tools may be used in harmony to organize the complexity of social life (even if in the hands of most of these writers such an approach did not add up, so that an overly fragmented view was the result). At the same time, Third World studies may work more fruitfully in the case of issue-oriented problems of comparative analysis, without the feeling that such efforts must ultimately vindicate either of those will-o'-the-wisps, a "general theory of action" or the notion that "all of recorded history is the history of class struggle." Simultaneously, there may be a renewed appreciation of works of art or history that, despite their lack of comparative focus (or indeed, because of it), are able to communicate so well the character of the Third World. In this way, perhaps something of the unity of the field may be resurrected—by the frank admission that the range of issues to be investigated admits of a variety of approaches such that discourse is facilitated, not ended. Still another frank admission must be that these concerns are not limited to the field of comparative study, but involve international relations as well. No matter how critical a comparative analysis may be today of the study of comparative development, its conclusions may also serve to clarify our thinking as to what is useful and what is possible—so that the field may once more experience the self-confidence that shows its revitalization to be at hand.

Books Written Under the Auspices of
CENTER OF INTERNATIONAL STUDIES
PRINCETON UNIVERSITY
1952-85

Gabriel A. Almond, *The Appeals of Communism* (Princeton University Press 1954)

William W. Kaufmann, ed., *Military Policy and National Security* (Princeton University Press 1956)

Klaus Knorr, *The War Potential of Nations* (Princeton University Press 1956)

Lucian W. Pye, *Guerrilla Communism in Malaya* (Princeton University Press 1956)

Charles De Visscher, *Theory and Reality in Public International Law*, trans. by P. E. Corbett (Princeton University Press 1957; rev. ed. 1968)

Bernard C. Cohen, *The Political Process and Foreign Policy: The Making of the Japanese Peace Settlement* (Princeton University Press 1957)

Myron Weiner, *Party Politics in India: The Development of a Multi-Party System* (Princeton University Press 1957)

Percy E. Corbett, *Law in Diplomacy* (Princeton University Press 1959)

Rolf Sannwald and Jacques Stohler, *Economic Integration: Theoretical Assumptions and Consequences of European Unification*, trans. by Herman Karreman (Princeton University Press 1959)

Klaus Knorr, ed., *NATO and American Security* (Princeton University Press 1959)

Gabriel A. Almond and James S. Coleman, eds., *The Politics of the Developing Areas* (Princeton University Press 1960)

Herman Kahn, *On Thermonuclear War* (Princeton University Press 1960)

Sidney Verba, *Small Groups and Political Behavior: A Study of Leadership* (Princeton University Press 1961)

Robert J. C. Butow, *Tojo and the Coming of the War* (Princeton University Press 1961)

Glenn H. Snyder, *Deterrence and Defense: Toward a Theory of National Security* (Princeton University Press 1961)

Klaus Knorr and Sidney Verba, eds., *The International System: Theoretical Essays* (Princeton University Press 1961)

Peter Paret and John W. Shy, *Guerrillas in the 1960's* (Praeger 1962)

George Modelski, *A Theory of Foreign Policy* (Praeger 1962)

Klaus Knorr and Thornton Read, eds., *Limited Strategic War* (Praeger 1963)

Frederick S. Dunn, *Peace-Making and the Settlement with Japan* (Princeton University Press 1963)

Arthur L. Burns and Nina Heathcote, *Peace-Keeping by United Nations Forces* (Praeger 1963)

Richard A. Falk, *Law, Morality, and War in the Contemporary World* (Praeger 1963)

James N. Rosenau, *National Leadership and Foreign Policy: A Case Study in the Mobilization of Public Support* (Princeton University Press 1963)

Gabriel A. Almond and Sidney Verba, *The Civic Culture: Political Attitudes and Democracy in Five Nations* (Princeton University Press 1963)

Bernard C. Cohen, *The Press and Foreign Policy* (Princeton University Press 1963)

Richard L. Sklar, *Nigerian Political Parties: Power in an Emergent African Nation* (Princeton University Press 1963)

Peter Paret, *French Revolutionary Warfare from Indochina to Algeria: The Analysis of a Political and Military Doctrine* (Praeger 1964)

Harry Eckstein, ed., *Internal War: Problems and Approaches* (Free Press 1964)

Cyril E. Black and Thomas P. Thornton, eds., *Communism and Revolution: The Strategic Uses of Political Violence* (Princeton University Press 1964)

Miriam Camps, *Britain and the European Community 1955-1963* (Princeton University Press 1964)

Thomas P. Thornton, ed., *The Third World in Soviet Perspective: Studies by Soviet Writers on the Developing Areas* (Princeton University Press 1964)

James N. Rosenau, ed., *International Aspects of Civil Strife* (Princeton University Press 1964)

Sidney I. Ploss, *Conflict and Decision-Making in Soviet Russia: A Case Study of Agricultural Policy, 1953-1963* (Princeton University Press 1965)

Richard A. Falk and Richard J. Barnet, eds., *Security in Disarmament* (Princeton University Press 1965)

Karl von Vorys, *Political Development in Pakistan* (Princeton University Press 1965)

Harold and Margaret Sprout, *The Ecological Perspective on Human Affairs, With Special Reference to International Politics* (Princeton University Press 1965)

Klaus Knorr, *On the Uses of Military Power in the Nuclear Age* (Princeton University Press 1966)

Harry Eckstein, *Division and Cohesion in Democracy: A Study of Norway* (Princeton University Press 1966)

Cyril E. Black, *The Dynamics of Modernization: A Study in Comparative History* (Harper and Row 1966)

Peter Kunstadter, ed., *Southeast Asian Tribes, Minorities, and Nations* (Princeton University Press 1967)

E. Victor Wolfenstein, *The Revolutionary Personality: Lenin, Trotsky, Gandhi* (Princeton University Press 1967)

Leon Gordenker, *The UN Secretary-General and the Maintenance of Peace* (Columbia University Press 1967)

Oran R. Young, *The Intermediaries: Third Parties in International Crises* (Princeton University Press 1967)

James N. Rosenau, ed., *Domestic Sources of Foreign Policy* (Free Press 1967)

Richard F. Hamilton, *Affluence and the French Worker in the Fourth Republic* (Princeton University Press 1967)

Linda B. Miller, *World Order and Local Disorder: The United Nations and Internal Conflicts* (Princeton University Press 1967)

Henry Bienen, *Tanzania: Party Transformation and Economic Development* (Princeton University Press 1967)

Wolfram F. Hanrieder, *West German Foreign Policy, 1949-1963: International Pressures and Domestic Response* (Stanford University Press 1967)

Richard H. Ullman, *Britain and the Russian Civil War: November 1918-February 1920* (Princeton University Press 1968)

Robert Gilpin, *France in the Age of the Scientific State* (Princeton University Press 1968)

William B. Bader, *The United States and the Spread of Nuclear Weapons* (Pegasus 1968)

Richard A. Falk, *Legal Order in a Violent World* (Princeton University Press 1968)

Cyril E. Black, Richard A. Falk, Klaus Knorr and Oran R. Young, *Neutralization and World Politics* (Princeton University Press 1968)

Oran R. Young, *The Politics of Force: Bargaining During International Crises* (Princeton University Press 1969)

Klaus Knorr and James N. Rosenau, eds., *Contending Approaches to International Politics* (Princeton University Press 1969)

James N. Rosenau, ed., *Linkage Politics: Essays on the Convergence of National and International Systems* (Free Press 1969)

John T. McAlister, Jr., *Viet Nam: The Origins of Revolution* (Knopf 1969)

Jean Edward Smith, *Germany Beyond the Wall: People, Politics and Prosperity* (Little, Brown 1969)

James Barros, *Betrayal from Within: Joseph Avenol, Secretary-General of the League of Nations, 1933-1940* (Yale University Press 1969)

Charles Hermann, *Crises in Foreign Policy: A Simulation Analysis* (Bobbs-Merrill 1969)

Robert C. Tucker, *The Marxian Revolutionary Idea: Essays on Marxist Thought and Its Impact on Radical Movements* (W. W. Norton 1969)

Harvey Waterman, *Political Change in Contemporary France: The Politics of an Industrial Democracy* (Charles E. Merrill 1969)

Cyril E. Black and Richard A. Falk, eds., *The Future of the International Legal Order*. Vol. I: *Trends and Patterns* (Princeton University Press 1969)

Ted Robert Gurr, *Why Men Rebel* (Princeton University Press 1969)

C. Sylvester Whitaker, *The Politics of Tradition: Continuity and Change in Northern Nigeria 1946-1966* (Princeton University Press 1970)

Richard A. Falk, *The Status of Law in International Society* (Princeton University Press 1970)

380

John T. McAlister, Jr. and Paul Mus, *The Vietnamese and Their Revolution* (Harper & Row 1970)

Klaus Knorr, *Military Power and Potential* (D. C. Heath 1970)

Cyril E. Black and Richard A. Falk, eds., *The Future of the International Legal Order*. Vol. II: *Wealth and Resources* (Princeton University Press 1970)

Leon Gordenker, ed., *The United Nations in International Politics* (Princeton University Press 1971)

Cyril E. Black and Richard A. Falk, eds., *The Future of the International Legal Order*. Vol. III: *Conflict Management* (Princeton University Press 1971)

Francine R. Frankel, *India's Green Revolution: Economic Gains and Political Costs* (Princeton University Press 1971)

Harold and Margaret Sprout, *Toward a Politics of the Planet Earth* (Van Nostrand Reinhold Co. 1971)

Cyril E. Black and Richard A. Falk, eds., *The Future of the International Legal Order*. Vol. IV: *The Structure of the International Environment* (Princeton University Press 1972)

Gerald Garvey, *Energy, Ecology, Economy* (W. W. Norton 1972)

Richard H. Ullman, *The Anglo-Soviet Accord* (Princeton University Press 1973)

Klaus Knorr, *Power and Wealth: The Political Economy of International Power* (Basic Books 1973)

Anton Bebler, *Military Rule in Africa: Dahomey, Ghana, Sierra Leone, and Mali* (Praeger Publishers 1973)

Robert C. Tucker, *Stalin as Revolutionary 1879-1929: A Study in History and Personality* (W. W. Norton 1973)

Edward L. Morse, *Foreign Policy and Interdependence in Gaullist France* (Princeton University Press 1973)

Henry Bienen, *Kenya: The Politics of Participation and Control* (Princeton University Press 1974)

Gregory J. Massell, *The Surrogate Proletariat: Moslem Women and Revolutionary Strategies in Soviet Central Asia, 1919-1929* (Princeton University Press 1974)

James N. Rosenau, *Citizenship Between Elections: An Inquiry Into The Mobilizable American* (Free Press 1974)

Ervin Laszlo, *A Strategy for the Future: The Systems Approach to World Order* (George Braziller 1974)

R. J. Vincent, *Nonintervention and International Order* (Princeton University Press 1974)

Jan H. Kalicki, *The Pattern of Sino-American Crises: Political-Military Interactions in the 1950s* (Cambridge University Press 1975)

Klaus Knorr, *The Power of Nations: The Political Economy of International Relations* (Basic Books, Inc. 1975)

James P. Sewell, *UNESCO and World Politics: Engaging in International Relations* (Princeton University Press 1975)

Richard A. Falk, *A Global Approach to National Policy* (Harvard University Press 1975)

Harry Eckstein and Ted Robert Gurr, *Patterns of Authority: A Structural Basis for Political Inquiry* (John Wiley & Sons 1975)

Cyril E. Black, Marius B. Jansen, Herbert S. Levine, Marion J. Levy, Jr., Henry Rosovsky, Gilbert Rozman, Henry D. Smith, II, and S. Frederick Starr, *The Modernization of Japan and Russia* (Free Press 1975)

Leon Gordenker, *International Aid and National Decisions: Development Programs in Malawi, Tanzania, and Zambia* (Princeton University Press 1976)

Carl von Clausewitz, *On War*, edited and translated by Michael Howard and Peter Paret (Princeton University Press 1976)

Gerald Garvey and Lou Ann Garvey, *International Resource Flows* (D. C. Heath 1977)

Walter F. Murphy and Joseph Tanenhaus, *Comparative Constitutional Law: Cases and Commentaries* (St. Martin's Press 1977)

Gerald Garvey, *Nuclear Power and Social Planning: The City of the Second Sun* (D. C. Heath 1977)

Richard E. Bissell, *Apartheid and International Organizations* (Westview Press 1977)

David P. Forsythe, *Humanitarian Politics: The International Committee of the Red Cross* (Johns Hopkins University Press 1977)

Paul E. Sigmund, *The Overthrow of Allende and the Politics of Chile, 1964-1976* (University of Pittsburgh Press 1977)

Henry S. Bienen, *Armies and Parties in Africa* (Holmes and Meier 1978)

Harold and Margaret Sprout, *The Context of Environmental Politics: Unfinished Business for America's Third Century* (University Press of Kentucky 1978)

Samuel S. Kim, *China, The United Nations, and World Order* (Princeton University Press 1979)

S. Basheer Ahmed, *Nuclear Fuel and Energy* (D. C. Heath 1979)

Robert C. Johansen, *The National Interest and the Human Interest: An Analysis of U.S. Foreign Policy* (Princeton University Press 1980)

Richard A. Falk and Samuel S. Kim, eds., *The War System: An Interdisciplinary Approach* (Westview Press 1980).

James H. Billington, *Fire in the Minds of Men: Origins of the Revolutionary Faith* (Basic Books 1980)

Bennett Ramberg, *Destruction of Nuclear Energy Facilities in War: The Problem and the Implications* (D. C. Heath 1980)

Gregory T. Kruglak, *The Politics of United States Decision-Making in United Nations Specialized Agencies: The Case of the International Labor Organization* (University Press of America 1980)

W. P. Davison and Leon Gordenker, eds., *Resolving Nationality Conflicts: The Role of Public Opinion Research* (Praeger Publishers 1980)

James C. Hsiung and Samuel S. Kim, eds., *China in the Global Community* (Praeger Publishers 1980)

Douglas Kinnard, *The Secretary of Defense* (University Press of Kentucky 1980)

Richard Falk, *Human Rights and State Sovereignty* (Holmes & Meier 1981)

James H. Mittelman, *Underdevelopment and the Transition to Socialism: Mozambique and Tanzania* (Academic Press 1981)

Gilbert Rozman, ed., *The Modernization of China* (The Free Press 1981)

Robert C. Tucker, *Politics as Leadership*. The Paul Anthony Brick Lectures. Eleventh Series (University of Missouri Press 1981)

Robert Gilpin, *War and Change in World Politics* (Cambridge University Press 1981)

Nicholas G. Onuf, ed., *Law-Making in the Global Community* (Carolina Academic Press 1982)

Ali E. Hillal Dessouki, ed., *Islamic Resurgence in the Arab World* (Praeger Publishers 1981)

Richard Falk, *The End of World Order* (Holmes & Meier 1983)

Klaus Knorr, ed., *Power, Strategy, and Security* (Princeton University Press 1983)

Finn Laursen, *Superpower at Sea* (Praeger 1983)

Samuel S. Kim, *The Quest for a Just World Order* (Westview Press 1984)

Gerald Garvey, *Strategy and the Defense Dilemma* (D.C. Heath 1984)

Peter R. Baehr and Leon Gordenker, *The United Nations: Reality and Ideal* (Praeger Publishers 1984)

Joseph M. Grieco, *Between Dependency and Autonomy: India's Experience with the International Computer Industry* (University of California Press 1984)

Jan Hallenberg, *Foreign Policy Change: United States Foreign Policy Toward the Soviet Union and the People's Republic of China, 1961-1980* (University of Stockholm 1984)

Michael Krepon, *Strategic Stalemate: Nuclear Weapons and Arms control in American Politics* (New York: St. Martin's Press 1984)

Gilbert Rozman, *A Mirror for Socialism: Soviet Criticisms of China* (Princeton University Press 1985)

Henry Bienen, *Political Conflict and Economic Change in Nigeria* (London: Frank Cass 1985)

Library of Congress Cataloging-in-Publication Data

Main entry under title:

Political system and change.

The essays in this book appeared originally in the quarterly journal World politics.
1. Political sociology—Addresses, essays, lectures. 2. Political science—
Addresses, essays, lectures. 3. Social change—Addresses, essays, lectures.
I. Kabashima, Ikuo, 1947-   . II. White, Lynn T.   III. World politics.
JA76.P596   1986   320   85-43377
ISBN 0-691-07698-7 (alk. paper)
ISBN 0-691-02244-5 (pbk.)